JUN 2   2005

11/05 - 4x

DESPITE
THE
SYSTEM

ORSON WELLES
Versus the Hollywood Studios

CLINTON HEYLIN

CHICAGO REVIEW PRESS

An A Cappella Book

Library of Congress Cataloging-in-Publication Data
Heylin, Clinton.
  Despite the System : Orson Welles versus the Hollywood studios / Clinton Heylin.— 1st ed.
      p. cm.
  "An A Cappella Book."
  Includes bibliographical references and index.
  ISBN 1-55652-547-8
  1. Welles, Orson, 1915- 2. Motion picture producers and directors—United States—Biography. 3. Actors—United States—Biography I. Title.
  PN1998.3.W45H48 2005
  791.4302′33′092—dc22   2004015959

For Jaime, who, like Homer, opened the door.

© 2005 by Clinton Heylin
All rights reserved
First edition
Published by Chicago Review Press, Incorporated
814 North Franklin Street
Chicago, Illinois 60610
ISBN 1-55652-547-8
Printed in the United States of America
5 4 3 2 1

CONTENTS

PREFACE

Dorian Gray in Reverse

"The one thing most people still ask about Welles is: what happened after *Citizen Kane*?"

—**Peter Bogdanovich, *This Is Orson Welles***

"If there was a downfall, then it was entirely of [Welles's] own doing. I mean, nobody stopped him from producing more *Citizen Kane*s."

—**John Houseman to Barbara Leaming**

O rson Welles was all too aware, in his later years, that posterity would judge his life to have been essentially a failure: that it would construct a neat parabola of decline that would arc down from his youthful masterpiece, *Citizen Kane*, to the wine advertisements he used to fund his latter-day imbibing. Not merely parabolic, but parablesque. In quieter moments, "between projects," Welles occasionally endeavored to fight these forces, while he had the strength, correcting the more extreme misrepresentations from film critic Pauline Kael, the psychobabble-as-criticism of Charles Higham, and the ostensibly autobiographical reconstructions from that "benign mandarin," John Houseman.

And still the obituaries of the man, who died peacefully in his sleep at his home in L.A. in 1985 at the age of seventy, rarely deviated from convenient myth into inconvenient history. Welles had become an anachronism before his time, a Dorian Gray in reverse whose physical corpulence was equated with some more cerebral

obesity. The failures of this most baroque of filmmakers were attrib-
uted to an excess of appetite and ego that, ergo, led to his fall.

Welles once ruefully observed, "I came to Hollywood saying, 'If
they let me do a second picture, I'm lucky.'" They let him make a
second movie (*The Magnificent Ambersons*), they just never let anyone outside Pomona and Pasadena see it. His determined attempts
to "get back to the [original] position" he found himself in pre–*Citizen Kane* lasted for some seventeen years, from 1941 to 1958, at
which point he had made six films for the studio system. The sixth,
Touch of Evil, was taken away from him at the editing stage and recast
as another uniform *noir* thriller, as had been the case with *The Lady
from Shanghai* (1948) and *The Stranger* (1946). It was the last straw.

Hollywood, in the end, ate up its "would-be genius" (gossip-
monger Louella Parson's little joke at Welles's expense) and spat him
out. Yet seventeen years after Welles's death, and forty-five years
after he last directed a film for a Hollywood studio, there is precious
little sign that the facts underlying Welles's largely unfulfilled career
as a Hollywood director are about to triumph over the lackadaisical
mischief-making of Pauline Kael ("Raising Kane"), Charles Higham
(*The Films of Orson Welles*), or, more recently, Simon Callow (*The
Road to Xanadu*), David Thomson (*Rosebud*), and Peter Conrad
(*Orson Welles: The Stories of His Life*).

Of these weighty tomes, Callow's has been perhaps the most
damaging. An actor and director of some note in his own right, and
a sympathetic biographer of Charles Laughton, Callow came to his
task with some credentials. Unfortunately he was hamstrung by his
own oxymoronic approach ("my book . . . is simultaneously a synthesis and a deconstruction"), and a profound inability to sort the
historical from the mythological (he is particularly suspect when
using the testimonies of the notoriously unreliable John Houseman
and Michael MacLiammoir).

As it is, *The Road to Xanadu* (1995), in seeking to rekindle dying
embers of myths about Welles's profligacy, "fear of completion," and
credit-stealing, was a weighty semibiography short on original
research and long on authorial judgements. As things stand, Cal-

low's "biography" of Welles is somewhat more incomplete, and a whole lot less representative, than most of Welles's so-called "unfinished" works; even as word arrives that another installment (of the now three-volume opus!) is all but finished.

Callow's hefty doorstop—coming a mere six years after Frank Brady's extremely well-researched, even-handed if largely overlooked, wholly fulfilling biography—was remarkably well received. Perhaps the gestalt was still against Welles, despite the steady accumulation of evidence in the decade since his demise, from which a more reasoned reevaluation could have come.

The first half of the 1990s had seen the dissemination of a wealth of new material on Welles, beginning in low-key fashion in 1990 with Bret Wood's meticulously researched bio-bibliography (Greenwood Press), a starting point for all Welles scholars. Two years later, Harper-Collins generated considerably more of a splash with the long-awaited *This Is Orson Welles*, four hundred pages of fabled "on the record" conversations between Welles and Peter Bogdanovich, undertaken in the late 1960s and early 1970s for a never-completed portrait by the modern film director with the greatest empathy for his subject. Accompanying these interviews were a number of private documents—memos, correspondence, and the like—to substantiate much of what Welles claimed to have happened to him and his films; and a detailed chronology of his career compiled by Welles authority Jonathan Rosenbaum, who was also responsible for editing the original 1,400-page manuscript down. A four-cassette set of audio tapes was issued simultaneously, with some material that had not been included in the book.

The following year Robert Carringer published a follow-up of sorts to his definitive account of *The Making of Citizen Kane*. *The Magnificent Ambersons: A Reconstruction* used much the same material he had drawn upon previously for a laser disc version of Welles's second movie, finally putting into the published domain the complete "cutting continuity" script for the Welles version of the film, as well as excerpting much of the correspondence that the ham-fisted editing of the movie had generated between Welles and the studio.

(Meanwhile the three best commentaries on Welles's films to date—Andre Bazin's *A Critical View* (1972), James Naremore's *The Magic World of Orson Welles* (1978), and Joseph McBride's *Orson Welles* (1972)—were all deemed worthy of republication (the latter two in revised editions), taking advantage of the same window of interest; along with Michael MacLiammoir's invaluable journal, kept during the making of *Othello*, *Put Money In Thy Purse* (Virgin Books, 1994).)

At the same time an appreciation of Welles's filmmaking was enhanced by three documentaries that addressed the films he had left unfinished. The first of these, *Don Quixote*, released in 1992, was a partial "reconstruction" of the project that had occupied Welles for much of the last quarter of a century of his life, painstakingly put together by Jesus Franco. The following year, another film "based on an unfinished film by Orson Welles," *It's All True*, was screened at selected cinemas. It was in part a reconstruction of Welles's fabled 1942 pan-American quasidocumentary, as well as a documentary about that film's fate. It was widely reviewed, and the context in which the original film had been "abandoned" widely discussed.

Finally, two years later, Welles's latter-day companion Oja Kodar authorized a ninety-minute documentary, *Orson Welles: The One-Man Band* (later shown on British television as *The Lost Films of Orson Welles*), that collected together some of the more immediately arresting detritus from the last fifteen years of Welles's life, a period previously perceived as being almost entirely unproductive. Kodar also oversaw the publication of Welles's last two completed screenplays, *The Big Brass Ring* (cowritten with Kodar) and *The Cradle Will Rock*, further affirmation that being denied the means of moviemaking had not acted as a final curb on his imagination.

The publication in *Film Quarterly* in its Fall 1992 issue of an abbreviated version of Welles's fifty-eight-page memo to Universal studio head Ed Muhl, regarding the studio's edit of his last Hollywood film, *Touch of Evil*, set another cartwheel in motion. The memo in question established not only what the studio had imposed against Welles's wishes, but also how meticulously the director had worked to put together the kind of film he wanted and to what extent the studio had fundamentally undermined his organic conceit.

The memo, which was meant to constitute part of the 1992 edition of *This Is Orson Welles*, was finally included in its belated 1998 paperback edition (Da Capo Press). The publication coincided with the general release of a new version of the film in question, reedited according to Welles's own instructions in that memo by Walter Murch, under the supervision of Rick Schmidlin. The "new" version of *Touch of Evil* again generated debate about how much damage Welles's work had sustained at the hand of Hollywood's artisans and execs, prompting the question, why Welles?

Yet none of the recent biographers and commentators on the man's work—with the notable exception of Michael Anderegg (*Orson Welles, Shakespeare and Popular Culture* [1999])—have drawn upon this wealth of material to reevaluate the circumstances under which Hollywood's most gifted and original film director made just six movies for the Hollywood studios, five of which were duly mangled by "the system." My intention is to redress the balance.

◆   ◆   ◆   ◆

As with all things under heaven, there are reasons why the studios never got to grips with Welles and why he never retained a strong enough grip on the public to be allowed to make the films he wanted. Some people's motives and reasoning are lost now in the mists of forgotten memories and handfuls of dust, and cannot thus be subjected to any ongoing revisionism. Thankfully, though, there are shooting scripts, shooting schedules, and internal memos; on-the-record interviews with protagonists; private correspondence to and from Welles; his own conversations, published and transcribed; letters to the papers setting the record straight(er); and articles and lectures to the public at large.

All help fill in the gaps and steer one toward a thesis of reconstruction. By revealing the circumstance of history in context, for perhaps the first time, I hope to *deconstruct* the idea that the subconscious demons of one man—a dubious notion at the best of times—led to a series of events that were as inevitable as the trajectory of Sisyphus's boulder. Welles was undone by real people, with real motives, and by circumstances found in a single time and place—Hollywood at the end of its golden era.

That many people felt threatened by Welles and what he appeared to stand for is surely indisputable. Welles came to Hollywood with an approach to filmmaking that was anathema to the system, and everyone soon knew it. He wanted to make movies as psychologically sound as a good novel, with layers of meaning that only became apparent on repeated viewings and with what the dean of film criticism, Andre Bazin, typified as "the kernel of meaning [being] perceived . . . in its natural relationship to all the contiguous realities." This young man represented the greatest threat to Hollywood's way of making movies precisely because he made the kind of film that everyone in Hollywood wished they could make, just *their* way.

His many enemies rarely articulated their concerns in such terms. Many would have balked at the term "enemy," but Welles always knew the name of the beast. The studio system meant that those who felt (justifiably) threatened could compel him to deviate from his own aesthetic core or, failing that, had the means to remove that core. Yet it can be found in all of Welles's films, no matter how many trapdoors we may have to pass through. And this brings us to the second strand I aim to weave—to show what each film could and should have been, and to illustrate how enriched the parameters of American moviemaking would have been had Welles been able to consistently enforce his vision on the medium.

I came to feel that this story was not one that even careful readers of recent tomes on the man would recognize (hence my ill-disguised lack of regard for the slanted views of Callow and Conrad). It is the story of an intelligent, perceptive, passionate, egotistical man who, for all his failings as a person, was absolutely uncompromising in his art. The endearing public persona went "nae deep," but the director within always knew when to keep his counsel (hence the visceral shock when that authentic tone was revealed in the *Touch of Evil* memo).

Though he had more faith in the average moviegoer than an entire school of Hollywood producers, Welles was allowed just one opportunity to express that faith fully—in resources, critical acceptance, and, above all, total control of the work itself—and *Citizen Kane* has certainly proved to be a lucrative earner through the years (as has *Touch of Evil*, which on its 1998 restoration had lines around the block at New York's Film Forum for weeks on end).

Welles's attempts to play the game only ended in heartbreak, but he kept coming back for more, filled with (as he put it, after his sixth and final hand went bust) "a greedy need to exercise, in some way, the function of my choice: the function of a director." He never repeated himself as a director, and he never played his hand quite the same way twice. But he participated in the game as long as he saw even the slightest chance of that big win: renewing the contract with his audience made back when, with *Citizen Kane*.

The results were not always recognizably his—after *Citizen Kane*, they were never entirely his again, at least until he sacrificed Hollywood's resources for his "kind of control"—but the ten films that he made between 1940 and 1965 (six in Hollywood, and four raised digits to that cinematic colony) have more genuine daring than any of the worthy contemporaries who made three or four (or fourteen) times that number of movies (some random numbers here: Hawks made 43, Capra 45, Ford 132, Huston 38, Wilder 27, Hitchcock 57). Even the similarly star-crossed Preston Sturges made more forays as a Hollywood director.

With Welles, at no point is it a question of "never mind the quality, feel the width." Even *The Stranger*, the one Hollywood movie he subsequently all but disowned, began life in the land of Welles, only to be kidnapped by editor Ernest Nims and given a new identity by producer Sam Spiegel. Welles did not surrender easily on any of his films, but the forces mounted against him probably made each defeat inevitable. As a result he got the thin end of the wedge in later life, rarely able to exercise his true vocation. A decade and a half of innovative filmmaking merely rendered him a "risk," unbank-able, a loose cannon, for daring to make films that challenged the way films got made.

Yet Welles himself never claimed that it was impossible to make a good film, even a very good film, within "the system." He cited Ford as an example of a director who had consistently achieved that. And when he first came to Hollywood as the Boy Wonder in 1939, he hoped that he could prosper in the tradition of D. W. Griffiths, with some of the accessibility of John Ford. But he quickly realized that he didn't "want to make the kind of movie which [Hollywood] produc-ers want to produce." However many self-evidently superficial films he acted in to pay the piper, he never gave Hollywood what it craved—a Welles film with all the persona but none of the personality.

Despite constantly reinventing himself to fit in with the lay of the land, he was undone by the very message he sought to convey, each and every time—there are no happy endings. And yet, some-how, though he suspected the underlying truth in the Don Marquis saying, "If you make people think they're thinking, they'll love you; but if you *really* make them think, they'll hate you," hope for the human condition peeks through even the bleakest, most baroque Wellesian moments.

Welles wrote a number of epitaphs for his characters, but he only wrote one obituary for another director. It was Jean Renoir, his favorite filmmaker and a man who was prepared to fund his art with Art (his father's). He wrote it, for the *Los Angeles Times* of all news-papers, when he was sixty-four years old, and sensing that he would never get to paint a masterpiece again. The parallels to his own fate cannot have been lost on him, even as the appositeness of what he had to say rang loud and clear:

> Some of these [films] were commercial and even, in their time, criti-cal failures. Some enjoyed success. None were blockbusters. Many are immortal.

Amen.

—Clinton Heylin, November 2003

Reader, please note: In the text, where it is not clear whose critical opinion I am embracing (or refuting), initials in brackets have been preferred to the tiresome practice (for reader and author alike) of notating each and every source. Bibliographical details can be found at the end of the book. Meanwhile, the initials utilized denote the following commentators:

AB = Andre Bazin
TC = Terry Comito
PC = Peter Cowie
BL = Barbara Leaming
JM = Joseph McBride
JN = James Naremore
BW = Bret Wood
MA = Michael Anderegg
AS = Audrey Stainton

ACT ONE: FAITH

1

DEFINITELY NOT LOVE
IN THE TROPICS

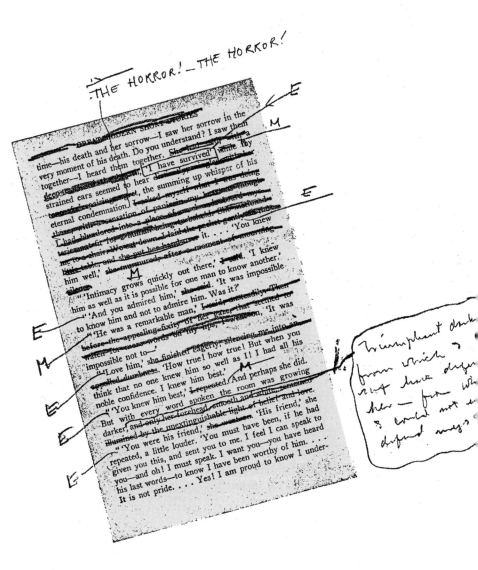

[Heart of Darkness]

"If you're walking along the edge of a cliff and you don't know it's
the edge of a cliff, you have perfect confidence. And I didn't
discover the cliff . . . in films until after I'd been in it for a while."

—Orson Welles, 1982

At the end of March 1939 Europe lay less than six months away
from its second universal conflict in a generation, after German chancellor Adolf Hitler reneged on a previous promise made to British prime minister Neville Chamberlain at Munich, annexing the Czechoslovakian rump into his ever-expanding vision of a Greater Germany. The ominously omnipresent rumble of these two powers mobilizing for war was unmistakable, even in a New York at last emerging from the Great Depression.

Even the latest Fred Astaire–Ginger Rogers movie—previously a guarantee of light, frothy escapism—ended with the death of Astaire's real-life character, shot down in the war to end all wars just twenty-one years earlier. The film in question, *The Story of Vernon and Irene Castle*, was due to make its New York premiere on March 30, 1939. As an RKO production, Radio City Music Hall was again booked to play host to this, the ninth (and last) Astaire-Rogers RKO movie.

It had been announced back in January that this would be the final film in the series. Director Mark Sandrich was leaving RKO, having never received any kind of percentage deal on the highly lucrative movies he had made with the pair. Fred Astaire was also at the end of his contract with RKO and was looking to change partners on a more regular basis in the future. Nor did the series' producer, Pandro S. Berman, look long for the organization. The simple fact was that the series had run its course, having been in irreversible decline since its sublime sixth installment, *Swing Time*, in the autumn of 1936.

RKO, though, hoped that returns from the ninth installment might tide them over until their new boss, George Schaefer, had his cherished independent production units up and running. After all, the Astaire-Rogers series of films had at times been almost single-handedly responsible for keeping the modest film studio afloat. After going into equity receivership in 1933, RKO had struggled to return to an even keel, held under by crippling mortgages on its theater chain for much of the decade. Thanks largely to the two toe-tappers, RKO had begun making a profit in the last three years, even if profits had again begun to fall after *Swing Time*, from $2,514,734 in 1936 to $173,578 on 1938's *Carefree*.

The initial receipts for the ninth Astaire-Rogers movie proved a little ominous. It looked as though the film could even end up losing money, an unheard-of phenomenon for a series that had consistently reaped large profits for RKO. The commercial failure of *The Story of Vernon and Irene Castle*, which ended up losing $50,000, was a severe jolt to the studio executives, Pandro Berman in particular. He had been associated with the pair since their second movie.

It was Berman who had agreed to replace Sam Briskin as RKO head of production—his second stint in the job—in the winter of 1938, having produced almost all of the studio's big earners through the Depression years. Aside from half-a-dozen successful movies with Astaire and Rogers, there had been the Hepburn-Rogers vehicle *Stage Door* and Rogers's solo vehicles such as *Vivacious Lady* and *Fifth Avenue Girl*, where she branched out from duo-dancing duties. But Berman disliked his responsibilities almost as much as the lack of opportunities for hands-on producing and when Leo Spitz, with whom he had a good rapport, stepped down as president of RKO, he was looking to move on.

If there was a man who might have persuaded Berman to stick around, it was never going to be the new president of the corporation. The forty-nine-year-old George Schaefer, previously sales chief at Paramount and United Artists, and with twenty-four years' experience in the industry, was brought in at the behest of major RKO shareholder Nelson Rockefeller. But Schaefer had no experience in film production, though he had some grand ideas, few of which found favor with Berman.

When the *Hollywood Reporter* suggested in an October 1938 bulletin that Schaefer intended to "step in with both feet," Berman was already set against him. Schaefer promptly announced that the RKO lot would soon move to an independent unit basis, with each production unit financed by one of the banking groups connected to majority shareholders Atlas-Lehman. Berman despaired of the innovation and as early as February 1939 was asking to be released from his contract. He vehemently disagreed with Schaefer's approach, which he felt was creating an organization divided against itself. However, feeling that he needed time to bring his schemes to fruition, Schaefer persuaded Berman to stay on until December, by which time he hoped that Berman's departure would pass largely unnoticed.

The new boss certainly had some grand plans for a company yet to come out of equity receivership. RKO remained far weaker than the four big Hollywood studios with whom they were competing commercially. If Paramount, Fox, MGM, and Warners all had substantial lots in Hollywood itself, sizeable theater chains across the States, and worldwide distribution, RKO had less Hollywood real estate, a smaller theater chain that was a constant drain on resources, and international distribution that was spotty at best.

Schaefer remained unperturbed. In June 1939, at the annual RKO sales convention, he proceeded to announce a new season of fifty-eight features and an increase in the production budget of around 40 percent. He was also trumpeting a deal he had signed with two eminent Broadway producers, Max Gordon and Harry Goetz, by which he was to acquire Robert E. Sherwood's Pulitzer-winning play *Abe Lincoln in Illinois*, along with *The American Way*, a work designed to appeal to the patriotism of a country still ambivalent about entering a war it would prefer to ignore.

Schaefer boasted to his salesmen that he had paid half a million dollars for these properties and was "prepared to spend up to three million to produce them." Paying such sums made a splash, even if the films would not. Evidently, the new RKO boss was in love with the idea of serious movies and was turning to Broadway producers to help him achieve new credibility for a studio generally associated with dance and song.

As Schaefer sat in the stalls at Radio City, watching the swan song of the old RKO's most reliable pairing, less than half a mile away Orson Welles's troupe of Mercury actors was preparing for a live recording of their weekly offering for the *Campbell's Playhouse* radio series, an adaptation of Edna Ferber's play *Show Boat*. The *Playhouse* series of hour-long, weekly shows had taken over from the *Mercury Theatre on the Air* after twenty-one sponsorless shows, thanks to a particularly notorious Halloween prank played by Welles on his unsuspecting listeners, under the guise of his namesake's *War of the Worlds*.

The twenty-four-year-old Welles had, in just over two years, become the wunderkind of New York theater, thanks primarily to two startling reinterpretations of Shakespeare plays, a "voodoo" *Macbeth* and an antifascist *(Julius) Caesar*; as well as a production of the radical, pro-labor play by Marc Blitzstein, *The Cradle Will Rock*, made under the auspices of the Federal Theater Program but then subject to an unsuccessful putsch by the WPA itself.

In all of these endeavors he had worked in collaboration with an older and more experienced theatrical producer and cofounder of the Mercury, the seemingly besotted John Houseman (Welles later told fellow director Bogdanovich, in private conversation, that Houseman was "a closet homosexual." His indulgences of his protégé certainly bear out such an interpretation, even though Houseman repeatedly applied more benign motives in his own account of these days, *Runthrough*). Houseman gave Welles an early insight into the ways in which a producer could be a valuable organizer and financier, as well as the price to be paid: a share in creative input wholly at odds with any likely aptitudes or insights.

These theatrical productions had established the name of the Mercury Theatre in New York City and on the Eastern Seaboard, but it was only after Welles came up with the startlingly simple (yet entirely original) idea of presenting H. G. Wells's *War of the Worlds* as a series of increasingly frantic news bulletins on an otherwise innocuous showtime radio program that his fame spread as far as the West Coast, as did his weekly audience. The week before, Mercury's weekly broadcast had attracted some 4 percent of radio-owning Americans; the week after, some 7.4 percent of the listening public tuned into Welles's first adaptation of Joseph Conrad's novella *Heart of Darkness*.

In fact, the Mercury Theatre was in need of a fillip after its first theatrical flop, a production of George Buchner's *Danton's Death*, which premiered less than a week after the infamous broadcast but ran for just twenty-one performances. Their weekly radio show, too, was under threat of cancellation from a Columbia radio network unamused by the Halloween ruckus—that is, until they reached an agreement with Campbell's to sponsor the show for the remainder of the season, commencing in its new guise with Daphne du Maurier's *Rebecca* on December 9, 1938.

Welles, though, had already indicated that he might prove a most unwilling sponsoree. In an interview for the *New York Times*, two months before the *War of the Worlds* broadcast, he suggested that "While I have no quarrel with the commercial sponsorship of radio programs . . . I do find fault with the fact that the broadcasters, in presenting a program, develop it along lines pleasing to the sponsor, rather than to the radio audience itself, for whom it is really intended."

Unfortunately, Welles knew all too well that he needed this sponsorship deal, even though it quickly became apparent, in John Houseman's words, "that our life with Campbell's Soups was going to be less agreeable than when we were our own masters." Welles already had an outlandishly ambitious theatrical production in mind for Mercury's spring presentation, a segue of Shakespeare's four War of the Roses plays into a single evening of *Five Kings*, so he needed the heightened profile to entice investors after Danton died a death.

A week of dress rehearsals in Washington, D.C. in March and a further week in Philadelphia merely confirmed the impracticality of the whole *Five Kings* project. Faced with a form of financial hemorrhaging that even recently replenished revenue from radio could not stem, Welles was obliged to abandon a second consecutive flop before it limped into New York. Another failure, on or off Broadway, would have applied an irredeemable taint to the troupe's burgeoning reputation, so the *Five Kings* was quietly put to sleep (to be awakened when Welles's career as an American director was over, recast as the story of Falstaff in the bittersweet *Chimes at Midnight*).

Not that Welles abandoned his pet project easily. Seventeen tons of scenery were shipped to New York, initially, and then into the limbo of storage; while Orson himself announced that he would not shave off his new goatee beard until he had appeared as Falstaff on a New York stage. Just when it seemed that any further sources of income had dried up, Welles found himself being courted by the new boss at RKO, hoping to convince the maverick director to make a pair of films for the ailing studio.

Welles expressed very little interest and almost no knowledge of the film medium, while demanding total artistic control of any project he might turn his hand to—whatever the media. Schaefer, who had seen the Mercury on stage, was greatly enamored of Welles's theatrical productions and was looking for a personality to help stamp his own imprint on the company he had barely begun to oversee. Common ground was found.

Schaefer seems to have quickly realized that much of Welles's professed indifference was a sham, though his demands were not. He also knew Welles had been approached by more prestigious studios, who continued to rely on the usual come-to-Hollywood-and-sell-your-soul patois to persuade their man. Schaefer's edge lay in the independence he was prepared to offer the young man, the limits of which grew ever less stringent with each rejected offer, as Welles continued to play hardball until he got what he wanted—the right to the final cut of whatever film he chose to make. Now there was a radical idea!

For all his studied disinterest, Welles had learned enough about Hollywood to know that trust was a surgical appliance one wore after a hernia operation and honor was another term for "judge." He also knew far more about movies than he was letting on. Indeed, he had attempted to shoot his first "short" the previous fall, when he had hit upon the idea of prefacing a farce (*Too Much Johnson*) he planned to present at a summer festival with what *Billboard* called "a motion picture prologue, to let the audience [in] on what's happened before the start of the play." According to Welles, he actually screened this "short" for RKO executives as proof that their faith would be well placed.*

If we can believe an anecdote Welles later related in a syndicated column (and, contrary to Callow, not all such stories smack solely of mythmaking), he had enjoyed a brief spell as an anonymous film critic in his youth, replacing a "drunken movie critic in a city which shall be nameless—and a newspaper which should be. I was his ghostwriter for a time. I got real money for this and he was well pleased with my work, since he was never sober enough to read it." (This suggests a possible inspiration for the memorable scene in *Citizen Kane* where Kane rewrites Leland's review of his mistress's opera debut).†

There certainly seem to be far too many allusions to the movies of his youth in later comments for the myth of Welles the virgin moviegoer to still endure. As it happens, a contemporary namecheck had already given the game away. At the end of a Mercury radio performance of John Buchan's *The 39 Steps* on August 1, 1938, Welles took the first of a number of little "pops" at Alfred Hitchcock's balloon:

> Ladies and gentlemen, if you missed Madeleine Carroll in our "stage" version of *The 39 Steps*, the young lady in the movie, in common with almost anything else in that movie, was the child of its director's own unparalleled and unpredictable fancy. If you missed anything you must blame Mr. Alfred Hitchcock.

---

*Sadly, the last surviving copy of the *Too Much Johnson* short was lost in a fire at Welles's home in Spain in 1970.

†Mankiewicz liked to relate a similar incident when he was theater critic for the *New York Times* in October 1925 and failed to review a particularly bad production of *School for Scandal* due to being thoroughly intoxicated.

Welles later professed to be a great fan of Hitchcock's *The 39 Steps*, bemoaning the fact that he then "gave in to Hollywood and . . . lost all the charm of his English style." *He* had no such intention of giving in, having already identified the central problem with the studio system, which he shared with a symposium on Hollywood in the fall of 1939, while he awaited the opportunity to begin shooting his own Hollywood debut:

> What I don't like about Hollywood films is the "gang" movie and I don't mean the Dead End Kids. I mean the assembly-line method of manufacturing entertainment developed in the last fifteen years or so, and I share this prejudice with practically everybody whose craft is the actual making of a movie, and not just . . . the business of selling it. When too many cooks get together, they find, usually, the least common denominator of dramatic interest.

Welles was careful to hide his own cinematic influences from the new RKO boss, but they are fully demonstrated by two documents from the 1950s, after he had found Hollywood too rich for his poet's blood. These documents suggest an early interest in, and appreciation of, the medium. In 1952 Welles was one of a number of directors asked to supply a personal top ten for the first *Sight and Sound* poll of best films. Of the ten films he selected, just one—a decidedly obscure movie by Vittorio de Sica, *Shoeshine* (1946)— postdated Welles's own immersion in the art form. The other nine, in chronological order, were as follows: *Intolerance* (1916); *Nanook of the North* (1922); *Greed* (1923); *Potemkin* (1925); *Our Daily Bread* (1928); *City Lights* (1931); *Le Grand Illusion* (1937); *The Baker's Wife* (1938); and *Stagecoach* (1939). The relevant directors—Griffith, Flaherty, Von Stroheim, Eisenstein, King Vidor, Chaplin, Renoir, Pagnol, and Ford—represented Welles's personal pantheon of influences. They also suggested someone whose appreciation of the art form preceded any contribution of his own.

Welles's view of the important figures in film hardly changed in the ensuing years. In a list given to his French secretary, Maurice Bessy, the directors he considered originators of the major branches of cinema were as follows: Georges Meliés, D. W. Griffith, Charlie Chaplin, Erich von Stroheim, Mack Sennett, F. W. Murnau, Jacques Feyder, Sergei Eisenstein, Jean Renoir, Ernst Lubitsch, and Robert Flaherty. Exempting himself from the four branches he delineated—storytellers, poets, filmmakers, and entertainers—Welles saw his own work as a form of inheritance from Meliés and Griffith.

If Welles reserved little time for those who came after him, he had prepped well for this unexpected opportunity. He implicitly recognized the power of the medium before he ever cranked a camera. As he wrote in *Stage*, three months before *Citizen Kane* premiered, "Hollywood is still a frontier. That it should be after all these years . . . is to the movies' shame and our advantage. . . . The dramatist—newly equipped with an imagery which is simply the image itself—more literal than sight and more eloquent than modern language . . . is again capable of poetry."

And it was fortuitous timing in another way too. By the time Schaefer began to whisper in his ear, Welles was already starting to despair of the New York theater and audiences that expected exciting, innovative fare twice a year. His view of the "casual theatergoer," as expressed in an article written for *Billboard* the previous November, shortly after the failure of *Danton's Death*, suggested a man who was no longer certain what that audience wanted:

> No matter how well a theater may succeed in organizing the organizable audience, its success or failure must be measured to a great degree by the desire of the casual theatergoer to see its individual productions . . . [for] he wants to see a good show at the least possible expense with the greatest possible convenience. . . . It is the necessity for educating this type of playgoer which is the greatest problem facing the practitioners of repertory.

In radio he could be more brazenly experimental, knowing that an unsuccessful broadcast was not the be-all and end-all. There would always be a chance to redeem oneself the following week. However, the particular deal with the devil he had made back in December 1938 as a means of ensuring the continuance of the Mer-

cury Theatre on the Air had brought him nothing but frustration. Though Welles never lost his ability to charm and cajole, it was Campbell's Soup, and in particular Diana Bourbon, program coordinator for *Campbell's Playhouse*, who had the final say on story selection and content.

Welles found he was frequently obliged to remind Bourbon that it was *his* show, on one occasion informing her in writing "that whatever gives our format individuality, beyond regular interest attaching itself to our guest, is my own extremely personal, rather particular style, which must needs express authentically my own enthusiasm and tastes." And yet he remained unsure enough about his Hollywood option to sign on for a second Campbell's season just weeks before Schaefer did indeed offer him what he was looking for.

Bourbon was unimpressed by Welles's displays of belligerence and they would tangle a few more times before the second series, which began in September 1939, ran its course in March 1940. When the end was in sight, Welles told one reporter why there would be no third season: "I'm sick of having the heart torn out of a script by radio censorship."

He was determined to ensure that he did not make the same mistake when it came to making movies. Though RKO retained the right to story refusal, with Welles they were contractually obliged to exercise "utmost good faith" and could not compel him to make any given film, or address specific subject matter. Welles already knew whom he wanted to emulate and how. As he duly informed *Stage*:

> I think a movie needs a boss. There has never been a motion picture of consequence that has not been, broadly speaking, the product of one man. This man has been the producer, could be the writer . . . [but] should be the director. . . . Good pictures . . . bear the signature . . . of this dominant personality: . . . Selznick, Zanuck, Thalberg, Guitry, Von Sternberg, Von Stroheim, Vidor, Capra, Ford, Menzies, Sturges, Chaplin, Sol Wurtzel. . . . This dominant personality is the essential of style in the motion picture art. When it is absent, a motion picture is a mere fabrication of the products of various studio departments from

the set builder to the manufacturer of dialogue, as meaningless as any
other merchandise achieved by mass production.

Schaefer hoped for something unique from the "dominant personality" Welles was determined to be, having asserted in a memo
to fellow executives, that "I was [only] able to secure Orson . . .
because of my sympathy with his viewpoint that he did not want to
. . . be tagged and cataloged." He needed Welles to make his mark
on RKO *and* Hollywood without delay. As John Houseman tersely
observes in *Runthrough*, "RKO was a maverick operation, the victim
of a long series of financial manipulations and changing manage-
ments . . . and [its] insecure boss . . . had little to lose and a lot to
gain by putting a good many of his eggs into the hands of the Wonder Boy of Broadway and radio, who just might come through with
a winner for him."

And so, on July 22, 1939, Orson Welles signed a provisional
two-picture deal with the Hollywood studio. The deal, finalized four
weeks later, comprised three separate contracts: a production agreement with "the Mercury Theatre" to "produce, direct, and write the
screenplay for two pictures"; an employment agreement with Welles
as actor; and a guarantee that Welles would personally deliver everything contained within the production agreement. It also provided
for Welles to receive $35,000 as producer and $30,000 as actor, plus
20 percent of the net profits, for his first film; and $35,000 as actor
and $25,000 as producer, plus 25 percent of the net profits of any sec-
ond film. Most significantly, and controversially, it contained a "final
cut" clause unprecedented in Hollywood history: "the distributor
shall be entitled to confer with the producer on the final cutting
and editing of each of the pictures prior to the delivery thereof, but
the control of such cutting shall vest in the producer."

Though this was not the carte blanche contract that initial
reports suggested—and even the usually circumspect *New York Times*
had reported that "the studio will exercise no supervision over the
picture, merely footing the bill"—the simple fact was that a twenty-
four-year-old theatre director, with no experience in film, had been

given the kind of contract for which the very directors Welles cited in *Stage* would have sold their families into slavery.

Such a contract was bound to create its own obstacles, even before Welles arrived in the West Coast colony to begin work. As he told one interviewer in 1966, "The real problem was that contract . . . I had too much power"; and another, in 1975, "The first contract I had when I came out here to this town was a kind of defiance of everything that was established in the Hollywood industrial system . . . [but] I thought if I asked for [the] impossible they'd leave me alone."

At the same time Welles was obliged to convince those around him that any such jealousy was as water off a platypus. Joseph Cotten, one of the Mercury troupe that insulated him from much of the envy and animosity, even suggested in his autobiography that, though "green eyes were watching him; [and] claws were being exposed, I am not sure he realized it." Welles knew all too well what happened when one set about threatening the status quo. After all, he'd been doing it for quite a while now:

> ORSON WELLES: I represented the ghost of Christmas future. Here was this guy with a beard who was going to do it all by [him]self. I was what was going to happen to that town. So I was hated and despised, theoretically, but I had all kinds of friends among the real dinosaurs, who were awfully nice to me, and I had a very good time. [1973]

At least the wannabe director got to enjoy a certain disinterest from those threatened with change for the first month of his stay. Although Welles arrived in town on July 20, the final draft of the fabled contract would not be agreed until August 21. Only then did its details become common knowledge. Meanwhile, he kept himself busy making and renewing contacts of his own. Almost his first social engagement was at the house of the Huxleys, Aldous and Maria, in Pacific Palisades. On July 30 Welles was one of a dozen guests invited to celebrate Huxley's forty-fifth birthday and the completion of his latest novel, *After Many a Summer Dies a Swan*, set at a thinly veiled San Simeon, where a Hearstian mogul spends his days with a young, flirtatious mistress, and his money on ways of delaying death (a theme Welles tackled head-on in the television pilot *Fountain of Youth*, where the professor's Austrian partner is even compared to an old, ugly monkey, à la Huxley's lost lord).

It seems inconceivable that Welles did not inquire about his host's latest work; nor Huxley ask about the film projects Welles had in mind, from *Cyrano de Bergerac* to a Joseph Conrad novella about a man's journey into the jungle to find another lost soul. Huxley, who had settled in Hollywood less than two years earlier, already an eminent literary figure and bestselling author of influential dystopia *Brave New World*, doubtless had his own words of warning for Welles. He had already found that the only reputation worth having in Hollywood was one earned there.

Another soul happy to befriend Welles in those early months was Preston Sturges. According to Welles, they had first met when he was just thirteen, staying "great chums . . . right up till the end of his life" in 1959. He would be the only American contemporary Welles cited in his "Major Branches of Cinema"; as well as warranting a mention as one of the "dominant personalities" of cinema in Welles's February 1941 *Stage* article, at a time when Sturges had just two credits as a writer-director to his name (*The Great McGinty* and *Christmas in July*).

Sturges was also awaiting his first opportunity to prove his worth as a writer-director when Welles arrived in town, having come to Hollywood as a successful playwright-turned-screenwriter back in 1932, one of the legions who never intended to stay but somehow never left. As he memorably recalled in his autobiography, "It took me exactly two days on the job as a hired writer, or until I met my first director, to find out that I was in the wrong racket."

Despite being credited with inventing something called "narratage" a year after his arrival for his nonchronological, told-in-flashback screenplay of a tycoon's rise and fall, *The Power and the Glory*, Sturges had spent a frustrating further six years trying to convince first Universal and then Paramount to let him direct one of his own scripts. Only when he made it clear that he would actually quit the studio, in the early months of 1939, did Paramount head of production William LeBaron finally relent and allow Sturges to direct a low-budget movie of a script he had written straight after *The Power and the Glory*, *The Vagrant* (a.k.a. *The Great McGinty*).

The contract for Sturges to make his own movie on his own terms, albeit with a Paramount producer as chaperone, was signed just two days after Welles's more fabled document. If Sturges envied Welles his contract, it never interfered with their friendship; and in those months before they started their tiny revolt against the hegemony of producers they doubtless compared strategies. Both would win their only Oscars for the original screenplays of their directorial debuts.

From the day he arrived in town Welles was obliged to tie his mast to Schaefer's sail. The RKO ship, though, was never a steady one, and Schaefer had at least as many green eyes watching him. When in September it was announced that Welles's first project—an adaptation of Conrad's *Heart of Darkness*—had a provisional budget of $750,000, *Hollywood Reporter* editor James Wilkerson questioned Schaefer's sense of priorities in print: "Mr. Schaefer evidently does not think an investment of $750,000 or more with an untried producer, writer, director, with a questionable story and a rumored cast of players who, for the most part, have never seen a camera, is a necessary cut in these critical times."

If Schaefer was obliged to play the diplomat, it was not Welles's style to go out of his way to smooth his own path. After he threw the traditional Hollywood arrival party, to which, *Vogue* cruelly claimed, "nobody who was anybody came. . . . In fact, nobody who was nobody [came]," Welles abandoned any attempt to ingratiate himself. When he had his tie cut in Chasen's restaurant by B-movie actor Ward Bond, "we went out in the parking lot and had it out."

Though Welles would later claim that "Hollywood has more to say against me, and says it, than I have to say against Hollywood," his ambivalence about the place continued to perplex him. When asked to write about Hollywood for *Esquire*, shortly after his return there in the 1950s, he did not spare his feelings re the place, nor his longing for the frisson New York always gave him:

> The metropolitan air is what one misses. Neither the theater nor its artists are at their best work in a suburb. Or a gigantic trailer camp. Whether we work before a camera or behind the footlights, actors are, by nature, city people. Hollywood is most precisely described as a colony . . . [and] colonies are notoriously somewhat cut off from reality, insular, bitchy and cliquish, snobbish—a bit loose as to morals but very strict as to appearances.

If he does seem to have had "a very good time" initially, he would ruefully reconsider the place in later life, after reading "a group of books about Hollywood that [my daughter] bought . . . When I take my own life out of it, and see what they did to other people, I [can] see that the story of that town was a dirty one."

It seems amazing that Welles should exclude himself from those it wronged, but he never envisaged becoming one of those long-term Hollywood habitués, "deeply tanned but unresigned to the sunshine and the flowers . . . confidently expect[ing] to take the next boat home." He was already informing some, "If they let me do a second picture, I'm lucky." As of September 1939, it looked like they might not even let him make his first.

◆   ◆   ◆   ◆

He had settled upon Joseph Conrad's *Heart of Darkness* as the raw material for his first film, believing it to be, as he later introduced it on the radio, "a downright incantation, [in which] we are almost persuaded that there is something essential waiting for all of us in the dark areas of the world." He seemed to be taking precious little notice of the clause Schaefer inserted in his contract, which stated that, though he had free rein on subject matter, his first film could not be "political or controversial." Welles already envisaged *Heart of Darkness* as an antifascist allegory, in which the looming threat to world peace from Europe's right-wing dictators was personified in the character of Kurtz. Also implicit would be the case for America's intervention and against international isolation, reflected in the actions of the film's narrator, Marlow.

In Welles's screenplay, Kurtz was made to espouse the view that "the leader, the strong voice of authority, is the highest expression of our culture—the fulfillment of superior race," which owed far more to Nietzsche than Conrad. Marlow, meanwhile, was made out to be a perennial fence-sitter. When asked about his politics, at the outset of the script, he insists, "I have no sympathies one way or another. I'm just here to run a boat." Only after he has traveled into the heart of a personal darkness does he come to understand the threat that men like Kurtz represent; and only then does he turn to the viewer—the only time Marlow's face would have been seen in the film, almost filling the screen as he looks directly into the lens—to say:

> You can't understand [a man like Kurtz]. How could you? With solid pavement under your feet, surrounded by kind neighbors ready to cheer you or to fall on you, stepping delicately between the butcher and the policeman, in the holy terror of scandal and gallows and lunatic asylums—how can you imagine what particular region of the first ages a man's untrammeled feet may take him into?

I somehow doubt that Welles highlighted these elements in his personal "pitch" to Schaefer. As long as he required Schaefer's approval to proceed, he preferred to keep the themes of the film vague, though he informed his own publicist, Herb Drake, that "the picture is, frankly, an attack on the Nazi system." RKO received no such guidance, even if a September 15 memo, ostensibly from Welles's mouthpiece, Drake, admitted that the film was "definitely NOT love in the tropics . . . Everyone and everything is just a bit off normal, just a little oblique."

But Welles was a man who had managed to make parallels between the murder of a would-be dictator two thousand years ago and events today in his highly praised précis of Shakespeare's *Julius*

Caesar. So perhaps such a leap should have been expected. He could hardly deny it once the script appeared. Indeed, when the film entered its production phase and Welles was obliged to come up with a press release, he was unabashed about its contemporary relevance, "[*Heart of Darkness* is] the story of an ordinary guy (Marlow) thrown into the company of evil men . . . representing every variety of the fascist mentality and morality. They are the vicious but not very intelligent class of person which is now attempting to take control of the world."

Though he would ultimately be obliged to abandon *Heart of Darkness*, Welles would continue to address the threat of world fascism in projects he presented to RKO. In the screenplay for *The Smiler with a Knife*, another possible pre–*Citizen Kane* project, he had Strangeways, a Wellesian figure, suggest that the American people may let a dictator in though the back door: "They'll never give a politician that much power. [But] how about a hero? We like heroes over here. And this one won't talk like a dictator. He'll look like a movie star, and everybody will love him." And in *The Way to Santiago*, a political thriller he intended to shoot immediately after *Citizen Kane*, one character Welles based on Lord Haw-Haw outlined a crash course for just such a coup d'état:

> Mr. England: Everything must move at the same time. We found that out in Europe. The terrorist provocation must break out simultaneously all through the country so that the public will be stunned and bewildered. They'll realize that only a strong man with dictatorial powers can save them . . . There'll be opposition from the unions and the peasant leagues. If there isn't, we'll make it. We'll jail the leaders, install our own people as the executives, rig a case against the head of the labor movement for misappropriation of union funds, and there we are. Purpose accomplished, minimum of discomfort for everybody.

During the early stages of the *Heart of Darkness* project, though, Welles was careful to tone down any overt didacticism. The September 15 memo, if anything, reads like an extended send-up of the atypical Hollywood thriller, rather than what it really was: an exercise in revealing as little as possible about the real themes its director intended to address. The memo may even have played a small part in starting the myth that Welles never had a firm handle on this film, nor a clear idea of how it might get made:

> The story is of a man and girl in love. They are separated by his career at the moment and the girl is coming to find him. The man is exploiting the river as a trader and as an explorer and is the head man of a whole company that is doing this in the name of a nonnamed foreign government. Girl goes to help rescue him since he has gone beyond the point reached by any of his assistants and has been missing for some months. There is a hell of an adventure going up the river. The action takes place largely on board a rusty stern-wheel paddle steamer at the stations of the trading company along the shore. There is an unhappy ending which we won't need to mention, man dies and the girl goes away unfulfilled. There are cannibals, shootings, petty bickerings among the bureaucrats, native dances, a fascinating girl, gorgeous, but black, a real Negro type. She has an inferred, but not definitely stated, jungle love life with our hero. There is a jungle in flames and heavy storms of a spectacular nature. . . . It all builds to a terrific climax in story when the man, Kurtz, is found at last. The jungle is set on fire and quenched by a storm. . . . We feel that once we get the audience in the theater it will go away completely thrilled and satisfied by the film even though [it] is not exactly in the boy-meets-girl tradition.

In those summer months Welles continued to work hard on this script that was hardly "in the boy-meets-girl tradition," contradicting Houseman's claim in his autobiography that, after arriving in California at this time, "every member of the organization . . . [wished to take] me aside to tell me that there was still no script for *Heart of Darkness.*" Welles delivered a first draft at the end of October 1939, shortly after spending his first night with a real movie camera in a genuine Hollywood studio. It ran to over 200 pages (most scripts ran between 120 and 140 pages.). If anything, Welles may have applied himself too much to this part of the process. He later informed Peter Bogdanovich that he "did a very elaborate preparation for that [film], such as I've never done again . . . I [may even have] shot my bolt on preproduction of that picture."

Certainly the studio staff was unused to the kind of demands this whippersnapper of a workaholic made on them. Starting in mid-August, there was a constant stream of requests for films to obtain for screening, some of which were simply intended to provide Welles with the requisite perspective. Along with the rushes for the second-most expensive film RKO had made to date, *The Hunchback of Notre Dame*, these included two of the films Welles later included in his top ten, Jean Renoir's *Le Grand Illusion* and John Ford's *Stagecoach*.

Much has been made of the multiple screenings of *Stagecoach* that Welles now undertook, but the fact is that it gave him an excellent template with which to understand the practical relevance of the various types of camera shots contained in a handmade textbook his assistant, Miriam Geiger, had compiled for him. As Welles later informed *Cahiers du Cinema*, "I didn't need to learn from somebody who had something to say, but from somebody who would show me how to say what I had in mind; and John Ford is perfect for that."

However, it was the search for good jungle footage that increasingly occupied Welles in the months of August and September, as he sought both for an effective approach to shooting such scenes and a way of reducing the potentially substantial costs (inserting existing footage where feasible). He already knew enough to be concerned about the likely cost of shooting such a film largely on location.

One internal memo, from some RKO employee searching for a film called *White Gods*, reports, "Can't find print as yet. [But] well-photographed picture of the Equadorean jungles; the life and customs of the Abarishi Indians—primitive men who never glimpsed a white man." After weeks of scurrying, a handwritten note informs, "9/7 Orson will see in NY." Another film, entitled *Wajan*, is damned with faint praise as "best Bali film yet produced. Additional advantage of good sound and photography." When Welles asked about a possible insert, though, the best Balinese cinema had to offer proved too much for his purse.

Welles had another, more pressing problem—one entirely of his own making. He had hit upon a wholly original way of shooting *Heart of Darkness* that would be in the spirit of Conrad and also announce him to Hollywood. He just wasn't sure it would work, and if it did, how much effort it might entail. That September 15 memo alluded to the story being "told in an entirely new way," while admitting that said methodology was "in the experimental stage, so [Welles] doesn't wish to mention it until we can find a convenient formula to express its meaning."

Welles had now decided to shoot the film as if the camera represented Marlow's line of vision—to make the first film in history that not only told its tale in first-person narrative but took the actual vantage of its narrator. Though he had yet to figure out how he might arrive at "a convenient formula," Welles knew it would not be easy—or cheap. Less than a month later, he arranged to send an undated memo, marked simply "Camera," detailing for the denizens of RKO just how one might go about shooting such a film:

> In filming *Heart of Darkness* the intention is to operate the camera so that, aesthetically speaking, there will be no interruption of action at any time, no cuts . . . [because] the camera has to function not only as a mechanical recording device but as a character. . . . Since the camera will be a character for the first time in its existence, it is going to have to undergo some changes . . . including several new gadgets[:] . . . a baby crane-trick calibrating device to handle the business of the "feather wipe" and a camera with a gyroscope mounted on it. . . . With cameras now in use, "tests indicate" a feeling of terrible stiffness, a mechanical effect, is noted. With the gyroscopic camera held in the hands of the cameraman himself a more casual effect is produced. . . . The feather wipe is a wipe on texture, say a wall. . . . The devices used will include dissolves but the action will never be interrupted for a second. This means, instead of cutting the picture here and there, you can only remove a whole sequence if you wish to shorten it. This operates to the

great advantage of the scenario since it means absolute perfection of preparation before any camera turns. It is not possible to shoot "off the cuff," nor is it possible to start a camera with only half the script written. This also means a tremendous saving in actual film.

Schaefer's reaction to this memo has not been recorded, but he must have been a mighty worried man. However, until he saw an actual screenplay, he was unable to comment on the practical realities. After all, the memo's author wisely observed, "it is not possible to shoot 'off-the-cuff,' nor is it possible to start a camera with only half the script written." Schaefer awaited the first draft with interest. Welles, meanwhile, was brimming with ideas, as he ripped into his copy of Conrad, writing and rewriting the novella to fit in with a preordained structure all his own.

In a story outline drawn up in the early days of the project, Welles divided the tale into six stages, each stage having its own visual metaphor, provided by the jungle itself. In the first stage, the jungle would be teeming with life, whereas the second and third stages would see the river close in, until the river became "nothing but a place cut out of this ghostly world by the steamer itself." By the fourth stage, dead cypress trees would envelop the boat; and by the fifth, the river would have become little more than a marsh, until it finally all but disappeared at the final outpost.

A version of this scheme was still in place when the memo of September 15 was written. It speaks of how the "jungle . . . changes in mood and intensity as the boat travels up the river. Said river gets narrower, the terrain changes from Savannah and open plains to woods, from woods to forest, from forest to jungle and all the time the excitement grows. . . . At the end, the boat is actually pushing aside the overhanging vines and creepers as it makes its last dash to the final station." But Welles's imagination was already running away with him, and he eventually had to abandon the six-tier scheme as impractical, reverting to subtler gradations of the jungle's decay as the boat makes its way into the interior. This meant another revision of the draft screenplay.

Welles had initially turned to his Mercury cofounder, John Houseman, for help with the script. Houseman recalls in his own book how "we wandered around the sound stages and talked about *Heart of Darkness,* which Orson had just announced—with considerable fanfare *and without consulting me* [my italics]—as his first picture." Houseman, by his own admission, was "frightened by the necessities of an unfamiliar medium" and was "unable to give him anything at all," so Welles was ultimately required to find his way alone.

If Houseman was no longer a necessary collaborator, Conrad proved an equally circumspect partner in the process. Welles had developed something of a reputation in New York for disrespecting source material. *New York Times* theater critic Brooks Atkinson had described his *Macbeth* as "a voodoo show inspired by the Macbeth legend"; while a *Billboard* report on the film prologue he intended to shoot for *Too Much Johnson* suggested that he had perhaps "succumbed again to his passion for chopping scripts to pieces."

Welles felt self-conscious enough about this reputation to insist on an essential reverence for his literary source in Mercury memos to RKO, asserting that, "while he is changing the locale from the Belgian Congo to an unnamed river and unnamed place, and . . . adding characters and moving the girl from Europe to the river, he is in no way violating Conrad . . . his treatment of *Heart of Darkness* [being] completely in the Conrad spirit." Perhaps so, but a loose-leaf page in Welles's marked-up copy of the novella (see illustration at head of chapter) contains a single scrawled sentence, in that unmistakeable hand, which turns the book's theme on its head: "Kurtz is the Byron of a totalitarian state—what Byron would be if he had become president of Greece."*

If Kurtz became recast as some would-be Byronic dictator, the role of Elsa, Kurtz's girlfriend, who only appears right at the end of the book, was dramatically expanded by Welles, who possibly felt

---

*Peter Conrad, in *Orson Welles: Stories of His Life,* suggests that Welles saw himself as a Byron, but the identification here is clearly between Kurtz and Byron, not Welles and Byron.

obliged to abide by at least one Hollywood convention. Rather than hearing of Kurtz's fate at the story's end, Elsa accompanies Marlow on his journey, providing not only the so-called "love interest," but adding another dynamic to Marlow's identification with, and envy of, Kurtz (made manifest by Welles's decision to play both parts).

The most dramatic amplification of this dynamic came when Welles turned Marlow's dream/vision of Kurtz at the book's end into a full-blown apparition, which dissolves (literally!) into a funeral procession for the great man. Whereas Conrad's Marlow simply "had a vision of him . . . with that wide immense stare embracing, condemning, loathing, all the universe," Welles's Marlow says instead, "I saw him again—months later, at the foot of the river—I saw him. With Elsa—I saw those eyes—that wide immense stare condemning, loathing the whole universe—piercing enough to penetrate all the hearts that beat in the darkness." The shot promptly dissolves into the dining hall of the river station. It is night, and it is raining. The camera pans toward the doorway, and we see, though only in silhouette, Kurtz being borne on a litter, with ivory-bearers behind and before:

> The door, in far corner of the room, opens now, throwing a dim angled pattern of light across the corrugated iron wall at the back, seen through the silhouette of Kurtz. This washes out the last impressions of the jungle and the campfires, but the silhouette of Kurtz's head remains, although it appears more faintly in the composition. Elsa comes out of the door and stops there, looking toward [the] camera. As she speaks, there sneaks in on the soundtrack—very, very faintly— the love strains of Elsa's waltz. . . . She carries the lamp with her as she moves toward camera until, as she speaks . . . the light of the lamp [is] showing her face and rendering the silhouette of Kurtz very pale so that as she moves in, it almost vanishes from the screen and only its outlines can be made out, framing her face. The appearance of the light, however, and its intensification is synonymous with the appearance in their proper proportions of the shadow of Kurtz's eyes, which gleam luminously into the lens.

ELSA (looking intently at Marlow): You were with him when he died . . .

[Marlow hears in his head Kurtz's last words:] The Horror! The Horror!

After Kurtz's voice is heard, the last indication of his silhouette dims off the screen and, as the sound of his voice fades away, his eyes glow out and disappear like dying coals. At the sound of his voice the tiny murmur of the waltz is no more.

This would be terrific stuff for a Huston or a Ford, at the top of their game. For a novice without a single film to his name it suggests somebody already capable of conceptualizing something remarkably cinematic. Even this early in his career, Welles had a real flair for dramatic staging, especially of funerals (most memorably in *Othello*). The *Heart of Darkness* script—which is all that remains of the film Welles had in his head—suggests that Kurtz's could have been another triumphant set piece.

Nor was Welles's visual imagination content to run its course there. After Marlow reassures Elsa with a white lie, hiding the awful truth from her, Welles sought to visualize the idea of the darkness closing in on them both. For Conrad, it was easy enough to say that "with every word spoken the room was growing darker." For Welles, though, this would not do. Initially, he added the following lines in the margin of his copy of Conrad, "triumphant darkness—from which I could not have defended her—from which I could not even defend myself," an insight into Marlow's thought processes.

The challenge remained: how to visualize such an idea. His solution was ingenious. As Elsa's eyes fill up with tears she begins to look beyond the lens of the camera, i.e. Marlow's eyes. Then, as the music fades in, she appears as in a spotlight on a stage. As the camera dollies back, "the set lighting dims out so that as this shot completes itself, Elsa is seen very small in the aperture . . . with nothing but darkness around her." At this point we return to New York harbor. Marlow is musing about whether he should have told her the truth. The night closes in and the credits roll. Even Conrad might have been impressed.

Where Welles was fully released from any textual reverence, self-imposed or otherwise, was in the prologue, through which he aimed to both introduce himself and lead the audience by its metaphorical hand into the heart of darkness. He hoped that by using a series of daring devices, the aware spectator might recognize that s/he was being, in Brecht's words, "put in a position where [s/]he can make comparisons about everything that influences the way in which human beings behave." As James Naremore notes in *The Magic World of Orson Welles*, the entire prologue was intended to "cut against the grain of the impersonal factory style, serving both as an entertaining device and as a commentary upon the illusory, potentially authoritarian nature of the medium."

This prologue would have begun with the disembodied voice of Welles, familiar to anyone who had a radio set in America. Almost immediately he asks the viewer "to divide this audience into two parts—you and everybody else in the theater," before placing the viewer at the end of a gun barrel, then as a reluctant talking parrot, and finally in an electric chair, as a convict about to face the death penalty. Even Welles cannot have expected to get the climax to the latter scene past the censorious Hays Office. "Sound of current being turned on. Screen goes into blinding red stain. Camera blurring its focus at the same time, moves quickly to electrician whose outline distorts terribly, melts into dirty violet, and sound of current [is] magnified into terrific metallic ring."

As the screen reverts to black Welles insists that "there is no cause for alarm." He was merely fulfilling an intention previously expressed in the memo, to demonstrate that "the audience plays a key part in this film." His next sleight of camera-hand would have involved turning the camera back upon itself, showing the viewer "what you ought to look like to me," before cutting to the interior of a movie theater as the camera pans down from the projection booth to the orchestra floor, to find that "the audience is entirely made up of motion picture cameras" (Welles uses the subjective camera in a similar way in *Citizen Kane*'s famous Chicago Opera House scene, where Susan the Camera peers out into an expectant auditorium, but only sees what one actually would, a black void). As he expresses the hope that we "get the idea," a human eye appears on the screen, then an equal sign and a capital "I." The eye winks and we dissolve into the heart of darkness.

Having indulged in such a shameless display of visual bravado, the opening scene of the film proper would have applied all that Welles had learned from his years in radio to make the film's sound-track as evocative and authentic to the spectator as its images. After a series of lap dissolves introduced the viewer to the familiar land-marks of New York, and as the parkways, boulevards, and skyscrap-ers were in turn illuminated, s/he would have heard the sounds of the city in "snatches of sound and music, the beginnings of life of the city at night":

> In Central Park, snatches of jazz music is heard from the radios in the moving taxicabs.
>
> The sweet dinner music in the restaurants of the big hotels further west.
>
> The throb of tom-toms foreshadow the jungle music of the story to come.
>
> The lament of brasses, the gala noodling of big orchestras tuning up in concert halls and opera houses, and finally, as the camera finds its way downtown below Broadway, the music freezes into an expres-sion of the empty shopping district of the deserted Battery—the mournful muted clangor of the bell buoys out at sea, and the hoot of shipping.

The idea of different musical themes bleeding into one another, their spirit immediately evoking a time and place, was one idea Welles filed away after *Heart of Darkness* went unrealized, to reappear in the "restored" *Touch of Evil*, during that memorable opening crane shot, as the cafes and bars vie with each other in a Mexican musi-cal spat.

For *Heart of Darkness* Welles planned to introduce a number of auditory innovations into a medium in which the soundtrack had for too long been considered a poor relation of the image. The overlapping dialogue that became such a feature of *Citizen Kane* would have been equally evident in *Heart of Darkness*. In his screenplay, Welles prefaced a crucial dining-room scene involving Marlow, Elsa, and the manager, Blauer, by stating that "there is no attempt to focus on faces for definite speeches; all the speeches will overlap preceding ones so that we will hear a jumbled conversation, [but] with important words and phrases . . . standing out distinctly on the soundtrack."

In another scene, where Kurtz is finally taken away from the natives, Welles intended to let the music ebb and flow, counterpointing events as they unfolded. When the camera panned to the crowd of natives thronging the shore, "music fills the soundtrack . . . so that the dialogue [on board the boat] cannot be heard." But when the boat has finally begun to pull away from the shore, "the music is heard—and the music itself expresses—the throb of the engines as the boat moves away."

The most potentially moving (if controversial) use of sound as planned would have come early in the film, as Marlow was walking up the hill toward the settlement. Here he would witness firsthand the way that his fellow white men treated the natives. Initially, as he turns to look back at the harbor, he hears a native "singing a mournful lament." As he sees a chain gang approaching, this lament continues and we register the identity of the singer. The chain gang then proceeds up the hill.

The next scene in the screenplay is of "a big, ridiculous hole in the face of the mud bank. In it, frying in the sun, are about thirty-five dying savages and a lot of broken drainpipes. Into some of these pipes the natives have crawled, the better to expire. The whole picture is one of terrible desolation and despair. As Marlow looks down to the singer, who is one of this number and who is lying on a little ledge, the camera pans down . . . registering . . . a Negro face, the eyes staring up into the lens." Here Welles has distilled the essence of Conrad, adding his own powerful visual image of the natives crawling into the pipes. But as Marlow walks away from the devastation, the lament continues to echo through the soundtrack, until

DEFINITELY NOT LOVE IN THE TROPICS 31

he arrives at the settlement itself and the "sound of the native's voice blends gradually into the tinkle of a piano which comes from the dining hall."

This was not intended to be the last we saw (or heard) of the dying. When Marlow meets the manager Blauer, he comes upon one of the white colonists, Brandenburg, in the last throes of a fatal fever, lying on a mattress in the outer office. Blauer, a true humanitarian, closes the door behind Marlow, saying, "The groans of the dying man make it difficult to work." It is a comment on all that Marlow has witnessed or will witness. As Blauer tells him about the man Kurtz, the soundtrack and camera work (sic) conspire to render his thoughts irrelevant:

> Blauer's voice . . . is now overwhelmed by music. This music makes reference to Blauer's voice, to the groans of the dying man, to the tinkle of Eddie's piano, to the somber overtones of the New York harbor. Blauer is seen to be still talking, but we cannot distinguish what he says. As this happens the camera starts to pull back, smoothly but swiftly. Simultaneously with this movement of the camera, Blauer's image begins to wash out. . . . When [the camera] gets outside door of Blauer's office [it] then starts to rise . . . gradually and solemnly, [before it] angles down to the floor so that we again see the dying man. This is the last clear impression we get on the fading interior.

If this depiction of man's indifference to man was not enough to send shivers down Schaefer's spine, Welles added precious few sops to Conrad's acid depiction of rank imperialism. Taken verbatim from Conrad was one speech Marlow recited in its entirety, "It's not a pretty thing when you look into it too much, the conquest of the earth, which mostly means the taking it away from those who have a different complexion, or slightly different-shaped noses than ourselves. What tries to redeem it is the idea at the back of it." Nor can Welles's reference to Kurtz's "inferred . . . jungle love life with a gorgeous [girl], but black, a real Negro type," have gone down well at the president's table.

Yet there is an even more shocking notion incorporated into the script by Welles, in a starker form than Conrad. The native crew on the white man's boat wishes to capture some of the primitives threatening them, with a view to dining on them. The white crew, though, hold no such appeal in the culinary department. Whereas Conrad contemplates the various reasons why they might be so unappetizing, Welles directly implies "that civilized man is no longer nourishing." As Bret Wood suggests in his bio-bibliography, this reference serves to underline "the idea that civilization corrupts the natural state of man."

The underlying idea expressed here may have eluded Schaefer (and most of his fellow executives), but they surely noticed one of the lines uttered by a frightened white crew member, that provided a neat summation of the essential plot to Welles's film, "We're going to be eaten by cannibals so you can rescue a corpse." Did Schaefer really have any intimation that this was what he was about to receive? Had he read the Conrad original, or was he relying on the Mercury radio adaptation, as he was later to do with *The Magnificent Ambersons*? Guerric DeBona is certainly right to suggest, in a 1994 *Cinema Journal* article on the project, that "Welles's film was shockingly unorthodox in its treatment of racial themes."

Though *Heart of Darkness* had been Welles's chosen project since August, being specifically named in the final contract he signed with RKO, Schaefer had to wait until the second week in November for his first sight of a complete script. A 202-page script was delivered to RKO for mimeographing on November 7. Copies were immediately forwarded to Budgeting, the Hays Office, and Schaefer in New York.

Welles's first draft had apparently been finished a couple of weeks earlier, but it had not conformed to the accepted form in its scene divisions or camera directions. So Amalia Kent, an RKO script supervisor, had been drafted in to work directly with Welles, who proceeded to describe intended camera movements to her in some detail. Kent obligingly translated this into recognizable screenplay dialect.

Nine days later Schaefer sent a note to Welles that was hardly the effusive response he might have hoped for. Rather, Schaefer predicted "a very unusual picture," before querying the sheer number of voice-overs and questioning the wisdom of making such obvious political parallels. He was unhappy with a couple of clear allusions to Hitler at a time when America was still ostensibly neutral in what would be (for two years yet) an essentially European conflict. Kurtz's dying tirade includes a particularly pointed reference, courtesy of Welles, "There's a man now in Europe trying to do what I've done in the jungle. He will fail. In his madness he thinks he can't fail—but he will."

By now, though, all the relevant studio wheels were in motion and Welles was confident that sheer momentum would keep everything moving forward. On October 18, he had breathlessly cabled Herb Drake, Mercury's one business head and unit publicity director, "Had my first night with the movie cameras a few hours ago and I am wildly enthusiastic about the business, Orson." In early November, he undertook a further four days of test shooting, using the scene at the First Station when Marlow first encounters Elsa.

These vitally important tests did not go so well. According to Amalia Kent, Welles's assistant assigned by RKO, "it was an enormously laborious and time-consuming process because of the elaborate camera movements and the intricate repositionings and measurements needed for the feather wipes." The scene in question required six of these feather wipes, which Welles had devised as a way of making shots look continuous even when a number of cuts were used. The technique involved, in Robert Carringer's words, "panning the camera to a stationary point, repositioning the camera but directing it at the same point, then continuing the pan in a new shot." It was all part of an elaborate pretense that Welles was obliged to maintain to give a sense of the camera-as-Marlow passing from one room into another. It was an ingenious solution, but horrifically time-consuming. And there were over fifty such feather wipes in the full script.

To what extent the budget department factored these fifty feather wipes into their eventual costs has not been documented, but when they finally delivered an estimated cost for the movie, it was $1,057,761. Welles's contract allowed for a budget per film of $500,000. To put all of this in perspective, Sturges's budget for *The Great McGinty* was $400,000. On the other hand, RKO made two films in 1939 that cost nearly $2,000,000 (*The Hunchback of Notre Dame*, at $1,826,000, a great success; and *Gunga Din*, at $1,915,000, an absolute catastrophe).

Welles was plunged into one of his great depressions, partially alleviated by a letter dated December 7 from RKO's Eddie Donahoe that detailed how an estimated budget of $910,740 for *Swiss Family Robinson* had been reduced to $596,000. Donahoe urged less despondency. "Whether we can take out that amount of money through a series of budget meetings and rewrite eliminations, is something we'll just have to go in and try, but it certainly isn't a hopeless task."

By then Welles had already trimmed twenty pages from his screenplay, delivering the "Revised Estimating Script" on November 30, two days after he had received RKO's own shooting schedule. The shooting schedule ran to eighty-two days; but special effects work would have to be completed beforehand, and principal photography matched to it, so there would be a significant delay before filming could begin. Meanwhile, there remained a gaping hole in the cast, as Welles's original choice for Elsa, Dita Parlo, was unable to leave Europe and he had failed to entice the newly arrived Ingrid Bergman to become her replacement.

Welles was undoubtedly still hoping (and expecting) to salvage the film as he flew to New York to meet Schaefer on December 9, to iron out the way ahead. However, the Mercury actors had already been informed that they would be taken off salary at the end of the week, prior to a further meeting on the fourteenth to discuss ways of trimming the film's budget. The deal he struck with Schaefer in New York was a typical Wellesian compromise: he would put *Heart of Darkness* on hold and would instead make a low-budget thriller for the studio, *The Smiler with a Knife*, for $400,000. Meanwhile, he would endeavor to overcome some of the logistical difficulties that the test shoots had thrown up, with a view to resuming work on Conrad in the spring. Welcome to Hollywood, Mr. Welles.

The *Hollywood Reporter* correctly predicted at the time that "*Heart of Darkness* won't ever be done." Where the gossip rags were proven wrong was in their prediction that "the current Welles confab with Schaefer in New York may end the whole works." They knew that the date when he was supposed to deliver his first film (January 1, 1940) was fast approaching, but Schaefer's faith in Welles's ability to deliver something startlingly original remained undimmed. For all its disconcerting aspects, the *Heart of Darkness* screenplay reaffirmed both an originality of thinking and a depth of understanding for the medium. Even in this rich period, how many directors working in Hollywood knew how to compact so much into each little scene, whether it be the rich use of sound, the dramatic use of light and shade, or an ineluctable instinct for the visually evocative?

> INT. PILOT HOUSE—NIGHT . . .
>
> The bamboo effect has stopped. . . . From the jungle comes a new sound, lower than the others, sustained and vibrant. With another giggle Carbs raises the bottle [of champagne] to his mouth, opens his mouth to blow [in imitation]. Then he freezes in that position, his mouth open, his eyes staring. [The] camera has focused on his face and now moves down very slightly to show a thin sliver of an arrow is through his neck. He drops the champagne bottle. Marlow hears it fall and watches him topple to the floor. [The] camera pans down to floor with the body. Marlow is still staring at Carbs' body when the Steersman falls on top of it, an arrow in his chest. The Steersman is dead but his eyes are on Marlow.

This was cinematic enough for Francis Ford Coppola to adopt the nub of the idea for the parallel scene in *Apocalypse Now*, his own not-so-respectful adaptation of Conrad. Back in 1939, though, few of Welles's doubters had seen the evidence of his first screenplay, or knew how hard he had strived to learn the RKO ropes. Even those who knew of his ability to transform raw literary material into something genuinely arresting were less than gracious about his perceived failure and concocted their own explanation for the reasons why. John Houseman, temporarily estranged from Welles, believed that he had fallen foul of the fame game and wrote a letter to that effect to composer Virgil Thomson:

> This new fame has grown in inverse proportion to the success of our [sic] recent artistic endeavors. . . . It is an appetite that grows as it is fed: in a creative artist, it becomes a compensation and a substitute for creation. . . . That is the main reason why, for seven months now, a picture (under one of the most magnificent contracts ever granted an artist in Hollywood) has been "about to be made."

But then, according to Houseman, there never was a script to *Heart of Darkness*, nor a shooting schedule, film tests, casting decisions, or budgetary restrictions. Welles himself, for better or worse, made no press pronouncement as to why the film remained stillborn, but simply kept moving ahead. Only many years later, in conversation with Barbara Leaming, did he suggest that it came down to the fundamental issue of control: "I wanted *my* kind of control. They didn't understand that. There was no quarreling. It was just two different points of view, absolutely opposite each other. Mine was taken to be ignorance, and *I* read their position as, you know, established dumbheadedness."

Welles felt that he could only make a film of *Heart of Darkness* his way, his how. Only now did he realize that it would require a degree of commitment from the studio—logistical and financial—that it would not (or, perhaps more accurately, no longer could) make. The cinematography alone would have required substantial expertise and considerable resources, and it was not something Welles felt confident would be done right. This realization probably first dawned during those four days of test shoots. By the time he saw the budget, and had heard firsthand from Schaefer how desperate the studio's business situation had become—thanks to the loss of markets caused by Europe's little fracas—he realized the game was up.

Though the Hollywood press cruelly dubbed *The Smiler with a Knife* "Mr. Welles's latest forthcoming picture," it was never conceived as anything but a stopgap measure. It was certainly never going to be the movie with which he intended to make his Hollywood debut. *Heart of Darkness* might have to wait until he had proved himself, but prove himself he would.

Schaefer was, meanwhile, hard at work shoring up his own position in the organization, after the departure of Pandro Berman at the beginning of December. The new chain of executive command he now constructed was designed to leave him firmly at the helm, with his own assistant, J. J. Nolan, promoted to vice president in charge of the studio and a former independent producer and agent, Harry E. Edington, placed in charge of high-budget films. Both were entirely beholden to Schaefer for these heady new powers and were expected to toe the line accordingly. Now all that Schaefer required was for his independent production units to begin to generate results, and in particular for the wunderkind from Wisconsin to prove all his carping critics spectacularly wrong.

THE WELLESIAN
MOSAIC

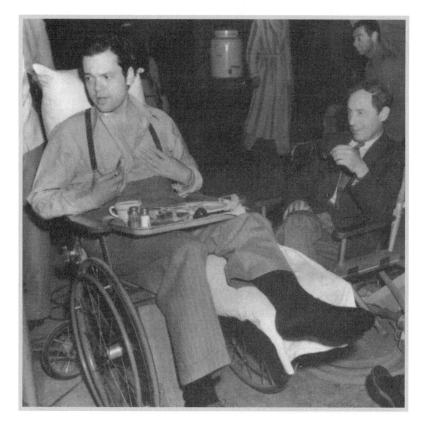

[Citizen Kane]

We were just ready to shoot [my screen test] when there appeared
suddenly six men in long overcoats and felt hats. I thought, my
goodness, these are gangsters who have come to stop the film. [But]
when they came closer, we realized they were RKO brass from New
York. After congratulating Orson on beginning the film, they called in a
dump truck, which deposited a ton of rank flowers on the floor. They
explained . . . they were sorry about the condition of the flowers, but
they had been fresh months ago when [*Heart of Darkness*] had first
been announced. Everybody laughed at the joke and shook hands.
But they didn't leave. Instead, they just folded their hands and said,
"OK, genius, show us. Start filming. Be a genius."

—Ruth Warrick [a.k.a. Emily Kane]

eart of Darkness had provided Welles with an invaluable
education in the ways of the West. Without that experience, *Citizen Kane* would have been a very different picture. But when one was lampooned as a "would-be genius," such a
highly publicized apprenticeship merely compounded the expecta-
tions of others, whether of failure or success, dissipation or vindication. So when, in January 1940, Welles found himself back at
something resembling square one, he knew that he had only one
option. As Francois Truffaut put it twenty years later, "He was
forced to make not a film which permitted him to get started in the
industry, but *the* film, the one which sums up and prefigures all the
others."

Not that Welles lacked ideas. He always had ideas, ways of
deconstructing set patterns of presentation to render them anew.
The one he had now, according to Mercury assistant Richard Baer,
first came up "in a conversation with Jack Houseman at the 21 Club
in New York." Baer, who signed a legal deposition to this effect,

wrote at the time of the film's release that "the idea of *Citizen Kane* was the original conception of Orson Welles, who in the early part of the year 1940 first discussed the idea [with John Houseman] and elaborated upon the same. The conception of the picture evidently appealed to Houseman, who suggested that both he and Welles leave for Los Angeles and discuss the idea with [scriptwriter] Herman Mankiewicz."

Baer's deposition is the only contemporary document we have as to the genesis of the film and is the sworn testimony of a firsthand witness without any obvious motive for perjuring himself. Sadly, he does not elaborate on the idea Welles espoused to Houseman, though it seems unlikely that the word "Hearst" had yet arisen in parentheses. Rather, it would appear that Welles's conceit was the more amorphous one he first highlighted in a statement made to the press in January 1941, with *Citizen Kane* barely completed:

> I wished to make a motion picture which was not a narrative of action so much as an examination of character. For this, I desired a man of many sides and many aspects. It was my idea to show that six or more people could have as many widely divergent opinions concerning the nature of a single personality.

Whenever he subsequently expounded on the source of *Kane*'s conceit, Welles consistently insisted that "we began on this idea of seeing it from various points of view." In a lecture given to the New York University Film School in October 1942, he would actually suggest, "I got the idea from the Bible; from the appearances of witnesses who came to testify to a man's character. [So] I don't know what is new about that." Before the film's premiere, he had suggested, that "the point of the picture is not so much the solution to the problem as its presentation."

Certainly the presentation, rather than its solution, was the one original aspect of a recent novel that Welles was "very fond of," *I Am Jonathan Scrivener* by Claude Houghton, first published in the United States in 1939. According to Welles's musical director,

Bernard Herrmann, "Orson was [certainly] influenced by . . . [this book]. All its characters talk about a man they know. In the last sentence, the doorbell rings and the butler announces Mr. Jonathan Scrivener. You never see him." It was an ingenious approach, fully enigmatic enough to influence our Orson.

Yet a more likely—asserted by some as undeniable—source for *Citizen Kane*'s approach lay not in testaments, old and new, or modern first editions, but in a film that had made the name of his good friend Preston Sturges in Hollywood. *The Power and the Glory* told the tale of a tycoon's rise and fall in flashback at his funeral. This so-called debt has been cited as fact in a number of Sturges studies, even though Welles denied point-blank to Peter Bogdanovich that he ever saw the film, dismissed it as "one of those coincidences," and insisted that Sturges himself "never accused me of it." In fact, however similar the fractured narrative structure of both films may be, *Citizen Kane* crucially relies on multiple narratives, as opposed to *The Power and the Glory*'s single narrator relaying "the visual action of a silent picture," as Sturges put it. It may well be that what Welles learned about structuring narrative came rather from hours spent watching films like D. W. Griffith's *Intolerance*, and drinking and conversing with "great chums" like Sturges, actor John Barrymore, and screenwriter and raconteur Herman Mankiewicz.

Herman Mankiewicz, in particular, seems to have greatly intrigued Welles. According to Houseman, the pair had first met in New York, probably in 1939, by which time Mankiewicz had long sold his soul to the Hollywood dollar. A part-time screenwriter, but a full-time alcoholic, Herman had been applying his two cents' worth to screenplays since the mid-1920s, being generally viewed as "a great paragrapher, [but] not really a picture writer," to quote fellow scribe and confidant Charles Lederer. If he almost never received sole credit on any of his Hollywood hackwork, the studios' "never too many cooks" ethos generally suited "Mank" just fine.

Increasingly considered a liability, as he devoted himself more and more to his true vocation, Mankiewicz was sour and bitter enough to enthrall Welles, who reveled in the stories of old Hollywood with which he was regaled. As Welles commented, "nobody was *more* miserable, *more* bitter and *funnier* than Mank." But Herman was also hard up, after recently burning down his last bridge on the MGM lot—playing cards with a recently secured loan from, and in full view of, studio boss Louis Mayer. He took up Welles's offer to work on the *Campbell's Playhouse* series, now in its second season.

Starting in November 1939 Welles hired his new drinking buddy to write five of the remaining Campbell scripts, as he saw out his contract with the tiresomely demanding sponsor. Mankiewicz couldn't help but sympathize with Welles when he heard of how his first film project had come to naught, and appeared anxious to collaborate on any future projects. He probably believed that Welles had little experience as an original scriptwriter, presumably unaware of clumsy early efforts like *The Marching Song* and *Bright Lucifer*. He may even have felt that *John Citizen USA*, Welles's working title, was a project he could make his own. He certainly chased the chance. According to Welles, "I didn't know how *not* to let him in since the essential idea of the many-sided thing had arisen in conversation with him," though Baer credits Houseman, not Mankiewicz, with that honor.

Film critic Pauline Kael, who turned her hand to the question of the "authorship" of *Citizen Kane* in a famous *New Yorker* article, "Raising Kane," in 1969, convinced herself that it was coauthor Mankiewicz who was responsible for "the prismatic technique" in *Citizen Kane*, which he somehow "turned into a masterly juggling act," despite almost never setting foot on the lot once shooting began. One of the many annoying little facts Kael overlooked to establish her thesis was that (*Citizen Kane* excepted) Mankiewicz never attempted, before or afterward, to deviate from the norms of Hollywood storytelling. On the other hand, the words "prismatic" and "juggling act" describe rather precisely the methodology of every Welles directorial effort.

Where the hand of Mankiewicz *can* be seen in the early drafts of *Citizen Kane* is in the diametrically opposed portraits the various witnesses originally painted, as if the man they were describing was some kind of undiagnosed multiple personality (as opposed to the "divided self" film critic Noel Carroll suggests Kane to be). Though Welles initially favored this approach, he later toned down the "more dramatic differences of point of view" when he realized that it simply was not going to work cinematically. As he put it in 1982, "the story got a little better than the gag."

Virtually all that remains of those extreme perspectives in the finished film is a single scene in the newsreel sequence, where Kane is denounced as a communist by his legal guardian and a fascist by a speaker in Union Square in almost the same foot of film; and then, surviving intact from the earliest known draft of *Citizen Kane*, predating even the so-called *American* script, a set of newspaper headlines announcing his death, "many of them . . . reveal[ing] passionately conflicting opinions about [Kane] . . . contain[ing] variously the words, 'patriot,' 'democrat,' 'pacifist,' 'war-monger,' 'communist,' 'traitor,' 'idealist,' 'fascist,' 'American,' etc."

If it was Welles who was largely responsible for conceptualizing *Citizen Kane*'s "prismatic technique"—which alone would have warranted a co-credit—it was in all likelihood Mankiewicz who first suggested the newspaper tycoon, William Randolph Hearst, as a possible template for the "big man" Welles wanted at the center of his labyrinth (as Welles said in 1978, "I suppose I would remember if it had been me"). Changing the provisional title of the script from *John Citizen USA* to *American* (the subtitle of a 1936 authorized biography of Hearst, and therefore a deliciously ironic title for such an unauthorized deconstruction) certainly smacks of Mankiewicz. Welles was immediately enamored of the idea.

Hearst was an ideal choice. He was known to both Mankiewicz and—through his late father, his guardian Dr. Bernstein, and drama critic Ashton Stevens—to Welles; he was a larger-than-life figure; and he represented a man whose isolationist stance was the antithesis of all that Welles most fervently believed. He had also enjoyed his share of scandals, including his peculiar marital arrangements, living with a long-term mistress but never divorcing his Catholic wife; an assassination attempt on President McKinley that many blamed on his newspaper editorials; and a particularly notorious, unsolved death that occurred on his private yacht in 1927. Mankiewicz, as a one-time regular at San Simeon, had rich anecdotal material on much of this, and most especially on Hearst's mistress, fellow alcoholic Marion Davies.

Attacking Hearst and his politics was nothing new for Welles. Five years before *Citizen Kane* he had starred in a play called *Ten Million Ghosts*, which contained a highly Hearstian antihero, espousing decidedly right-wing views. And he had doubtless been following with great interest the reception that greeted publication of his friend Huxley's novel, *After Many a Summer Dies a Swan*, the previous November. In Huxley's book, the Hearst character, Jo Stoyte, is an obsessive acquirer of things, who sees his pale horse approaching and promptly loses all reason.

Welles was equally intrigued by the dichotomy between the ultraconservative xenophobe Hearst had become by 1939 and the young swinger (Welles's word) his father had known. Mankiewicz's view of the man, now that his heavy drinking had finally resulted in expulsion from Hearst's kingdom, was a more jaundiced kaleidoscope of fear and loathing. It was Mankiewicz's bilious venom that Welles was ultimately obliged to tone down if not expunge from the script, if he was going to make Kane into the first of his sympathetic monsters.

And yet, as Welles told Mankiewicz's biographer Richard Merryman, "there was a quality to the film that was Mank . . . a kind of controlled virulence." There was also from the very outset, in Welles's mind's eye, "a certain tension: that [stemmed from the fact that] one of the authors hated Kane and one of them loved him . . . In his hatred of Hearst, or whoever Kane was, Mank didn't have a clear enough idea of who the man was. Mank saw him simply as an egomaniac monster with all these people around him. So I don't think a portrait of a man was ever present in any of Mank's scripts . . . I felt his . . . point of view [was] of a newspaperman writing about a newspaper boss he despised."

Certainly the initial script, *American*, represents "the point of view of a newspaperman writing about a newspaper boss he despised." In fact, Welles informed Merryman that the writer wanted to build the movie around the shooting of Thomas Ince on Hearst's yacht in 1927. Mankiewicz himself claimed, on the one occasion he talked "on the record" about the writing of *Citizen Kane*, a late 1940s deposition for a plagiarism suit brought by Hearst biographer Ferdinand Lundberg, that he had originally expressed to Welles his interest "in doing a picture based on Hearst and Marion Davies. . . . It wasn't really *Citizen Kane* at all, because we were going to do a great love story."

This "great love story" had, by the time of its earliest draft, come to include a scene in Italy where the Kane character is surrounded by "pimps, lesbians, dissipated army officers, homosexuals, nymphomaniacs and degenerates in general. [Kane], aged 25 today, is draped along the fireplace, talking to a hideous woman, under five feet in height and weighing 300 pounds, who is 65 years old and trying to look 25." This was to be the day that Kane came into his majority and inherited all.

The death of the Hearstian figure is treated in an equally sordid, unsentimental manner, with the camera not entering through Xanadu's window, but down a corridor, past a white hospital table on rubber wheels: "As it goes by, we catch sight of the sordid paraphernalia on it—a basin, some surgical instruments, some soiled towels—and the starched white skirt and the white shoes of the nurse who propels it." As the door to Kane's bedroom begins to close, we catch "the sound, faintly of a shrill, choked voice and the one word 'Rosebud!'"

At least in this original scene we know who it is that hears such a talismanic epitaph—unlike in the finished film. Its inclusion here confirms that the hook on which the film was duly hung was banged in early. It is a device that Welles always credited to Mankiewicz, for it is a perfect Hollywood solution to a cinematic conundrum: how to make the key and the search one and the same. If Welles accepted that "it was the only way we could find to get off," it is, as Brian O'Doherty has written, "a brilliant formulation. To treat it contemptuously is to have contempt for the popular audience, for it is the sled that takes them through the movie, and if they are not along for the ride, you don't have a movie."

If Rosebud appears to confirm Mankiewicz's key contribution to the genesis of the script, far too many commentators have accepted the contention, first voiced by the largely unreliable Houseman, that the first draft of *Citizen Kane* was wholly the work of Mankiewicz, off the top of his head as it were. This is despite independent testimony found in Richard Baer's May 1941 deposition, which bluntly states:

> As portions of the script were finished, the finished portions were sent in relays to Mercury Productions at RKO, where they were revised by Welles. Some of this original script which was periodically sent from Victorville is still in the files of Mercury Productions. The revisions made by Welles were not limited to mere general suggestions, but included the actual rewriting of words, dialogue, changing of sequences, ideas and characterizations, [as well as] the addition or elimination of certain scenes.

Baer expanded on this to Mankiewicz's biographer, stating that "Orson touched every scene. And I don't mean cutting a word or two. I mean some serious rewriting, . . . in a few cases . . . whole scenes." This blatantly contradicts Houseman, along with such modern biographers as Simon Callow, who suggests in *The Road to Xanadu* that Welles had barely any input on the script until Mankiewicz delivered the first complete draft of *American*, and when he did, simply "slashed through Mankiewicz's text, just as he had slashed through Shakespeare's and Dekker's. As with those writers, he added none of his own words." Simon says.

The less-than-sound basis for Callow's claim lies with a credulous acceptance of Houseman as a detached historian, not someone with repressed homosexual feelings for his fiercely heterosexual protégé. Confirmation for Baer's statement resides in the Lilly Library, a ninety-two-page draft that clearly predates the *American* script and includes Welles's own handwritten changes, one of which is from the original Charles Foster Rogers to Charles Foster Craig. Evidently, neither he nor Mankiewicz had yet hit upon the punning surname by which the character was eventually immortalized.

What this draft (which ends at page 92 because that was all that had been written at the time) also makes clear, as much by its very existence as its actual content, is that these pre-*American* drafts drew from something a lot more solid than mere abstract discussion about subject matter. Welles had not only expressed to his collaborator clear ideas about what he wanted represented in the film, but suggested specific ways in which he could realize central themes, communicating as much to Mankiewicz, though probably not in script form, before a word was written. As Welles informed the London *Times*, in response to Pauline Kael's wholesale attribution of credit to Mankiewicz, "the initial ideas for this film *and its basic structure* [my italics] were the result of direct collaboration between [the two of] us; after [which] we separated."

The *March of Time* sequence is just one instance assuredly included at Welles's instigation. Even the begrudging Mankiewicz admitted that the idea arose in discussion with Welles, and that the director wanted "to show an actual guy in a *March of Time* and then find out about that guy." As early as January 1941, in a lengthy press statement, Welles insisted that "it was . . . the [very] essence of my idea that the audience should be fully conversant with the outlines of the public career of this fictitious character before I proceeded to examine his private life." The newsreel scene achieves this with brevity and wit.

As Frank Brady notes in his excellent biography, Welles had already planned to use a newsreel sequence based on *The March of Time* in *The Smiler with a Knife*, the potboiler he had offered to RKO as a sop for his failure to deliver *Heart of Darkness*. In that script, the segment ended with the camera tracking back from the screen to a smoky theater (à la *Heart of Darkness*'s prologue, I presume), where a young couple is watching the timely trailer.

In *Citizen Kane* the sequence ends in a smoky screening room where the shadows of men converse about what they have seen. This in itself strongly resembles an idea Welles first expressed back in

1932, in an early script called *The Marching Song*, where the character Kagi finds himself in a meeting hall: "Strong light plays on the wall from the other room, and we can clearly make out the shadows of a group of men seated at a table." The ensuing conversation comprised a primitive form of overlapping dialogue.

So there really *was* a constant flow of feedback from Welles to Mankiewicz while the latter worked on that first full draft at Victorville, drying out in the desert with only John Houseman and a bemused secretary for company. One of the "bonuses" that Houseman's presence brought to proceedings was a devil-may-care attitude to conventions they could break, or subjects they might broach. He constantly pushed Mankiewicz to make Kane's portrait less Hearstian and more Wellesian.

There is even a sense in which the "kind of controlled virulence" that Welles found in much of the writing manages to combine the feelings of "Mank" for Hearst and Houseman for his former protégé. When Kane's guardian, Thatcher, says in the first draft, "He's hated me from the moment he set eyes on me. You'd think I'd taken things from him—instead of given him things," is it just me who can hear Houseman's whine? He certainly seems to have succeeded in coloring Mankiewicz's view of Welles, who later ruefully noted that "when Mank left for Victorville, we were friends. When he came back, we were enemies."

Welles, though, was only galvanized by the script's deliberate blurring of fact and fiction, subject and object. As Houseman states in *Runthrough*, "Far from resisting the resemblance, he pushed it even further when he came to shoot the film." Yet the director later felt obliged to challenge many of the similarities, claiming to a BBC journalist that "the notion that Kane himself is some sort of version of myself, I really fail to recognize; it may be out of blindness, but it seems to me that Kane is everything that I'm not—good and bad."

At the time Welles did not even shy away from the subject of "mother love," though he must have realized that it was Houseman who had prompted Mankiewicz to make Kane the same age he had been when his real mother up and died, at the point where Kane is sent away by his mother. The scene certainly had no parallel in William Hearst's life. As Welles commented in 1951, "Hearst was raised by his mother. He had a very happy childhood. My man Kane was raised by a bank. That's the whole point of the picture." But Welles needed that sense of inconsolable loss at the very outset, and so the scene stayed in.

Interestingly enough, Welles expressed a similar raison d'être to the one that prompted him to retain this scene in a conversation recorded by Michael MacLiammoir during the filming of *Othello*, when the unfortunate Suzanne Cloutier found herself on the end of some withering Wellesian wit. Presumably Cloutier was blithely unaware that she was treading on very thin ice as she began to address the subject of a mother's love:

> Orson lifted large, taurine, slightly bloodshot eyes and began to inform her in almost caressing tones that she was too big a girl to say things like this any longer and that it was, indeed, high time for her to remember that she had teeth in her mouth, and plenty of them, and could bite on life quite hard if she chose. What was more, continued O., warming to his subject . . . "Don't you realize, you great big cosmic mass of uncompromising egocentricity, that if you are foolish enough to wish to impress an adult audience with the assumption of an attitude that has nothing whatever to do with the facts about yourself, you could conceivably find better models for style than stories from the Girls Own Library or their probably inferior French equivalents? . . . So shut up about your Maman and your everything else, for if you felt as you wish us to think you feel, you'd never talk about it so easily. What is more, you are conspicuously failing to hold your audience."

For Welles, especially when playing a young, rather Wellesian Kane, everything was fair game as long as it held that perceived audience. After all, he still had everything to prove. And when Mankiewicz obliged, by delivering an almost complete draft in mid-April 1940, he felt that he had the raw material with which to deliver that proof. There were huge flaws in the script when it was delivered—it was far too long and there were too many literal reworkings of specific historical incidents from William Randolph Hearst's life—but Welles finally had a subject big enough for him to make "*the* film, the one which sums up and prefigures all the others."

Almost immediately three new scenes were added, the impetus for which surely came from Welles. Each of the scenes appeared in the second *American* draft, dated May 9, by which time Welles had shot his first screen test as Kane, on April 16 with Russell Metty behind the camera, and a further test on May 1, after the *Hollywood Reporter* sarcastically advised its readers that "this Saturday, no kidding, Welles is starting to make tests of different players at RKO."

Of the three new scenes in that May 9 script, the central one finds Kane's second wife, Susan Alexander, about to leave him. In the words of Maurice Bessy, he proceeds to destroy "her doll-like room . . . wreak[ing] his vengeance on the dolls of the woman who has escaped the tyranny of the spoiled child." The description of the team, which made it all the way to the shooting script, perfectly distills the one instance of uncontrolled virulence in the film, even down to its depiction of "Susie's whorish accumulation of bric-a-brac":

INT. SUSAN'S BEDROOM—XANADU—1929.

Kane, in a truly terrible and absolutely silent rage, is literally breaking up the room—yanking pictures, hooks and all off the wall, smashing them to bits—ugly, gaudy pictures—Susie's pictures in Susie's bad taste. Off of occasional tables, bureaus, he sweeps Susie's whorish accumulation of bric-a-brac.

Raymond stands in the doorway watching him. Kane says nothing. He continues with tremendous speed and surprising strength, still wordlessly, tearing the room to bits. The curtains (too frilly—overly pretty) are pulled off the windows in a single gesture, and from the bookshelves he pulls down double armloads of cheap novels—discovers a half-empty bottle of liquor and dashes it across the room. Finally he stops. Susie's cozy little chamber is an incredible shambles all around him.

He stands for a minute breathing heavily, and his eye lights on a hanging what-not in a corner which had escaped his notice. Prominent

> on its center shelf is the little glass ball with the snowstorm in it. He
> yanks it down. Something made of china breaks, but not the glass
> ball. It bounces on the carpet and rolls to his feet, the snow in a flurry.
> His eye follows it. He stoops to pick it up—can't make it. Raymond
> picks it up for him; hands it to him. Kane takes it sheepishly—looks
> at it—moves painfully out of the room into the corridor.

Mankiewicz was probably unsure about how best to deal with material pertaining to Susan Alexander, the film's fictional Marion Davies. That first draft omits all scenes concerning their early relationship, jumping to the point near the film's end where they have retired to Xanadu. Perhaps he felt guilty about portraying his drinking buddess, Marion Davies, in such an unappealing way. He probably left it to Welles to add the "half-empty bottle of liquor" to the above scene. It surely wasn't there when he gave a copy of the script to Marion's nephew, Charles Lederer.

Years later Welles suggested that it was "something of a dirty trick" to have put somebody so different in the Davies role. At the time, though, he may have been thinking along the lines of Aldous Huxley's floozy, in his Hearstian fable, rather than the real-life actress Hearst lived with (as has been pointed out a number of times, a closer model in Hearst's own biography can actually be found in his first love, opera singer Sybil Sanderson). As it is, the "Davies" character in *After Many a Summer Dies a Swan* bears for less resemblance to her nonfictional "inspiration," even if she seems equally able to whip her Hearstian magnate into a jealous frenzy. Indeed Stoyte's destruction of his secretary's office in the search for a set of keys has much the same sense of fury and regression present in Kane's demolition of Susan's bedroom:

> The elevator came to a stop. Mr. Stoyte darted out and hurried along
> the corridor to Miss Grogram's empty office. He thought he knew where
> she kept the keys; but it turned out that he was wrong. They were some-
> where else. But where? Where? Where? Frustration churned up his rage
> into a foam of frenzy. He opened drawers and flung their contents on

the floor, he scattered the neatly filed papers about the room, he over-turned the dictaphone, he even went to the trouble of emptying the bookshelves and upsetting the potted cyclamen and the bowl of Japan-ese goldfish which Miss Grogram kept on the window-sill. Red scales flashed among the broken glass and the reference-books. One gauzy tail was black with spilt ink. Mr. Stoyte picked up a bottle of glue and, with all his might, threw it down among the dying fish.

"Bitch!" he shouted. "Bitch!"

Then suddenly he saw the keys, hanging in a neat little bunch on a hook near the mantelpiece, where, he suddenly remembered, he had seen them a thousand times before.

"Bitch!" he shouted with redoubled fury as he seized them. He hurried towards the door, pausing only to push the typewriter off its table. It fell with a crash into the chaos of torn paper and glue and goldfish.

At this point in the scriptwriting process the influence of Hux-ley seems more apparent. In one instance, Raymond the butler seeks to imply that Kane arranged for the murder of a rival for his second wife's affection; much as Huxley's Stoyte, after finding the key, acci-dentally shoots Peter Boone dead in a jealous rage at his mistress's (otherwise channeled) infidelities. By the end of the writing process, though, Susan Alexander had been rendered a fairly pathetic shrew, the temptress element having been quietly dropped.

A second new scene again involved Susan, though only as its ostensible subject. The actual scene featured Welles and a supposedly drunk Joseph Cotten, unable to bring himself to express his true feel-ings about her singing. The comatose Leland's incomplete review of the boss's wife had a precedent in Mankiewicz's past, an incident from his days at the *New York Times*. However, the idea of writing a slam review in that situation was Welles's, who later commented that "Mank fought me terribly about that scene . . . Oh, how Mank hated my version!"

The third new scene never made it to the shooting script, though it was one that Welles most reluctantly cut, addressing as it did two of his favorite themes, mortality and loss (also central themes in Huxley's novel). In the movie itself, we pass immediately from Susan's departure to Kane's death, eleven years later, meaning that Kane's true decline into dotage is never seen (it is only alluded to by Raymond). Originally there would have been another scene, shot in Kane's private chapel, where he has come to bury his only son, Howard, who has been killed during an attempted fascist coup in Washington, D.C., leaving Kane at the end of his life without an heir to inherit "the loot of the world."

Again Welles excelled himself in conceptualizing a funeral, albeit a very private one, attended by a single mourner, Kane; his butler, Raymond; and "a group of ordinary workmen in ordinary clothes [who] are lowering a very expensive-looking coffin into [the private] crypt." As the workmen depart, Kane asks Raymond if he likes poetry. He is noncommittal. Kane tells him that Mrs. Kane liked poetry, and for a minute Raymond isn't sure which Mrs. Kane he means. Kane clarifies, "Not my wife—not either of them." He is talking about his mother, whose grave now sits alongside his son's. At this point, he asks Raymond whether he knows what is written on the crypt wall, itself imported from Persia. He proceeds to translate the poem's desolate message:

> The drunkenness of youth has passed like a fever,
> And yet I saw many things,
> Seeing my glory in the days of my glory,
> I thought my power eternal
> And the days of my life
> Fixed surely in the years
> But a whisper came to me
> From Him who dies not.
> I called my tributary kings together
> And those who were proud rulers under me,
> I opened the boxes of my treasure to them, saying:
> "Take hills of gold, mountains of silver,
> And give me only one more day upon the earth."

But they stood silent,
Looking upon the ground;
So that I died
And Death came to sit upon my throne.

As here conceived this would have been a powerful last appearance for Kane, and an especially cogent representation of Welles's worldview, given his perennial fascination with Mr. D. At the end of his own life, he even penned a proposal for a film of *King Lear* which suggested that "death is our only dirty word . . . in our consumer society we are encouraged to forget that we will ever die, and old age can be postponed by the right face cream." This was the same Welles who felt obliged to inform Maurice Bessy, "We do not live on the edge of the abyss, but in its depths, and there is neither faith nor philosophy which can touch the souls that still breathe beneath the ruins."

Sadly the chapel scene, an early instance of the invasive darkness that permeates Welles's films, would become one of the elements he was obliged to sacrifice at the end of June, when budgetary restrictions required him to trim some $300,000 from the film's budget, as the preliminary budget on his second attempt at a "first" picture again topped a million dollars ($1,082,798). The crypt proved to be one set too many, and so another funeral scene was lost to the red-pen men. Other scenes were also pruned, though none quite so powerful or pertinent.

One of the scenes cut at this stage skirted dangerously close to its historical equivalent, as Kane is seen in the composing room of the *Enquirer* making up the next day's headline. Only when he turns away would the viewer have seen the headline—"OIL THEFT BECOMES LAW AS PRESIDENT WITHHOLDS VETO." This would have been followed by a montage of further attacks on the president until a hand is seen reaching into a side pocket, containing a copy of the *Enquirer*—and a gun. The hand fires the gun, a struggle ensues, and then "we see the White House beyond," thus realizing it is an attempt on the president's life.

Hearst had hounded President McKinley through his papers and, when there was an actual attempt upon the president's life, was vilified from every corner of the country. If the above scene, presumably written by Mankiewicz, owes much to Lundberg's version of events, the next scene was surely all Welles:

EXT. STREET OUTSIDE *ENQUIRER* BUILDING—NIGHT—1902
An angry crowd seen from the window of Kane's office. They make a deep threatening sound which is audible during the following scene. Across the heads of the crowd are two great squares of light from the windows above them. One of these disappears as the blind is pulled. As the dissolve completes itself, the second square of light commences to reduce in size, and then the entire street is cut off by a blind which Leland pulls down, covering the entire frame.

Kane is now a scared man. Even he realizes that he has gone too far. He asks his wife, the president's niece, to stand by him. She refuses. The following scene, which was to have been shot in their son's nursery, would have reinforced Kane's regression, as he once again finds himself excluded from the mother-son bond. In the script, "Kane, unwanted, ignored, looks on," as Emily soothes their child. Providing a further symmetry, Kane's own plea to Emily directly mirrors one he will later repeat to Susan, "Emily, you mustn't leave me now—*you can't do that to me.*" Here is someone who through every life-altering trauma proves unable to change his essential nature.

As Welles reworked Mankiewicz's material, he found it necessary to delete or refine a lot of segments self-evidently based on events in Hearst's life, like the assassination; the rigged election (in the film Kane is beaten fair and square); as well as Raymond's account of the death of Susan's suitor, which played on a common rumor about the death of Thomas Ince on Hearst's yacht, and which even Kael called "a nasty version of the scandal."

Welles's own criteria for applying changes and cuts retained one absolute test. As he expressed in a press statement four months before the film's premiere, "[*Citizen Kane's*] dealings with these events were determined by dramaturgical and psychological laws which I recognize to be absolute. They were not colored by the facts in history. [Rather] the facts in history were . . . determined by the same laws which I employed as a dramatist." Richard Baer, in his contemporary deposition—while admitting to certain Hearstian parallels (and a course of reading about "the lives of many publishers" by Mankiewicz *and* Welles)—confirmed how Welles invariably deferred to the laws of drama:

> While it is impossible to deny that some of the incidents in the picture have a similarity to episodes in the life of Hearst . . . I feel it would be untrue to say that because of such similarity there was any calculated attempt to picturize the life of Hearst. On the contrary, in such conferences I attended . . . the dialogue, scenes, sequences, and events were all discussed from the standpoint of their dramatic values in relation to the primary thought in the story, and their particular value with respect to whether or not they should be included in the story.

Ironically, the man who seemed most perturbed by these changes—which probably saved him (and the studio) from a suit—was coauthor Herman Mankiewicz. When he got his hands on a copy of the revised draft, he forwarded his complaints, and a copy of the script, to John Houseman in New York, who immediately recognized the dramatic worth of what Welles had done. Cabling Mankiewicz back, Houseman replied, "After much careful reading I like all Orson's scenes including new montages and Chicago opera scenes, with exception of Kane-Emily sequence." So much for his Victorville ally.

Nor did comments Mankiewicz made after viewing early rushes suggest he was cut out to play a film critic. Phoning Mercury publicist Herb Drake, he complained, rather tellingly, that "there are not enough standard movie conventions being observed, including too few close-ups and very little evidence of action. It is too much like a play." Perhaps it wasn't his movie, after all.

If, as he would assert to Mankiewicz's biographer in 1978, Welles felt that the original script "had a curious iciness at its heart . . . I was always conscious of the sound of footsteps echoing in some funny way," his attempt to inject flesh and blood into Kane may have been altogether too successful. No longer "resisting the resemblance[s]," Kane was slowly but surely mutating into a darker version of Welles himself. Bernard Herrmann, whose memorable score for *Citizen Kane* would result in his first Oscar nomination, concluded that, "*Citizen Kane* was arrived at through an inner compulsion on the part of Orson Welles. Having known him as I did, I would say that it was part of the fiber of the man." Welles's latter-day secretary Maurice Bessy concurred: "*Citizen Kane* is first and foremost an attempt to assemble the pieces of the Wellesian mosaic, a formidable, unifying projection of his multiple personalities."

In fact, once Mankiewicz realized just how important this film might prove to be, he promptly forgot about all of his caveats and began to inform his (many) drinking buddies in the Hollywood nexus that he was the one and only author of *Citizen Kane* (even though he had previously signed over all rights, including any credit, to Mercury Productions). He even accused Welles, in a message doubtless sent when he was the worse for wear, of being a "juvenile delinquent credit stealer, beginning with the Mars broadcast and carrying on with tremendous consistency." (Given that Welles had come up with the one and only *original* aspect of that *War of the Worlds* script, he was quite entitled to feel outrage at Howard Koch for taking all the credit when the script appeared in a Princeton University academic study in 1940.) Now Koch's replacement as Mercury scriptwriter was opportunistically dredging up that ol' crock-o'-crap!

Mankiewicz's intent was clear—to take all the credit for *Citizen Kane*. And, unlike Welles, he consistently claimed throughout his remaining years that *he* was responsible for (on a generous day) at least 98 percent of the script. Welles left him to it and only felt obliged to relate his version of events, in a 1971 letter to the London *Times*, after Kael bought into the late Herman's bilious bent:

When Mr. Mankiewicz, in Miss Kael's words, "raised so much hell" . . .
this was not an attempt to secure himself against anonymity. Quite the
opposite. What he wanted was sole credit. . . . There are usually two
sides to any story, but in working up her case against me, [Kael] has
not availed herself of any testimony which might tend to spoil it. . . .
My own secretary can show that just as I did not write any of Mr.
Mankiewicz's script, he did not write any of mine. . . . Placing his name
first [in the credits] was my own free decision, made out of the sin-
cerest feelings of gratitude and regard. Any ill-feeling was entirely on
the side of some few of Mankiewicz's partisans. It takes nothing from
his contribution to that film—which was in every sense perfectly
immense—to admit that he did indeed have a collaborator.

Not only did this "juvenile delinquent credit stealer" willingly
put Mankiewicz first in the relevant credits, but he took the unprecedented step of placing full-page ads, at his own expense, in *Variety*
and *Hollywood Reporter*, calling Maurice Seiderman "the best makeup man in the world" for his work on *Citizen Kane* (he was unable
to credit Seiderman on the film itself as he was not a union man).
He also insisted on placing cinematographer Gregg Toland's name
alongside his own directorial credit, in recognition of the huge debt
he owed him. These are hardly the actions of a man bent on taking
all the plaudits.

Though those plaudits were some time coming, when they did
Welles made no attempt to devalue others' contributions. Indeed
the reverse is demonstrably the case. The insightful if acerbic
Bernard Herrmann put the whole *Citizen Kane*–credit debate in its
most apposite context, in an interview conducted shortly after Kael's
polemic appeared:

If Welles hadn't created *Citizen Kane*, he would have made some other
equally remarkable picture. Mankiewicz's credits don't show any other
remarkable scripts. His only moment in the sun was when he came
across Orson Welles. . . . Film being a mosaic art . . . doesn't alter the
fact that it's still Welles's film. . . . What Miss Kael doesn't understand

is that . . . the damn screenplay really . . . is [only] the springboard.
Nobody goes to look at *Citizen Kane* just for the story. It's how it's done.

◆   ◆   ◆   ◆

The process by which it became "Welles's film" had barely begun
when the Third Revised Final Script was mimeographed to all RKO
departments on July 16, 1940. The production department took just
three days to come up with a shooting schedule that provisionally
ran from July 30 to October 19. At last, Welles was getting to shoot
a real movie. No more dry runs. In preparation for this he began to
arrange regular morning meetings with art director Perry Ferguson
and cinematographer Gregg Toland—eminent enough to insist on
being assigned to Welles—to discuss the sets, the props, camera positioning, and the like. Constantly affirming every aspect of its visual
presentation, Welles surrounded himself with yet more reminders.
Joseph Cotten remembered, in his autobiography, the layout of
Orson's office at this time:

> The largest bare wall of Orson's office was covered with rows and rows
> of sharply defined drawings . . . visuals, they were called. . . . Orson
> explained that he was preparing a movie, and these visuals on the wall
> allowed him to "see" the film, just as the words in the manuscript
> allowed him to "hear" it. The visuals ran along his wall in sequence,
> and he used them as an experimental jigsaw puzzle, substituting a
> two-shot here for a close-up there.

Toland, who had worked with everyone from Richard Boleslaw-
ski to William Wyler, was impressed by the sheer desire for experimentation with which Welles imbued the filming process, and the
fact that he "instinctively grasped a point which many other, far
more experienced directors and producers never comprehend: that
the scenes and sequences should flow together so smoothly that the
audience should [never] be conscious of the mechanics of picture
making." According to camera grip Ralph Hoge, Toland was occasionally obliged to explain why, after Welles had "rehearse[d] a scene

as he would do it for the stage, . . . it could not be done for the screen in the same way," but the relationship seems to have remained one of unerring mutual respect.

Welles knew that he would need every ounce of Toland's expertise if he was going to successfully translate that Mercury Theatre ensemble approach to this demanding new medium. He had been quick to realize that the extreme depth of field that Toland's innovations with camera lenses made possible, and that the cinematographer had willingly presented as a solution to some of Welles's conundrums, enabled the actors to play the scenes much as they would on stage, engaging in those long takes that were destined to become something of a Wellesian trademark. Hence, presumably, Mankiewicz's bitter retort that what he had seen was "too much like a play." But Welles's unsparing use of lap dissolves, avoidance of direct cuts, placement of actors in extreme foreground and background—à la Mercury stage productions—were all part of a grand scheme, worked out in advance, and executed by Toland according to Welles's precise instructions:

> Gregg Toland: Before actual shooting began, everything had been planned with full realization of what the camera could bring to the audience. We arranged our action so as to avoid direct cuts, to permit panning or dollying from one angle to another whenever that type of camera action fitted the continuity. . . . Scenes which conventionally would require a shift from close-up to full shot were planned so that the action would take place simultaneously in extreme foreground and extreme background. . . . Our constant efforts toward increasing realism . . . [meant that] most of the transitions in *Citizen Kane* are lap dissolves in which the background dissolves from one scene to the next shortly before the players in the foreground are dissolved. This was accomplished rather simply, with two light-dimming outfits, one for the actors and one for the set. [1941]

With Welles every innovation served a purpose, above and beyond mere gimmickry. As David Bordwell has written, in the best of innumerable essays on *Citizen Kane*, "The glitter of the film's style reflects a dark and serious theme: [for] *Citizen Kane*'s vision is as rich as its virtuosity." Though this distinction has become lost over decades of unstinting praise for the film's technical innovations, it was never lost on Welles. As Toland stated at the time, "the *Citizen Kane* sets have ceilings because we wanted *reality*." It is this "rich fusion of an objective realism of texture with a subjective realism of structure"—to quote Bordwell again—that still sets the film apart from all but a handful of Hollywood's hand-me-downs.

The demands Welles placed on RKO's technical crews may have been such as they had never previously encountered, but not everyone responded with sour complaint. A few folks let out huge sighs of relief when provided with the opportunity to express themselves more fully than the studio system usually allowed. The soundman on *Citizen Kane*, James G. Stewart, emphasized just how unusual Welles's approach was: "The motion picture business as a whole had no concept of the possibility of sound, and [when] you fall into a pattern, it [becomes] difficult to deviate from that pattern because it costs money. . . . With Orson, deviation from the pattern was possible because he demanded it."

One way that Welles achieved such a deviation from the studio pattern was by circumventing RKO's library of sound effects. He preferred to bring in one of the sound specialists who had worked with him in radio, creating a unique set of special effects, which he deposited separately in the RKO sound library. Editor Robert Wise was one of those overwhelmed by "his masterful use of sound, stretching the [very] boundaries of how I thought sound could be used [in film]."

From the very first scene shot—in the projection room at RKO—Welles began using overlapping dialogue and spatial placement, achieving a new realism in that oft-overlooked soundtrack. Nor was he afraid of the overdub. When the positioning of overhead microphones threatened to inhibit the movement of Toland's cameras in the final sequence in the Great Hall the entire sequence was shot silently, with the actors dubbing their dialogue onto the scene during postproduction. For Welles, postproduction was not for dotting *i*'s and crossing *t*'s, it was for enriching the entire vocabulary of the movie.

If the head of the RKO special effects department, Vernon Walker, was appalled when Welles requested certain effects to be done three, four, five, even eight, times before he was happy, it was because he was a Hollywood department head, essentially concerned about costs incurred versus effort expended. Welles knew all too well when something fell short of the highest achievable standard and continued with his demanding ways.

If Welles in time came to feel that there was "a kind of unjustified visual strain at times in *Citizen Kane,*" this was the view of a man who had grown to know his medium but could never quite recapture that initial thrill of it all. For those who had long yearned to see the medium approached with such devil-may-care daring there was, as Dilys Powell incisively observed in her review of *Kane*'s belated British premiere, "no question here of experiment for experiment's sake; it is a question of a man with a problem of narrative to solve, using lighting, setting, sound, camera angles, and movement . . . with the ease and boldness and resource of one who controls and is not controlled by his medium."

What can easily be forgotten is just how refreshing such a daring use of resources seemed to early viewers and reviewers of *Citizen Kane*, of which the perceptive Powell was one. Their strong reaction was itself an implicit condemnation of the way Hollywood continued to waste its remarkable resources, human and otherwise. Cedric Belfrage, reviewing the film on its release, commented on not only "the excellencies of different kinds—lighting, composition, direction, dialogue, acting, makeup, music and sound, editing and construction—which are present simultaneously at almost any moment in the picture," but also "how rusty [one's] faculties for apprehending all the qualities of a motion picture have become, through long experience of striving to find even one good quality at a time." That visceral shock ensured its initial critical acceptance, though it is only because Welles's vision remains as enduringly three-dimensional as the film's virtuosity that it retains its grip on audiences.

Along with what James Naremore calls "this richness, this seven-layer-cake profusion, that . . . distinguishes his work in Hollywood," Welles sought a psychological depth to his characterizations more commonly found in novels than film (*Time* was quick to praise the film for being "as psychiatrically sound as a fine novel"). At the time, Welles willingly discussed Kane's psychological profile, how the character "never made what is known as 'transference' from his mother—hence his failure with his wives." And though he subsequently dismissed this as "dollar-book Freud," he was still using the same terms six years later, when obliged to make a deposition in a suit brought by Lundberg for plagiarism:

> We postulated a fairly classic psychological setup involving the loss of a mother, and the [resultant] need to wield power as an expression of ego. . . . In other words, we wished to show a man with an urge to assume a position of responsibility in public affairs but having himself no sense of responsibility, only a series of good intentions, fuzzy sentiments, and numb, undefined yearnings.

"Dollar-book Freud" it may have been, but such a "classic psychological setup" made Kane into something more than another cinematic cardboard cutout. Welles even chose to adopt Freudian phraseology when describing to the studio boss, in the spring of 1940, that pivotal scene in the film where Kane impulsively rejects the offer of the grubby politician Gettys. In a memo to Schaefer, he wrote of Kane's "enraged conviction that no one exists but himself, his refusal to admit the existence of other people with whom one must compromise, whose feelings one should consider, whose ability to damage one he must take into account."

Yet by the time he actually shot the scene this kind of profiling had become little more than background interference. Welles had found a more effective way of conveying the dynamics of the various relationships with a camera, as Bordwell observes:

> Inside Susan's bedroom, the angles crisply build the tension. First, a shot frames Emily in the foreground, Susan in the middle ground, and

Gettys and Kane facing each other deep in the shot. But as Gettys explains the power he has over Kane, he advances to the foreground, dwarfing his rival; Emily says that apparently Kane's decision has been made for him; Kane, in the distance, seems overpowered by circumstance. But when Kane decides to assert his will, the shot cuts to an opposite angle: he dominates the foreground, and Gettys, Susan, and Emily taper off into the background.

The symmetrical patterns with which Welles crisscrossed his debut provide[d] the viewer with all the information they need[ed] to make their own judgments about the characters and their motivations. Welles does not lay this information in the viewer's lap, like so many of his contemporaries, but asks of his audience that they meet him halfway if they wish to truly discern his intent. All credit then to Tangye Lean, reviewing the film barely six months after its release, for having noticed as much as she did:

> We are forced by [various] devices to lay our own emphasis on the data, to make our own selection. Orson Welles even takes a perverse, sometimes slightly cheap, delight in heightening our difficulty. As an instance I would say that it is of the greatest possible relevance that Kane fell in love with Susan immediately after he had seen on her dressing table a crystal ball containing a snow-covered shack and a sledge. It is this crystal which reminds him of "Rosebud" when his wife leaves him, and which he holds when he dies. But the crystal has the same lack of prominence on the screen as Susan's hairbrushes, and most of the audience, if they noticed it, would probably not agree with me in thinking it of greater interest. Orson Welles likes this confusion, [which] he extends . . . beyond the technical management of light and sound.

Heart of Darkness may have been devised to divide up into six stages, but *Citizen Kane* had a neater division, being essentially the rise and fall of a man incapable of love—pivoting around the scene with Gettys. The symmetrical patterns that weave in and out of the latter film consciously reflect both the stasis of the characters, fixed in their time frame by the film's informants, and the movement of events.

In Welles's grand scheme those little touches, like the crystal ball on the shelf in Susan's room, are not so much clues to a mystery as refractions of some aspect of that person's identity. As Bret Wood states in his thorough bio-bibliography, Welles's "visual symbols are not puzzles to be deciphered by the viewer, but reflections of elements clearly presented in the film . . . used to remind the viewer of aspects of the story which make the entire film more significant when considered in relation to that scene in which it is surreptitiously placed."

If, as Peter Cowie suggests, "practically every movement has its complement at another point in the film," those complementary movements are almost always in the opposite direction. The very first shot in the film, the camera's passage over the gates and into the realm of Xanadu—finally intruding on Kane even on his deathbed—is exactly reversed in the final shot, as the camera zooms up and out of the Great Hall and back to its starting point.

The shot of Susan's door at the end of the Gettys confrontation is imperceptibly frozen—an actual, pukka feather wipe—only for the camera to pan back, showing that it has become a picture of the door in a newspaper, under the headline, "THE HIGHLY MORAL MR. KANE AND HIS TAME SONGBIRD." This reverses an earlier effect, when a still photograph of the rival *Chronicle*'s staff comes to life as the new *Enquirer* staff. As per, the reversal signals a reversal in Kane's fortunes.

It took me several viewings (shameful, I know) to notice that not only does Kane's shadow envelop Susan the morning after her opera debut, shrouding her in his presence, asserting his will over her, but that he also attempts to swallow her in his shadow during the grand picnic in the Everglades. This time, though, Susan does not allow his shadow to encompass her, signaling her growing independence and culminating almost immediately—in the film, that is—in her leaving Kane. This visual motif—another reversal of a previous effect—is simultaneously expressed through narrative and dialogue, to convey a sense that she has started to pull away. To weave such intricate motifs convincingly takes enormous self-confidence, as well as a degree of preplanning. That there was an absolute precision to *Citizen Kane* requires only a single screening to affirm. This subtlety of tone may not be apparent to any but the most attentive viewer, but it is what makes the film's rich imagery recur in the imagination, demanding further viewings.

Welles, though, was not about to rely solely on visual motifs to underpin the narrative thrust of his tale. His audacious use of the soundtrack extended to its crucial musical element and again stock sounds would simply not do. Rather than have a score commissioned after the film was finished (a Hollywood norm), obliging the composer to fit the music to the film, he ensured that, in the words of his chosen composer, "many of the sequences [were] tailored to match the music."

Welles already knew he had a true ally in Bernard Herrmann, a man almost as prickly as his boss, and just as physically and psychologically demanding. Having worked together closely in radio and theater since 1936, their understanding of each other's strengths and weaknesses was total, as was Welles's confidence in his musical collaborator. Herrmann was given the freedom (and an unprecedented fourteen weeks) to deliver the appropriate score. Welles asked Herrmann for two (musical) motifs, vying with each other throughout the film. Herrmann explained their common intent in the *New York Times* at the time:

> Leitmotivs are used in *Citizen Kane* to give unity to the score as a whole. I am not a great believer in the "leitmotiv" as a device for motion picture music—but in this film its use was practically imperative, because of the story itself and the manner in which it is unfolded. There are two main motifs. One—a simple four-note figure in the brass—is that of Kane's power. It is given out in the very first two bars of the film. The second motif is that of Rosebud. Heard as a solo on the vibraphone, it first appears during the death scene at the very beginning of the picture. It is heard again and again throughout the film under various guises, and if followed closely, is a clue to the ultimate identity of Rosebud itself.

These musical motifs begin to incline toward darkness and dissonance as the film accelerates to its conclusion, culminating in both motifs blending into a single melody when the "ultimate identity of Rosebud" stands revealed at film's end.

Other "minor" motifs incorporated into the score help define characters in *Kane*. The opera part Susan sings at the Chicago Opera House was one of Herrmann's own, Welles having asked him to compose an aria in a key too high for her (or, more accurately, Jean Forward's overdubbed) voice. Just as Susan is straining for notes destined to remain out of reach, so she strains for the love of Kane. In this sense, Herrmann's intent—to create "the feeling that she was in quicksand"—serves to underline the whole relationship. And so, when Susan is recovering from her suicide attempt, brought on by Kane's refusal to let her stop singing, the street music playing outside her hotel window is a muted rendition of her operatic solo.

Every day that Welles worked on *Citizen Kane* he grew ever more convinced that he had chanced upon his true vocation. The challenges were immense, but so was his determination to find solutions. On the set itself the studio was not allowed to interfere, and after that unnerving experience at Ruth Warrick's screen test, Welles never allowed RKO's "gangsters" to faze him again. When executives came to see how work was progressing, Welles would shut down the set and entertain them with card tricks until they went away. They eventually took the hint, leaving behind a "front-office spy" who was only expelled after John Ford pointed him out to the director when visiting the set for a day, a gesture of immense significance to Welles.

As Welles told Dick Cavett, during a memorable television appearance in 1970, "I didn't have anybody [on the set] saying, 'You can't do that!' I just had a sort of a pause and then, 'Well, that's never been done, but we're gonna try it.' So I had a marvelous spirit. The battle was in the front office among some enemies—you always have them in any [Hollywood] picture—and this was the gang that was getting ready to take over the studio. . . . That faction was spreading it about that I didn't know what I was doing, that I was gonna be taken off the picture any day." But as long as Schaefer kept faith, and held onto his job, Welles knew he would get to finish his film.

Unfortunately, Welles's attempts to keep the ostensible subject matter of *Citizen Kane* a close secret met with less success. Those front-office enemies may have thought that once the film's primary biographical source was known, it would be put on hold, much like *Heart of Darkness*. According to film historian Harlan Lebo, it was RKO executive J. R. McDonough, openly an opponent of Welles (and, through him, Schaefer), who sent a copy of the *Citizen Kane* script to RKO's New York office some time in August, where it was copied and, in fairly short order, leaked to the press.

The first magazine to make any direct allusion to Hearst was a short-lived weekly scandal sheet, *Friday*. On September 13, 1940, their magazine ran a "puff piece" called "Wellesapoppin'" (oh dear!), which previewed the film and reproduced six film stills taken from production. Though Hearst was not named, the caption for actress Dorothy Comingore described her character as "a [dead] ringer for Marion Davies." Uh-oh.

In what appears to have been a ruse to deflect attention, Welles and/or RKO somehow managed to convince *Newsweek* to run a story the following week to the effect that "the script of Orson Welles's first movie, *Citizen Kane*, was sent to William Randolph Hearst for perusal after columnists had hinted it dealt with his life. Hearst approved it without comment." No such script was ever sent, though given Hearst's longstanding friendship with Will Hays, he may well have seen a copy of the script that was sent to the Will Hays Office for their approval the previous July. Anyway, the ruse appeared to work, along with further assurances made by Welles to Hearst columnist Hedda Hopper. The story duly faded away and work continued on postproduction through December.

However, it was inevitable once the film was finished that Hearst would become aware of the fact that he was the primary template for Kane. According to Schaefer, interviewed by Pauline Kael, "Hearst personally sent [a message] to me at the studio and asked to see a print, and we let him have it . . . there was no response, no comment." Presuming that Schaefer remembered correctly here, this request surely followed a hysterical phone call from the generally hysterical Hopper, who found out that she had been duped when *Friday* concocted another story about the film for its January 8, 1941, issue, in which Welles allegedly said of Hopper, "Wait until the woman finds out that the picture's about her boss." This sounds like Welles, but was probably an aside uttered to a friend during a late-night binge that was overheard by a *Friday* "spy." It was certainly never said to any reporter "on the record."

If Hearst was making "no comment," his minions now did. As ever, at the front of the line, was Hopper in a huff. Her January 15, 1941, column predicted trouble ahead for the beleaguered studio: "All kinds of rumors are flying about town. First, that the RKO studio will be ignored editorially by all of Mr. Hearst's papers. That is being done. Next, that the refugee situation will be looked into. Nor are the private lives to be overlooked. These rumors have become so frightening . . . that it's now become an industry affair and will be dealt with accordingly."

The threat implicit in that final sentence did not take long to reveal itself explicitly. The other studio heads had their own motives for wanting the film suppressed, which were not necessarily down to pressure from Hearst or Hopper. When one of the Warner brothers apparently let it be known that RKO would have to put up a one-million-dollar bond to protect their movie houses against possible suits, he was simply providing himself with a get-out clause should it become politic not to screen the film in their theaters (Schaefer resolved the matter by threatening Warners with an antitrust suit). Welles never forgot this, and would later write for his *New York Post* column, "Jack [Warner] claims that one of his theaters will play one of my pictures as quickly and cheerfully as it will give the time to one of his. I say that's spinach."

Meanwhile, a close associate of Louis B. Mayer, agent Frank Orsatti, was orchestrating a whispering campaign accusing Schaefer of anti-Semitism, hoping to unite the other Jewish movie moguls against the RKO studio head. Mayer's motives were invariably self-serving, but he had long maintained a healthy friendship with Hearst, and continued to be a regular visitor to San Simeon. According to *Newsweek*, Hearst had only recently held a private meeting with Mayer regarding the possibility of reentering the film industry via a production deal with his old ally. Whether at Hearst's instigation or not, Mayer was soon making a binding offer to buy the film from RKO with a view to suppressing it. This prompted an aside in *Variety* on March 6 "that an $800,000 bonfire of prints and negatives [for *Citizen Kane*] is not impossible."

Around this time Schaefer found himself summoned to New York for a meeting with Nicholas Schenck, chairman of the board for Loew's International, responsible for distribution of MGM's pictures, who informed him, "Louis has asked me to speak to you about this picture. He is prepared to pay you what it cost, which he understands is $800,000, if you will destroy the negative and all the prints." The actual cost of the movie, and therefore the offer, was $805,527.53. Schaefer, to his immeasurable credit and Schenk's absolute consternation, refused. Nor did he refer the offer to his own board of directors because, as he revealed to Kael, "he had good reason to think they would tell him to accept."

Schaefer knew what he had. He also undoubtedly realized that *Citizen Kane* was set to become the defining moment of his RKO presidency. Equally, he *must* have known that Welles, who had known few setbacks to date and had never been unduly concerned about making enemies, would not sit idly by and watch his film be destroyed; and that the contract Welles had with the studio gave him far more rights and recourse than the standard Hollywood deal. Calling a press conference at the Ambassador Hotel in mid-March, Welles issued a press statement of his own, threatening to make the film's release a cause célebre. In so doing, he placed the RKO board between a solid rock and a concrete block:

> I have at this moment sufficient financial backing to buy *Citizen Kane* from RKO and to release it myself. Under my contract with RKO, I have the right to demand that the picture be released and to bring

legal action to force its release. RKO must release *Citizen Kane*. If it
does not do so immediately, I have instructed my attorney to commence proceedings. . . . Strong pressure is being brought to bear in
certain quarters to cause the withdrawal of my picture because of an
alleged resemblance . . . [to] incidents in the life of Mr. William Randolph Hearst. Any such attempts at suppression would involve a serious interference with freedom of speech and with the integrity of the
moving-picture industry as the foremost medium of artistic expression
in the country.

Welles's first biographer, Roy Fowler, suggested that this threat
of legal proceedings against the studio (and by implication Hearst
himself) was actually a ruse arrived at in cahoots with Schaefer. Barbara Leaming also implies as much, in her 1985 biography, suggesting that the threat had "in fact . . . been most carefully calculated to
give Schaefer the leverage he needed against [those] of RKO's con-
trolling stockholders who opposed releasing the picture." (One presumes Leaming is here operating as a cipher for Welles's own point
of view.)

If the press conference was a device thought up by the pair in
tandem, such a plan only arose after a heartfelt cable from Welles to
Schaefer the day after *Variety*'s worrisome report. Here Welles
accused Schaefer of "deliberately avoiding me . . . [or perhaps] pursuing some policy the nature of which must be kept secret . . . [So]
don't tell me to get a good night's rest and keep my chin up . . . I've
been leading with it for more than a year and a half." Welles had
come to rely on Schaefer's unequivocal support, and as he put it
many years later, "RKO had read the script and . . . went ahead [any-
way] . . . so they then should have been willing to go all the way."

Welles knew that he had delivered the goods in the face of much
petty jealousy and envy from Hollywood on high. So did Schaefer,
who had wisely begun, in early February, to arrange a series of private screenings of the completed *Citizen Kane* for the great and good
of the city of Los Angeles. Among the producers and directors who
attended were the recently Americanized Alfred Hitchcock, David

O. Selznick, Ernst Lubitsch, Frank Capra, Hal Wallis, and Cecil B. DeMille. Few left these screenings less than astonished, and, as Frank Brady recalls, "Welles [personally] received direct commendations from William Wyler, John Ford, and Sam Goldwyn." However much these commendations mattered to Welles himself, though, the main object of these screenings was to reverse the tide in Tinseltown against the film, centering the debate on the *quality* of the film, rather than its alleged subject matter. As such, the figures who acquired invites to these screenings were generally there because they exercised power or represented prestige.

Certain friendly press-men were also allowed into these sneak previews, prompting the anti-Hearst *Time* to proclaim in March "that Hollywood [is] about to destroy its greatest creation." At the same time, *Newsweek's* John O'Hara reported how "it is with exceeding regret that your faithful bystander reports that he has just seen . . . the best picture he ever saw . . . Reason for regret: you, my dear, may never see the picture." O'Hara was promptly fired by the pro-Hearst weekly. But the tide had turned. Even Hearst realized he had more important battles to fight, and the film at last received its New York premiere at the Palace Theatre on May Day, 1941.

If Welles, and more especially George Schaefer, had held their nerve in the face of unprecedented pressure, the one figure who wilted like a late-summer breeze was Herman Mankiewicz. After lodging a complaint with the Screen Writers' Guild—who actually held no jurisdiction, as his contract was with Mercury Productions, not RKO—demanding full, and it would appear sole, credit for the *Citizen Kane* screenplay, Mankiewicz suddenly withdrew his protest when the war of words broke out in January 1941.

Some weeks later "Mank" asked fellow screenwriter Ben Hecht, "Do you think . . . that Willie Hearst will figure it's about him?" Hecht's response has not been recorded, though it was doubtless in the affirmative. Mankiewicz promptly insisted, "I didn't write it about him, but about some of our other mutual friends—a sort of a compendium." In fact, it had been his coauthor who had taken his virulent portrait of William Randolph Hearst and turned it into "a sort of . . . compendium," and a three-dimensional one at that, in the process creating the script that would win Mankiewicz his only Oscar.

However, that success did not turn Herman's fortunes around. He remained what he had always been, a "great paragraph writer" and an even greater liability, who would be dead from booze by 1953. He would write just two screenplays in the last eight years of his life. Welles, on the other hand, seemed destined for greater things.

3

JOURNEY INTO
DARKNESS

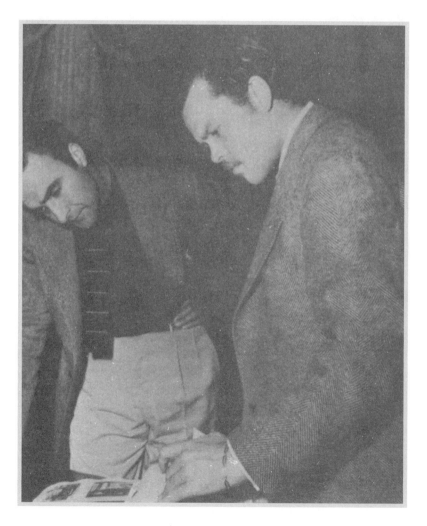

[*The Way to Santiago* and *The Magnificent Ambersons*]

I came to Hollywood saying, "If they let me do a second picture,
I'm lucky." They didn't—and since that time I've been trying to
get back to the position I was in when I first arrived.

Orson Welles

It would take just fourteen months from *Citizen Kane*'s much-feted premiere, at New York's Palace in May 1941, for Welles to be dubbed a profligate wastrel and his much-vaunted Mercury unit to be unceremoniously booted out of their offices at RKO. In that time he would manage to complete a movie that may well be the equal of *Citizen Kane* (we'll never know for sure); cowrite, produce, and star in the first of his noirish thrillers; and then work long and hard on a South American travelogue, at the behest of the U.S. government, that challenged many prejudices and upset quite a few. At the end of it, he would be an unemployable director who, by refusing to trade on his "bankability" as an actor, was consigned to a limbo from which he only slowly—and never fully—recovered.

For RKO it all began to go pear-shaped before the receipts were even in for *Citizen Kane*, which was an unprecedented critical success from the very outset—unlike, say, The Beatles' *Sgt. Pepper's Lonely Hearts Club Band,* another so-called milestone of pop culture, which was unceremoniously slammed on the day of release in both the London *Times* and *New York Times* for being pretentious twaddle (hats off, Messrs. Cohn and Goldstein). More than twenty years earlier, even the *New York Times'* Bosley Crowther, one of Welles's most constant critics, gave the director his one and only good review, the day after the film's premiere, calling *Citizen Kane,* "far and away the most surprising and cinematically exciting motion picture to be seen here in many a moon . . . [In] fact, it comes close to being the most sensational film ever made in Hollywood."

Crowther couldn't quite bring himself to endorse such a view for long, and after heaping such effusive praise on the young whippersnapper, wrote a second, altogether more begrudging re-review of Welles's extraordinary debut a few days later. By that time, it mattered not. The reviews were in, and were almost universal raves. The *New York Post* confidently predicted that "this is the picture that [will] win the majority of 1941's movie prizes in a walk, for it is inconceivable that another will come along to challenge it."

But at RKO's New York HQ the plaudits failed to change the big picture—which was one of mounting losses that *Citizen Kane* only compounded. After finally emerging from equity receivership the previous January, it was galling to major shareholders like Floyd Odlum and Nelson Rockefeller to find the company already slipping back into the red. Nor was *Citizen Kane* the only one of Schaefer's independent productions failing to turn positive reviews into currency in RKO coffers. William Dieterle's confusing film version of *The Devil and Daniel Webster* (*All That Money Can Buy*) had encountered surprisingly strong market resistance when it opened earlier in the year. *Citizen Kane* was destined to fare no better. It turned out that certain chains who had agreed to take the film then refused to screen it due to the climate of fear that continued to surround the film and its ostensible subject.

The film's one chance of taking on a second lease on life was if it grabbed one or more of the major categories at the Academy Awards for 1941. *Citizen Kane* was nominated in nine categories, with four personal nominations for Welles: best picture, actor, director, and screenplay; as well as cinematography, art direction, sound recording, editing, and music score. For all the rancor Welles seemed to inspire, *Citizen Kane* was widely expected to win most, if not all, of its nine nominations.

However, just as Welles divided Hollywood opinion in general, he polarized the members of the Academy, and when the votes were counted, the only Oscar that Welles ended up receiving was as coauthor of the original screenplay that Mankiewicz had gone to such lengths to suggest he wrote single-handedly. That Welles's film had been expected to sweep the board was indicated by the headline of *Variety*'s Oscar feature that year—"ORSON WELLES'S NEAR-WASHOUT RATED BIGGEST UPSET IN ACADEMY STAKES."

If Welles was seeking vindication from the Academy, he did not show it. By the time of the annual award ceremony, in February 1942, Welles had not only completed his follow-up to *Citizen Kane*; but had left for Brazil to begin work on the film after that. Aiming to single-handedly undermine the Hollywood production system, he had as yet no actual vocational experience of Hollywood producers. But he seemed in no doubt that they were the cause of most evils, expressing his thoughts to the press with *Citizen Kane* barely completed:

> If an actor [on the stage] can do without a director, a camera can't. Call directing a job if you're tired of the word "art," [but] it's the biggest job in Hollywood. It should be anyway, and it would be, except for something called a producer. . . . The producer is not a necessary evil. He's unnecessary, and he's an evil. . . . In Hollywood, he is the man who interferes with a movie, . . . [who] negate[s] all other potential dominant personalities.

Welles must have been talking to his fellow directors, some of whom were having a torrid time with this all-powerful breed. Hitchcock's battle with David Selznick over who would be the "dominant personality" at the helm of his first American movie, Daphne du Maurier's *Rebecca*, had already passed into legend less than a year after their spat. Ironically, the conflict was mostly Welles's fault. After he had ticked off Hitchcock for the liberties he had taken with Buchan's *The 39 Steps*, his own faithful radio adaptation of *Rebecca* in December 1938 prompted Selznick to send Hitchcock a transcription disk of the broadcast, with the following message:

> Last week's radio broadcast of *Rebecca* . . . created a minor sensation in this country. . . . I think it was exceptionally well timed, and there are certain phases of it which I should like you to study. In particular, I have been thinking about the idea of the first-person method of telling

the story in part, which you will note Welles . . . used, following the book in this method. It has never, to my knowledge, been used in a picture except to a minor extent in [a] Fox picture of some years back called [*The*] *Power and the Glory*[!].

Hitchcock did not take kindly to Selznick's suggestion and when, six months later, he produced a draft screenplay (with Philip MacDonald and Joan Harrison), it was another *39 Steps*. Selznick promptly demanded a complete rewrite of what he described as "a distorted and vulgarized version of a provenly successful work," again insisting that Hitchcock follow Welles's example:

The medium of the radio is certainly no closer to the novel form than is the motion picture. And yet Orson Welles, throwing together a radio script . . . in less than a week's time, had one of the greatest dramatic successes the radio has ever known. . . . A clever showman, he didn't waste time and effort creating anything new. . . . I hope we will be equally astute.

This time Selznick got his way, prompting Hitchcock to remark to Francois Truffaut, "It's not a Hitchcock picture." As if to reinforce the point, when *Rebecca* won the Oscar for best picture in February 1941 it was Selznick who collected the Oscar, not the British director.

Selznick may have been one of film's "dominant personalities" in his own right, but Frank Capra was experiencing similar difficulties at Columbia, having been the studio's most consistent director for over half a decade. The studio head at Columbia, Harry Cohn, was a bad-tempered bruiser with all the aesthetic sensibilities of a Venus flytrap. If Hitchcock recognized his tenuous position in Hollywood's hierarchy, Capra did not need to be so gauche. After *Mr. Smith Goes to Washington* provided Columbia with another box-office bonanza in 1939, Capra finally told Cohn what he could do with his studio.

And yet, despite being one of Hollywood's most consistently bankable directors, beginning with *It Happened One Night* in 1934,

Capra's demand for complete artistic control of his first independent production, *Meet John Doe*, led the likes of Louis Mayer and Daryl Zanuck (at MGM and Fox respectively) to not even throw their hats into the ring. Eventually Capra and his partner Robert Riskin were obliged to raise $100,000 each of their own money before that old brave heart Jack Warner agreed to cough up the necessary film-making funds. Such was Hollywood, at the end of its most golden decade, awash with great directors still being treated like spoiled children.

While still enjoying a unique immunity from unnecessarily evil producers, Welles continued to take potshots from the cheap seats at their interfering ways. When he found himself in a question-and-answer session with the Sigma Delta Chi fraternity of newsmen in November 1941, he felt compelled to observe that Hollywood producers continued to insult the intelligence and artistic maturity of film audiences, and that this perhaps indicated it was the producers who were immature, not the public.

This would become something of a theme with Welles's more satirical writings over the years (notably a script he was to write in the late 1940s, *The Unthinking Lobster*). A pseudonymous portrait of one Hollywood mogul (probably Harry Cohn) in one of his syndicated articles written near the end of the war, at a time when he may have been dreading the prospect of his first directorial assignment under a producer's thumb (*The Stranger*, with Sam Spiegel), suggests that his despair at the lack of ambition displayed by studio heads did not fade with time:

> The hero of this story [is] his gorgeousness the Bey of Beverly Hills. . . .
> I have a bowing and scraping acquaintance with this royal personage
> and . . . he runs a factory where they turn out very expensive motion pic-
> tures . . . yet he is a man of simple tastes. Look at his movies and you'll
> see what I mean. . . . But the champ has finally met his match. . . . The
> Bey himself [was recently] backed against the wall by an outlander, the
> merest female tourist . . . [and] she was heard speaking to the Bey of
> Beverly as follows, "Why don't you make better pictures? . . . I think it's

because you make too much money, or rather because you don't lose
enough to learn anything. . . . I'm tired of having you tell us we have
twelve-year-old minds. . . . America is now the strongest nation the world
has ever known and the movies are a greater power than the atom
bomb. If you deserve exclusive rights to this whole empire of ideas, why
don't you prove it by growing up a little?"

Back in the summer of 1941, in the afterglow of *Kane's* critical
triumph, Welles was still hoping to prove that it was possible to abide
by many of Hollywood's cherished cinematic conventions, and make
money, without presuming that one's target audience had "twelve-
year-old minds." It was an ambition that he would ultimately be
obliged to abandon, and with it Hollywood. For now, though, he
thought he could convince RKO to let him address more populist
genres in a way as adult in its depiction as *Citizen Kane.*

One way that Welles felt he could show what a productive little soul he could be was to make a low-budget thriller, along the
lines of the now abandoned *The Smiler With A Knife*. A Mexican
melodrama (Welles's term), provisionally entitled *The Way to Santiago*, was his new plaything of a script. Written with every Hollywood thriller convention in mind, it was planned as a "quickie"
between more portentous statements.

In fact, Welles was in the early stages of planning what he hoped
would become a kind of production repertory company, with Amalia
Kent as his special writing assistant, and Perry Ferguson and Gregg
Toland also along for the ride. This was hardly a new idea for the
director. In the days of the Mercury Theatre, he had happily flitted
between *Julius Caesar* and Thomas Dekker's farce *The Shoemaker's
Holiday*; while *Danton's Death* had been intended to vie with a slap-
stick version of *Too Much Johnson*. The logic was partially financial,
as he wrote in *Billboard* back in 1938, "The Mercury must pay its
own way. The small profit we rolled up on the performances of *Caesar* paid for the production of *Shoemaker's Holiday*, and these two in
turn paid for the production of *Heartbreak House*." In Hollywood, he
saw it as a way of bargaining with the studio.

The Way to Santiago—entitled simply *Orson Welles #4* on the Third Revised Continuity Script, dated March 25, 1941—represented another attempt at transposing issues of personal identity, the threat of dictatorial power, and America's political isolation (themes already addressed in the unrealized *Heart of Darkness*) to the nearest of America's Latin neighbors, Mexico, couched in the context of what James Naremore calls "a Hitchcock-style, 'wrong man' thriller."

Reminding fellow Americans that there was a lot going on beneath the bland surface Mexico presented to every well-heeled tourist, Welles poked fun at a busload of American tourists who first fail to notice the presence of the notorious Mr. England in their midst, and then, when shunted into an up-market nightclub reserved solely for the likes of them, are overheard to say, "This is the way to see a country. *You* know—get right under its *skin!*" Such satirical intent would flower more fully when Welles finally got to film in Mexico for real in *The Lady from Shanghai*.

As with *Heart of Darkness*, Welles's intention with *Orson Welles #4* was demonstrably didactic. The viewer was to be educated along with the central character as to what exactly fascism is and why it must be opposed. Welles planned to play an amnesiac whose opening line in the movie, as his face fills the first frame, is, "I don't know who I am." He is unfortunately mistaken for this Mr. England character (a thinly disguised Lord Haw-Haw), a right-wing English agitator who is in Mexico to incite a revolution.

Elena, the love interest, is made to represent Welles's own liberal leanings through a series of speeches designed to convince "Me"/"Mr. England" that he can be a force for good. When "Me" finds out that he is apparently a fascist and has to ask Elena what that means, she replies ("with great sincerity," says the script), "It means tyranny. It means everything that isn't human or beautiful. It means—it means the anthill. Darkness and death."

The Way to Santiago has its moments but, as scripts go, does not work as well as *Heart of Darkness*, despite occupying Welles off and on throughout his tenure at RKO. It was quite simply an early attempt to write a "popular" script, a distinction that comes from Welles himself (he later said of *Mr. Arkadin*, "it was the best *popular* story I ever thought up"). Perhaps he sensed that Schaefer was already breathing down his neck. The sentiments Schaefer expressed to Welles in a cable after the first *Magnificent Ambersons* preview presumably did not spring fully formed from that experience, but rather reiterated something already voiced: "Orson Welles has got to do something commercial. We have got to get away from 'arty' pictures and get back to earth. Educating the people is expensive, and your next picture must be made for the box office."

Welles, though, was never a sure-footed populist, and in *The Way to Santiago* it shows, as he puts in elements that *he* equates with a "popular audience," such as the hero's bout of amnesia and the absurdly contrived "love interest," that rarely combine in a convincing way. Throughout, our protagonist is made to feel that he dare not sleep, lest he should wake up and remember just who he had been, which in his mind is some fascist thug with whom Elena won't fall in love (it's an idea Hal Hartley, presumably consciously, appropriated for his film, *Amateur*):

ME: I don't want to ever close my eyes again.

ELENA: Some time you must.

ME: And wake up with a past?—My past?—That'd be some hangover.

Just as later proved to be the case with *Mr. Arkadin* and *The Big Brass Ring* (an original script Welles spent his last years trying to turn into a film), the "populist" elements in *The Way to Santiago* replace the baroque gothicness of *Citizen Kane* with little more than a mundane pitter-patter of accentuated Hollywood "situations." This kind of "populist" script failed to work not because Welles was a "bad" writer, as Callow seems to suggest (and he should know), but precisely because his strengths lay elsewhere.

It is doubtful whether *The Way to Santiago* would ever have made much of a film. Where it does work, in script form, is during what Naremore depicts as "a wonderfully atmospheric journey through the jungle toward the radio station," and it works here because at this point it is, to quote a certain memo, "definitely NOT love in the tropics . . . [and] everyone and everything is just a bit off normal, just a little oblique."

Welles always yearned to be a popular artist. At the end of his life, he chastised Peter Bogdanovich for thinking he was under attack when Orson attached the epithet "popular director" to his name (which, at the time, he was), "I'm not putting you down, Peter . . . I'm just trying to draw a line between yourself and me." This was after previously confiding, to the same trusty chronicler, that the artists he personally "enjoyed the *most* are popular artists. I *wish* I were one—but I'm not." He even admitted at the end of the 1970s that "what made [*Citizen Kane*] finally popular" was the "audience-identifiable reasons for what happened to Kane, [which was] part of Mankiewicz's contribution." If he had been left to his own devices, the film "would have been much more concerned with the interior corruption of Kane."

Welles's growing fascination with the interior corruption of his characters certainly seems to have coincided with a lessening commercial profile. However, he continued to admire those who succeeded within the system, and in a talk he gave to some film students in France in 1982, he sincerely expressed a hope that "some of you . . . [who] wish to be *metteurs en scene* . . . will realize that the other branches of movie-making are just as much fun and are just as important and, above all, much less of a headache." The comment was addressed as much to himself as his reverential audience.

At the beginning of his film career, though, Welles still believed that he could be both "a petit maître of an art form which has not yet entirely proved itself to be an art form" *and* a successful Hollywood director. He also hoped that he might yet take a popular audience with him as he peered over the precipice, down into the abyss. The great test of this belief, and the watershed in his Hollywood career, was his original, "director's cut" version of *The Magnificent Ambersons*, made in the last few months of 1941, as the storm clouds of world war began to roll across the Pacific.

The *Magnificent Ambersons* was just the kind of popular classic that Welles sincerely believed could bridge the great divide in Hollywood between art and commerce. However, his take on Booth Tarkington's novel was no more faithful to the original than his Conrad. The man just seemed to draw out all the dark elements from whatever he turned his hand to. Michael MacLiammor, a close friend who had given Welles his first job in the theater at the age of seventeen, probably came closest to capturing the inner divide in the man, and therefore his art, that prompted him to try and produce *The Way to Santiago* and *The Magnificent Ambersons* under the same mercurial umbrella, when describing him for *Sight & Sound* some years later:

> The ironic part of his career is that what to me seem slum and marsh are the very qualities that the public, which has given him fame, prefers to the palace and the mountain, and that he himself in many ways seems to agree with the popular viewpoint. He has an unwholesome regard for his lesser gifts; his real ones thrust him on a tightrope. They fill him with a dreaded sense of solitude and uncertainty; there is no net spread out below to catch him if he should fall.

With *The Magnificent Ambersons* Welles planned to make a film entirely without a safety net, and paid for it with his RKO contract. Just as with the *Citizen Kane* script, he came uncomfortably close to aspects of his own biography in Booth Tarkington's tale of small-town life in the Midwest at the turn of the century and, like *Citizen Kane*, "far from resisting the resemblance[s], he pushed [them] even further when he came to shoot the film." Any measured consideration of the film Welles actually made cannot help but detonate Robert Carringer's unsound suggestion that, because the *Ambersons* story welled up a series of conflicting emotions in Welles, he somehow subconsciously set out to sabotage his greatest film. Such conflicts lie at the heart of all great works, but the point of walking a tightrope is to get to the other side.

Welles had to go to some lengths just to get the project approved, even by the usually magnanimous Schaefer. Times were getting tougher than tough, due to the pesky war. Thankfully, another change at the top now worked in Welles's favor. In July 1941 Joe Nolan surrendered his duties as RKO production chief, to be replaced by the nemesis of many a moviemaker, Joe Breen, previously in charge of the Hays Office and therefore effectively American cinema's chief censor.

Breen, though, was no Harry Cohn in censor's clothing. At an informal press conference, announcing his new role at RKO, he informed those attending that he was looking to secure the services of some of the finest directorial talent available, and proceeded to drop the names of Gregory La Cava, Leo McCarey, and John Ford. When Welles's name came up, Breen made it clear that "the wizard of RKO" would be staying, and would be making three or four movies a year, starting with "a Mexican picture he wanted to make," followed by another, unspecified film, which Breen insisted would not shock Hollywood.

Breen was an important ally as Welles set about convincing Schaefer to approve the Booth Tarkington novel as his next pukka project. Going on one of his charm offensives, Welles visited Schaefer in person and played him the Mercury Theatre's own radio adaptation of *The Magnificent Ambersons*, which ended on an upbeat note with Eugene the content widow, and George and Lucy reconciled. To sweeten the deal, Welles offered to write and produce a third movie gratis. (Initially he intended this to be *The Way to Santiago*. It became an even more hokey template of the same "innocent abroad" genre, *Journey into Fear*. Based on an Eric Ambler novel, it would be directed by Welles's protégé, Norman Foster, under his supervision. He would also star in this vehicle, forgoing any acting fee.)

Acquiring the film rights to *The Magnificent Ambersons* proved unproblematic. The studio that owned them, Warners, seemed surprisingly anxious to sell them on. They had already realized something Schaefer had yet to consider—that the novel might not translate easily to celluloid. As V. F. Perkins has written, regarding the RKO director's adaptation of the novel:

Welles delivered what we must suppose he had promised, a remarkably close adaptation of Booth Tarkington's 1918 Pulitzer prized novel.
All the problems that the film encountered were predictable if anyone
at RKO had taken the trouble to read *The Magnificent Ambersons* . . .
[Booth Tarkington]'s text [even] carries a warning against dramatiza-
tion; a young audience in the theater would, he says, be "not only
scornfully amused but vaguely angered" by his tale.

Though *The Magnificent Ambersons* had been a great success
when first published, it had already failed to set the silver screen
alight. A silent version had been made in 1924, under the title *Pam-
pered Youth*, and even at this early date the ending of the novel, in
which Eugene contacts his late love, Isabel, via a séance, was deemed
unconvincing, not to say incredible. The alternative ending of *Pam-
pered Youth* had enfant terrible George Minafer give his blessing to
the union of his mother, Isabel, with Eugene, thus defeating the
whole thrust of the original novel. Yet the film was still a failure;
and an attempt to revive the story in 1938 only got as far as a draft
screenplay before Warners pulled the plug. So it was with something
between a sigh of relief and open arms that they greeted RKO's
request for the film rights.

However, even a finally persuaded Schaefer insisted on one intsy
lil' gesture from Welles before giving the project the green light—
that he surrender the right to the final cut. It was asking a lot of
Welles, but Schaefer and Breen reassured him of their faith in his
abilities, and that he would still have the right to edit the film, as
well as preview it in his own, "approved" version. Welles was already
too in love with the idea of the film to say no, though he undoubtedly hoped that he might never have to formalize their verbal agreement, reached on July 7, 1941.

◆   ◆   ◆   ◆

It is possible that Welles had not as yet informed Schaefer of his
intention to direct and write *The Magnificent Ambersons*, but not to

star in it. The decision was certainly viewed at the time as surprising, though it is hard to see what part he could have played on the big screen. He had played George Minafer in the radio broadcast, where his physical presence was not a factor, but was aware enough to realize that his on-screen persona would conflict with the character as he envisaged it. Instead, he cast Tim Holt as the stuffed shirt of a young man, a role he had already played convincingly at RKO, in the 1939 Ginger Rogers vehicle *Fifth Avenue Girl*. Welles later informed the BBC's Huw Wheldon, "It was a joy not to have to . . . build a film around my own personality, which . . . imposes certain limitations on any story that I'm in."

The resultant freedom seems to have inspired him to turn the self-absorbed son of Isabel Minafer into "an intensely ironic version of his own . . . dark alter-ego,"[BL] able to show his own brattish inclinations on screen without compromising his role as the film's at-times-ironic narrative presence. That narrative presence was intended to guide the audience into the story. But—unlike the Mercury's radio adaptations, usually conducted in the first person singular—his presence on the soundtrack always stands at a remove from the events that change the town. In fact, he removes himself from the story when the family's fortunes start to decline and is not heard again until after Isabel's death. And throughout the film the narrator speaks of "*their* splendor . . . *their* town," for as V. F. Perkins observes, in his British Film Institute monograph on *The Magnificent Ambersons*, "this narrator is not telling us about his own life and memories and he will never come into the film as an I."

In other words, Welles's narrative function is essentially to bookend the story of George's "comeuppance," which lies at the center of this winding labyrinth, wrapping it in a detached depiction of the town "Then" and "Now." Unfortunately, as Joseph McBride suggests, "Welles's distance from the characters is slightly greater than Tarkington's," and those ironic touches in the film were not necessarily destined to be viewed as such. For what Welles was attempting with this daring technique was something more commonly found in popular song than cinema (a good example being

Hank Williams's "The Stones That You Throw"): a narrative presence *at odds* with the characters' perceptions of themselves. Sometimes the characters also become commentators, as in a (deleted) scene in Eugene's stable early on in Welles's version, after the last of the great Amberson balls and Lucy's first encounter with George. Lucy presses her father for an explanation as to why he is "so conceited and bad-tempered." Eugene proceeds to explain all about a boy he, too, has only just met:

> EUGENE: Lucy, you need only three things to explain all that's good and bad about George.
>
> LUCY: What?
>
> EUGENE: He's Isabel's only child. He's an Amberson. He's a boy.

If, as Brett Wood puts it, "there are no villains in the film other than time," you wouldn't know it from this early part of the film, where George Minafer is portrayed as "spoiled enough for a whole carload" of children. Even the narrator seems to be suggesting that we will in time get to see "the day when that boy would get his comeuppance."

Welles's real aim, though, seems to have been the inverse of what he had attempted in *Citizen Kane*—in which a headstrong boy is expelled from Eden, charms his way into the hearts of many, but turns into a cold-blooded monster because he cannot come to terms with the loss of his mother. In *The Magnificent Ambersons*, he prefers to challenge the natural sympathies of the cinema audience by creating a monster in George, who finally comes down from his lofty tower at story's end.

What George and Charles Foster share is a childhood that was indeed Edenic, for as Welles has stated any number of ways, "that Eden people lose . . . is a theme that interests me." However, an essential difference between George and Charles Foster is that "Kane's snow scene is brief, tense, claustrophobic, punctuated by small, sharp camera movements. His childhood is over in minutes. George's Eden lasts years longer, and his expulsion is delayed for thirty minutes on the screen . . . [but it] ends with a long iris-out, a tribute . . . to the passing of an age" [JM].

Of course, the Hollywood handbook made no mention of how Welles might achieve such a transformation. If he wanted to make a villain out of a good guy, that was easy enough because film audiences expected that sort of thing. But the natural sympathies of moviegoers were bound to be sorely tried at the outset of *The Magnificent Ambersons*, as George is shown to be both demanding and needy in the ballroom scenes with Lucy, insisting that she let him escort her for the whole evening:

> GEORGE: Give me the next [dance] and the one after that, and give me every third one the rest of the evening.
>
> LUCY: Are you asking?
>
> GEORGE: What do you mean, "asking"?
>
> LUCY: It sounds as though you were just telling me to give you all those dances.
>
> GEORGE: Well, I want 'em!
>
> LUCY: What about all the other girls it's your duty to dance with?
>
> GEORGE: They'll have to go without. (With vehemence) Here! I want to know. Are you going to give me those . . . ?
>
> LUCY: Good gracious! Yes!

Afterward, a bemused Lucy asks of her father, how come George "does anything he likes to, without any regard for what people think, [but then seems to] mind so much when the least little thing reflects on him, or on anything or anybody connected with him?" Eugene observes that, "the most arrogant people I've known have [usually] been the most sensitive." This measured assessment is lost from the finished film, and so the final "redemption" of George Minafer comes across as wholly unexpected and largely unwarranted.

Another marvelous scene cut from the released film was designed to illustrate how even George did not entirely buy into his own stuffed-shirt persona. It comes after George has been sitting on the veranda with his mother—now estranged from Eugene at George's behest—and his aunt Fanny, whose increasing hysteria counterpoints George's stoic acceptance of all that life has begun to throw at him. He is sitting alone, thinking about Lucy, from whom he is also estranged, thanks to his treatment of her father.

Welles's shooting script here provides a better sense of his intent than the bone-dry cutting continuity, published in 1993.* In it, Lucy vividly appears to George, "in old-fashioned transparency (the shadowy ghost figure from the silents) [and] throws herself on the steps at his feet." She begs for George's forgiveness, telling him, "Papa was utterly wrong! I have told him so, and the truth is that I have come rather to dislike him as you do, and as you always have, in your heart of hearts." When George asks for further assurances, she insists, "I will never listen to Father's opinions again. I do not even care if I never see him again!" George magnanimously pardons her, at which point the vision departs.

However, this is not the end of the scene. George duly realizes that the whole scenario he has just acted out in his mind is "strikingly unlikely in substance. Abruptly he swings his feet down from the copestone to the floor of the veranda . . . [and] pictures Lucy as she probably really is at this moment: sitting on her own front porch in the moonlight with four or five boys, all of them laughing most likely, and some idiot probably playing a guitar . . . Harassed by his thoughts, [he] begins furiously to pace the stone floor," muttering about riffraff.

Such self-awareness seems at odds with the depiction of George certain critics have chosen to construct, especially those who have endeavored to add a Freudian subtext to the Isabel-George relationship (like Stephen Farber, who has written of George's "destructive, vaguely incestuous relationship with his mother"). It seems to me that they do so at the expense of Booth Tarkington's and/or Welles's

---

*A copy of the shooting script for The Magnificent Ambersons resides in the film archive at the Museum of Modern Art in New York. It provides an important counterbalance to the cutting continuity.

intent. Nothing in the movie or book that I can discern suggests any obvious Oedipal intent. Indeed, as James Harvey observes in *Movie Love in the Fifties* [sic], "There are . . . none of the expected Freudian glosses. . . . The [*Ambersons*] feels, even looks, like it should be a 'psychological melodrama'—but it is not." When Joseph Cotten wrote to Welles after the film's two previews and suggested that the film was "filled with some deep, though vague, psychological significance," it only prompted a firm rebuttal from the director.

George expects his mother to play the eternal widow, but happily carries on with his own determined pursuit of Lucy. Indeed, when his mother rushes to his aid, in front of Lucy, after they tumble from their sleigh in the famous snow scene, he pointedly tells her, "Don't make a fuss, Mother! Nothing's the matter," and when she perseveres, he insists, "Let me alone!" Hardly the actions of a mama's boy.

Robert Carringer has gone several stories higher than most, suggesting that Welles was enacting some kind of modern version of *Hamlet*, indeed that "the central conflict in *The Magnificent Ambersons* . . . is borrowed from *Hamlet*." That sure must be some "bad" quarto the eminent professor knows! Aside from suspecting Freud of coauthoring the play as we know it, he suggests that when Booth Tarkington quotes from Hamlet, he is "openly acknowledg[ing] one of his primary story sources."

In fact, as Welles brings out in the shooting script, which adapts the novel's characterization of George faithfully, the quote from *Hamlet*—delivered by George on his return to his bedroom after persuading Isabel to give Eugene up—is designed to show a growing self-awareness (illustrated here by that common Wellesian motif of the mirror) that is at odds with any mock identification with the hopelessly tragic prince:

> She runs from the room. A little while after she has gone, George rises and, happening to catch sight in his pier glass of the picturesque and medieval figure thus presented in his dressing gown, he pauses to regard it; something profoundly theatrical in his nature comes to the surface. His lips move.

GEORGE: (half aloud, whispering)
Tis not alone my inky cloak, good Mother,
Nor customary suits of solemn black . . . .

His own mirrored princely image with hair disheveled on the white brow, the long tragic fall of black velvet from the shoulders, reminds him of that other gentle prince and heir whose widowed mother was minded to marry again.

GEORGE: But I have that within which passeth show;
These but the trappings and the suits of Woe.

This little vignette is absent from the cutting continuity. Welles evidently intended to drop it from the film, probably because he felt that the purpose of the scene would not be sufficiently transparent to a popular audience. The scene in question also worked against a main plank in his architecture: George having to learn to roll with the punches. Only as the financial underpinning of the Ambersons' fortune begins to collapse does it becomes clear that Welles intends to portray George as the victim of societal flux, not a villain per se—a man out of time, ill-equipped for the world as it changes, leaving behind him and his mother, wrapped up in her own romantic reveries. Indeed, Isabel is so wrapped up in her reveries that she fails to notice when Eugene comes to call on her one afternoon, and George, determined to snuff out the faintest whiff of scandal, drives him away. Eugene is now a man about town, and it is her son who has become "the queer-looking duck." The description of the scene in the shooting script makes the contrast plain:

EXT. AMBERSON MANSION—DAY

Angle past George peering through the drawing room window curtain, toward front of the house. An automobile stops, and Eugene jumps lightly down from it. The car is of a new pattern, low and long, with an ample seat in the tonneau; a professional driver sits at the wheel, a strange figure in leather, goggled out of all personality and seemingly

part of the mechanism. Eugene's appearance affords a debonair contrast to that of the queer-looking duck capering at the Amberson ball
in an old dress coat; today he is richly in the new outdoor mode: his
motoring coat is soft gray fur; his cap and gloves of gray suede, and
he wears them easily, even with a becoming hint of jauntiness. Even
his face is changed—for a successful man is seldom to be mistaken.
Eugene looks like a millionaire. What is most evident about him as he
comes up the path is his confidence in the happiness promised by the
errand; the anticipation in his eyes could be read by a stranger. George
leaves the window.

George dresses Eugene down before sending him on his way,
while Isabel is elsewhere, absently humming the words of a song. It
is the old English ballad of "Lord Bateman," in which an English
lord (believed to have been based on Gilbert a'Beckett, father of
Thomas) travels to the Crusades and is captured by a Turkish noble,
whose daughter frees him on the understanding that she may be his
bride. He returns to England, forgets all about his female savior,
and arranges to marry an English lady. But on his wedding day the
Turkish lass appears, and reminded of his obligation, he duly mar-
ries her.

The choice of this ballad is clearly designed to reflect Isabel's
dewy-eyed view of the world, where true loves entwine like the red
rose and the briar. At the same time George is putting an end to all
of his mother's dreams, reinforcing the central theme of the film,
which is the loss of innocence. Even during its occasional idylls,
what V. F. Perkins calls "an attachment to the past, and the piercing sense of its loss" remains omnipresent. At the fabled Ambersons
ball, which beautifully captures the end of an era, the dialogue is
replete with ironic references to "old times" and "new times." Then,
just when "everything seems to be in harmony . . . at the very peak
of gaiety and light—at the instant when the Amberson ballroom is
filled with busy joy—the image dissolves" [JN].

In another scene trimmed from the film, during the resumed
courtship of Isabel by Eugene, the pair are sitting together in the

arbor. Isabel is prevaricating about whether to tell George about the two of them (a fatal delay, as it happens). Uncharacteristically, she begins to talk of the dissolution of things, "I mean the things we have that we think are so solid—they're like smoke, and Time is like the sky that the smoke disappears into. You know how a wreath of smoke goes up from a chimney, and seems all thick and black and busy against the sky, as if it were going to do such important things and last forever, and you see it getting thinner and thinner—and then, in such a little while, it isn't there at all."

But the essential metaphor for the themes of time and loss in *The Magnificent Ambersons* is the town itself, which is never formerly identified, being made to represent every Midwest town that has "spread and darken[ed] into a city." When referring to the movie he had just made, at a talk in New York in October 1942, Welles said it "was . . . about a town, [not just] a family of people. Originally it really was very great, depicting realistically a changing town and a changing world." By then Welles knew all about time and loss, having had central scenes totaling a third of its running length ripped out of his film by the editor he had assigned to preside over its completion, the young, ambitious Robert Wise.

One of these lost scenes was designed to show how the motorcar has destroyed the still of night, contrasting the automobile's speed with the motionless Ambersons, representatives of a fading world in their formal evening dress. Meanwhile, the grounds of their mansion are being turned into another building site (a necessary source of revenue as their fortunes decline) for this ever-expanding town. On the basis of production stills, the scene would have been shot almost entirely in shadows, save for George's white collar, the kind that Isabel observes, "we don't see . . . any more, except on the stage and in the magazines":

> George is sitting with his mother and his Aunt Fanny on the veranda. He sits on the copestone of the parapet, his back against the stone pilaster; his attitude not comfortable, but rigid, and his silence not comfortable either, but heavy. However, to the eyes of his mother and

his aunt, who occupy wicker chairs at a little distance, he is almost indistinguishable except for the stiff, white shield of his evening frontage.

The five new houses on the lawn have progressed some in the construction; one is already completed. In the street the evening life of the Midland city is beginning. Through the moonlit darkness flashes the firefly lights of silent bicycles riding by in pairs and trios, striking their bells, the riders' voices calling and laughing. Surreys rumble lightly by with the plod-plod of honest old horses, and frequently there is a glitter of whizzing spokes from a runabout or sporting buggy. Interspersed, disrupting the peace of the night, comes an occasional racketing auto—causing bicycles and people to scatter for cover.

This scene foretells the static family's fate, as they are left behind by movers and shakers like Isabel's former paramour, Eugene. George, who first appears in the movie charging through the town in a buggy, recklessly out of control, "causing . . . people to scatter for cover," and predicting that he "will own this town . . . when I grow up," at film's end will be obliged to walk the streets of an unfamiliar city, a complete unknown.

The walk home threatened to be the film's most powerful moment—the dawning of self-realization. Finding himself buggyless and alone, George walks past unfamiliar faces and new storefronts as he returns from the station where he has said his last farewell to a broken Uncle Jack. For once, the shooting script not only adds a great deal of descriptive color to the cutting continuity, but provides a quite different sense of Welles's intentions, revealing the fact that "we [are supposed to] see the following . . . in a slow moving shot (with a sort of slight dissolve or wipe from one scene to the other, but retaining a moving-forward speed) for the camera, which is now George, is slowly walking along the street." Evidently Welles originally planned to shoot these scenes using the "subjective camera" technique he devised for Heart of Darkness. As the script indicates, "we are seeing what George sees." When we hear the comments of strangers, they all seem strangely pertinent:

A shabby, stone-faced house behind a fence, its double front doors, of carved walnut, once glossily varnished, have been painted smoke gray, but the smoke grime shows; over the doors a smoked sign proclaims the place to be a "Stag Hotel."

Other houses that have become boardinghouses too genteel for signs, but many are franker, some offering "board by the day, week or meal," and some, with the label: "Rooms."

One, having torn out part of an old stone-trimmed bay window for purposes of commercial display, showed forth two suspended petticoats and a pair of oyster-colored flannel trousers to prove the claims of its black and gilt sign: "French Cleaning and Dye House."

Its next neighbor also sports a remodeled front and permits no doubt that its mission in life is to attend cosily upon death: "J. M. Rolsener, Caskets. The Funeral Home."

A plain old honest four-square, gray painted brick house decorated with a great gilt scroll on the railing of the old-fashioned veranda: "Mutual Benev't Order Cavaliers and Dames of Purity."

At this point in the script the camera was to move up National Avenue to Amberson Boulevard. However, when it stops at the intersection and we get a close-up of the street sign, we see that it has been renamed 10th Street. A car comes to a stop, very close to the camera, a premonition of George's imminent auto accident, and we hear a young lady say, "One sees so many nice-looking people one doesn't know nowadays." The camera pans across to the car. It is "a red one, glittering in brass, with half a dozen young people in it whose motorism has reached an extreme manifestation in dress. The ladies of this party are looking favorably at the camera":

YOUNG LADY: This old town of ours is really getting enormous. I shouldn't mind knowing who he is.

YOUNG MAN: (loudly) *I* don't know. I don't know who he is, but from his looks I know who he thinks he is: he thinks he's the Grand Duke Cuthbert.

[George is now seen . . . from [the] angle of the people in the car]

GEORGE: (scornfully) Riffraff!

This sequence was ultimately replaced, probably for purely technical reasons, by one where Welles uses the (returning) narrator's voice over a series of visual segues, designed to illustrate how the town has changed into a city, but not as a personal revelation experienced by George. He still arrives at the Amberson mansion itself, which we learn from the narrator's voice is about to be repossessed, and through which he now plans to walk one last time. Again, the original plan, as outlined in the shooting script, retained the use of the subjective camera:

> Camera wanders slowly about the dismantled house—past the bare reception room; the dining room which contains only a kitchen table and two kitchen chairs; up the stairs, close to the smooth walnut railing of the balustrade. Here camera stops for a moment, then pans down to the heavy doors, which mask the dark, empty library. Hold on this for a short pause, then camera pans back and continues, even more slowly, up the stairs to the second floor hall where it moves up to the closed door of Isabel's room. The door swings open and we see Isabel's room is still as it has always been; nothing has been changed.

At this point the narrator returned to the soundtrack, speaking of a ghostly image of "a young man kneeling in the darkness . . . clutching the covers of a shadowy bed." How Welles intended to handle this visually is not clear from the script. Presumably it would have been the subjective eye glimpsing a hologram of itself, resembling the earlier vision of Lucy on the veranda.

George is no longer the "lofty person" Lucy first met. He has been humbled by experience, and all the sense of propriety he inherited from his mother, who rejected her most eligible suitor and ruined her own life because he "embarrassed" her one night by getting drunk and falling on his bass, has only brought him and his family ruin.

The question no one can answer, save perhaps the handful who saw the original Wellesian creation, is whether Welles succeeds at the end of *Ambersons* in making George a sympathetic ex-monster. If he failed, as some of the comments at the Pomona preview might suggest, then he failed Booth Tarkington, for the story centers around George's troublesome passage into self-awareness. The original "subjective camera" sequence would have brought this home to even the most inattentive cinemagoer.

And yet Welles changed his mind at some point about using (or attempting) such an extensive "subjective camera" sequence. The scene in his mother's bedroom has been substituted in the released film by a brief shot of "George" (shot from the back, as Holt was not available) kneeling, asking for forgiveness, and the narrator's voice speaking of how he "had got his comeuppance . . . three times filled . . . and running over." This scene also appears in the cutting continuity (albeit in longer form), so was evidently included at Welles's behest.

Why the change of mind? On the basis of the two extant scripted representations of Welles's film, i.e. shooting script and cutting continuity, the sequence was replaced with something less original and effective. And Welles must have been aware that it was less impressive. There is enough external evidence that the sequence in the mansion was definitely shot "subjectively" by cameraman Stanley Cortez (seen comparing notes with Welles on page 75). (Cortez suggested to Charles Higham that it was actually his idea. However, unless the cameraman was also responsible for writing that part of the shooting script, this cannot have been the case.)

As we know, Welles had been itching to utilize this technique since first coming to Hollywood, and he already knew the amount of preparation required. According to Carringer, "Cortez and a crew spent four days working out the elaborate mechanics of the shot." Higham gives some idea of just how complex the sequence was in his *Films of Orson Welles*. It required a sixty-five-pound camera to be strapped to a camera operator's chest and for the man to walk slowly, but precisely, trailing cables, in and out of the rooms and up stairs for four full minutes. Also, "mirrors had to be reversible on hinges, so that they would not show the cameras. They had to be twisted back, then returned to their original position, with split-second timing, [and] each room had to have an entirely different kind of lighting, to convey the fact that the Ambersons, following a contemporary custom, liked to have each of their rooms in a different style."

The results, even after four days' work, were unusable. According to Frank Brady, when the original rushes came back, the images were blurred because of the vibrations of the operator's movements. Cortez then had the operator remove his shoes and the camera was more tightly strapped, thus solving this problem, though perhaps not to the director's exacting standards. Welles at some point gave up on the whole "'subjective camera'" sequence, or simply ran out of time, and had to come up with an alternative in a hurry, surely the only credible explanation for Tim Holt's absence from his own walk home. As long as Welles intended to film the sequence subjectively, Holt was not required; but by the time it became apparent that this original scheme was impractical, Holt appears to have been unavailable.

Despite Welles's highly effective narration, the replacement scene has none of the power of the sequence in the shooting script (this whole sequence is marked in the cutting continuity as "Transition No. 1," in what Carringer calls an "unfamiliar notation," clearly suggesting it was a last-minute insert). Welles's narration, which pays witness to George's act of contrition in the mansion, was presumably dubbed in Miami, where he would stop on his way to South America to do postproduction work on Ambersons, including voice-overs, in early February 1942.

If Cortez, Welles's original choice for cameraman, proved unable to execute his boss's demands on this key sequence in the film, it might explain why he was replaced as principal cameraman by Harry Wild at some point. The director subsequently held Cortez's chronic slowness (Welles's phrase) largely responsible for the film overrunning its shooting schedule by fourteen days. Cortez seems to have been caught up in an impossible situation, anxious to meet Welles's demanding requirements, but unable to combine fastidious exactness with any of the instinctual swiftness of Gregg Toland.

Though we do not know how much of the film Cortez shot, as a period piece it is gloriously evocative and richly atmospheric in all the right places. Andre Bazin gave Cortez the credit when championing the film's "look," enthusing about "the lighting of Cortez . . . [which] serves in one respect to restore the ambiance of gaslight, and in another respect, enables Welles to let the actors evolve in a luminous heterogeneous space, where the alternations of clear and shadowy areas restore, within the immobility of the sequence shot, a sort of . . . dramatic rhythm."

"A luminous heterogeneous space" was necessary because the whole design of the film centers upon the mansion, which takes on a life of its own, residing at the psychological heart of the film right up to its controversial ending. As Mike Prokosch notes, it is "[this] unity of space within the Amberson mansion [that] makes [Welles's] dramatic method possible. In its grand interiors Welles can include all the characters in one frame, or track in for a close shot, or include close-up and long-shot in a single set-up—as when George and Lucy sit on the stairs during the opening party, the background filled with dancers . . . More than [merely] a metaphor for the family's unity, it is a dramatically self-sufficient world."

Given such cinematic ambition Welles was bound to require that much of the mansion be constructed to scale, enabling camera movement to take the place of actual cuts. All of which suggested that *The Magnificent Ambersons* was likely to prove a (very) expensive film. Indeed, as Carringer notes, the single biggest outlay in the budget was set construction, at a cost of $137,265.44, a sum larger than that expended on RKO's set-intensive, hugely expensive 1939 version of *The Hunchback of Notre Dame*. But there was simply no way around these costs, given the precision in Welles's design.

The inevitable budget cuts would have to come elsewhere. Though a preliminary budget estimate came to $987,024, cost cutting and trimming, much of it cosmetic, reduced the figure down to $853,950, which was all but the actual cost of *Citizen Kane*. Though there was an ostensible ceiling of $750,000 recently imposed on any new RKO production, Schaefer again made an exception for Welles, and at the end of October 1941, shooting began on his second Hollywood production.

Unlike *Citizen Kane*, where shooting proceeded quite smoothly, the opening day's shoot on *The Magnificent Ambersons* was a disaster, as Welles attempted to get the actors to mime their lines with a view to overdubbing more precise dialogue at a later date. As one might expect, it proved beyond everyone in the cast, who were used to matching the rhythm of speech to their facial expressions. The innovation was one novelty too many and was quietly sidelined, though not on every scene. Two scenes *were* shot silently, with dialogue being dubbed on at a later date. Of these two scenes, one was part of the lengthy ballroom sequence, where the huge camera cranes creaked across the original soundtrack. The other was the snow scene, which needed more work than the special effects department was used to providing:

> James G. Stewart: It was a massive job. . . . I was very proud of it, and I ran it for Orson. This was our normal procedure. I did the work first and then ran it for him. And he sat there for a moment, and [then] said, "Jimmy, it's fine, but I don't have any sense of motion of the horseless carriage in their voices." And as soon as he said it, of course it was immediately apparent. But he was very conscious of [such things]. . . . So I did it all over again . . . with a twelve-inch plank suspended . . . [and] myself sitting on it, bouncing it up and down, while the actor or actress sat on the same plank.

Welles had shot this scene in a disused Los Angeles ice plant, in order to show the breaths of actors from the cold air. Unfortunately, the usual bulbs used in filming broke in the subzero temperatures and, when replaced with more durable ones, the increased wattage began to melt the snow. The cold also caused the actors real problems. A couple of days into the shoot, Ray Collins (Jack Amberson) contracted pneumonia, delaying the filming further. But Welles persevered, and at the end of twelve days he had the scene as he wanted it, complete with actors' icy breaths.

Welles's motive, in seeking to shoot under such difficult circumstances, cannot have been merely "a fetish for authenticity," for as Perkins suggests, "The setting [itself] has throughout a beguiling artificiality. . . . [However,] the condensation of the actors' and horse's breath on the air . . . creates an image of new-minted purity to contrast with the smoke that befouls the air as it issues from the exhaust of Eugene's horseless carriage." Fortunately, RKO were not apprised of Welles's reasoning for shooting the scene under such exacting circumstances, as surely even Schaefer would have balked at the cost.

The part of the snow scene where the sled carrying George and Lucy overturns also had to be shot using the actors themselves, rather than their stunt "doubles," as Welles insisted on a close-up of their faces as the sleigh tips over, focusing on their expressions all the way down to the bottom of the slope. At the end of it all, Welles had one of the most powerful scenes in the film, but at such a cost that even the $850,000 budget was beginning to look decidedly optimistic.

The ballroom scene took almost as long to shoot, occupying nine days, averaging ten hours per day, with close to a hundred operators using cranes and cameras, as Welles went for his most ambitious use of the long take to date. Indeed, he would claim to his biographer Barbara Leaming that, as shot, the ballroom sequence was "the greatest *tour de force* of my career." Carringer mouthwateringly describes how Welles's "shooting plan involved a series of backward-moving camera shots that traversed the third floor of the Amberson mansion, where the ballroom was located, along a circular course, twice. . . . Perhaps the most lamented of the lost footage [was] a four-minute, single-take, horseshoe-shaped tracking shot. . . . The [released version] not only destroyed the rhythm of this plan but also rendered the physical layout of the space incomprehensible." The full sequence would have run for a full reel, over ten minutes.

When George Schaefer was shown the ballroom scene in all its uncut glory—along with the dinner at the Ambersons' for Eugene, and the subsequent encounter between George and Aunt Fanny on the stairs—on November 28, 1941, he was effusive in his praise, sending messages of warm congratulation to Welles. This important reassurance convinced the director everything would work out fine. Also in attendance that day, to see these three key sequences, was Joe Breen, who was equally impressed by Welles and his work. The would-be genius, it seemed, had nothing to worry about.

Except that Welles had kept one little secret to himself. The end of the film. It would appear that he *never* intended filming the finale that appears in the shooting script (the final two scenes in the released film do in fact come close to Welles's original version, albeit with an extra truckload of sugary intent). The original script was scheduled to end with Eugene entering his library, going to his bureau and taking out his diary, in which he proceeds to write (and recite), as the music swells:

> Dearest Isabel, your boy was hurt in a street accident today—run down by an automobile. I thought at first I wouldn't go to see him at the hospital, but of course I did. I thought it would be hard not to be bitter but I found it was easy—he looked so much like you, dearest one. As I came in, he lifted his hand in a queer gesture, half-forbidding, half-imploring, then let his arm fall back on the covers. He said, "You must have thought my mother wanted you to come so that I could ask you to . . . to forgive me." Lucy was beside him and she shook her head. "No," she said, "just to take his hand—gently." She was radiant. . . . But for me another radiance filled the room—and I knew I'd been true at last to my true love, and that through me you had brought your boy under shelter again.

This is better than what we actually get (a scene which has Agnes Moorehead's Aunt Fanny walking away from George's hospital room to hear how he is!?!). It also comes close to the ending used in the Mercury radio adaptation, where it worked effectively, resembling the equally contrived ending that Booth Tarkington had hit upon in 1918. However, Welles knew that the logic of the story, especially as framed by him, did not lend itself to such a convenient wrapping up of loose ends.

And there is evidence to support the notion that it was Welles's abiding intention not to end the film so. As Perkins points out, "The storyboards drawn by Joe St. Amon to visualize the first draft screenplay are extensive and detailed, but they run out at the point where George is a stretcher case about to be taken to hospital. . . . Their absence suggests that Welles was not yet ready to commit himself to an ending." In truth, Welles probably already had an ending in mind, one that tied no neat ribbon bows, but realized the resistance such an ending might incur if presented to the powers that be ahead of shooting.

After all, this time RKO had script approval. And Welles had the all-too-recent example of Frank Capra's *Meet John Doe*, premiered earlier that year, which had been shot with at least three different endings, all of which were tested out on preview audiences—including the only logical one, in which the John Doe character kills himself. But the audiences hated this ending, despite a number of obvious Christ analogies throughout the film, and Capra was obliged to give the film an altogether more implausible, upbeat ending (much as Evelyn Waugh had been obliged to write an alternative, "happy" ending to his *Handful of Dust* for the American edition of his novel, three years earlier). Rather than give RKO such an option, Welles intended to give them just one ending, and a bleak one at that.

Welles's preferred ending took most of the words Eugene entered in his diary and transposed them to a monologue delivered to Aunt Fanny on returning from the hospital to visit George. However, the effect was diametrically different and altogether more downbeat. Eugene finds Fanny in a boardinghouse. As he tells her about his visit and reconciliation with George, she begins to rock backward and forward, just as she has in much of the film when her emotions have threatened to get the better of her. Now, though, she has simply shut down, her deadpan response failing to register with the man she once carried a torch for, Eugene Morgan. Meanwhile, a comedy record plays in the background. It tells the story of one calamity after another befalling a man who has gone away to rest, only to find on his return that he has lost everything. The whole vignette is delivered as a dialogue between the man and his colored servant, who says there is "No news," despite the fact that his dog died, his house burned down, his mother-in-law died, and his wife ran off with the chauffeur— "but outside of dat dey ain't no news." Calamity upon calamity, just like the story of the Ambersons.

Fanny just keeps rocking through it all. Finally, Eugene gets up to leave. The parting shot, according to the cutting continuity, would have been quite banal: "[Eugene's] car parked at right before boarding house—Tall buildings at end of street in background—Light in windows—Music heard—Car starts—Drives to background—Traffic passing on across street in background—Car turns corner in background—Exits." Hardly the great lost ending one might have expected from the man who gave the world Rosebud, though Jonathan Rosenbaum champions it "as a kind of chilling, tragic diminuendo that has few if any counterparts in the American cinema." I subscribe to an alternate point of view, based on the crucial recollection of composer Bernard Herrmann, who was not only one of the chosen few who saw Welles's original, but worked on the film score prior to the fateful preview screening and, when the film was butchered, had the integrity to demand his name be removed from the credits. His recollection of the "real" ending returns us to the still center of the story:

> After the car accident and George's injury, the picture then goes to what we don't really realize until the end has been once the home of the Ambersons. It is now a home for aged gentlefolk. Eugene comes back from the hospital to visit Aunt Fanny. . . . An old gramophone, a wind-up, is playing a record . . . called "The Two Black Crows." . . . Eugene pleads with Fanny to come look after him, to live with him. And she says, "No, I'm very happy here." Remember this in context with the picture. She takes Eugene to the door and opens it, and that's when you realize this has been the Amberson house. He kisses her

goodbye, he stands at the doorway on the porch, and he looks all around him. Where before in the film it was all surrounded by beautiful country, we see the city. . . . And in every direction the Ambersons are being swallowed. He walks down the stairs, into the city, and in the background we hear "Two Black Crows" getting smaller and smaller, and the sound of the traffic getting bigger and bigger, until it finally smothers the whole screen.

It seems unlikely, given Herrmann's pivotal role and fierce intellect, that his memory here is confused. His version certainly feels like the way Welles would have wanted to end such a saga—with a salutary depiction of the Amberson mansion being swallowed whole by the new age. And yet, the director must have realized that he was taking a big, career-threatening gamble as he placed his faith in his own expressive imagination and the power of the medium. He later told Leaming, "There was just a built-in dread of the downbeat movie, and I knew I'd have that to face, but I thought I had a movie so good—I was absolutely certain of its value . . . that I had absolutely no doubt that it would win through, in spite of that industry fear of the dark movie."

Already, though, control of events was passing from his hand. At the end of 1941, he found himself with not one but two movies to finish before departing for South America to begin work on a government-sponsored project dear to his heart. The "other" film, *Journey Into Fear*, according to Welles's assistant, Richard Wilson, "was a studio-initiated and -scheduled project, taken away from another producer by Schaefer, who asked Welles to do it in August of 1941." Seeing it as an opportunity to show how the Mercury could evolve into a production repertory company, Welles shelved *The Way to Santiago*.

The Ambler novel was given a thorough rewrite by Cotten and Welles, who informed director Norman Foster prior to shooting, "Don't read the book . . . we've changed it." And though Foster remained ostensibly in charge on *Journey Into Fear*, Welles found it hard to sit back and watch. His input was soon evident to everyone on the set. According to cameraman Karl Struss, Foster and Welles discussed every scene in detail before shooting began. Struss was apparently maddened by the constant retakes demanded by Welles in the scenes in which he appeared, probably unhappy with the way he came across as a very hammy chief of police.

Not surprisingly, the strain of keeping two film shoots going soon began to tell on Welles, who became prone to the kind of fitful outbursts he had previously displayed in the theater whenever an opening approached. Robert Wise informed Barbara Leaming that Welles was directing *The Magnificent Ambersons* in the day and shooting his scenes for *Journey Into Fear* at night, only to then return to *The Magnificent Ambersons* set in the morning to view the rushes. Wise is not alone in expressing amazement at how Welles kept going.

But Welles was on a nonmoveable deadline. He needed to finish *The Magnificent Ambersons* to his satisfaction, save for some "minor" postproduction work he was prepared to leave to Wise—as well as his part in *Journey Into Fear*—by the end of January 1942, when he knew he had to be ready to board a plane for Miami, and then Rio. He was planning to shoot the legendary Carnaval, a central joist to a film he hoped to make there called *It's All True* (a title Welles registered long before he had this film in mind).

What is not clear is why Welles was so keen to shoot the carnival. According to Charles Higham, it stemmed from a suggestion by Nelson Rockefeller, who aside from being a major RKO stockholder was also now the Co-ordinator of Inter-American Affairs, and therefore responsible for ensuring good relations with (and continuing neutrality from) South America's more powerful states. It was he who persuaded Welles to go to Brazil and make a film designed to reflect how much the two Americas had in common.

Welles, for whom the Latin countries had long held a strange fascination, saw a chance to realize a project he had previously only sketched out in his mind, a series of stories that would combine folklore, song, and dance, all now entwined in Welles's mind with the Rio carnival. According to Richard Wilson, "The pressure to get there fast and actually see what he was supposed to be making a picture about was exerted mainly by Orson . . . [because] no script was possible until Welles had actually seen the carnival . . . RKO and the Co-ordinators Office understood this, and these were the ground rules accepted by all."

Part of the agreement drawn up between RKO and the Department of Inter-American Affairs obliged the government to indemnify RKO against any losses (up to $300,000) that the film might make. Though there was no actual budget, Welles felt he could make the movie he had in mind for perhaps double that figure. So, contrary to legend, he was hardly risking a great deal of RKO's depleted reserves on this celluloid adventure.

The last thing Welles needed to do before leaving L.A. at the end of January was to make sure that work on *The Magnificent Ambersons* would proceed according to precise instructions he had already laid down. Schaefer reassured him that, when the time came, Robert Wise would be sent down to South America with a Moviola, to complete the cutting of *The Magnificent Ambersons* under Welles's direct supervision.

The suggestion made by a number of film critics, with no more experience of filmmaking than the RKO janitor whom Welles once whimsically suggested edited the released version of *The Magnificent Ambersons*, is that he was a fool for leaving *The Magnificent Ambersons* unfinished and at the mercy of the studio. He did not act like a fool. He simply failed to conceive of a situation akin to the one that transpired.

Welles must have suspected that the film had gone well over budget—and indeed over the red-light figure of a million dollars—but probably thought that this would work to his advantage. The studio was bound to want to start recouping such a massive investment as soon as possible and however much the new ending might take the executives by surprise, any further changes would only incur greater expense and further delays. In fact, no other ending made sense of the story, as Warners had already discovered to their cost.

He also had good reason to believe that as long as Schaefer and Breen were making the decisions, his wishes would be not only considered but respected, and the quality of what he had achieved fully appreciated (they had, after all, been bowled over by the scenes they had viewed at the end of November). At the point when he was packing his bags, why would Welles have even considered the possibility that Schaefer and Breen might not be the ones making the decisions about the film's fate?

Confident as he was of the strength of his relationship with this powerful pair, Welles still played a little game of brinkmanship, hoping that he might not be required to ratify in writing the verbal agreement he had made back in July, requiring him to surrender the right to make the final cut. He continued to play this game until the propellers on that plane began turning, only putting his name on the fateful document on January 29, 1942 (having presumably been threatened with an embargo on his trip to Brazil unless he signed on the dotted line). After he finally, begrudgingly signed, he still expected, as he later observed, "that what I [might have to] say still carried some weight." Little did he know.

THE SPOILED BRAT GETS
HIS COMEUPPANCE

[The Magnificent Ambersons and It's All True]

HOTEL GRANDE LOBBY (RECEPTION DESK)

ELDERLY MAN: Do you find [enough] material for motion
pictures in our country, Mr. Welles?

ORSON WELLES (grins): Señor, I don't know where to
begin—or where to stop. This whole continent . . . you could
make a thousand pictures here.

It's All True draft, September 2, 1943

In one sense at least it was an opportune time for Welles to skip town. The fact is that *The Magnificent Ambersons* had gone some $160,000 over budget. When the set closed down on January 22, 1942, they were fourteen days. Over schedule, despite Welles's breakneck work schedule at the end.

If Schaefer was initially sanguine about the overrun, it is unlikely that Welles's enemies in the RKO executive were anything other than delighted. Welles had let them down badly with *Citizen Kane*, delivering a masterpiece that received rave reviews, nine Oscar nominations, and considerable prestige for the small studio. If early reports were anything to go by, this was more like it, horrendously expensive and hopelessly uncommercial. It is certainly hard to believe Welles's later claim that "there wasn't a tiny cloud . . . in my mind when I left that there would really be trouble with that picture," even if he clearly felt that once the film was completed, everyone would again see that the cinematic bar had been raised.

In order for that to happen Welles had to meet with Robert Wise at the Fleischer studios in Miami in early February, to record his narration and ensure that Wise understood how the remaining postproduction work should be completed. At the end of an intensive three days of work, Welles signed a memo authorizing Wise to act as his mouthpiece in all decisions made on the film back in Hollywood. However, he still expected Wise to bring the completed film to Rio for the final OK and he asked Wise to ensure that every possible dissolve, alternate shot, and music track was available to him, should he wish to make last-minute changes (as late as March 11, six days before its fateful preview, Welles was still issuing instructions to wise).

Unfortunately, though Schaefer initially approved Wise's travel, his application to leave the country was refused at the last minute due to wartime restrictions. According to Welles's assistant, Richard Wilson, "Bob [Wise] was ready to leave for the airport with the film when the government put an embargo on nonmilitary travel. That ended RKO's effort to fulfill the promise." Nor does there really seem to have been any concerted effort to get Wise and the film to Welles in the weeks leading up to its preview, even though a further request, expressed in the right language, reminding the government of the reason for Welles's visit, would surely have freed up a plane.

Schaefer probably felt that if both Wise and Welles were in Brazil it would be a recipe for further delays, and on March 1 he cabled Welles to say that *The Magnificent Ambersons* had to be ready for the Easter break, traditionally a good time for movies, because it had to make its money back sooner than soon. Indeed, such was RKO's determination to get the film quickly into a releasable state that they had already booked ads in *Life, Look, Time, The New Yorker,* and *Good Housekeeping* over the Easter weekend.

Necks were on the line, Schaefer's included. Breathing down his collar was a new, "temporary" production head, Charles Koerner, who was no ally to the cause. Koerner, who had previously been in charge of RKO's theater chain, was apparently brought west at major shareholder Floyd Odlum's behest when Joe Breen left for Mexico shortly after Welles's departure. Breen's departure was not merely ill timed, it was unexpected. Though ostensibly a short vacation, he appears to have been away from Hollywood for at least six weeks, by which time Koerner was in no mood to take his shoes off Breen's desk.

A natural pugilist, Koerner had orginally come to RKO at the instigation of then-president Harold B. Franklin in the early 1930s.

By the time he was elevated to temporary production manager, he had detached himself from the deposed Franklin and attached himself to Floyd B. Odlum instead. Odlum, ostensibly a supporter of Schaefer, had begun to lose faith in his chosen man, and Koerner was keen to encourage his passage into apostasy.

Koerner was a businessman whose loyalties lay with the parent theater company that controlled RKO Radio Pictures. As he told press men on his promotion to head of production, "When we decide to make a picture, I try to think of what the exhibitor can put up in his lobby to sell tickets." He was precisely the man needed to reorganize the company and galvanize the sales force; but as production head, he would be responsible for making decisions about films when every inner fiber cried Bottom Line.

His one idea was as blunt as the man himself, a bludgeon with which to beat all RKO filmmakers. Koerner believed in value for money, double booking films few would pay to see individually, a drama with a comedy, a weepie with a screwball, two B movies rather than one A movie. Hence the "obvious" pairing of *The Magnificent Ambersons* with *The Fleet's In*, a rabble-rousing wartime musical, at its first preview on March 17.

By this date Koerner was probably thinking not *if* but *how* to trim three-quarters of an hour from the $1.2 million saga, making for a far more distorted refraction of its creator's intent than any Shakespeare play ever trimmed by Welles. Koerner had already organized his own preview of *The Magnificent Ambersons* at the studio the day before its first public preview. The cable Wise sent Welles on the sixteenth hardly conveys the sense of panic that this screening undoubtedly caused: "Mr. Schaefer unexpectedly requested running *Ambersons* today for himself *and Koerner* [my italics] and 4 other men unknown to me, probably Eastern executives. Following showing Schaefer inquired regarding shortening length."

Reading between the lines, it seems clear that Koerner (at Odlum's behest) had brought along executives from the parent company to shore up his own position and to provide him with the necessary clout to override any protests from Schaefer. As to what

Koerner saw that day, one witness, Jack Moss's young assistant Cy Endfield, remembers it well. He had no doubts about its quality, "It was a picture done like music, so smooth, the choreography of camera and actors so beautiful. It was the best I'd ever seen. But I also knew it was boring other people. It didn't hold them. We came out, and Jack Moss said, 'We've got a problem.'"

Simply put, Koerner wasn't looking to salvage the movie, he was looking to savage it. He had done his homework and knew that Welles had, in the words of RKO's own counsel, Ross Hastings, "the right to make the first rough cut of the picture or to cut the picture in the form of the first sneak preview, if it is to be previewed. Thereafter he agrees to cut the picture as directed by us." So he was going to oblige Welles with a preview in the most inhospitable circumstances his closed mind could conceive. Second on the bill to a Dorothy Lamour musical in Pomona, California, sounded just fine and dandy.

The preview system itself was based upon a very skewed form of faith in the innate wisdom of the paying public. David Selznick highlighted the fallacy it played upon when writing about the possibility of previewing *Rebecca* in December 1939. His comments apply just as well to *The Magnificent Ambersons*:

> [It] is a very tricky picture, with very peculiar moods and a very strange sort of construction and playing. I don't want to take the chance of finally editing it according to the reactions of an audience that has come to see a Marx Brothers picture, or even a Joan Crawford picture, as might be the case at previews. I think the whole preview system is wrong, in that it is the equivalent of trying out a Eugene O'Neill play on the road by advertising to the public that they are going to see the Ziegfeld Follies, and then having the reactions of a Follies audience determine how the O'Neill play should be cut.

By screening *The Magnificent Ambersons* at this stage RKO were probably also in breach of their agreement with Welles. The fact is that the version screened on March 17 (and presumably the sixteenth) was *not* Welles's preferred cut. Having only just received a print of the film five days earlier, still without its musical soundtrack fully integrated, how could he have approved the print for preview in the time allowed? Indeed, someone at RKO must have been concerned about this because, as Carringer notes, "as a protection against possible legal complications, the negative trims and outtakes were held for a time in the vaults." Welles, though, was never apprised of their existence and eventually the material was burned, along with composite material for Hitchcock's *Suspicion*.

Before Welles had even run the movie for himself, he was ordering Wise to make the so-called "big cut," trimming the film from around 132 to 110 minutes, an altogether more palatable length. All the scenes between Isabel receiving Eugene's letter, begging her to confront her son with the truth about their relationship, and the one in which everyone gathers outside her room as she approached death were to be deleted, to be replaced by a single scene in which George enters his mother's room immediately after she receives Eugene's letter, to find her unconscious. She dies shortly after, without regaining consciousness, rent apart by the kind of conflict that filled those ballads she liked to hum.

Robert Carringer, without the benefit of a single screening of the Welles edit, may feel that the director's "impulsive second guesses were not always improvements." I find it hard not to side with Welles, who considered himself "totally without self-doubt [when it comes to] the technical side of . . . movies." And yet, as recently as January 2002, a long feature on *The Magnificent Ambersons* in *Vanity Fair* claimed that "the first blow against this version was dealt not by RKO but by Welles himself, [who] before he'd even received the composite print . . . impulsively [sic] ordered Wise to cut twenty-two minutes from the middle of the film."

Welles had learned an important lesson early on in his career: that the test of a good director is whether he is willing to throw out his most beautiful shots. Even though much of what this director was prepared to lose in the so-called "big cut" was exquisitely shot,

V. F. Perkins puts his finger on that metaphorical button when he finds "a lot of merit in the single hefty cut volunteered by Welles. This would have eliminated all the material dealing with George and Isabel's absence in Europe, so that her illness and death would result immediately from George's rebuff to Eugene and the strain of the conflict between love for her son and love for Eugene."

The whole European sojourn reads like a segment from a bad eighteenth-century novel, in which the lady has retired to the country with "the vapors" only to return home looking pale and wan. Isabel dying because she is unable to reconcile her divided feelings is equally contrived, but far more aesthetically satisfying. It also makes George's rejection of Eugene as his mother's suitor an impulsive act, the tragic consequences of which happen too soon for him to recant his initial course of action.

This "big cut" was apparently made in time for the Pomona preview,* as was the new scene Welles asked to be shot, in which George comes upon his unconscious mother. Unfortunately, the scene as filmed by Wise was deemed unsatisfactory by Welles, who sent Jack Moss a cable a few days after the preview, informing him that "New scene Bob shot . . . not well enough done. Absolutely insist Norman direct it. Must have intensity punch." Presuming that these views were communicated to Wise, they surely put our nascent director's nose out of joint. Instead of following Welles's directions, Wise unilaterally decided to restore the scenes removed before Pomona in time for the people of Pasadena's own preview three days later.

The Pomona preview has over the years become typecast as something of a disaster, largely because of a letter Schaefer wrote to Welles four days later, describing how "in my twenty-eight years in the business, I have never been present in a theater where the audience acted in such a manner. They laughed at the wrong places, talked at the picture, [even] kidded it. . . . I don't have to tell you how I suffered, especially in the realization that we have over a million

---

*Carringer discusses at length the differences between the two versions screened at Pomona and Pasadena on pages 284–5 of *The Magnificent Ambersons: A Reconstruction*.

dollars tied up." He returns to this central theme later in the letter, pointing out how "if you cannot satisfy . . . the younger element . . . you just cannot bail yourself out with a million-dollar investment." He goes on to inform Welles that his next film "must be made for the box office."

Schaefer's concern throughout this letter is more the cost of the film than the reaction of a particularly unsuitable demographic chosen for its first preview. So was the audience reaction really bad enough to sabotage the precise design Welles had applied to Booth Tarkington's novel and replace it with, to put it kindly, a film with a split personality? Jonathan Rosenbaum, in his recent *Movie Wars*, sees fit to challenge the "Schaefer" version of events, and those who continue to take it at face value:

> Carringer accept[s] without qualm the conclusion of studio executive George Schaefer that the first preview of *Ambersons*, when a version approximating Welles's own version was shown, was a "disaster." . . . I've seen most of the 125 "comment cards" myself—fifty-three of which were positive, some of them outright raves ("a masterpiece with perfect photography, settings and acting"; "the best picture I have ever seen")—and would conclude that declaring the preview a "disaster" on the basis of those cards is a highly subjective matter, very much dependent on what one is predisposed to look for.

What Charles Koerner was "predisposed to look for" was evidence that the film was a box-office turkey. In fact his most persuasive evidence could be found in the asides of those who *were* impressed, even bowled over by the movie they had seen:

> Very good. . . . Far too high for general consumption, however.

> I enjoyed it but . . . I don't think it will have much box office appeal. A good psychological study. Photography excellent but the darkness gets on ones nerves.

This picture is magnificent. The direction, acting, photography, and special effects are the best the cinema has yet offered. It is unfortunate that the American public, as represented at this theatre, are unable to appreciate fine art.

I liked it, but I feel that it was above the audience.

Koerner also found vindication among fellow Luddites. Those whose command of English was almost guttural were unanimous in their distaste ("Boys your slipping. I was ribbed"). As Bob Wise informed Welles in a letter mailed on March 31, there was even "some laughter at the first preview on the Major's wonderful speech [staring] in[to] the fireside," though there are no more than a handful of scenes as affecting in the whole Hollywood pantheon.

Schaefer was mortified. Yet, as Perkins correctly concludes, he "should have seen it coming." It was the cost of the film, not its quality, that now counted. The outcome had been predetermined, as the results of a second preview in Pasadena on March 20 confirm. Even though the studio had restored twenty-two minutes of film—the "big cut"—to a movie already described by one preview audience as "too long and drawn out," of the eighty-five cards collected at Pasadena, just eighteen were unfavorable, an impressive response for such a "downbeat" movie.

Schaefer proceeded to inform Welles that, despite "the reaction at Pasadena [being] better than Pomona, we still have a problem." Quite simply, Schaefer's nerve, so important to *Citizen Kane's* survival, had deserted him. With the new head of production carving out his own little corner, the studio boss had become a worried man. The letter Schaefer sent Welles on the twenty-first confirmed this catastrophic loss of nerve. Richard Wilson was with Welles when the letter arrived and subsequently told Carringer that he "always remembered his utter devastation and the deep gloom into which he sank." To compound Welles's sense of despair, he almost immediately received a cable from Jack Moss that confirmed his worst fears:

Schaefer and his associates advocate many drastic cuts mainly for purposes of shortening length Stop Bob Wise Joe Cotten and myself have conferred analyzing audience reactions exercising our best judgement and we believe the following suggested continuity would remove slow spots and bring out heart qualities of picture.

The trio's detailed suggestions were brutally uncinematic, made by people who saw a movie not as a totality but as a sequential series of scenes. Included were a couple of swinging cuts to the ballroom scene and much that was duly adopted by the studio. However, to its credit, after George's "comeuppance," this so-called compromise plan suggested "play[ing] on through to end as in Pasadena preview." In other words, the film would have retained its downbeat direction, just minus the steady rhythm Welles had sure-handedly imposed. Welles's response was remarkably restrained. He simply reiterated the need for Wise to bring the film to him, "My advice absolutely useless without Bob here. Sure I must be at least partly wrong, but cannot see remotest sense in any single suggested cut of yours, Bob's, Jo's Stop."

But Welles already sensed that those he had previously considered allies were slipping across the lines one by one. Three days later he received another blow to his self-esteem: a letter from Joe Cotten that hit home, but missed the point by a mile, as he wrote of "the emotional impact in the script [having] lost itself somewhere in the cold visual beauty before us." Welles subsequently said he felt that Cotten "had become, with the best will in the world, an active collaborator with Wise, and whoever else was busy screwing [the film] up. They used him." Cotten would ultimately comply with the studio reshooting the finale in a vapid hospital corridor.

By this time Welles had already cabled eight pages of suggested alterations *and cuts* to Wise, a prompt, precise and practical response to the March 25 cable; which, as Carringer suggests, "represents Welles's most sustained effort to reassert control over the production." These are to *The Magnificent Ambersons* what the fabled fifty-eight-page memo became to *Touch of Evil*. Yet a letter from Wise, four days later, detailing responses from the previews, makes no mention of Welles's eight pages of suggestions; and by mid-April it was being communicated to Wise by the studio that he should do whatever was deemed necessary to get the movie into releasable form. What is not clear is whether he was told at this point to make sure the finished film clocked in at under ninety minutes. Such an instruction, though, remains the only logical explanation for such a defiantly illogical, not to say abrupt, ending.

Welles quickly forgave Cotten, but he never forgave Wise. Never a vindictive man, it was an uncharacteristic Welles who, when asked by Joseph McBride if he felt the writer had blamed the editor unduly for the destruction of *The Magnificent Ambersons*, replied, "You can *never* be too hard on Robert Wise." Wise, who would go on to become a successful Hollywood director—making the usual mixture of the atrocious (*The Sound of Music*, for fuck's sake!), the respectable (*The Day the Earth Stood Still*), and a single classic (*West Side Story*, a terrific stage show he managed not to louse up)—has often changed the medley of excuses for what he perpetrated on *The Magnificent Ambersons*, but never the tune: "I can tell you, everybody strived as hard as they could to retain every bit of feeling, the quality of what Orson was trying to do" (and all in eighty-eight minutes!); "I simply couldn't follow his instructions, they made no sense" (actually Welles's cables are perfectly intelligible and consistently focused); and, most recently, to *Vanity Fair*, "I think, someplace down the line, he got tired of dealing with [*The Magnificent Ambersons*]. . . . He kind of forgot about the film, lost interest. It was pretty much, 'You take care of this, Bob. I have other things to do'" (the April 18 cable refutes such a claim).

The wanton curtailing of the ballroom scene in the released version is the most damning evidence that the (re)editing of the film by Robert Wise, at the behest of the studio, was not—as Wise has consistently argued—conducted with due care and diligence, but was an almost random assault on the film's sense and sensibility, designed to get it down to that all-important eighty-eight minutes, and damn any deleterious effect upon continuity and rhythm. By then, Schaefer must have become little more than a bystander to permit this to happen, given his enthusiasm for the scene when viewing the rushes.

In all likelihood, Wise read the writing on the wall, sensing that a change at the top was in the offing. There was certainly nothing "gentle, tireless, and careful" about the changes he eventually made, whatever he claimed to Welles in correspondence that spring. Welles did not know this, and when he sent those detailed changes to Jack Moss on April 18, he specifically refers to one "cut [that] Bob must monkey with" and how "exact means of cutting [one scene] must be [left] up to Bob." He was still expecting Wise to act in the film's best interests. By the time he found out that this was not going to be the case, it was too late.

The April 18 cable ran to four typed pages and made sixty-six specific suggestions, thoroughly belying Wise's claim that he "lost interest." A number of these related to the musical soundtrack, especially during the all-important ballroom scene, which Welles was still unhappy with and hoped Wise would rectify: "Downstairs music should not build after 'someone in congress,' upstairs orchestra should begin at that point"; "Transition between two orchestras should be brighter more interesting dramatic"; "Watch all ups music thru out picture for Wagnerian assertiveness."

Sadly, Wise was not the only person party to the March 25 "compromise" plan who now abandoned Welles. According to Cy Endfield, his boss, Jack Moss, the Mercury's main mouthpiece in L.A. and recipient of the April 18 cable, also surrendered the cause:

> A telephone with a private line had been installed in Moss's office in the Mercury bungalow that had a number known only to Orson in Brazil. For the first few days [after Pomona], he had a few discussions with Orson and tried to placate him; then they had started arguing because there were more changes [being made] than Orson was prepared to acknowledge. After a few days of this, the phone was just allowed to ring and ring.

If anyone still hoped to reach some kind of compromise, it was Schaefer. He imposed a moratorium on further changes to the film at the beginning of April, while he attempted to convince Welles to cooperate in the film's (de)construction. But Schaefer was beginning to feel that he was in an impossible situation, held accountable for Welles's "excesses," yet unable to make things happen that might salvage the situation. A cable sent to Welles in Rio about the cost of color film suggests how much of a stew he believed he was in:

Dear Orson Tremendous amount of personal embarrassment Stop Hope black and white material can still blend in with Technicolor Stop Most anxious you bring this [film] thru at least possible cost Stop I want you to believe me that I am personally on the hook for the whole South American adventure Stop

The cables Welles began to receive from Schaefer at this time can hardly have calmed his shredded nerves. On April 13, he received a seemingly unprompted rant from Schaefer about how costly his current project was proving—"I am rapidly coming to conclusion you have no realization of money you spend and how difficult it is to recoup cost"—that reads more like a belated admonition for *The Magnificent Ambersons*. The subtext of this cable was that Schaefer was losing control of the organization. The cable ended with a "most anxious" plea that "you phone me not later than Wednesday this week." When no such conversation had transpired by the Thursday, Schaefer spelled it out, "With respect to my own apprehension, I must contact you by phone within 24 hours as there are some developments that look very unpleasant in many directions."

Schaefer was now locked in a power struggle to the death. If Welles still wasn't fully aware of how serious the situation was, it was brought home to him one morning in mid-April when, according to Richard Wilson, "Orson and I were surprised by ads in the financial pages of the Rio morning papers which declared in beautiful Portuguese that RKO would no longer be responsible for debts incurred by Orson Welles or Richard Wilson. . . . Orson's vigorous private protest direct to Schaefer went unheeded."

Though Joe Breen had returned to RKO at the end of March, Charles Koerner maintained joint control of production, evidently intent on bringing matters to a head with Breen, who, in the words of Charles Higham, "wanted a policy of high-quality pictures, carefully sold on particularized publicity campaigns one by one, and was [wholly] against the cutting of [The Magnificent] Ambersons." Koerner was convinced that the board would see things his way but still asked RKO's legal counsel, Ross Hastings, to look at some numbers for him. On April 7, Hastings gave Koerner the answer he wanted: "Certainly a strong case can be made that the loss of world markets makes it unfeasible to produce motion pictures of the type and cost which Welles wants to produce."

These were the circumstances in which Wise continued to slice and dice The Magnificent Ambersons until the film was ready for yet more previews on more of Koerner's double bills. A preview in Inglewood on May 4 suggested that they had failed to remove enough vestiges of Welles. Perhaps, even at this late date, it retained the original ending, as suggested in Wise's compromise plan at the end of March. By May 12, when it received its final preview at Long Beach, that was certainly not the case. What was screened that evening was truly a shell of the former shell, an emasculated eighty-eight-minute excerpt of its Pomona self. As almost his last act for the organization Schaefer cleared the film for release. Welles never spoke to him again.

Little of Welles's The Magnificent Ambersons remains, even in the first half of the film, where his intent at least remains discernible. As he said to the BBC's Leslie Megahey, "Everything that is any good in [The Magnificent Ambersons] is . . . really just a preparation for the decay of the Ambersons. . . . It was the purpose of the movie to see how they all slid downhill in one way or another; and . . . how they turned away from each other." That sense disappears between the joins, and with it Welles's film.

Talking about the importance of editing in filmmaking some years later to *Cahiers du Cinema*, Welles spoke of "work[ing for] months and months [on] *Ambersons* . . . so all that work is there, on the screen—but for my style, for my vision of film, editing is not an aspect, it is *the* aspect." *The Magnificent Ambersons*, as it has come down to us, is in that all-important aspect the work of Robert Wise, the man who would go on to be the auteur of *Curse of the Cat People*, *The Andromeda Strain*, and *The Sound of Music*.

Meanwhile, back in New York another power struggle was playing out at the parent company, involving three extremely powerful individuals: Floyd Odlum, president of the Atlas Corporation, who had bailed the studio out once before, back in 1939; Nelson Rockefeller; and David Sarnoff, head of the Radio Corporation of America. With a hundred million dollars of the Atlas Corporation's money, Odlum had the resources to make his views count and Koerner was now his man on the West Coast. Assuming ever-greater control with the steady purchase of more and more shares, Odlum had by June 1942 acquired 47 percent of RKO and with it effective ownership of the parent company.

By then Breen had resigned from RKO, returning to the Hays Office, and Koerner was confirmed as sole head of production; while Schaefer, who was left with a title but no power, was soon to follow, to be replaced by another Odlum man, Peter Rathvon. Such was Koerner's confidence in the eventual outcome that he personally visited the *Hollywood Reporter* in mid-May to tell its editor Billy Wilkerson that "you can take it from me that RKO will not renew Orson Welles's contract after the current deal under any circumstances." These views were passed on to Welles by his ex-guardian, Dr. Bernstein, and confirmed in a letter from Jack Moss at the beginning of June. Welles already knew he had lost the battle for *The Magnificent Ambersons*, but soldiered on with *It's All True*, hoping against hope that it might not suffer the same fate.

Yet Welles retained an almost begrudging respect for Koerner. He felt that the new boss was committed, "by the simple logic of

[his] position, to enmity." Somehow, one doubts that it was mere strategy. The new boss, who died in 1946 after a highly successful stewardship of the studio, never actually understood what Welles was trying to do. Koerner turned the studio around, but his tenure resulted in very few decent movies, and the Big Four studios were never again threatened on the quality front.

◆   ◆   ◆   ◆

It was against such a backdrop of anti-intellectual "enmity" that Welles found himself in Rio that spring, trying to complete a movie with no specific budget, without any real studio support and with the very real possibility looming that he and his crew might be yanked out of there at a moment's notice. The saga of *It's All True* could fill a book (and, assuming I'm correctly informed, imminently will—courtesy of the redoubtable Catherine Benamou).

The story of *It's All True* begins before *The Magnificent Ambersons*, with Welles's plans for a production repertory company under the RKO umbrella. In the spring of 1941, aside from planning a low-budget thriller to be shot just as soon as he settled on a story, Welles had an idea for a film comprising a series of short stories in a documentary style, bound together by the unifying theme of *It's All True*. The opening credits to the so-called "Love Story" segment of the film, scripted by John Fante in August 1941, introduced it as "a story of simple people. It begins when your mother and mine were girls. It teaches no moral and proves nothing. But it really happened."

Though the disparate elements that made up the prototype *It's All True* never coalesced into an actual shooting script, it had by the summer of 1941 acquired three, or perhaps four, components:

1. "The Story of Jazz";
2. "Love Story," an original story by John Fante;
3. "My Friend Bonito," based upon a short story by Robert Flaherty; and, possibly,
(4. "The Captain's Chair," also based upon a Flaherty story.)

Of these, the first element was the one closest to Welles's heart. He had embraced jazz enthusiastically during his time in New York, getting to know the likes of Duke Ellington and Louis Armstrong, and he was fascinated by the origins of this authentically "American" sound. Its evolution soon became a part of his suite of stories, as Welles conceived of an effective way of conveying the elements intrinsic to the jazz sound through visual montage. Described thus in Bret Wood's bio-bibliography, "The ["Story of Jazz" segment of the] film was to open with a montage of shots tracing the evolution of jazz. A jungle ceremony establishes a steady drum rhythm. As the beat continues we see a ship on the ocean and inside it a galley of slaves, the chained men singing with the slow beat, which continues through a slave auction. In a cotton field, the pickers hum a melody and in New Orleans, after the end of slavery, the blacks play instruments and sing for their own pleasure."

Welles was reusing an idea from the opening of *Heart of Darkness*, with its "snatches of jazz music . . . heard from the radios in the moving taxicabs . . . [and] the throb of tom-toms foreshadow[ing] the jungle music of the story to come." This time it would have had a slightly grander purpose than mere scene setting, showing how, as Wood puts it, "jazz evolved from a way of life and continued to change as those who created it went through different situations." When *It's All True* became a more pan-American odyssey, this potted history of jazz would give way to the story of samba.

The one element that survived its transition south was Robert Flaherty's retelling of a Mexican fable about a boy who befriends a baby bull and watches it grow, only to see it sent to die in the bullring. However, because of the bull's exemplary courage it is spared by the crowd. Welles had already begun work on the tale of Bonito the Bull before the approach by the Department of Inter-American Affairs in December 1941. The opening scenes of "My Friend Bonito" comprised a test run for his protégé, Norman Foster; who went with Welles to Mexico in late summer 1941 to compile a cast and crew and be coached by Welles in the style he wanted the film to adopt. With Foster left to get on with it, Welles returned to California to begin work on *The Magnificent Ambersons*.

At this juncture, though, Schaefer approached Welles about the possibility of taking on *Journey Into Fear*, and Foster was recalled from Mexico for his first full-blown directorial assignment, again under Welles's supervision. Meanwhile, the young boy who was to play Chico, the bull's friend, was brought to America to be educated, with a view to returning to Mexico as a more grown-up boy, where he witnesses Bonito's heroic appearance in the bullring. At the same time, Welles quietly put "Love Story" to bed, having presumably realized that the story of a young Catholic girl relentlessly pursued by an unpromising suitor held little potential. He apparently never even revised Fante's original August 1941 script, which is all that remains of that planned segment.

Just when it looked like another ambitious project might go the way of previous schemes, Welles was approached by Nelson Rocke-feller, a major shareholder at RKO, who had recently been put in charge of the Department of Inter-American Affairs. He needed a cultural envoy of sorts who was willing to travel to South America and remind everyone of the many common bonds binding the Americas in these troubled times. Welles, who evidently felt he should be making a more active contribution to the war effort, was just such a man.

Though the whole trip to Brazil became wrapped up in the saga of the film Welles "failed to finish," *It's All True* was only envisaged as one part of his mission. A long letter from Tom Pettey to Herb Drake back in L.A., dated March 27, 1942 (the day Welles sent eight pages of changes for *The Magnificent Ambersons* to RKO), refers to "the Orson Welles project in South America [being] of such magni-tude that it is difficult even for Welles to outline its many facets . . . [though it] embraces the making of a motion picture in a form yet unknown to the screen, transmission to North America and a large part of Brazil of regular weekly radio shows . . . [and] lectures before social, civic and charitable organizations."

The regular weekly shows never came to pass, though on his return to the States Welles did record a series of radio shows about his South American experiences, and occasional lectures only occupied him when he was stalled on the film due to logistical difficulties. And yet he continued the demanding regime he'd maintained back in the States, burning the candle at both ends, then blowtorching it in the middle. According to Grand Otelo—a Brazilian performer whom Welles befriended, then co-opted into his film—he, Welles, and nightclub owner Herivelto Martins would talk (and drink) into the night about the samba and the carnival.

These talks were not just a way of killing time. George Fanto, the cinematographer on the latter part of *It's All True* (and most of *Othello*), recalls how Welles retained all of the essential details from these conversations, and, when he began shooting each morning, would know exactly what he wanted, having "cataloged everything in his mind." As for Welles's work ethic, Otelo recalls how, "when Herivelto and I would arrive at the studio, even if it was 7:15 in the morning, Orson would already be there [and he would be] pointing at the clock. He'd already started working. . . . He seemed to work twenty-four hours a day."

Welles may have flown down to Brazil with no script and only an imprecise idea of how he was going to make "a picture that is neither a travelogue, a documentary film, a boy-meets-girl romance, nor a glorified newsreel," but within a month he had a treatment that linked the social and musical dimensions he wanted to explore, which was promptly forwarded to RKO:

This is the way I visualize [it]—Beautiful shots Rio, and I start kind of travelogue, looks like going to be boring and I say a few words, rush expensive music, Copacabana crowds of bathing girls and suddenly close shot of couple girls under umbrella looking out at water. . . . Guys stand up and look. . . . Make cuts showing tiny sail out in the bay, no explanation for all this. Few more cuts people noticing, kids, crowds beginning to form and look at what is apparently refugees or guys on raft caught in storm. Sail keeps coming in. Show Copacabana Palace Hotel. Crowds of people around front, don't see President, then jangadeiros come through crowd. Then I either appear on screen or speak and say, "This is what happened when we were in Rio and we didn't

understand who these people were. We found out and it is the best
story in America."

Welles "found" the remarkable story of the *jangadeiros*, fishermen
who sailed a thousand miles on rickety rafts to petition the president
of Brazil for improvements in their working conditions, in an article in *Newsweek* that he read on the plane down. It gave him something he felt to be truly epic; epic being, as Welles himself put it, "a
word advisedly used, because the people shown, their world and their
behavior in it, is of a simplicity and nobility truly Homeric." But he
still needed a framework with which to link it to the story of samba,
which now overwrote "The Story of Jazz."

By the end of March he had hit upon a structure that would fuse
these elements, outlined to Herb Drake in Pettey's March 27 missive.
According to Pettey, the film would now comprise "My Friend
Bonito," "a short episode concerning the conquest of Peru," which
Welles planned to shoot after he left Brazil, and the stories of the *jangadeiros* and of the samba, which would come together at that all-
important Carnaval. Pettey described the way Welles planned to
bring the stories together:

> The Welles voice, which has been carried throughout the earlier parts
> of the film, has turned into what the audience suspects to be a trave-
> logue lecturer. Suddenly . . . the voice fades out and the cameras turn
> from the scenic beauties of Rio de Janiero to a group of pretty girls on
> the beach at Copacabana. The camera discloses the little group of
> girls gazing seaward. Soon boats put toward the little craft in the dis-
> tance which resembles a log raft. Four men can be seen riding the
> logs. The audience has no idea who they are and what they are. There
> is no commentary. The camera follows the four men and the hundreds
> of fishing boats escorting them into the docks, up the avenue to the
> Presidential Palace. Then the scene shifts to Fortaleza, home of the
> *jangadeiros* where the story of the fight of these brave fishermen for a
> bare living is told. Finally they start for Rio to demand social legislation
> and better working conditions. The cameras follow. Back in Rio one of

the fishermen sits in front of the camera and tells his story, then excuses himself and remarks that he has never seen a Rio carnival and that he intends seeing this one. The carnival sequence follows with the unfolding of the story of the samba, the story of a music-loving people gone mad quite happily from New Year's until the first day of Lent. Finally the carnival ends, it is dawn and the street cleaners are sweeping the last confetti from the sidewalks. A huge plane flies toward the rising sun circling beautiful Rio harbor. Inside are the *jangadeiros*—59 days en route to Rio aboard their *jangada*—[who] are flying home in a day.

Pettey also insisted that Welles already "knows . . . exactly what he wants to do in South America, and how to do it." However, even at this distance from the studio, there were forces within RKO that were working to undermine the man and his mission. The film's production manager, Lynn Shores, whom Welles never trusted enough to involve in any discussions about the film's format, was by the end of March suggesting to Walter Daniels at RKO in Los Angeles that "Welles wants to shoot a few miles of film and let the cutter try and make a picture out of it."

Shores had his own reasons for wanting to undermine Welles. As Richard Wilson observed, he "was not our nemesis out of innate villainy . . . but was representative of an interesting species . . . The Old Hollywood Hand. . . . This type resisted both youth and outsiders, [and] for Lynn Shores, Orson was the enemy all rolled up in [one] outsized [figure]." Shores's enmity was as real as Koerner's. Indeed, according to the *Encyclopedia of Orson Welles*, it was prompted in part by a request from Charles Koerner "to compile negative information about Welles, so RKO could shift the onus in possible lawsuits from RKO to Welles."

Shores proved to be a most willing trooper in this larger campaign. Welles's own assistant, Wilson, was repeatedly obliged to complain to Los Angeles about Shores's malignancy, which extended to dealing "with [the] Brazilian people rudely and emotionally." When he sabotaged the filming of a crucial scene at the

Urca nightclub, the all-important link between the carnival and the story of samba, Wilson fired off his most strongly worded memo to date:

> From [early in the project] Shores seemed to have taken the attitude of opposition toward Welles and the staff that represented him. . . . He said very often that he didn't think there was a story in the "whole God damn thing," and that nobody wanted to look at "a bunch of niggers." . . . In each case he has exercised a very limited personal judgement, without giving any vision to the complex details of what Welles was trying to do . . . He has been aided in his work and thinking by Leo Reislor, the assistant director . . . [and], without consulting the producer . . . sent unauthorized information and estimates, particularly . . . about the Urca [nightclub], which by his presentation that it would cost $50,000 and then editorialized for a six-minute scene, caused the Urca sequence to be called off . . . shortly thereafter.

The suspension of the all-important Urca scene resulted in a showdown of sorts with Schaefer, who appears to have taken Shores's "presentation" at face value and refused to honor any obligations Welles had made attempting to make it happen (ironically, the scene was finally shot the first week in June and was completed the very day Schaefer was obliged to clear his own desk). Welles was understandably furious, and cabled Schaefer on April 12, predicting disaster if his authority continued to be undermined from within:

> As to Urca commitments I made them personally in no wise acting in excess of my authority. . . . As producer I should be consulted before their validity is questioned. . . . The front office would take no steps regarding any motion picture being made in Hollywood under my responsibility without first and at the very least referring such action to me, its producer. Here real disaster will be the consequence of heedless assaults on my authority. . . . Our carnival story is built entirely around and up to the [Urca] casino scene.

At this juncture neither party was prepared to give up entirely on the other. Welles, in particular, still hoped to salvage *The Magnificent Ambersons* with Schaefer's help. So Schaefer's reply, three days later, must have filled him with a despair similar to the one that his earlier cable on *The Magnificent Ambersons* preview had induced. It alleged that RKO "records indicate you spent $33,000 in March. This is out of [all] proportion to what we ever estimated. We cannot go along on that basis even if we have to close down show and ask you to return. This is how serious situation is."

Evidently, something had happened on the West Coast to alter the basis on which RKO was prepared to subsidize Welles's mission. The $33,000 estimate, if accurate, was hardly an outlandish expenditure for such a difficult project, shot almost entirely "on location," in a country with no one to facilitate filmmakers but plenty of petty bureaucrats hindering them (as a report for Rockefeller's government department at the end of April made plain, "the difficulties accompanying a major production are enormous and are [quite] impossible to overcome in a few weeks"). Those difficulties were now being compounded by RKO itself. When Welles ran out of color film on May 15, it took two weeks to supply more, and then it was only a single two-thousand-foot can. Welles, it seemed, had slumped beneath the studio's radar. Schaefer's April 15 cable crossed with one from Welles, pleading for the opportunity to reaffirm what he was capable of:

> Here our costs are actually not high even during shooting this sequence including Technicolor and particularly considering disastrous transportation delay. When I finish this picture you will see what I mean. Must however be allowed to finish it as I wish to. I have added nothing to original project . . . [and] unless I can finish film as it must be finished for [it to have] entertainment value the entire expenditure of time and effort and money will be total loss.

The supply problems, though, continued. When film did arrive, and was used, it was not necessarily processed efficiently. At the vortex of most logistical headaches was still Shores. A memo from

Wilson at the end of April suggested that Shores had now become openly obstructive, convinced on the basis of his own sources of information that he would prevail in the end: "[Shores] said . . . he'd seen fifteen directors like Orson—he'd seen them come and go. He was feeding half of them right now in Hollywood. . . . He said the whole [project] was silly, that there had to be an end of the shooting of these 'niggers,' [and that] everything would be thrown out in the end. I asked him why he thought so. He said he just knew so." Inside information, presumably. The above certainly suggests that Shores was in cahoots with Koerner.

Not surprisingly, "the shooting of these niggers" was where Shores and Welles most frequently and vociferously clashed. Theirs were two inextricably opposed points of view: one forward thinking and open to experience; the other, regressively conservative and closed to other cultures. In his letters to Walter Daniels, Shores was unrelenting in his racist distaste for Welles's modus operandi, complaining in one letter, dated April 14, how "last Friday, [Welles] ordered day and night shots in some very dirty and disreputable nigger neighborhoods throughout the city," an allusion to Welles's repeated efforts to film in the shanty towns that still cling to the hills around Rio, the *favelas*. Two weeks later, he was generalizing the film's content to Daniels as "just carnival nigger singing and dancing."

When it came to voicing prejudices, Shores did not confine such views to fellow workers. He was willing to actively sabotage the efforts of Welles to film among the *favelas*. On April 11 Shores sent a message to Dr. Alfredo Pessoa of the Brazilian Department of Propaganda, informing him that he was "holding the negative of this film [of the *favelas* that Welles had shot], and [am] not shipping it through for development until I can perhaps have a talk with you on this subject, to be sure that I am not unduly alarmed over its possible consequences." Shores suspected that the upper echelons of Brazilian bureaucracy were likely to take an equally dim view of Welles compiling documentary evidence of their "dirty and disreputable nigger neighborhoods."

Shores even seemed prepared to endanger the lives of Welles and his crew. By informing Brazilian officials of the areas where Welles was filming, he must have known the possible consequences. Welles later referred to one hairy night when "we tried to photograph one of the tenement districts in the *favelas*. Thugs surrounded us and after a siege of beer bottles, empty of course, stones, bricks, and I hate to think what else, we retreated to a more photogenic district." Whether these "thugs" had been officially co-opted to make sure he did not get any further filming done, we'll never know.

If Wilson already suspected Shores of entering into an agreement with the Brazilian Department of Propaganda not to ship these scenes, he later claimed that "we managed to calm local fears and shake the film loose from his grasp." And yet none of the scenes from the *favelas* have emerged from the Paramount vault (where most of the surviving footage lay until the mid-1980s, when it was finally cataloged). So perhaps Shores really did ensure that certain reels went astray between Brazil and L.A. Welles makes no reference to this footage in correspondence about the film in the years 1942–43, though the *favelas* do feature in his September 1943 treatment for the film, written after he had viewed much of the then-extant footage at RKO.

Shores remained determined to undo much of the sterling work undertaken by Tom Pettey, who had been spreading necessary disinformation in order to give Welles the freedom to film where and what he wanted. Pettey personally informed Herb Drake at the beginning of May, "I have had to lie and lie for the last two or three weeks to keep the local reporters away from the studio. If they ever got in and saw some of the Rio shanty life we are doing they would write Orson out of town."

The worldly Pettey was hardly exaggerating. When one journalist, Gatinha Angora, did find out where Welles had been shooting and ran a story in the *Cine-Radio Journal*, he castigated the American director for filming "no-good half-breeds . . . and the filthy huts of the *favelas* which infest the lovely edge of the lake, where there is so much beauty and so many marvelous angles for filming," a story that undoubtedly played its own part in cooling relations between the various official departments and Welles's much-pressed crew.

For Welles, though, the *favelas* were the very nub of the story he wanted to tell. As he put it in one of the radio broadcasts he made back home later in the year elaborating upon his experiences in South America: "There's another side of Rio, . . . not a seamy side—not at all, even if smart isn't the word for it. No, indeed. If Rio's backyard isn't exactly [gala], it's even gayer than Rio's front lawn. There isn't a jazzsmith up north who could ever express it. It's set to music—but it's all its own; rich, deep, Brazilian. It comes rolling down to Rio from the hills. It throbs in the streets. It's called Samba." This reiterated sentiments already voiced in the earliest treatment Welles prepared on his South American odyssey:

> Music is the basis of our picture. . . . [Its very aesthetic] is based on the conception of an illustrated musical constructed of Brazilian popular tunes. . . . Our music had to be native and truly of carnival, and our picture had to be true to the music. We had to discover what Samba was before we found an architecture for our film. Samba, we learned, comes from the hills, so our picture had to be oriented to the hills.

It was in the hills that the *Escolas da Samba* were to be found, as a fifty-five-page draft of *It's All True* makes clear. Unfortunately this draft, the most complete, if belated, representation of the director's intended structure for the film, dates from almost eighteen months *after* filming in the *favelas*—September 2, 1943. In it, though, Welles devised a carefully interlinked series of scenes to convey just how samba "comes rolling down to Rio from the hills." It was to begin at samba school, among the *favelas*, at the very fount of the samba sound, and would end at a Rio tennis club, where "an expensively jazzy version of a Samba is just finishing."

The contrast was to be emphasized by the opinions of Welles's companion on his journey, and immediate audience, a dazzling Chilean senorita named Dorothea who finds herself in the hills above Rio with Welles, where she (and the audience) was to be given an education in Brazil's indigenous sounds. Dorothea is that familiar figure in Welles films, the innocent abroad, who learns to embrace a better way. As the pair follow the setting sun up a mountain road, they see Rio "sumptuously spread out beneath them." A Brazilian station is broadcasting homegrown sounds on the radio:

DOROTHEA: I like that. That's the music here they call Samba.

WELLES: Samba is what Carnaval is made of . . . .

DOROTHEA: I like Samba almost as much as I like swing.
(Dorothea is a jazz afficionada, which warms Welles up on the subject of Samba.)

WELLES: I'll show you where it comes from.
(Welles has stopped the car and switched off the radio.)

WELLES: Listen—there's the real thing.

EXT. MOUNTAIN ROAD DUSK

They are up in the *favelas* now. Music rises from these hill communities like mist—weird, wonderful, strangely darkly African—broodingly sweet as the fading twilight itself. . . . The two have strayed into the real jungle, which still makes long hopeless war on the capital of Brazil. But even here the conquering city, the improbable, the sparkling, the profuse equatorial metropolis is on gorgeous display—its bays, its beaches, its skyscrapers—[Behind], and yet beyond, are the elegant and sinister monuments of other hills—Here, in its own special place, marked out from other dwellings by its wide fenced-in yard—is a typical Escola da Samba.

Welles brings Dorothea to a place where she can watch, and tells her things concerning what she sees. Folk music has produced nowhere else a comparable phenomenon to these Samba schools. Flourishing everywhere in the *moros* of suburban Rio, they serve a generous diversity of social purposes. They are community meeting places, clubs, but always and first they are serious musical societies. . . . Cheerfully unaware of their high cultural importance, the Samba schools are earnestly dedicated to the preservation of a great tradition.

After the duly educated pair leaves the school, they descend down the mountain road, Dorothea listening anew to the samba as it plays through the car radio speakers. Meanwhile Welles demonstrates various musical instruments he unwraps from a paper bundle—each one a samba instrument. Welles plays them one by one, giving their names and functions, developing what he calls "the anatomy of samba." At this point the pair is overtaken by "a very sleek roadster," whose occupants turn out to be young male friends of Welles. As the Brazilian boys pile out of the car to say hello they grab the instruments Welles has been clumsily using for illustration "and quickly identifying the remainder of the catalogue, play them to the radio's lead."

The scene dissolves into the dawn of another day, the first day of Carnaval. Once again Welles aims to reinforce the idea of samba, this time personified. And so rolling down from the hills "into the city come the people of the Samba schools, early rising outlanders, whole clubs and neighborhoods at a time—in *cordoes* and *blocos*; all costumed, all dancing and singing—in pairs and in battalions." During Carnaval itself Welles planned to keep up a running commentary, explaining the difference between a samba and a *marcha*, and how each float is made to represent a particular song. Finally, Welles pulls the crew away and heads for the Rio Tennis Clube and an arranged meeting with Dorothea. But when he arrives at the Clube, and locates Dorothea, he is "just too late to stop a handsome Brazilian youth from whirling her off into a Samba." End of script.

So how representative of Welles's intentions back in the spring of 1942 is this script from September 1943? Or am I, like Welles himself, rewriting history by even connecting this document to the Brazilian adventure itself? Structurally, the script conforms almost exactly to the treatments he sent from Brazil. However, the September script rarely suggests that this is an actual record of what was "in the can," being confined to either a general description of raw, silent footage or the rudimentary scene setting of someone trying to connect up the joins. The one exception is the samba sequence, which does not conform to either type.

In fact, we know from Welles's own correspondence that at least part of the "Carnaval" sequence had been "put together and combined with the soundtrack" by the beginning of 1943; and that by the following year Welles had made a seven-reel edit of "Carnaval" for his own purposes. So it does seem likely that the September 1943 samba sequence was based on a genuine knowledge of what RKO retained. Though a number of links in that September were (intended to be) the kind of scenes it would have been easy to reshoot on a studio lot, the scenes with Dorothea—from the hills, via the school, to the tennis club—do not fit easily into this category. It is certainly hard to see how Welles might have "faked" the scene at the *Escola da Samba*.

What is noticeably absent from that September script is the big Urca finale, which we know (from a letter Welles wrote to Brazilian sidekick Fernando Pinto) had been processed as early as the fall of 1942. This finale was intended to resolve *It's All True* in a dramatically satisfying fashion. According to Richard Wilson, the ending focused on a lost child who has been cropping up throughout "Carnaval." He represents the spirit of Carnaval, which as Welles wrote in 1945, "calls for the aimless exuberance of childhood." As dawn breaks our child is asleep under a lamppost:

> As distant figures of street sweepers appear with their brooms, a policeman tenderly picks up the sleeping boy, asks his name and where he lives. The boy's answer is a sleepy murmur of his favorite Samba. . . . Their walk away is intercut with Otello . . . saying farewell to Plaza Eleven as [his] song . . . plays like an echo. The lamp above the street sign goes out. Silence. Carnaval and its film are over.

Before he could get RKO to provide the funds (and film) to shoot his finale, though, Welles was expected to address the lack of a formal script—even though, according to Richard Wilson, the studio knew full well that "there had never been a script on which to base . . . Welles's estimate that the picture would cost between $850,000 and a million dollars." Welles decided to remind the studio and his main backer, Nelson Rockefeller, of the terms under which he had agreed to the assignment; and how fastidiously he had stuck to them. The result was a forty-seven-page document that gave a breakdown of all activities to date. Copies were sent to Schaefer, Rockefeller, and John Hay Whitney at the Department of Inter-American Affairs.

On May 2, though, Schaefer cabled Lynn Shores. The message was terse and to the point: "Abandon Four Men On Raft Film. Continue to completion Carnival. Make no [further] commitments . . . [Phil] Reisman coming to act for company." Shores had continued to stir up trouble for Welles even after the latter fired assistant director Leo Reislor for aiding and abetting Shores in his machinations. Another missive three days later, this one from Pettey to Drake in L.A., suggested just how bad things had gotten: "All of this coupled with the RKO home office harassment of Welles is enough to make the boy go off the deep end. Then, too, somebody has been turning in a detailed report on Welles in Rio and it has not been flattering."

No prizes for guessing who that somebody had been. What perturbed Welles most was the fact that Schaefer accepted Shores's version of events over his own. When Reisman, the RKO vice president for foreign sales, arrived (for the second time) a few days later, he delivered to Welles a long, condemnatory letter from Schaefer. Though Reisman had some sympathy with Welles's point of view, he quickly set about laying the groundwork for a release to the South American press explaining that Welles had to go back to Hollywood to work on *The Magnificent Ambersons*, but that a smaller group, including the director, would shortly return to Brazil to complete work on the film.

Just when it looked like *It's All True* was doomed, a genuine tragedy handed Welles an unexpected remission. The leader of the *jangadeiros*, Jacare, was drowned on May 19 while reenacting their heroic arrival into the harbor in Rio. Suddenly a summary recall of Welles and the crew back to L.A. seemed likely to send the Brazilian press into a frenzy of anti-American sentiment. At the same time, according to Wilson's wife, Elizabeth, "Orson was so undone [by the death of Jacare] that he . . . made the decision at that point that he would make the film no matter what."

RKO, in the middle of its own ructions, was obliged to show some kind of good faith, and finally the film and funds necessary to complete the Urca sequence were released. On May 30, shooting at the Urca commenced. Everything in Rio was wrapped up by June 8. Reisman, meanwhile, imposed a solution on Welles that gave him precious film and six weeks of shooting time in the village of Fortaleza, home of the *jangadeiros*, but did not give him any leeway as to the kind of equipment or crew with which he might work. Funds of $10,000 were supplied (deposited in a Brazilian bank in Wilson's name) along with a silent Mitchell camera, forty thousand feet of black and white film, and the services of a young Hungarian cameraman, George Fanto. Welles had forty days before his flight home and the unstinting support of the Wilsons, Fanto, and his secretary Shifra, with which to shoot the necessary footage at the *jangadeiros'* village.

As Wilson states in his own memoir of those days, "By June 13th our little group was in Fortaleza, two thousand miles away, near the mouth of the Amazon. But our equipment arrived a whole precious week after we did, and our camera was without the lens that everyone knew Welles used the most. We worked from before dawn to after darkness fell for some six weeks." The defective equipment rendered much of the footage unusable, but that marvelous funeral featured in the 1992 restoration suggests that there was still enough "in the can" to "complete" the story.

By the time they returned to the West Coast in late August, Welles was not alone in suspecting that the studio was looking for a way out of honoring their agreement with him, the Department of Inter-American Affairs, and the people of South America. Wilson reminded Reisman, in a memo written on their return, of how "we pled for better and safer equipment . . . We lost time every day because we had trouble with the poor motor we got in Rio . . . The spare motor we rented in Rio was finally sent to us mounted backwards, so it was no use at all. Worse than that, after two weeks of hard and careful composition work we discovered that the Academy aperture in the RKO spare camera had been removed." Wilson's subtext is plain: if the studio really wanted a releasable film, how come it did everything it could to deny Welles the means to complete it?

Welles and Wilson found plenty of evidence on their return that RKO's ill will was not confined to mere technical interference. A letter from Herb Drake, that arrived the week before they headed into the hinterlands, had put Welles under notice that "there is a widespread, nurtured campaign to prove you have been spending too much time and wasting too much money in Brazil; that *Ambersons* is no good, and [*Journey Into*] *Fear* ditto. This has gone so far as a personal visit by Koerner to the *Hollywood Reporter*."

While Welles was incommunicado in the interior, the Mercury troupe were summarily ejected from their office on the lot. Even with *Ambersons* emasculated, Koerner seemed determined to put the kibosh on each and every project of Welles's. As Welles put it, "proving my incompetence would have won [his] cause . . . It was a cold-blooded political maneuver." But there seems a spitefulness to some of the actions Koerner took upon assuming full control of studio production the second week in June. *Journey Into Fear*, which Welles had only made a Mercury production as a favor to Schaefer—and was never his work, per se—was taken away from the Mercury; and its director, Norman Foster, excluded from the editing process. When Jack Moss wrote to Koerner in measured tones to complain, suggesting that "courtesy alone should be enough to cause Mercury to be included in any function concerning *Journey Into Fear*," he received the curtest possible dismissal from Koerner:

Dear Jack,

Believe me, I realize your situation very definitely and clearly. . . . In fact, the extent of RKO's [previous] help to Orson Welles and The Mercury Productions would, in many circumstances, be considered somewhat fantastic. In regards to *Journey Into Fear*, I simply followed very definite and clear-cut instructions. . . . As far as I'm concerned, the matter is permanently closed.

Sincerely, Charles Koerner

In fact, the matter wasn't closed because these "definite and clear-cut instructions" were so nonsensical that the studio had to plead with Welles to return to Hollywood in October and shoot several retakes in order to finish the film. The contract they were obliged to enter into before he would agree to shoot these scenes included a clause that showed how little he now trusted the studio. It recognized the existence of "a controversy over your employment by us in the making of the picture *It's All True*, [and] it is expressly understood . . . that the additional work on *Journey Into Fear* . . . shall in no way affect this."

Despite Welles's generous gesture, the editing of *Journey Into Fear* was a shambles and so was the finished film, which duly became another RKO double-bill B movie. Again studio scuttlebutt suggested Welles was to blame, as he was transformed into the scapegoat for all of the studio's ills during the reign of the late, but little lamented, George Schaefer. If *The Magnificent Ambersons* and *Journey Into Fear* suffered at the hands of the studio's ever-obliging editors, it would be some time before footage from *It's All True* was even processed.

And yet, according to the generally reliable, firsthand testimony of Richard Wilson, by the end of June all of the filming on "Carnaval" had been completed, most of "My Friend Bonito" was in the can, and all two thousand feet of film was being used in Fortaleza. Enough to make a movie? Welles would never really find out. Not only was all the footage embargoed, so was the true cost of *It's All True*, which was subject to every exaggeration the new status quo could apply. Though the total expenditure to date was $531,910—of which $300,000 had been vouchsafed by the government *provided the film got a release*—the RKO, which now preferred "showmanship instead of genius" (its new motto), added an overhead charge of $146,275, then scrapped the project entirely, at an ostensible cost of $678,185.

The alternative—allowing Welles the facilities necessary to finish the film—stood to recoup RKO at least half of the actual cost from the government. It was barely considered. The decision to scupper the film had already been made, without Welles even being permitted to sync sight and sound to show what he had. In the light of these stark facts it seems that Welles got most essentials right when he told Dilys Powell of the *Sunday Times*, twenty years later, what really happened to *It's All True*:

ORSON WELLES: I was to shoot, among other things, a giant Technicolor documentary on the carnival in Rio. No script, no story line, and a budget of a million dollars. A mammoth Hollywood crew and tons of equipment were shipped to Brazil and we started in recording the carnival, and documenting the samba. The material was interesting. But back in Hollywood . . . the film we were sending them looked fairly mysterious. No stars. No actors even. "Just a lot of colored people [sic]," to quote one studio executive, "playing their drums and jumping up and down in the streets." Meanwhile there'd been a great shake-up at RKO: Rockefeller's men were out. The idea was to make a case against the old administration, and my million-dollar caper in Rio, without even a shooting script, made a perfect target. I never really lived that down. [1963]

And he never did.

ACT TWO: HOPE

5

THE NATURE OF
THE ENEMY

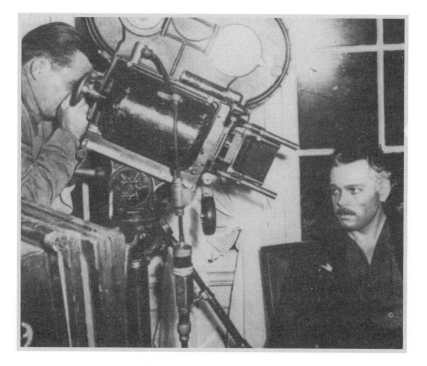

[It's All True: Carnaval in Rio]

I have got to be free to make the pictures I want to make, as I
want to make them. I have always taken this stand, and
regardless of any good advice I may get to the contrary, I shall
continue to take it, and *must*, as long as I am going to do
good work in the films.

Orson Welles to Nelson Rockefeller, October 20, 1942

According to subsequent statements, it was a number of years before Welles got to see the butchering of *The Magnificent Ambersons*, at a special showing in Paris in the 1960s. When he did, he made it through five or six reels, thinking, "Well, that isn't so bad." And then, as he put it, "All hell broke loose." When he saw it again with Peter Bogdanovich, in the 1970s, he had to turn away when the film became a medley of random scenes, tears filling his eyes; and by the time he sat and watched it with Henry Jaglom in the early 1980s, he couldn't even stand the thought of the film ending the way it did. As Jaglom recalls, "about twenty minutes before it ended, he grabbed the clicker and turned it off. . . . He said, 'From here on it becomes *their* movie—it becomes bullshit.'" A year or two later, BBC producer Leslie Megahey asked him, "Do you ever get over something like that?" He replied, "Not really, you don't."

If *The Magnificent Ambersons* was a lost cause, Welles still hoped that *It's All True* might be saved. And so began a series of vain attempts to salvage that film, and prove (again) his worth to Hollywood at large. It was never the easy option. He had not gone out of his way to make friends in this West Coast colony, and even now he was not adverse to publicly criticizing the system he needed to play. At a lecture given at the New York University union less than two months after his return, he made a reference to the need for greater experimentation in Hollywood, and even suggested the studios find a form of funding to provide it:

Hollywood expects you to experiment on a film which must make
money, and if they don't make money you are to blame because your
job is to make money. Movies can only go forward in spite of the motion
picture industry. I don't want you to . . . believe that Hollywood is a
place where a good picture is made as a normal course of things
because it is made against more odds than you could possibly guess.
. . . It is too bad that there is no money spent in Hollywood for experiment. If you take any other large industry . . . you spend at least 10
percent—maybe 20 percent—of your profits on a laboratory where
experimentation is done.

It was a theme he would return to a number of times, notably in
his regular column for the *New York Post* in the first half of 1945,
when his initial target was the Academy of Motion Picture Arts and
Sciences, which he accused of being "as snobbish as a Hollywood
hostess. Did you ever hear of a B picture getting one of the prizes, or
even a nomination? . . . A valid academy . . . would be a laboratory
for experiment [rather than] for the manufacture of a product. . . . I
love movies . . . but don't get me wrong—I hate Hollywood."

A couple of months later he was back on the attack, contrasting the first part of Sergei Eisenstein's magnum opus, *Ivan the Terrible*, with "the pallid stylelessness of [Hollywood's] 'realistic' school,"
before accusing American "arts and artists of . . . hav[ing] been so
busy for so long . . . teaching the public to reject anything larger
than life, unless it be stated in the special language of glamour and
charm, that I'm afraid many good citizens will laugh out loud at
Eisenstein's best moments." Such disrespect for the precepts of cinematic realism, consistently espoused by Hollywood, set Welles apart
from all but a handful of contemporary American filmmakers.

He returned to the same theme, two columns later, suggesting
that American filmmakers' obsession with realism came at the
expense "of an exclamatory and resonant beauty . . . to which our
school [of filmmaking] cannot [even] aspire." Welles's avowed aspiration for the same "courageously radical stylization" as Eisenstein
could not have helped his chances of securing another directorial

opportunity out west, no matter how much he talked about wanting to make movies "so meaty, so full of implication that everyone will get something out of it." Welles may have retained a personal faith in the intelligence of the average filmgoer, believing implicitly that "once they are interested, they understand anything in the world," but he was up against the kind of men who "always tend toward the . . . entertainment world, [where they] combine a morbid preoccupation with the public with a devastatingly low opinion of the public mentality and moral character." This was Welles's description of Charles Foster Kane in a 1947 deposition, but he encountered much the same traits in the various "ex–pushcart peddlers" who reinvented themselves as Hollywood moguls.

Such an outburst was prompted by more than three years of bitter frustration; at a time when it looked like he would have to play the game according to Hollywood rules, or remain, like his mentor D. W. Griffith, forever ostracized. One way of putting himself in the studios' good books would have been to refrain from comments like, "[Film] is the great art form of our century. It is just too bad it is . . . so very meaningless most of the time. When I tell that to people in Hollywood they get mad at me." Mad they were likely to remain as long as they continued to read quotes from Welles like "I don't acknowledge the existence of a job called producer." (Nor did he deviate from this view, which he reiterated thirty years later to the producer of *The Other Side of the Wind*, who was informed that "there are no producers, only bankers.")

Nor was Welles alone in denigrating the Hollywood producer's worth. Even in the mid-1940s a growing tide of articulate critics of the Hollywood system was beginning to demand the right to write (and direct) without an intolerable degree of interference. And yet, "the making of a picture, [which] ought surely to be a rather fascinating adventure . . . is not; it is an endless contention of tawdry egos, some of them powerful, almost all of them vociferous, and almost none of them capable of anything much more creative than credit stealing and self-promotion." Such was the view of crime novelist Raymond Chandler, in an article on "Writers in Hollywood," published in *The Atlantic Monthly* six months after Welles's review of *Ivan the Terrible*.

Chandler had come to Hollywood in 1943 to work as a scriptwriter for Paramount Pictures. His first script, for Billy Wilder's *Double Indemnity*, was promptly nominated for an Oscar. Yet he quickly learned that even "so far as the writing of the screenplay is concerned . . . the producer is the boss; the writer either gets along with him and his ideas (if he has any) or gets out." As for the producers' actual worth, Chandler characterized most of them as "low-grade individuals with the morals of a goat, the artistic integrity of a slot machine and the manners of a floorwalker with delusions of grandeur."

Chandler had most of his prejudices confirmed when he arrived at Paramount just in time to see the studio head, Frank Freeman, effectively fire (i.e. not renew the contract of) their most successful director, Preston Sturges, because he insisted upon a thirty-day option at the end of each picture when he could leave the studio if he was unhappy with the cutting of a picture. As Sturges put it, "This right to leave was . . . intended . . . merely to cause their production head [Henry Ginsberg] . . . to treat me with the courtesy due a grown man of known integrity and not like an irresponsible child . . . My proposal was deemed unacceptable." Ostracized by the big studios, Sturges would direct just three more films in Hollywood before his death in 1959.

Like most writers Chandler was initially enthused about Hollywood as a subject for a novel, but couldn't conceive of anything that wouldn't end up largely satirical, "like one of these South American palace revolutions conducted by officers in comic opera uniforms." Welles, too, came to feel that satire might be his strongest weapon when addressing Hollywood's many absurdities. It was probably around this time that he first conceived the idea for a script called *The Unthinking Lobster*, which centered on a producer/mogul by the name of Jack Behoovian, first cousin to Bey of Beverly Hills, a cigar-chomping entrepreneur without the slightest pretense to artistry. Welles's first full-blown satire on Hollywood, *The Unthinking Lobster* portrayed a producer obsessed with commercial hits who fires a female star and replaces her with a secretary from the typists' pool. The secretary proceeds to play a saint who heals the lame—except that she actually *does* heal them. At this point Hollywood turns into another Lourdes, until no one is able to make any more movies. Finally, our producer has to go into conference with the archangel Gabriel, who agrees to allow him to resume his ill-gotten pursuit of Mammon if the Hollywood studios will agree to stop making religious pictures.

In later years, though, Welles came to paint a quite different, almost rosy picture of his time in Tinseltown. In conversation with Kenneth Tynan in 1966, he claimed that the majority of "the old studio bosses—[like] Jack Warner, Sam Goldwyn, Darryl Zanuck, [and] Harry Cohn—were all friends, or friendly enemies I knew how to deal with. They all offered me work. Louis B. Mayer even wanted me to be the production chief of his studio . . . I was a maverick, but the studios understood what that meant and if there was a fight, we both enjoyed it." He even typified these "ex–pushcart peddlers [who] turned into Hollywood moguls" as "by and large honest salesmen," who thought that they were giving the public what they wanted, never "seriously invading the artist's life unless the artist was willing to make that concession."

Welles still hoped he might never have to "make that concession," even as he continued having dinner with Goldwyn, Warner, or indeed David Selznick. He hoped against hope that "with an annual output of forty pictures per studio, there [might just] be room for one Orson Welles picture." For now, Hollywood's version of Chinese whispers continued to denigrate his credentials. Charles Koerner was still shoring up his position by putting Welles down (his final act of spite came in December 1942, when he ordered all of the footage cut from *The Magnificent Ambersons* to be destroyed). Meanwhile vials of vitriol continued to pour from Herman Mankiewicz, who now privately claimed sole authorship of *Citizen Kane* as a way of generating work from the barren field of film scripts left in him (he still found the nerve to ask the ever-obliging Welles to appear as a character witness in a 1943 lawsuit over a drink-and-drive incident involving Ira Gershwin's wife).

Where Welles remained a potentially potent box-office draw was as a leading actor. Whatever his personal doubts about his acting abilities, he realized, as he told a *New York Times* journalist, that he had "a small public . . . whose interest in me is sufficient at the box office to make my appearance on the screen a necessary adjunct to my writing and directing." Here was where he endeavored to apply what leverage he had, hoping to make Welles actor-director the kind of package a studio might buy. The results were not encouraging. Fox offered him a lead role in the movie *The Moon Is Down*, but Welles's insistence on directing it as well eventually led them to abandon negotiations. Other offers foundered on the same demand.

At the end of 1942 he was "considering" a number of offers, of which a multipicture deal with 20th Century Fox appeared to be the most promising. They were even apparently prepared to take on his South American odyssey *It's All True* sight unseen. However, it was made clear that a producer would preside over him. As Welles wrote at the time, the deal would have been "at such cost to my own future independence *as a producer* [my italics] that after much thought we turned down the offer. . . . Any deal of the kind Twentieth can offer represents a serious mortgage on the coming years . . . [and] I have got to be free to make the pictures I want to make." The issue of control remained crucial to the man's well-being, setting him apart from others who carped at the system for lack of an alternative.

By the winter of 1943, with his own coffers running dry, Welles was finally obliged to accept an extremely well-paid offer to play Rochester in *Jane Eyre*, under the watchful eye of Selznick, for which he demanded top billing and an associate producer credit. He also required access to a Moviola so that he could work simultaneously on his South American picture—which he did, "with whatever material I'd been able to get, trying to show people a part of it to persuade them that it was worth finishing." He hoped such evidence would persuade some potential investor that he could still be a

worthwhile risk behind, as well as in front of, the camera. If he
needed "to be free to make the pictures" he wanted to make, he continued to view *It's All True* as the clinching evidence that he still had
what it took.

One of the extraordinary facets of Welles's personality that continues to be misrepresented in print is the man's sheer tenacity. That
someone like the academic Peter Conrad can write, in a hefty, self-
important tome published by Faber in September 2003, "conception
mattered more to him than accomplishment—once he had an idea,
its execution was either impracticable or a dreary anticlimax," suggests a blatant disregard for any facts that fly in the face of a useful
myth (one that my fellow English writers, in particular, seem intent
on propagating).

The saga of *It's All True* proves, once and for all, that Welles
never willingly abandoned projects. As he later observed, "If I'd
just forgotten [*It's All True*] . . . I would have been way ahead. But
I kept trying to be loyal to it." The choice of the word "loyal" is
highly significant. He felt a connection with *It's All True*, and with
the people who had helped him in Brazil, that was as personal as it
was professional. His commitment to finishing the film appears at
times as almost a matter of honor. It certainly comes across that
way in a letter sent to Brazilian coconspirator, Fernando Pinto, in
February 1943:

> As you may know, my quarrel with RKO has assumed virtually Homer-
> ic proportions. Since its completion last August, they have steadfastly
> refused to release the picture. Five months passed before I could even
> so much as look at the film. Now I have finally persuaded them to
> allow me to cut it at my own expense, which formidable project occu-
> pies the better part of our time these days. . . . I have yet to see the
> result of all our work in Sierra. Just now, however, by virtue of signing
> to do another picture with 20th Century Fox, we have raised enough
> cash to run the negative through the laboratory, and by next week I will
> have seen enough to know whether we have as worthwhile a film prop-
> erty as I expect it to be. We are hoping that, after the whole movie is

cut together, that some studio will like it well enough to buy it outright
from RKO. If this doesn't work we shall simply go on saving money until
we can bring it out ourselves. Too much effort and real love went into
the entire project for it to fail and come to nothing in the end.

An earlier missive to Pinto gives a glimpse of the sheer willpower
Welles had to expend when dealing with his old studio, even when
enthusing about the worth of the footage he had been allowed to see.
He rhapsodizes about "the film we made on Carnaval, [which] is
breathtakingly beautiful. So far the whole Urca sequence is completely put together and combined with the soundtrack. It is so exciting and so satisfying that whenever my spirits are low I go to see it."
Those low moments continued to multiply.

In his letters Welles continued to express his personal frustration
at how much of the footage was still awaiting development half a
year after the fact. In his February 1943 missive to Pinto, he admitted that RKO "wouldn't even develop" the footage from Fortaleza.
He also revealed that he was using the money paid for his appearance
in *Jane Eyre* "to run the negative through the laboratory," rather
than to shore up personal finances. Another of Welles's independ-
ent-minded working practices was thus established, even as attempts
to complete the film placed impossible financial demands on him.

Welles, though, was convinced that he could make something
out of the material he had so far screened and which RKO continued to hold. This was considerably more than what eventually found
a home at Paramount, to be salvaged in the mid-1980s. According
to an RKO inventory from November 1952, the studio then retained
twenty-one reels from "My Friend Bonito," fifteen reels of the *jangadeiros*, plus some two hundred thousand feet of unprinted Technicolor negative from "Carnaval." Aside from all of this apparently
unprocessed material, two sequences did pass through an editor's
hands—in the case of "Carnaval," Welles himself. (Catherine Benamou, in her "Persistence of Vision" article, seems to suggest that this
was not done until 1944, though Welles refers to the Urca sequence
as "complete" in December 1942.) In the meantime, RKO's Jose

Noriega made a preliminary edit, 1,968 feet long, of "My Friend Bonito."

Even though we do not know how much of the footage Welles had actually viewed since returning from Brazil, he evidently felt that he had seen enough to warrant a detailed treatment for the film, such as he completed in early September 1943. As Frank Brady suggests, this script seems to have been intended to provide "a rationale for salvaging his film . . . [though we are] never clear . . . whether the actions described are actually on the film Welles thought he had shot." Where Welles's script *does* imply something solid to work with is in the two sequences for which we know there were preliminary edits, i.e. the samba sequence (discussed in the previous chapter), and "My Friend Bonito."

The September 1943 script of "My Friend Bonito" suggests a belief that something of real quality lay in those twenty-one film cans. He claimed that what he had amounted to not only "a complete camera account of the life of Bonito, the great fighting bull, and of his little friend, Jesus, [and] the saga of their curious comradeship throughout their years of growing," but also "a lyric celebration of the changeless pastoral world of ancient Mexico—a human story, simple, tender, and warm, unfolding before a backdrop of the land itself; the very Mexican earth and the lift it supports—a climate of the spirit, solemn, beautiful, and unutterably strange."

Though something "solemn, beautiful, and unutterably strange" can be discerned among the fragments of "My Friend Bonito" utilized for the 1992 documentary film *It's All True*, it seems to have been compiled from scraps of the scraps Welles had to work from immediately after the South America debacle. Unfortunately, nothing of the story's climax features in the 1992 version, though Welles's script depicts a finale in which the boy climbs into the bullring, hardly a scene he would have found easy to restage:

And now Jesus speaks very gently, with no fear in his small voice, "Hi!—Bonito!" The bull moves forward, quickens—but then stops. We can't tell whether the child is certain of his friend or not. Whatever he feels, he turns deliberately away, his back all this while to the bull, and walks to the entrance doors. He turns only to open the door. He holds it open. The bull starts toward him—breaks into a run—a charge—at the child?—No! Through the door and out! As he slams the gate we see his face. The big Indian eyes are suddenly full of tears. Such a shout goes up as never was heard before, even in the Plaza de Toros of Mexico City.

Leaving aside the elements of "Carnaval in Rio" and "Bonito," the September script mostly comprises a series of amusing links—which Welles presumably envisaged filming in a studio setting—along with a general description of the other elements necessary to bind the film together. These appear to have been largely bereft of dialogue. Thus Welles's description of "the epic of the *Jangadeiros*" is little more than a bare prose outline of the visual poetry he intended to bring to the screen:

We are shown the life of the fishing community, with special reference to the romance, and finally the marriage of Sebastian and Francesca. Sebastian is the fifth member of a Jangada crew, the four of which made the historic voyage to Rio. His death by drowning leaves his family, and Francesca's too, without support. . . . After the funeral—a weird and impressive ritual—a meeting is held by the men of the community. Something must be done for the families of those who die in the perilous profession of fishing by Jangada. . . . Here was the motive and purpose of one of the bravest voyages ever made by man.

The 1992 *It's All True* reconstruction was intended (in part) to tell the story of the film (less successfully, I feel, than the episode of *The RKO Story* devoted to Welles). Drawn from elements salvaged from Paramount's vault, it included some of the *jangadeiros* footage that Welles complained RKO would not process. These reels were presumably among the thirty-seven boxes of negative Technicolor, black-and-white film, and positive prints deposited in a storage unit in Salt Lake City in Welles's name at some point in 1944.

Prior to this development Welles signed a promissory note for $197,500, obligating him to repay this sum to RKO over two installments, in September 1945 and 1946 respectively, should he wish to finally secure the footage for good. Again, he must have felt that there was enough there to make some kind of film for him to potentially put his future finances in hock. Unfortunately, without Welles's narration, or the fify thousand feet of music sound negative RKO never relinquished and eventually destroyed, the 1992 composite version can only hint at what might have been possible—with a fair financial wind—in 1944.

In Welles's mind, he hoped *It's All True* might return rhythm of sight and sound to the language of cinema, having anticipated many of the technical difficulties the footage presented. If the silent composition of much of the footage had been the only logical response to the trials and tribulations of filming in South America, the September 1943 treatment is full of little visual gags reflecting those (past) difficulties. One sequence shot on a "perilous Andean road" features "the unlikely spectacle of a motor car inching gingerly around a curve. Indians on foot, ahead of this machine, and behind it, supervise its tentative progress. Welles, sitting up in the back, is busy with a hand camera. At closer range we see Welles run out of film." Just as the audience is beginning to ponder how come the image remains, Welles reveals it to be another sleight of hand, "our camera show[ing] us what it was he wanted to photograph."

Another scene, supposedly shot in Welles's hotel room, involves Orson, his assistant Shifra, and a New Yorker named Harry. We find Harry gingerly plugging in a portable movie projector while Welles self-consciously pontificates about the kind of movie he feels he should be making. "You can't make a movie out of skyscrapers and scenery. We're after *people*." Shifra and Harry finally get Welles to sit still long enough to show him some footage they have compiled of the *jangadeiros*. When the fishermen are introduced to the president in Rio, the film breaks, at which point "Shifra tosses Welles a clipped sheaf of typed pages." It is Jacare's own story in his words, recorded before the fatal accident.

At another point Welles intended to "explain" why the film jumps into Technicolor just as it becomes carnival time (*Wizard of Oz*, it ain't). As the story of the voyage of the *jangadeiros* comes to a close, a moving title was supposed to inform the audience that "THE FILM JUST SHOWN OF THEIR STORY WAS ALMOST COMPLETE WHEN TECHNICOLOR EQUIPMENT ARRIVED FROM THE STATES, IN TIME FOR *CARNAVAL IN RIO*." The last three words suddenly become Technicolor, as a "richly orchestrated, glamorous and ultrapunchy" samba bursts on to the soundtrack. The silent part of the picture is over, as Welles seeks to subvert the style of the documentary travelogue as pithily as Monty Python's John Cleese declaiming, "More fucking gondoliers!"

During the filming Welles had informed various folk that he envisaged a film that—to quote a May 1942 press release—"will be comprehensible to the eye and not necessarily the ear of the audience. It will not be necessary to be able to read to understand. This means a venture into the revival of silent film techniques." The September 1943 script adopted the self-same aesthetic, which Welles lucidly expressed later to a roomful of French cineasts: "We were luckier . . . when we didn't have sound, but we have been moving steadily backward as we've improved technically—*dans le sens* poetry." In striving for "*le sens* poetry" with *It's All True*, Welles hoped to reflect a certain quality found in many of his favorite films from the silent era.

Welles knew that whatever film he ended up making, the joins would be showing. And so, like the opening sequence to the aborted *Heart of Darkness*, a certain visual bravado was necessary in order to overcome resistance to such an overt departure from Hollywood's dictums on continuity. In fact, *It's All True* was always intended to be "incomplete" for the simple reason that, as Welles pointed out to the elderly gentleman in the Hotel Grande, "You could make a thousand pictures here."

The acquisition of the footage from RKO may have spurred Welles to the breach once more, but the September 1943 treatment appears to have been his last attempt to stay true to the original concept. In January 1945 he approached Francis Alstock, coordinator of

Inter-American Affairs, hoping to convince him that his original vision might still serve a purpose. Alstock was unconvinced, and at this point Welles seems to have realized it was no longer practical to resurrect all three tiers. Instead, he conceived of a film that centered on Carnaval, for which he presumably intended his seven-reel edit to serve.

Initially this change of tack manifested itself in a treatment for a film called *Carnaval in Rio*, a.k.a. *Samba*. Written in the spring of 1945, it was shown to a few folk, blending ideas that reached all the way back to the August 1941 "Love Story" element:

> Jack is the hero of the story. (That's me. And, if you don't think I can play it, wait 'til I take off another forty pounds.) . . . The time of the story itself is two or three years before the time of the opening of our picture. The story is told to the Stranger by the Countess on the morning of the first day of Carnaval. It's the story of another Carnaval, some years ago. . . . It's a love story. The Countess tells it because, with a new Carnaval about to begin—and a couple of drinks under her belt—she's feeling sentimental. In Brazil they have a better phrase for the way she feels, it expresses the mood of the frame of this picture. "Saudades" is the word. . . . "Saudades" . . . The remembrance of things past. . . . This frame, remember, is a café on the morning of next year's Carnaval. . . . Here we meet the incidental personages of the love story and see what became of them. . . . Otello plays a major part in the regular Carnaval footage and is important to the story itself. He's a little ebony imp with as much talent as anybody I've ever met— a black blend of Mickey Rooney and Charlie Chaplin. (He's available and we can bring him up here for very little money.) Otello comes often to the café to shine the shoes of the customers. Like many of his sort in Rio, he's an authority on the music and manners of Carnaval. In a special way he embodies its essential spirit—the true Carnaval of the streets. In our story he's go-between and critic, observer and performer. He helps the Countess tell the story. . . . Most importantly, he winds up the old Carnaval and says a long farewell to the old days it stood for.

One of the fortunate few privy to this *Carnaval In Rio* treatment at the time was writer-producer Anthony Veiller, who would end up receiving scriptwriting credit for Welles's next movie, *The Stranger*. Veiller, a friend and collaborator of John Huston's, was probably a name Welles had been given as a potential producer for the Carnaval film. Certainly a letter from Veiller in May 1945 suggested he had been sold on the idea, as he thanked Welles "for a nice sleepless night, thinking about your damned picture. It is the most exciting film I've ever seen, and it seems a damned shame to have to muck about with it. However, if a story must be injected into it, it seems to me that it should be one in which Carnaval itself is the leading character and is dramatized as such." The quality of the seven-reel edit—which must have been what Veiller saw—was evidently impressive enough to generate hyperbole from an industry professional.

Veiller, though, had no more joy than Welles in finding a willing investor among the studios, and when Welles failed to find the $100,000 he needed for the September 1, 1945, installment, it was only a matter of time before he lost the footage again, this time for good. On May 22, 1946, RKO brought action against Welles in the state of Utah, demanding foreclosure on the loan made to him and the return of all thirty-seven boxes of film. The bulk of this material—the seven-reel edit of *Carnaval* included—appears to have ultimately joined Jacare at the bottom of the ocean.

By May 1946 Welles was in dire financial straits, with the collapse of his stage production of Jules Verne's *Around the World in Eighty Days*, which personally cost him a couple of hundred thousand dollars, and was in no position to fight RKO over the enforced return of those thirty-seven boxes, much of it unprocessed (and destined to remain so). Ever the optimist, though, Welles still informed the *New York Times* the following December that he hoped "to buy from RKO the footage he shot for *It's All True*, and complete the picture, just to prove he was right." That passing reference is the last we hear of Welles's attempts to revive the project. Finally, and most reluctantly, he had to let it go.

If Welles never returned to an even keel financially, his career as a celebrity continued apace. On September 7, 1943, he had married America's favorite fantasy figure, Rita Hayworth, during a break from *The Mercury Wonder Show*, a variety show staged for American troops based on the West Coast. The following December, he starred in his first romantic lead role on the big screen, as Rochester in *Jane Eyre*, a distracted, broody performance that proved surprisingly popular, despite being cast alongside perennial celluloid wallflower, Joan Fontaine.

Welles's intellectual concerns, though, found focus elsewhere. In January 1944 he embarked on a lecture tour, arranged by the William Morris Agency. His subject matter was "The Nature of the Enemy," dissecting the fascist mentality that meant "darkness and death" for everyone. At last he was in accord with the whole country when delivering prophesies of doom and gloom. Even Hollywood had reverted to typecasting every German as a Nazi, and every European émigré as a martyr. In such a fevered climate, with every studio scrabbling to make the ultimate patriotic statement, Welles hoped he might interest somebody in a reworking of certain themes from *Heart of Darkness*, *The Way to Santiago*, and *It's All True*.

His last attempt to find a home for all that expensive Technicolor footage shot in Rio was yet another new screenplay, also called *Carnaval*. This time the carnival footage was ancillary to the story, though part of the action revolved around the Rio Carnaval and the film was intended to feature a samba version of "Ave Maria." The two central characters were Michael, an American engineer, and his "true love," Ludmilla Koren, who has fled from the Nazis in Czechoslovakia with enemy agents hot on her heels. Michael, the familiar innocent abroad, knows little of this and remembers even less, for he is a reincarnated "Me" from *The Way to Santiago*, another amnesiac who by "gradually piecing together the past . . . find[s] an inspirational logic in it" [BW], so that as the truth is uncovered, he finds the necessary motivation to support the war effort.

Though this Carnaval story seemed to suffer from the same curse as its predecessors, it showed Welles's abiding interest in certain

themes addressed in previous projects, and which he was understandably unwilling to wholly discard. The most important of these
was the fascist mentality itself, which prompted some rather virulent
prose when he began writing a regular column for the *New York Post*
in the winter of 1945. Calling for the trial of "every clothed anthro-
poid between the ages of 18 and 80 who has violated the accepted
standards of civilization" in one column, he went on to praise the
screening of footage from the recently liberated concentration camps
in another:

> If your stomach is weak, you are the one they were after when they
> decided to show these films in the movie house. It is figured that peo-
> ple who don't like to see such things may not like to remember what
> they hear and read. Such things must be *seen*. . . . The thought of
> death is never pretty but the newsreels testify to the fact of quite
> another sort of death, quite another level of decay. This is a putrefac-
> tion of the soul, a perfect spiritual garbage. For some years now we
> have been calling it Fascism. The stench is unendurable.

Welles continued to feel that this concentration camp footage had
not been screened widely enough. Six months later, he inserted some
of the more innocuous snippets from these newsreels into his next
movie, *The Stranger*. However, he obliged us to focus our attention
throughout the scene on the reactions of Loretta Young's character,
Mary, who turns to her accuser, Edward G. Robinson, and asks "Why
do you wish me to look at these horrors?" Though Welles knew that
he would never get actual "scenes of concentration camp horrors"
(mentioned in the shooting script) past American censors, he found
almost as effective a way of making his point to "people who don't
like to see such things."

The *New York Post* columns, which occupied Welles for much of
1945—after enthusiastically campaigning for Roosevelt's reelection
the previous fall—generated a certain amount of controversy.

Within eight days of their start, Welles was proudly informing his readers about how he "already has a fat scrapbook full of indignant newsprint, demanding his immediate return to the seclusion of the playhouse." He proceeds to remind *The New Yorker*, who had accused him of a dilettantish distaste for fascism, that he "has been concerning himself with matters of State and the hope for an abundant peace for just about as long as the editors" of that esteemed magazine. Longer, actually.

When the general manager of the *New York Post*, Bob Hall, who had hoped to recoup much of Welles's substantial retainer by syndicating his columns, suggested to the new columnist that he was writing far too much on world affairs and that the people (and the *Post*) expected more showbiz gossip and outrageous anecdotes, Welles promptly disabused him of any such notion. The unfortunate Mr. Hall was informed that "this would [indeed] build an audience, but . . . it wouldn't be the audience I want to address. There is a serious public. I believe that time could teach that public to take me seriously."

Despite such belligerence, Welles was obliged to become more circumspect about some of his views. Though he described his *Post* job as "a political column" in his very last interview (on the night of his death), the column did subsequently strike a kind of balance. Where a balanced view was entirely lacking was in his view of Germany and its people. He believed that there was something deeply rotten in the state of Germany and that "while every German is not a storm trooper, your 'democratic German' has taken orders from his masters for so long now that when he gets the chance, he can't say no to a Nazi." This view, expressed in an April 1945 column, was the very antithesis of Welles's usual libertarian persona. Yet it was reinforced on a number of occasions, as Welles argued repeatedly for "a hard peace for Germany [based] on this very proposition: That there are no tyrants without the sufferance of the enslaved. . . . If we exempt a people from the guilt of their leaders, we libel progress itself."

Welles continued to believe that Nazi elements in German society were "laying the fuel for another conflagration, even as their hopes in Germany die in the embers of World War II. . . . Stealthy as before and shrewd as ever, the Nazis of 1932 are plotting for 1952." In a May 1945 column he ventured to suggest that the threat remained as great as ever, predicting that the "fascist world conspiracy" would seek to hide behind a set of new slogans, which might run to something like, "Germany is no more, finished, done with forever. Let all agents promote this with no variation until further orders. Germany is kaput."

These views hardly modified with time, or peace. When Welles was interviewed for a French newspaper in 1949, during a stint with his own little theatrical review, he baldly stated, "I don't find many anti-Nazis in Germany today." When he took that review to Germany in 1950, he included in *An Evening with Orson Welles* his own version of the Faust legend called *Time Runs*. In this version, which Welles described as a "collaboration of many authors, among them Milton, Dante, and Marlow," he "refused to countenance the idea that a diabolical genius could lead a man or a country astray." Rather, as Peter Conrad recently highlighted, he preferred "to disabuse the Germans of their infatuation with a Faust who was sublimely errant."

As so often with Welles, such views were given flight in the centerpiece to his next film, *The Stranger*. It is here we find the Nazi who has wheedled his way into the heart of an archetypal small-town U.S.A., Franz Kindler a.k.a. Charles Rankin the schoolteacher, sitting at dinner with his new wife's family, being asked about his view of Germany by the ever-so-curious Mr. Wilson, the agent sent to track down this war criminal (played by Edward G. Robinson). In the shooting script, Rankin's father-in-law has already prepared us for the views he is about to espouse by referring to "rumors . . . [of] men drilling by night . . . underground meeting places . . . pagan rituals."

This memorable scene contains its share of allusions to the dinner scene in *The Magnificent Ambersons*, where George makes himself equally unpopular by expressing his views on the infernal internal combustion engine; and, more willfully, to a similar scene in Hitchcock's 1943 movie *Shadow of a Doubt*, in which the serial killer uncle, played by Joseph Cotten, reveals a disturbingly sociopathic view of widowed women. The scene as shot by Hitchcock lacks any obvious trigger for Cotten's unhinged monologue, making it cinematically satisfying but psychologically unconvincing. Kindler's response, on the other hand, was intended to project the idea of someone self-consciously trying to be anti-Teutonic. Certainly not a Nazi! Welles-as-Rankin-as-Kindler-as-Welles even claims at its very outset, "I have a way of making myself very unpopular when I start on Germany," a possible dig at critics of his own column.

Kindler proceeds to talk of a world "peopled with warrior gods, marching to Wagnerian strains, their eyes fixed upon the fiery sword of Siegfried" and how "in those subterranean meeting places . . . the German's dream world comes alive" (Welles here retains the double meaning of dream as both "ideal" and "fantasy"). This was the voice of Welles-in-the-*Post*, the skeptical tone that disguises Kindler's "true" view, which only slips out when Noah mentions Marx, and Kindler, in measured tones, mutters, "Marx wasn't a German. Marx was a Jew." The divided self stands revealed, not as in Hitchcock, writ large, but in a slip of the tongue that even Wilson initially fails to notice.

As such, it should have come as no great surprise when Welles agreed to direct and star in *The Stranger*. As Bret Wood notes, "The story line of *The Stranger* provided the perfect vehicle for . . . the expression of Welles's late World War II political concerns—namely the survival of fascism." And yet the suggestion that this represented an untypical project has gained a hold in print, based, it seems, on the film's final form, a generic Hollywood thriller with only occasional flashes of originality.

Welles himself may have welcomed an opportunity to take a little potshot at Hitchcock, whose *Shadow of a Doubt* remains a close template for the movie (though one should not entirely discount John Huston's input into the screenplay. Clearly identified as the coauthor of the August 9, 1945, draft, Huston is removed from the final credits. It is Huston, after all, as director Jake Hannaford, who utters the immortal line in *The Other Side of the Wind*, "Pure Hitchcock! If you'll pardon the language").

Francois Truffaut has written about how the two films share "the same realistic and everyday portrait of a small town in America; the same succession of peaceful, familiar, and familial scenes presented in contrast to the central character's terrible secret; the same construction on the principle of the vise closing in. One even finds the ladder rungs sawed through with the intention of making the heroine fall!" But as the worthy French director also observed, at another juncture, "In Welles's case . . . the spirit of contrariness is so strong that . . . influences show themselves more readily in an inverse fashion; that is, I suspect him of having watched other films not to gain inspiration, but rather to take systematically the opposite course." This was certainly the case with *The Stranger*, which operates at times as some kind of antithetical *Shadow of a Doubt*.

If Welles felt that "everything [Hitchcock] did in America is dry, empty, weak . . . [for] he . . . lost all the charm of his English style," *The Stranger* might perhaps qualify as a Wellesian version of one of those early Hitchcock movies. Welles certainly had fun with the thriller elements of the story, constructing a convincing profile of the Stranger who insinuates himself into the very interior life of a small town, yet whose presence fails to raise the necessary questions until another outsider intrudes to expose his misdeeds. His original shooting script even had a guest at Mary's party speculate about the identity of Meinike's murderer in classic Hitchcockian dialogue:

> MRS. LUNDSTRUM: The murderer's a fiend, who'll turn out to be a highly respected member of the community. He's too intelligent to do away with residents of Harper . . . They'd be missed, so he picks tramps and the like. [gestures to the window] There may well be ten . . . or a dozen . . . graves out there in the woods.*

Here can be found the other central theme Welles introduced into—or, given the question mark over its authorship, highlighted in—*The Stranger*. The enemy within, specifically the fascist world

---

*Though much of the dialogue spoken by Mrs. Lundstrum in the shooting script is trimmed in the released film, Welles retains her reference to "Jack the Ripper and that Frenchman, what's his name, Landru." Charlie Chaplin had yet to shoot *Monsieur Verdoux*, the film based on Landru's exploits, which originated with an idea by Welles.

conspirator, was a theme already featured in a number of unrealized projects, of which *The Way to Santiago* remains its closest kin. In one scene from that earlier screenplay the nosey, Lundstrum-like Mrs. Mallory, one of a busload of American tourists, is too busy seizing her tour guide by the arm to notice what—or whom—is right under her nose:

MRS. MALLORY: What do they call him?

THE GUIDE: I beg your pardon.

MRS. MALLORY: That Fascist organizer . . .

THE GUIDE (distracted): I don't know, Madam. There must be lots of them.

MRS. MALLORY (interrupting him): No—*the* one.

GUS: Goebels?

MRS. MALLORY: The one next to him. He turned up suddenly here in Mexico this afternoon.

MR. MALLORY: Oh, Lillian.

MRS. MALLORY: Well, he did and he was killed.

THE GUIDE (slowly and with emphasis): Eleven. Twelve. Thirteen.

MRS. MALLORY: Well, not exactly killed. Some radical attacked him . . . The clerk in the Reforma told me all about it. His picture's in the paper. It was on the cover of *Life* last week.

INSERT—The paper in my lap. Prominent on the front page is a four-column photograph of me.

MRS. MALLORY: I'd know him anywhere.

In *The Stranger* references to the insidious nature of the Nazi threat litter Welles's carefully constructed trail, eventually leading Mary (and her fellow Americans) to the heart of the mystery—the true identity of Kindler. Her initial assessment of the man, though, proves to be wide of the mark, our unsuspecting heroine deeming him to have "an extraordinary quality. I've never met a person one trusts so implicitly, so immediately." Mrs. Lundstrum turns out to be the better judge, thanks to "read[ing] every mystery story in the last twenty years," though even she fails to conceive of the scale of the murders this "highly respected member of the community" has committed. For Kindler is the mastermind behind the attempted extermination of an entire race, against which calumny Hitchcock's serial killer in *Shadow of a Doubt* seems almost benevolent.

Welles thought that *The Stranger* would provide him with an opportunity to reestablish his credentials as a director. He certainly had a story that gave him scope to address all the issues he had raised and raged about in previous lectures, radio broadcasts, and newspaper columns, throughout a war he had seen all too clearly coming. After trying to address much the same theme in at least four stillborn projects—*The Smiler with a Knife, The Way to Santiago, Carnaval in Rio,* and *Don't Catch Me*—he would at last get to drive his point home in the medium that suited him best.

What he did not have was the kind of contract he had enjoyed at RKO, the one that had enabled him to at least *make Citizen Kane* and *The Magnificent Ambersons* without interference. *The Stranger,* as Welles informed Peter Cowie, was to be "the only picture I have made in which I did not at least expect to function as a producer (in the American sense of the word)." In fact, the contract he signed in order to make the movie tied him tighter than a Victorian corset.

Yet it had been Welles who had asked for the chance to direct, having been approached by Sam Spiegel to star in a film originally called *Date with Destiny,* from a story developed by Anthony Veiller and John Huston. Spiegel knew of Welles's extracurricular activities and the views he'd expressed in them, and thought that Welles would be an ideal choice as the Nazi on the run. Initially, it would appear that Huston was in line to direct the film, and it was probably during the brief period when there was the possibility of a genuine collaboration between these two fine directors (and friends) that they worked on the script in tandem.

However, when Huston went off to mine another vein, striking gold with *Treasure of the Sierra Madre* after signing away any credit on *The Stranger*, Welles asked Spiegel if he might direct the film instead. Spiegel sensed that Welles's request was an ultimatum in disguise and turned to his associate at International Pictures William Goetz for guidance. Goetz had recently completed a film called *Tomorrow Is Forever*, in which Welles starred as a decidedly tardy returning warrior that his wife, played by Claudette Colbert, fails to recognize. An awful, overwrought melodrama, the film was a great success, and Goetz had nothing but praise for Welles's professionalism.

Spiegel decided to take a risk, though the terms of the contract ensured it would not be the greatest of gambles. He would give Welles the opportunity to direct the film, but he would deny him any chance to be the "dominant personality." And should Welles prove himself unworthy of even this marginal degree of trust, he would be required to complete his role in the movie, irrespective of any duties that may be reassigned. The contract Welles signed on September 20, 1945, can be read as Hollywood's ultimate revenge on the Boy Wonder of 1939:

> We have the right to terminate your entire employment hereunder, terminate only your employment as actor or, alternatively, as director. Should we terminate your employment in only one of said capacities, and not in both, you shall nevertheless be obligated to continue to render your services hereunder in the capacity as to which your employment has not been terminated by us. . . . I [also] hereby agree to indemnify you . . . from all loss, cost, and expense . . . incurred by . . . both of you due directly or indirectly to any failure, refusal, or default on my part in the performance of said contract of employment between myself and said [parties]. As security for the foregoing agreement on my part, I hereby assign and transfer to you all wages . . . or other income . . . in excess of $50,000 per year.

As if this wasn't humiliating enough, Welles was obliged to get his new, wealthy wife, Rita Hayworth, to "hereby consent to the foregoing," indemnifying the studio should her husband default on any of the pernicious terms contained in the contract. Having been given the dream Hollywood contract at twenty-four, after which he made two of the most daring, original, innovative films in the history of the cinema, Welles was treated as if he was still wet behind the lens. The absurdity of the situation cannot have been lost on him.

So why did Welles agree to be bound by such strictures on his directorial art? He later said that he did it "to show people that I didn't glow in the dark—that I could say 'action' and 'cut' just like all the other fellas." There is undoubtedly some truth in this. However, Welles's most reliable biographer, Frank Brady, asserts that Goetz actually promised Welles, presumably verbally, that if he brought *The Stranger* in on budget and within deadline he could have a four-picture deal as producer-director, on subjects of his own choosing. If so, that was a huge incentive for the man to prove that he "didn't glow in the dark." Only by making the picture, though, would he find out if it was too high a price to pay or whether Goetz would be as good as his word.

A DATE WITH THE
SUPERCUTTER

[The Stranger]

*I didn't do [The Stranger] with a completely cynical attitude.
. . . Quite the contrary, I tried to do it as well as I could. But
it's the one of my films of which I am least the author.*

Orson Welles, 1958

B y the time that Welles signed the contract to make *The
Stranger*, he had already immersed himself in the themes of
the film, developing them in a more multilateral, Wellesian
way. Just four days after inscribing his moniker on the dotted line,
he delivered a 164-page final shooting script which bore telltale
thumbprints on every page. Seventy-two hours later there was a fifty-
three-day shooting schedule. Done and dusted, ready to roll, four
days hence.

Evidently, this project was some way down the pike when Welles
agreed to sign his directorial freedom away. What remains unresolved is his degree of input into early versions of the script; and
indeed at what point he became a cocollaborator with John Huston
and/or Anthony Veiller, whose initial treatment of a short story by
Victor Trivas had prompted International Pictures to obtain the
screen rights. We know that Welles was in contact with Veiller in
May of 1945 regarding his own treatment for *Carnaval in Rio*, and
that he had an ongoing relationship with fellow director John Huston; but it seems unlikely that he had any input into its initial treatment, still entitled *Date with Destiny*.

The earliest script we have for *The Stranger* is dated August 9,
1945. Identified as a "Temporary Draft," on its title page are just two
names, Orson Welles and John Huston, in that order. Welles had
now entered the project with both size-twelve feet, seemingly at the
expense of Mr. Veiller (who, nevertheless, was to receive sole
screenplay credit on the film itself). This "Temporary Draft" essentially accords with the final shooting script Welles produced six

weeks later, save for the deletion of twenty-five pages (or twenty-eight scenes) from the front-end of the film.

Even at this stage, Sam Spiegel was looking to test Welles's resolve. As such, preproduction, he had hired editor Ernest Nims to look at the script and construct "a completely preplanned pattern of editing." Welles was duly informed of the changes Nims felt were necessary, which had to be followed to the letter or he would be removed as director, yet obliged to remain on as lead actor. At what point this threat was made is not clear, but the September 20 contract confirms Spiegel's intention to enforce it.

In an interview in *American Cinemeditor*, Nims stated that he felt Welles "had a reputation at that time of being a very costly and rather unmanageable director . . . [and he] was very anxious to correct this impression." If Welles gave such an impression to Nims—and the editor consistently claimed to have had a good relationship with Welles—the man's true feelings came out in conversation with Barbara Leaming, to whom he described Nims as "the great supercutter, who believed that nothing should be in a movie that did not advance the story. And since most of the good stuff in my movies doesn't advance the story *at all*, you can imagine what a nemesis he was to me. [But] I fought him tooth and nail . . . and [thought that I] won in the case of *The Stranger*."

Initially, Welles hoped that his considerable powers of persuasion, aligned to a sure understanding of the medium, might hold sway; and that the film may yet closely resemble his intent. All the while he gave Nims the impression of total cooperation in the pruning process. When Nims told *American Cinemeditor* that he "suggested eliminating 32 pages of the script, including the first 16," he was presumably referring to the twenty-five pages that were trimmed from the "Temporary Draft."

A copy of the shooting schedule for *The Stranger* resides in the Welles collection at the Lilly. It designates set days to all the scenes in the September 24 shooting script, but then has a series of lines drawn through the scenes deleted from the film, perhaps suggesting their elimination at the outset. The shooting script itself suggests not. Most of its first forty-five pages were subject to revision *after* September 24, with these changes incorporated into a working script (in keeping with standard shooting practice). These rewrites date from September 26 through October 1, the first scheduled day of shooting. It strikes me as inconceivable that Welles would still be working on these scenes if Nims the Supercutter was already starting to swing his axe. In later life, Welles was adamant that the sequence in Latin America, which he proudly claimed to have written in its entirety and thought "was much the best thing in the picture," *was* filmed and that Nims only later "took out everything which is interesting in the great long sequence in Latin America." He even spoke of physical scars from shooting this sequence, cutting his leg badly "on a baby's coffin in one of the scenes" (the sequence runs from page 5 to 21A in the shooting script).

"The great long sequence in south America" would have come immediately after the film credits, beginning with Wilson, the agent played by Edward G. Robinson (after Welles's own suggestion, Agnes Moorehead, was rejected by Spiegel), demanding that Nazi-nobody Meinike is set free so that his trail might lead him to the greater prize, Franz Kindler, a thinly disguised, fictionalized Martin Boorman. Meinike immediately heads for South America, where he comes to face to face with the "Nazis of 1932 . . . plotting for 1952." Snippets of Meinike reaching port, being followed and then photographed remain in the final film, but they were originally part of a far grander exposition on "the fascist mentality." In the "Temporary Draft" we discover that Meinike has in fact recanted his evil ways and found Christ. One classic Wellesian moment illustrates this and can't help but suggest the famous entrance of Harry Lime in *The Third Man* four years later, the inspiration for which has remained a source of dispute for some fifty years:

A DESERTED STREET—NIGHT
Meinike, eyes glazed, moves down [the street], camera tracking ahead of him. His jerky shuffle, more loose jointed than ever, speeds him forward. His hand clutches the paper given him by Farbright [a fellow

Nazi]. His lips move ceaselessly in a soundless babble of near hysteria. Suddenly the darkness behind him is broken as a window shade flies up revealing a room lighted by an unshaded lamp bulb, hanging from the ceiling. It cuts a path [?thread] of light along the cobbled street past Meinike. In the window, stands a cheap and gaudy crucifix. Meinike stops, transfixed, his eyes staring at the ground before him. . . . Etched in the path of light is the misshapen shadow of the cross.

[On] the street Meinike [is] staring down at the symbol of man's redemption. He staggers towards it and falls to his knees.

MEINIKE (sobbing forth the words): I understand. I shall not fail. I understand.

The shade in the window is pulled down, a woman's coarse laugh breaking the silence.

Meinike is left staring at the dark cobblestones. He shakes his head to clear it . . . struggles to his feet . . . and shuffles on, anxiously.

In the light of this scene the brief sequence where Meinike demands that the photographer tell him the whereabouts of Kindler "in the name of . . . the All Highest," retained in the film, would have retained its ironic power. We would have been aware that Meinike means the Lord, whereas his fellow Nazi assumes the moniker refers to the Führer. This, though, was one of those diversions designed, in Welles's words, to "give reverberation and density to [an] ordinary narrative," but which (Nims presumably felt) "did not advance the story." Even the version that replaced this in the shooting script, presumably at Nims's behest, which had an old woman leading a (surely symbolic) goat down the street with a couple of milk pails around its neck, was ultimately deemed diversionary.

In the end all we get is a shot of Meinike sneaking into the morgue, unaware that he is being trailed by a female agent, whereas in the shooting script the female agent phones Wilson to tell him "not to be surprised if [Meinike] remains there, [for] from his appearance it's where he belongs." This comment holds a double irony. Meinike will soon end up on a slab, but not before the woman herself, who is wheeled into the morgue a few minutes later, having been set upon by the dogs from Farbright's kennels. The scene in which a covered corpse is brought in on a gurney and the female agent's earrings fall to the floor, thus revealing her identity, was clearly designed to put the audience in no doubt that these Nazis were "perfect spiritual garbage":

> We hear the door to the morgue open and footsteps begin to cross the floor towards [another Nazi] Guinazu and Meinike, who turns toward the sound. The bruisers, one the dog trainer from the Farbright Kennels, enter, carrying a body on a stretcher. It is covered with a rough cloth.
>   . . . We can see hair, long hair, hanging down from beneath the cover. As the men set the stretcher and its burden upon an empty table, there is a small thud as some object drops to the floor. One of the men from the kennels stoops and picks up an earring.
>   . . . The earring is [an] exceptionally heavy, very wide hoop of gold.
>   The man places the earring in his pocket. Guinazu uncovers the body and stands looking down at it. We cannot see what he sees.
>
> GUINAZU (looking down at what he sees): Poor woman . . . Dreadful accident . . . I wonder . . . How do you think it happened . . . (studying the matter) Dogs, maybe . . . a number of dogs . . . (he clucks regretfully).

Also explained in this tight little sequence would have been how Kindler made himself into Rankin, as the photographer proceeds to take a paper with Franz Kindler's name on it and draw a series of diagonal lines through the letters F, Z, D, L, E, R until it spells Rankin. He then shows Meinike a postcard of Harper, Connecticut, which he then sets alight in front of him. The next shot was supposed to have been of the clock tower and the iron angel, standing rigid, "sword in hand, almost in the center of the clock." From this, Welles planned to pan out and reveal the bucolic town itself, at the center of which was this incongruous Gothic tower (what we actually get is a cutesy cut from picture postcard to actual town, not even a feather wipe as the card itself springs into life).

Though Welles undoubtedly treasured the "South American" footage more—because of the cinematic challenges presented, the early footage of Rankin in Harper, Connecticut, also "pruned," had a more direct bearing on the structure of *The Stranger*. It included our first sight of the iron angel. Many of these deletions were not made willingly, and in at least one instance fundamentally affect the audience's understanding of events. This is the scene where Charles Rankin, a.k.a. Franz Kindler, is wooing his bride-to-be by the riverbank, and she admits to a very real phobia:

RANKIN and MARY reach a crossing. Boulders, rising above the rippling current, provide stepping stones to the opposite bank.

MARY: We'd better start back.

RANKIN: We can cross here and go home past the woods. It's quite a shortcut.

MARY (resignedly): Well . . . it may as well come out now as later. You'll have to know the awful truth sometime. I'm a fearful acrophobic.

RANKIN: Really?

MARY (seriously): Really. I have the most dreadful fear of falling. Let's go back the long way.

RANKIN (quietly): You need have no fear. [He extends his hand.] You won't fall.

She looks at him a moment, then puts her hand in his. He helps her across. On the opposite bank, they pause, look at each other, smile gravely. Then start towards home.

As the audience has not been apprised of Mary's fear of falling, the denouement in the bell tower, where Mary must face her fears and climb the ladder if she is to confront her husband and assuage her blood guilt, loses a great deal of its power. Though Welles inserted a reworking of this scene into the shooting script, he still lost it from the final film. Already, it would seem, he was being asked to make major concessions that Huston may not have made had he stayed a part of the project.

Like *Citizen Kane*, *The Stranger* was originally circular in construct. As Welles told one interviewer in 1974, "I like putting the end of a tragedy at the beginning . . . I find that it adds a lot." In fact, when Welles shot the scene in the clock tower (the film's finale), he originally envisaged showing its climactic moment first as the film's opening scene, but from the vantage point of the crowd below. Welles had assigned his favorite cinematographer, Russell Metty, to make sure that he covered all the angles from a crane. Before this moment, though, there was to be a scene in which Mary recalls Rankin's voice, saying, "Let's go through the fields—it's beautiful that way. It's my favorite walk. The cemetery, over the little brook," as she is seen making her way toward the church and her date with destiny, "carrying a small package, across the snow-covered cemetery, through the row of tombstones":

> Mary reaches the church in the center of town and climbs the ladder to the belfry. As she reaches the top an angry mob forms outside below, wielding sticks, rakes, etc. The camera joins them. A scream is heard from the bell tower and the people look up in time to see two people struggling high on the ledge above—a man and a woman it seems. Suddenly both of them fall to the earth and the crowd of townspeople swarm around.

At this point the title of the film would have appeared on-screen, against a glowing backdrop comprising "the distorted face of a grimacing demon. [The] camera races back to disclose [that] the demon [is] made of iron, emerging through a dark portal, through the side of the same massive clock we [just] saw on the belfry." As the credits roll, the iron devil moves "across the face of the clock [and] exits through the opposite portal as there emerges from the first another automaton, a gilded iron angel. Sword in hand the angel pursues the demon as the heavy chimes within sound stridently the hour of midnight." Having barely set the series of events in motion, Welles was already introducing important motifs—angels and devils, clocks and towers, mortality and time—to potential viewers.

❖   ❖   ❖   ❖

It was Welles himself who had found the physical centerpiece for the movie, the clock at the top of the church tower, sparing Spiegel a great deal of expense and giving the film a crucial component with none of that architectural mélange found in many films of the period. The clock had previously been in the Los Angeles County Courthouse, but as of 1922 had been left to gather dust in the cellar of the Los Angeles County Museum. Welles had it hoisted by cranes in two sections, before reassembling it in the 150-foot imitation tower built for the film.

Captured in picture-postcard freeze-frame on its first appearance, Harper represented an American town that had not spread and darkened into a city, but rather had stayed fixed in time. Indeed, when Rankin first encounters Mary and explains his ambition to fix the church clock and get it to run again—after two hundred years of stasis—Mary wonders aloud, "what the effect would be on Harper if it were to run and keep time. The whole character of the town might undergo a change. I'm sure it's not really very different from the Harper of the eighteenth century. Perhaps that's because the clock's hands have never moved." In *The Magnificent Ambersons*, the passage of time is inexorable. In *The Stranger*, it is staved off by the townspeople until the man from Strasbourg comes to set everything in unassailable motion.

Rankin, as the force of change, threatens to usher in the world at large. In the shooting script, he has already suggested sending

Mary's brother, Noah, off to see the world so that he may come to "recognize the necessity for change." At the same time, Rankin has picked this town precisely because of its otherworldliness, or rather unworldliness. This is a place where, as Mary reminds Rankin, "there is nothing to be afraid of." Rankin later boasts to Meinike, prior to murdering him, that "at six o'clock I shall be standing before a minister of the Gospel with . . . the daughter of a justice of the United States Supreme Court . . . [For] who would look for Franz Kindler in the sacred precincts of the Harper School?"

In sleepy Harper (in its "Temporary Draft" guise) there was even time for romance. Before we were educated as to the capabilities of Kindler and his kind we would have seen Rankin lead the quintessentially good, fundamentally passive, Mary from the path of righteousness—quite literally, according to Leaming, who says that in an early draft Mary first met Rankin on her way to church one Sunday and was convinced to walk off with him into the woods rather than attending Mass. No such scene appears in the August draft. Instead, we find Mary in church one Sunday, searching in vain for the mysterious man whose absence itself suggests a certain ungodliness:

> The choir, in their surplices, file out of their stalls and move down the center aisle of the church as they sing the Recessional. The rector brings up the rear of the procession, which Camera Pans To Follow until it has passed the Longstreet pew where it remains. Mary is alone with her Father. On the same side of the church are other citizens of Harper. On the opposite side, a large section of pews are reserved for and occupied by the students of Harper School. . . . Behind the boys, sit the Masters. Rankin is not present. Mary's eyes search the congregation. As it rises, she and her father start down the aisle. . . . Her greetings to acquaintances are friendly enough, but her eyes constantly return to their search.

When Mary does come upon Rankin, outside the church, he informs her he had "played hooky this Sunday, indulging an old fascination." He looks over his shoulder toward the clock tower. His interest in the church is architectural, not religious. The outsider in their midst, he only ever enters the church to climb its tower and look down on the God-fearing townsfolk with disdain.

The shooting script—certainly the best indication of Welles's intentions—suggests that the director intended to use the church's own iconography to reinforce the sense of an old-fashioned battle between Good and Evil, much of the conflict being fought out in the church itself. Rankin, a man who actually intones "Oh God of all Goodness . . ." as he is strangling Meinike, originally concocted his initial "explanation" to his wife for murdering Meinike in the church at night. As he "puts down his tools near the altar and Mary sinks to a pew, the moon [is] shining through the stained glass windows on her face. There is a pause before Rankin speaks. He walks slowly toward her, his feet echoing on the stone floor of the church." Likewise, when the film is moving toward its final confrontation between the two forces, Mary is supposed to enter the church to confront her murderous husband, only to find it "full of ghostly shadows and half tones from the moonlight, diffused through stained glass windows." Welles was obliged to unravel these threads. Stripped of such atmospherics, the finished film barely hints at his original design, though one instance remains. It comes when Noah tells Wilson that Mary has disappeared and an arched windowpane casts a shadow behind the pair, indicating precisely where she has gone.

If Mary represents all that is God-fearing (she even comes from a family named after Biblical characters, such as her father, Adam, and her brother, Noah), Rankin derides all that she holds sacrosanct. One scene that Welles was obliged to cut—probably at the behest of the censor—comes after he has made a martyr of Meinike, hastily covering up the corpse. Rankin promptly realizes that the paper trail the boys from the Harper School have laid leads to the spot where he just killed his former comrade. He spies the Bible in Meinike's hand and picks it up. Seeing the sacred work as a mere means to an end, he tears "pages from it, [and] runs in a wide arc, establishing a new trail to carry the chase away from Meinike's body. Out of breath, he returns to stand guard. His eyes watch the chase as it branches off to follow the new trail. The boys disappear in the distance. Rankin looks down at Meinike's lifeless body and begins to kick leaves over it. He dry washes his hands." No blood guilt here. All he feels is a sense of satisfaction at a job well done.

In its celluloid alternative we at least get a glimpse of Welles's cinematic genius, even if the Bible no longer serves as the means by which he diverts the boys from his guilty secret. Revealing a sense of visual power play similar to the Getty scene in *Citizen Kane*, he transforms Kindler in seconds from the all-powerful overseer of life and death to the furtive criminal he really is. This volte-face is achieved by a dramatic crane shot that ends with the camera looking down pitilessly on his attempts to cover his tracks. Later, Welles intended us to see how this related to the film's central premise, when Wilson quotes Ralph Waldo Emerson to the citizenry of Harper congregating at Rankin's house, "Commit a crime and it seems as if a coat of snow fell on the ground, such as reveals in the woods the track of every partridge and fox and squirrel and mole. You cannot recall the spoken word, you cannot wipe out the foot-track, you cannot draw up the ladder."

Welles's penchant for using his camera to visualize the dynamics of interpersonal relationships, presaged throughout *Citizen Kane*, is only occasionally allowed to flower here. Before Mary learns that for evil to prevail all that the good need do is nothing, she is portrayed as the dutiful wife. But her passivity, like Susan Alexander's, disappears the very instance she realizes that she is married to a monster. Bret Wood highlights the changing dynamic in his essay on the film:

> The violation of Mary through her marriage to Rankin is shown as he enters Mary's bedroom one night, first seen as a shadow over Mary's bed, then in silhouette as he moves to her, towering over her, the camera looking down on the helpless woman from Rankin's shoulder. Reverse shots look up at Rankin's half-shadowed face. The scene ends with Mary cowering in her bed, compared to the dog imprisoned in the cellar (we hear its yelps and whines), both a prisoner of Rankin. . . .

[However,] when she hears of the murders, Mary stands and for the first time takes the dominant position of looking down on Rankin.

In keeping with recent Hollywood convention, it was originally Mary's subconscious that first recognized the truth about her husband, manifested in a particularly hallucinogenic dream, precisely described in the shooting script. The medium's potential for depicting the surreal logic of dreams had long fascinated Welles, and though *The Stranger* was originally intended to be his first foray into this field, it would not be his last. The thin line between everyday reality and a nightmarish netherworld serves to inspire most Welles films from this point forward. None would be stranger than *The Stranger*, for which he had devised an entire "impressionistic montage":

In Mary's eyes, the room tilts crazily. . . . Noah catapults towards the Camera, his face filling the screen. . . . Superimposed over this is the strong, black silhouette of a high ladder. This falls with Noah and stops with him just ahead of his face. He grasps a rung of the ladder. It breaks and Noah falls out of scene. Camera tilts to follow his hands. . . . They clutch first at one rung, then at another . . . rung after rung shatters under his weight—finally a rung holds—the last. Beneath it the two shafts of the ladder stretch down into space like a pair of cosmic stilts. Red, the dog, is at the base of this lunatic machine (seen very distantly because Mary's delirious eye is viewing this scene from a great height). He howls furiously and claws at the foot of the shaft. . . . His baying echoes and merges strangely with the music. Noah, clinging to the last rung, looks as if he were treed. But now [the] Camera closes in on him and shows us suddenly that it's not Noah after all! It is Rankin.

Welles's multilayered approach to filmmaking provided further challenges on the soundtrack he designed to accompany this "impressionistic montage"; for "above the queer music . . . we [were supposed to] hear [a] dialogue. It . . . quite realistically [details] what goes on in the Rankin living room from the moment Mary faints."

The dialogue, involving Dr. Lawrence, Noah, and Wilson, would have taken on its own hallucinogenic quality inside Mary's dream as Noah and Wilson's discussion of how to stop Rankin crosscuts with the doctor's comments on his unconscious patient.

Like a good little citizen of Harper, the doctor asserts that we "need have no fear," which in Mary's delirious state reminds her of the earlier scene where Rankin used the self-same phrase to cajole her across the stream. At this point "the realistic sequence of dialogue" within her dream comes to an end, and we find ourselves "totally within Mary's delirious dream," as the line is repeated not by Dr. Lawrence but by her husband, who is "still clinging perilously to the last rung," insisting, "You won't fall, you won't fall—fall—fall," an apposite reminder of her acrophobia.

Seemingly innocuous lines spoken earlier by Rankin begin to assume a new resonance in her dream: "failing to speak . . . you become part of the crime"; "these . . . same hands that have held you close to me"; "the incongruity of a Gothic clock in a Connecticut clock tower." Throughout this delirious vision the camera was supposed to slowly close in on Rankin "until only one of his eyes fills the screen, monstrously." Eventually his eye grows "so large that only the pupil remains . . . [which] changes queerly into the face of the clock." On the soundtrack, "the music is heavy with the rhythmic grinding of the works. The shadow of the iron demon falls over the screen and now we commence to hear distinctly and strangely the tolling of the clock." Finally the music ceases, and we see a shot of the bedroom ceiling on which "a macabre pattern of the moonlight" plays. For one instance it looks like "the grimacing demon, [but it] is really the twisted shadow of the tree."

The camera moves down to Mary, whose eyes are open. We have returned to the very moment with which Welles intended to open the picture. Mary rises and heads out of the room. She now knows where Rankin is. At this point, the clock ceases to chime, another portentous reminder of a key motif. Mary's prophecy that "the whole character of the town might undergo a change" if Rankin sets the clock in motion is about to come to pass.

It is possible that none of this was even filmed. The shooting schedule had Mary's dream down as one of the last scenes to be filmed, and as of November 12—three-quarters of the way through shooting—when Welles drew up a list of scenes to be shot, it was still awaiting completion. But Welles may have decided against using this device to reveal Kindler's guilt in the wake of recent premieres of two Hollywood productions, both of which had long and elaborate dream sequences that supposedly provided the male lead with an explanation of his past and a guide to the future. Such was the power of Freud!

Of the two films, Welles would have been the more keen to avoid comparison with Hitchcock's latest, *Spellbound*, which made its screen debut in October and featured a memorable dream sequence designed by Salvador Dali himself. And yet the other dream sequence was the more ambitious, a sixteen-minute "dream ballet" performed by Fred Astaire in the Arthur Freed musical, *Yolanda and the Thief*. A musical homage to Dali and his fellow surrealists, it was a seemingly random assortment of ideas from the movement's manifestos. Perhaps Welles felt that a third such sequence would be chancing his arm with the critics, most of whom seemed impressed by Dali's contribution to *Spellbound*, but were left cold by Freed's pseudo-psychobabble.

In the film itself, the moment when Rankin does at last succeed in getting the church clock to work comes immediately after Mary has informed him of Wilson's suspicions. As per Welles, at the moment of Rankin's great triumph, with "jubilation [still] in his eyes," things have already begun to implode. Time, for Kindler at least, has already begun to slip away.

The script indicates that Welles wanted the instant where he "turns back to the clock [and] suddenly it is in motion," to be signified on the soundtrack by a regular, steady beat "throughout the [remainder of the] scene . . . indicating the passing of the seconds." This inventive notion did not survive the Supercutter, and Welles was obliged to file it away. It appeared a decade later, in his one and only TV pilot, *Fountain of Youth*, where an audible ticking serves as a sardonic reminder of the characters' own mortality; and, more memorably, in that meticulously choreographed opening to *Touch of Evil*, where the steady, audible tick of the bomb counts down to the big bang.

As Harper emerges out of its Amberson-like state it finds that the world has become a noisy place, leading one bystander to ask Rankin, as he makes his way through the curious townsfolk, "How's a person to get their sleep?" Not only has the sleep of the just been disturbed by Rankin's intervention, but the local gossipmongers are finding it difficult to tittle-tattle. The following day's party at Rankin's house, during which Mary becomes visibly unhinged, was originally interrupted by pealing chimes striking five, "the noise mak[ing] conversation impossible. Everyone . . . start[s] shouting to make themselves heard. Mrs. Lawrence's rises above them, 'Charles Rankin . . . I wish you'd left that clock alone. Harper was a nice quiet place until it began banging.'"

Indeed, Rankin's relationship with clocks throughout the film was intended to reflect his view of people, but Nims and/or Spiegel remained suspicious of any such psychologizing, and so the viewer of the released film is left searching for the slightest clues as to the inner struggle going on in Rankin. In one cut speech, Mary confirms Wilson's growing suspicions by telling him about her husband's depiction of "the ideal social system in terms of a clock . . . [in which] the force that runs the clock, the spring . . . is the head of the State. The pendulum is his government which transforms his inspiration into law . . . [and] the train of gears are the working masses." Rankin tellingly intercedes to explain his system's version of progress, represented by the clock's hands, "which would not occur by fits and starts, but according to the laws of harmonic motion." When Wilson begins to ask whether, as such, he is an "admirer of democracy," Rankin says he is "a complete democrat"—in the here and now. These ideas are intended for "a thousand years from now"—i.e. the coming Reich.

However, Rankin proves unable to apply the precision he brings to timepieces to events surrounding his impulsive murder of

Meinike. Whenever he is required to maintain the greatest self-control, he looks to his clocks. Thus, when his wife's father asks her to come to his house alone, Rankin is seen winding up a grandfather clock, as if this will somehow restore order and hold back the forces of fate. At the same time he comments to his wife (and his own self), "You must get a tight hold of yourself."

But his precious clocks cannot save him. When Mary starts to tell her husband about the burgeoning friendship between Noah and Mr. Wilson—who Rankin now knows has come to track him down—his divided self stands briefly revealed (after its initial appearance at the dinner table). His temporary loss of self-control results in the clock losing its head of state:

LONG SHOT—HARPER SQUARE—WILSON AND NOAH

Camera, shooting from Mary's angle, over her shoulder, down into the square, shows Wilson and Noah talking together. They appear very small, standing near Potter's.

MARY's voice: See them down there talking so earnestly? It's a fine experience for him . . . the companionship of an older man like Mr. Wilson.

As she looks down into square from tower.

MARY: You know, everywhere I go I seem to see them together.

We hear the sound of a spring breaking.

The mask has started to slip. The threat this relationship represents is not lost on Rankin, but he remains powerless to stop it. As his cherished, ordered world begins to disintegrate, Welles intended us to witness Rankin viewing the pair from his vantage point in the clock tower. At this point we would have caught a glimpse of the unequal battle in his solitary features—in a rare Welles close-up—as he "sinks down on the ledge. The job of being Charles Rankin, a school teacher, is becoming almost too much for him. He is terribly, terribly tired. His eyes turn dull, his mouth hangs loose. He sits there among the works of the clock. His breath comes long and heavy." When he devises an "accident," designed to remove the one link that connects him to the murder of Meinike—his wife—he is seen idly doodling a swastika on a notepad at Potter's store. When the plan goes wrong, he is again seen winding the grandfather clock at his home, but this time he seems fit to bust its springs. Yet his capacity for self-denial survives to the bitter end. Virtually the last words he utters are, "I'm not a criminal."

But for Nims and Spiegel establishing the actual character of characters was unnecessary. Thanks to their pre- and postediting, the movie lost as much from the front end as *The Magnificent Ambersons* lost from its rear. Though Welles hardly considered the loss as great as *Ambersons*, we are left with the least Wellesian of his films, from an original script bearing many of his trademarks, unfiltered by any respect for its literary source. Even in its bastardized state, it is fair to say—as the recent *Encyclopaedia of Orson Welles* does—that "*The Stranger* has been seriously underrated in the Welles canon."

◆   ◆   ◆   ◆

Unfortunately, both forms of editing undermined much of Welles's grand design, depriving him of many little strokes he'd planned to apply to his thematic canvas. The process of removing Wellesian motifs willy-nilly left a rather uniform Hollywood thriller, as producer and editor intended. If Welles considered "editing *the* aspect," Nims's editing exemplified the Hollywood snip. *The Stranger* as released hastily moves on from scene to scene, without respite or opportunity for reflection.

What was deemed superfluous was often the director's own unique mortar, notably several vignettes involving store owner Potter, intended to represent the everyday life of the town. Getting a feel for the place went against the Hollywood grain; and, as Welles caustically remarked to Leslie Megahey, "Scenes didn't go to supporting actors in Hollywood in those days, unless they were featured players . . . [And] here was an unknown actor given great hunks of scenes that should have gone to the money, you know."

Some of the losses were subtle, but profound. In the scene where Mary stalks out of her father's house, Welles intended for us to hear "her footsteps sounding on the graveled walk. Judge Longstreet looks after her sadly. *There is the sound of her running footsteps . . . then the slam of a car door . . . the grinding of a starter . . . the clash of gears . . . the motor racing as she speeds away.*" These (italicized) discordant elements—a familiar Welles device designed to reflect Mary's mental anguish—were deemed ancillary to the film's headlong rush to its date with destiny.

Mary's angst-ridden departure followed a private screening at the judge's house of the filmed evidence of Kindler's atrocities back in the fatherland. Again, Mary's entrance follows immediately on from a phone call to her home. Welles, though, intended to show Mary just as divided from her real self as her husband. Her inner struggle was to be revealed by her pausing on the threshold. "Visibly braced for any emergency, [she] crosses to the entrance of her father's study. She hesitates a moment. Then throws open the door. . . . Silhouetted in the light from the hallway behind her, [she] stands on the threshold of a dark room."

In the finished film Mary is made to watch some "hard to stomach" footage from the concentration camps, while the camera focuses on her reaction. The horrors she is shown are not all that she must come to terms with. She must confront her husband, or hide what she is beginning to feel from him. Her real self now cannot help but recoil. When she returns home, and Rankin sweeps her into his arms, "some instinctive reaction that she herself doesn't understand makes her body tremble." She proceeds to blame her shudder on nerves and asks for her husband to hold her close.

But in the shooting script, at the point where Rankin kisses her she suddenly slumps in his arms. She has fainted. Her inner struggle to keep her true feelings hidden has failed. Rankin is also losing his own struggle to keep a lid on his true self. After Mary passes out, "all expression falls from his face. His eyes grow dull and his mouth hangs slightly open. . . . He lays her down and stands looking down at her. Unconsciously, his fingers flex themselves. He knows now that she, too, must die."

What Welles planned next was a little mock "murder" scene, aping one in Hitchcock's *Suspicion*. Rankin convinces Mary to drink a glass of milk he has drugged, though not with a fatal dose, just enough to buy him some time. By the time she awakes, Rankin has a plan, but he also has a wife who appears to have resolved her own inner struggle. We were supposed to see Mary "slowly . . . bring[ing] her hands together and dry wash[ing] them in the immemorial gesture of blood guilt . . . [as] she [finally] acknowledges her complicity in the crimes of [Franz Kindler]."

Mary's method of resolving her conflict, atoning for her sense of "blood guilt," was to clamber up to Kindler's domain and confront him. This time it is her husband who misreads his spouse's motives and lets her up. No longer charmed by her husband's hobby, Mary aims a gun at her husband but accidentally shoots the clock mechanism, sending it spinning wildly out of control, instigating the collapse of Kindler's ordered universe. However, in Hollywood, Connecticut, any suggestion that Mary's capacity for action has been aroused, or that the experience has permanently altered her, must be removed. Wilson's final line in the movie—"Good night, Mary. Pleasant dreams"—surely would have originally carried an altogether more ironic undertone.

With so much of Welles's conception lost between the cracks of pre- and postediting, the critics again seized on the "flaws" in his portrayal of Rankin as indicative of the man's failings as an actor, and not a general determination on Hollywood's part to treat its audience as if "we have twelve-year-old minds." Welles's own "courageously radical stylization" of Kindler and Mary as "divided selves" was as lost on the media as the film's editor and producer. Walter Kerr, perhaps Welles's least favorite critic, wrote disparagingly of "the spectacle of Mr. Welles, as a disguised Nazi spy, walking through the film with an expression on his face which would have brought out the entire staff of Bellevue in an instant." One presumes he had not been following Welles's columns in the *New York Post*, and was unaware of an already voiced disregard for the Hollywood school of realism:

> When the American movie-maker becomes aware of a discrepancy between his film and the appearance of life, he corrects the difference in favor of "realism." . . . The Russians go out for the effect itself—and when they find what they're after—they manage moments of an exclamatory and resonant beauty on a level of eloquence to which our school cannot [even] aspire.

From this point forward Welles would invariably aspire to such moments, and this profound change required a new mind-set from his audience. As Michael Anderegg has recently observed, "the key to understanding what Welles [sets out to] achieve in *The Stranger* lies in seeing . . . the actor and the character [being] locked in an irresoluble conflict: Welles's desire to expose Franz Kindler as a mad Nazi [operates] in direct opposition to Kindler's desire to keep that fact well hidden." Without this "key to understanding" Welles's intent, clarified as it was by a number of "lost" scenes, his characterization makes little sense.

If there was a literary model on which Welles based such an outlandish approach, it was the writings of Bertolt Brecht (though one should not entirely discount the influence of Eisenstein). Any debt came not from contact with Brecht—their brief association was still some months way—but from articles the playwright had written; perhaps most obviously, a 1935 essay called "Alienation Effects in Chinese Acting." Its supposed influence on *The Lady from Shanghai* has frequently been cited, but Brecht's aesthetic approach is just as evident in the shooting script for *The Stranger*. Like Welles's own essay on Eisenstein, Brecht's 1935 essay was essentially an attack on the Western theater of "realism":

> The Western actor does all he can to bring his spectator into the closest proximity to the events and the character he has to portray. To this end he persuades him to identify himself with him (the actor) and uses

every energy to convert himself as completely as possible into a different type, that of the character in question. If this complete conversion succeeds then his art has been more or less expended. Once he has become the bank-clerk, doctor, or general concerned he will need no more art than any of these people need "in real life." . . . [In China] there is not the same automatic transfer of emotions to the spectator, the same emotional infection. The alienation effect intervenes, not in the form of absence of emotion, but in the form of emotions which need not correspond to those of the character portrayed.

Many of Brecht's theoretical writings were destined to remain scattered for some years yet, inaccessible to an English speaker like Welles. However, this particular essay was published in English, in a London periodical, *Life & Letters Today,* in the winter of 1936. Given Welles's intense involvement with the New York stage from 1936 to 1939, at a time when the aesthetics of performance were taking on a new importance, it seems inconceivable that he would not have encountered Brecht's ideas, especially his dispositions on "the alienation effect," a theory which devolved down to making "what is *natural* . . . have the force of what is startling." Elements of this approach even encroach into *Citizen Kane* and *The Magnificent Ambersons,* without dominating Welles's overarching design.

Though Leaming claims that prior to working with Brecht on an aborted version of *Galileo* in 1946, "Orson had never paid much attention to his essays," his discussion of Eisenstein in the May 1945 *New York Post* articles suggests otherwise. It bears all the marks of a man conversant with Brecht's expressed distinction between dramatic theater and epic theater, first voiced in his notes to the 1930 opera *Aufstieg und Fall der Stadt Mahagonny.* In all likelihood, Welles *actively* sought Brecht out those several months later, having already worked on a script for *The Stranger* that was symptomatic of the epic as Brecht conceived it:

    I. [Reliance on] narrative
    II. [which] turns the spectator into an observer, but

   III. arouses his capacity for action
   IV. forces him to take decisions
   VI. [and so] he is made to face something
  VIII. [and] brought to the point of recognition

Unfortunately, Welles's inability to assert himself as the "dominant personality" meant that *The Stranger*, as released, focuses rather on those elements with which Sam Spiegel, William Goetz, and Ernest Nims felt comfortable. Brecht would have identified theirs as the so-called "dramatic" approach, with its emphasis upon:

    I. [A] plot
   II. [which] implicates the spectator in a stage situation
  III. wears down his capacity for action
  IV. provides him with sensations
  VI. [and though] the spectator is involved in something
VIII. instinctive feelings are preserved

If Leaming believes that "Orson's study of Brecht's theatrical theory in this period would bear a decisive . . . influence on the next film he would make in Hollywood, and on much of his work in film thereafter," her dismissal of *The Stranger* suggests that her knowledge of the finished movie was somewhat greater than its genesis.

At the end of the process, having proven his worth and professionalism, Welles presumably hoped to resume persuading Nims and Spiegel that his instincts were true(r), even though he knew to steer clear of their conceptual basis. Ideas, though, like "each scene for itself—man as a process—social being determin[ing] thought," all components of Brecht's epic theater, were lost on their creed. Their eyes were ever on the finish, as one scene moved seamlessly into another, with a plot that reflected a clear linear development, and characterizations based upon the idea that man was a fixed point, whose thoughts determined "being." A hundred and eighty degrees removed from the Brechtian ideal.

Perhaps Brecht was able to sympathize with Welles about the fate of this film when they finally spent time together, a few months later, as *The Stranger* awaited a release slot. By then, Welles felt he had been obliged to grit his teeth one time too many, as he again saw plotlines left trailing, themes half-expressed, subtleties sacrificed for a peculiarly subjective, only nominally consistent paciness, indicative of the kind of *ur*-thriller *The Stranger* was never meant to be.

If the film that now carried his name was not the one he had hoped to make, Welles hoped it would help him make others he might prefer. *The Stranger* was already another lost cause, though the film did come in under budget and a day short of its projected schedule. Welles's own edit—now lost—ran to 115 minutes, as opposed to 95, post-Nims.* If it was the only instantly successful movie Welles ever made "within the system," grossing over three million dollars, on a million-dollar budget, it was everything he had already condemned in the *Post*. Without its first act, stripped of set pieces and those wonderfully Wellesian digressions, it was assuredly "the one of my films of which I am least the author."

Welles probably suspected all along that he would never be given the opportunity to make the kind of film he knew he could for a producer like Sam Spiegel. Now he *knew* for sure just how inimical his ideas were to the Hollywood producer's mind-set. Meanwhile, Goetz predictably reneged on his offer to let Welles write and direct films of his own choosing, making the effort seem to have been largely wasted. Hence his personal disregard for the finished film, which still contains its share of Wellesian moments.

If *his* version of *The Stranger* had made three million dollars, he would have felt a certain vindication, but the "success" of *The Stranger* proved only that Hollywood studios never "lose enough [money] to learn anything" about the potential the medium still held.

Welles would never sign such a deal again. If their game was the only game in town, better to find another town. His next movie

---

*Unfortunately no cutting continuity has been located for the 115-minute version of the film, and so one can only speculate what was cut during the final edit.

would be a richly cynical, self-consciously surreal exposition on the very genre *The Stranger* mundanely defined: the Hollywood thriller. This time, though, he would make it all but impossible to remove the director from the equation. Deconstructing film noir itself, he would make *Black Irish*, as it was initially known, his most profound distillation of that antithetical worldview.

THAT QUALITY OF
STRANGENESS

[The Lady from Shanghai]

I believe that the only good work I can do is my own particular
thing. I don't think I'm very good [at] doing *their* thing.

Orson Welles, *Tomorrow Show*, September 1975

Of the six movies Welles completed within the Hollywood
system in the years 1941–58, three were contemporary
thrillers. The war years also saw him peddle unrealized projects like *The Smiler with a Knife*, *The Way to Santiago*, and *Don't Catch
Me*, designed to be political-but-populist thrillers. Yet he later dis-
paraged this kind of pulp fiction in word and deed. In a long letter
to the *New Statesman* in May 1958, he sought to explain why he
kept making movies in this "discredited" genre:

> I have only twice been given any voice at all as to the "level" of my sub-
> ject matter. In my trunks stuffed with unproduced film scripts, there
> are no thrillers [sic]. When I make this sort of picture—for which I can
> pretend to no special interest or aptitude—it is "not for the money" (I
> support myself as an actor) but because of a greedy need to exercise,
> in some way, the function of my choice: the function of director. . . . I
> have to take whatever comes along from time to time, or accept the
> alternative, which is not working at all.

And yet, in the spring of 1946 it was Welles who convinced the
notoriously difficult head of Columbia, Harry Cohn, to provide him
with his largest-ever budget in order to transform the utterly conventional potboiler *If I Die Before I Wake* by Sherwood King into *The
Lady from Shanghai*. This venture took place against an unpromising
backdrop, in which his first completed Hollywood thriller, *The
Stranger*, was trimmed of any radical accoutrements. Meanwhile, he
was in intense discussions with Sir Alexander Korda, the London-
based producer, about a number of potential projects, of which a ver-

sion of Oscar Wilde's *Salome* seemed the most promising. (Welles, in typical fashion, promptly started work on a screenplay, to which he would return in 1950.)

The biblical Salome seems like a long way from a noirish novel set on Long Island, in which a naive adventurer is seduced and deceived by the archetypal femme fatale of the genre. Later pronouncements by Welles are not much help here either, hiding his true agenda behind one of those wonderful tall stories he liked to devise and embellish, until the truth became lost in a fog of the purely anecdotal. This particular tale went through a number of verbal drafts before it arrived at the one he expounded to Leslie Megahey in 1982, in which he finds himself needing $55,000 to pay for costumes on the opening night of his stage version of *Around the World in Eighty Days*, and can only think of one man with that kind of money who would be prepared to wire it to him—Harry Cohn. "[So] I called him up . . . He said, 'What is it? What do you want?' I said, 'I've got the greatest story you've ever read,' and I turned the paperback around that the girl in the box office was reading. . . . I said, 'It's called *The Man I Killed* [sic]. . . . You get me $55,000 to Boston in two hours and I'll make the picture. I'll write it and direct it and act in it.' [The $]55,000 came."

He told Peter Bogdanovich a similar story, and it is tempting to discount it as merely one more Wellesian smoke screen (which it partially is). However, as Bernard Herrmann once observed about the man's mischievous mythmaking, "anyone who believes he has caught him in a fantastic lie is apt to find that the fantastic story is the truth. And some unimportant statement, like just having bought an evening paper a half-hour ago, is the lie."

In fact, we know that Welles's ever-loyal assistant, Richard Wilson, cabled Lolita Hebert at the Mercury offices in Hollywood on April 26, 1946—the day before *Around the World* opened in Boston—begging her to "try desperately to get *If I Die Before I Wake* to Harry Cohn immediately. Perhaps Franchot Tone has book. Tell him we need it for picture deal."

To discover why this request had become a matter of urgency we need to rewind a few months, all the while reminding ourselves that

Welles's greatest ally in Hollywood—even as their marriage was coming apart at the seams—was "the missus," a.k.a. screen siren Rita Hayworth. For some time Rita had been personally pleading with Cohn for her husband to be permitted an opportunity to make a movie at Columbia. She hoped that such a move might save their marriage as well as enable her to develop the range first glimpsed in *Gilda.* Cohn asked Sam Spiegel if he thought Welles could deliver a film on budget, and Spiegel said that he could.

Welles, though, was understandably wary of Cohn, a meddler supreme and master of the Hollywood chapter of Grand Philistines. He had already brushed up against his bullying ways when pursuing Rita. After Cohn insisted that his prize star withdraw from Welles's magic show for the troops in August 1943, Welles was quoted as saying, "We had hoped that reason might prevail, but Mr. Cohn is adamant, a chronic condition with that gentleman. Needless to say, I shall never appear in a Columbia picture."

Years later, though, he claimed a certain liking for Cohn because although "he was a monster, . . . almost all of them [were] who ran their own stores in those old days of Hollywood. . . . He couldn't be as bad as his first impression, so everything was a pleasant surprise after that. He would snarl at you as you came in the door, [but] you could gradually throw him little goodies and he would quiet down and lash his tail." And in 1946 Welles still hoped and prayed he might find a way to make his "own particular thing" within the studio system, with all its resources and know-how at his disposal.

As such he tentatively sounded Cohn out on a project close to his heart—a modern version of Merimée's *Carmen.* Incorporating elements that remind one of Welles's September 1943 treatment of *It's All True,* his *Carmen* began with an American professor's encounter with a local bandit during his travels through Central America. The bandit saves him from a gypsy woman, who is about to rob him and slit his throat. He later runs across the bandit again, now awaiting execution, and hears firsthand of how he had first married and then murdered a gypsy temptress named Carmen, who had finally betrayed him hoping to save her own skin. Welles intended to use the carnival festivities he'd filmed in 1942 as a centerpiece of the film (he had not yet been obliged to surrender those reels to RKO). It is at Carnaval that the bandit finds his wife in the arms of a picador named Lucas. When the bandit returns to Carmen's house to kill her, he finds her waiting there, almost welcoming her fate (much like Du Maurier's Rebecca).

The appeal of the story to Welles was obvious, but Cohn was uncomfortable with the idea of a female lead being cold-bloodedly murdered by her husband at film's end; and he was even less willing when he realized that his favorite femme fatale was angling to play the part of the would-be murderess. Welles, already reconciled to such disappointments, promptly shelved the project and returned to New York, where he put his whole being into his return to the stage, in Jules Verne's immortal story.

Enter William Castle, whose film *When Strangers Marry* Welles had previously championed in his *New York Post* column. After a gratified Castle wrote to thank him, they began to exchange the odd call and occasional letter. Welles, in his usual way, suggested that they work together in the future, which Castle seems to have interpreted as some strong commitment on the notoriously flighty director's part, duly sending him a ten-page treatment of a novel he had previously purchased the film rights for on the cheap. The novel in question was Sherwood King's *If I Die Before I Wake*. Welles appears to have received the treatment in the early spring of 1946.

Castle claimed in his autobiography that he also sent Welles a copy of Sherwood King's novel, though this fails to explain Richard Wilson's manic search for a copy that April. Anyway, Welles's massive commitment of time and energy in his fated production of *Around the World in Eighty Days* hardly afforded him time for pulp fiction. The treatment is probably all that Welles read for now (though his marked-up copy of King's novel now sits in the Lilly, so it was ultimately consulted). He seems to have found within a way of making his modern-day *Carmen*. In *If I Die Before I Wake*, Welles felt he had the kind of raw material he could *transform* into "a contemporary film noir . . . that was little more than *Carmen* in modern dress" [BW].

Castle had already apparently pitched his movie idea to a Columbia story editor while Cohn was on holiday. Somewhat presciently, the editor in question informed him that Cohn would never agree to make such a film because it depicted the leading lady as a murderess. A dispirited Castle seems to have sent the treatment (and the novel?) to Welles, hoping he might adopt the idea. Almost immediately, Welles cabled him back, saying, "About *If I Should Die* [sic]—I love it . . . I have been searching for an idea for a film, but none presented itself until *If I Should Die*, and I could play the lead and Rita Hayworth could play the girl."

Welles *and* Hayworth was certainly a powerful package. But Welles seems to have been as wary of letting Castle in on his plan to remake *Carmen* as Cohn. However, his powers of persuasion did indeed prove greater than Castle's. He duly convinced Cohn to advance him, as his "directorial fee," the $25,000 he needed to keep his stage musical afloat (that part of the anecdotal version appears to be accurate). As an actor it was agreed that he would receive $2,000 a week, plus an additional $100,000 after Columbia recouped its full negative costs, and 15 percent of all profits made by the film. Welles did not forget William, requesting that Castle, a contract director at Columbia, be made associate producer.

In his own autobiography, *Step Right Up!*, Castle seems to imply that Welles's approach to Cohn was slightly underhand, even though it was Welles who ensured the film got made. Castle cannot have been unaware of Welles's working methods, and must surely have realized that by sending him the treatment he would be surrendering to the great man's conception of the film (according to the writer Fletcher Markle, Castle actually worked with Welles on a draft script during the New York run of *Around the World in Eighty Days*, suggesting that he quickly accepted Welles as the driving force behind this project).

Over the years Welles would give the impression that he did not intend for *The Lady from Shanghai* to be such a big production; that he had intended to make an A-movie aesthetically with a B-movie budget (like Castle's *When Strangers Marry*); and that he intended to film it in and around New York, hopefully during a successful run of his stage musical (Welles's initial screenplay, entitled *Black Irish*, was largely set in New York, as opposed to Long Island, where the original novel had been set). He even told Bogdanovich that he never intended for Rita to play the female lead, having Barbara Laage in mind instead. Cohn, though, was never going to buy that suggestion; and, anyway, Hayworth's name appears in that original cable to Castle. With Hayworth as the femme fatale, all things became possible, including a budget of $2,300,000.

As for the original novel, one would be hard-pressed to argue with Bret Wood's assessment that Welles "used the source material as a basis to build an original film with little regard to the novel." For the film to have that "seven-layer cake profusion" found in all of Welles's finest work, he knew that he was going to have to contribute more from his imagination than Sherwood King's. Talking about *The Lady from Shanghai* in 1982, Welles insisted he got easily "bored with stories that don't seem to be balanced dangerously. If you walk down a highway . . . instead of on a tightrope, I'm bored with it." So from the very first draft Welles devised a series of ingenious ways of negotiating that tightrope, making for one of his most challenging scripts, from one of the least promising sources. Andre Bazin offers almost a truism when he suggests that "*The Lady from Shanghai* is paradoxically the richest in meaning of Welles's films in proportion to the insignificance of the script [precisely because] the plot no longer interferes with the underlying action, from which the themes blossom out in something close to their pure states."

In fact, the book presented a number of problems that Welles was obliged to resolve if he was going to get the script approved by Harry Cohn (and by Joseph Breen, who was once again American cinema's chief censor). One of these was the suggestion that the lawyer-husband of Hayworth's character was homosexual. Another was the fate of "the girl" at film's end. What would be an appropriate punishment for this screen siren hell-bent on luring men to their doom?

Welles's first attempt at an appropriate ending never made it past the censor. On August 19, 1946, Joseph Breen, the man who had fought for Welles's original *Ambersons* when he was production chief at RKO, rejected the initial script because his character, Michael O'Hara, encourages Elsa Bannister to commit suicide. Even with all those American casualties in the bloodiest of wars, reality continued to be verboten on the silver screen.

In this *Black Irish* draft Welles once again embraced the idea of the divided self. At the end, Michael calls "Elsa" by her real name, Rosaleen, telling her that "it wasn't you I gave the gun to. . . . The gun's for Rosaleen. She knows what to do with it." Her inner struggle takes place behind Michael's back as he walks down the hallway of mirrors in search of an exit from the crazy house. The audience, though, would have seen Elsa raise the gun and aim it at his back, only to lower it just before he turns one last time, to hear her say, "Good-bye, knight errant. . . . Give my love to the sunset."

This was all Welles. In *Black Irish*, even Michael's escape from the cops in a drugged state—which has yet to involve a Chinese theater—prompts a chase sequence which is almost as hallucinatory as the hall of mirrors. Welles told Leaming that unless a film "becomes that kind of [hallucinatory] experience, it [just] doesn't come alive" for him. The finale to *Black Irish* was just such an experience, with Michael "fighting to wake up from the nightmare":

[Michael] steps, drugged, stunned, almost asleep. The voices of the commercial on the radio, the jam session, the billiard game, the congregation, the fight, blend weirdly together. Michael claps his hands over his ears. He suddenly looks up startled as he hears sirens in the distance. He runs down the street, his heart pounding. He plunges into the thickest part of the crowd. He slips, twists, turns in the midst of it, running faster, faster. The sirens come closer. . . . He stops abruptly. He looks up. The camera pans slowly from Michael to disclose an immense Negro fully eight feet tall. The giant is stripped to the waist, his black torso glistening with sweat. A white turban is wound about his head. This fearful apparition stands in the center of the street, bearing a white sign like a sandwich board. Nothing is on the sign except a picture of a huge white door. In his great hand, he clutches handbills which he gives to the passerby on the street.

The hallucinatory quality that Welles required to make some-thing "come alive" would run through all the incarnations of *The Lady from Shanghai*. If Mary's unseen nightmare in *The Stranger* had been a mere device to resolve her ordeal, in its successor we are never sure when or if we are seeing things as they really are. Hence, as Michael enters the Savoy Ballroom kitchen, the *Black Irish* script offers as an aside, "His nightmare never seems to end." And when he awakes from his ordeal, though he is no longer drugged, he still finds himself "in one of the queerest rooms ever built by man. . . . The floor is raked at an angle of the sheerest vertigo, the walls and ceiling are pure *Cabinet of Dr. Caligari* . . . He rises from the little pal-let that's been fixed for him, blinks his eyes, shakes his head and wonders—as we do—where in hell he is. For . . . Hell itself couldn't be a stranger place to look at. He staggers over to a cock-eyed door, and stumbles out," only to find himself in the hall of mirrors.

Welles intended the viewer to share the hero's increasing dis-orientation leading up to the hall of mirrors. Mirrors and mirrored surfaces constantly refract reality when the drugged hero is on the run, seeing everything through distorted vision. When he slips into the Savoy Ballroom to escape the police, we see the bottles on the bar reflected by a vast mirror. A close shot catches Michael viewing "the faces of the people around him reflected many times. The magic Mirror seems to push the walls back and back and reflects the light from the ceiling. The illusion in the magic mirror fascinates him as he gazes into it. [Meanwhile,] sirens sound outside." Just when it looks like he might be trapped, "the whole mirror is filled with the monstrous head of the giant [eight-foot Negro] Michael saw before in the street. The piercing black eyes stare at him. The head seems to come closer and closer."

Unbeknownst to an increasingly woozy Michael, this figure is there to help him evade the police. He ushers him into the kitchen, pursued by a detective, at which point events unfold refracted through a silver tray that Michael is pretending to wipe at the sink. The detective's "image in the tray grows bigger and bigger as he comes closer," but Michael is spirited away before the detective can get to him. He finds himself down a side street, on the verge of unconsciousness, staring at a huge white door, suddenly remembering what had been written on the card the eight-foot Negro was handing out on the street: "Sinners! Go Through the White Door. Find Refuge and Safety!!!" He takes this as his cue and, like Alice, enters the disproportionate portal, where he promptly collapses, to awake "in one of the queerest rooms ever built by man."

Welles knew from the very outset that Cohn was likely to prove a hard sell, but was determined to ensure that his fourth Hollywood film was not as fatally compromised as his second and third. The characterization of Elsa as the queen scorpion in this nest of vipers proved a problem from the very outset of the project—it had already prompted rejection of his version of *Carmen*. As with *The Stranger*, though, Welles wrote a script in the hope that many similarities to its "true" source would pass the producer by. That script was *Black Irish*. In this original version, Elsa's husband has no illusions about his wife. In a speech to Michael in the fun house that is overheard by Elsa, he suggests the power of money:

> I'm never satisfied—I'm what they call the jealous husband. If my wife couldn't love me, I wanted to be sure she wasn't capable of love. That isn't much, but I'm not very well, you know, and I simply had to have that. You took it away from me. Not her love—there wasn't any—just my poor little hope that Elsa could never truly love anything—except money. I think she loves you, Black Irish . . . but I know Elsa—she'll always be true to my money.

Michael himself has still not learned the truth about Elsa. By pronouncing the truth to the one true believer his wife has left, Bannister sentences himself to death. In this original shoot-out only Elsa has a gun, which she fires wildly at the mirrored images of her husband until, with her "final" bullet, she kills him. Bannister faces up to his fate "with a curious, relaxed kind of dauntlessness." Elsa insists that she "couldn't help it," as Michael "tears the gun out of her fingers." Defenseless, she clings to the hope that she can continue to ensnare Michael with candied words, claiming that she had done it because she couldn't stand her husband "say[ing] those things [i.e. the truth] in front of you." Michael, though, has finally awoken from his romantic reverie. He quietly points out, "There wouldn't be much point in killing him if he was lying." At the same time he hands Elsa/Rosaleen the gun. Immediately she reverts to type, and cries, "You *fool*!" But Michael knows that a witness, Bessie, is waiting in the wings. The cops have been called, and for once Michael will be relieved to see them.

As Michael exits from the crazy house, he mutters "almost to himself," "Like the sharks eatin' each other—there isn't one of you left." Broome, Grisby, Bannister, and Elsa are all dead. Michael waits for the approaching police in the early dawn. Welles even sneaks in a subtle allusion to another Marlow, the narrator of *Heart of Darkness*, recreating that script's opening as the finale to *Black Irish*: "From the sea-reaches beyond come the clangor and complaint of shipping in impatient anchorage, iron boats straining for voyages, eager for the conquest of oceans."

Did Welles *really* think he was going to get this kind of finale past Cohn? Even after he rewrote the script to satisfy the censor, making Elsa commit suicide of her own accord, he had scripted a movie in which Cohn's number one star stood revealed as an amoral manipulator of men. Noir or no noir, it was bound to mean trouble with Harry. Yet Welles's original solution remains the most satisfactory, because the impetus of the story leads directly there.

In this version, even after Elsa has killed her husband, she tries to convince Michael that they can get away, that she's "got money." Michael merely reminds her of what she has become, and who she is really running from. "Money? Sure, it won't get you away from yourself, *Mrs. Bannister*! And if I were you, ma'am, it's *myself* I'd be runnin' from. Not from the cops, or from a little bit of a gun, or all the devils in the black pit of hell." It was a daring inversion of the Hollywood norm.

Too daring, by half. Even after Hayworth's captivating performance as a less sociopathic femme fatale in *Gilda*, turning the beautiful woman into a murderess at film's end went against Cohn's (and Hollywood's) box-office instincts (Mary Astor in *The Maltese Falcon* remains a solitary exception). On some level, it was the fault of American filmmakers who, with the best motives in the world, shirked from depicting leading women as anything other than essentially passive figures, goddesses, or whores. Raymond Chandler's *The Big Sleep* depicts *both* sisters as vicarious, pleasure-seeking users of men; but Howard Hawks, in the 1946 film, has the elder daughter (and "love interest") tamed by Marlow.

◆   ◆   ◆   ◆

Cohn demanded further rewrites from Welles before shooting started, obliging him to search for an ending that made sense of the story, yet played to the gallery. Welles suspected that the problem lay outside the movie, though not the Columbia studio gates. There was the long-term damage done to the American psyche by "the West Coast dream factory," something Welles had already written about in his *New York Post* column, on one of those rare instances where his wife was mentioned. The couple had gone to see an evening of Mendelssohn, "when a young lady danced on from stage left and, moving center, commenced a highly personal interpretation of the music." Before the audience had quite got its bearings "the choreography was enriched by the appearance of two policemen." After the lady in question had been carted away, Welles and Hayworth fell into a discussion about what had possessed the young woman to humiliate herself so:

> My wife says the dancing lady could only happen here. Me, I don't think it occurred because the concert was in Hollywood. But I do believe that Hollywood's to blame. I think the young lady is the victim of a movie. The plot is all too recognizable. She's probably seen it all too often. It goes, you'll remember, like this: Talented unknown talks her way backstage and, as the mighty orchestra strikes up her favorite number, leaps before the eager crowd and does her stuff . . . As the music smashes to a finish, our heroine is greeted with a standing ovation. The conductor embraces her. Contracts . . . are immediately in

evidence. . . . Nothing we've manufactured in the West Coast dream factory of ours would equip her for anything but triumph. My heart goes out to her . . . wherever they've put her. It's tough to find out so very publicly that there isn't any such thing as a happy ending.

The happy ending never did come easy to Welles—not that he tried too hard. And *The Lady from Shanghai* was never going to be a remake of *Gilda* (where Hayworth finally wins the love of Glenn Ford, despite her many deceptions). Rather, as Bret Wood suggests, it takes its lead from *Carmen*, "tak[ing] a certain pleasure in antiromantically turning the beautiful woman into a murderous villain." In the shooting script Welles now applied himself to, Michael inquires accusingly, "Did you care for any of the others?" meaning fellow victims of her feminine wiles. Elsa turns on the waterworks and insists, "I'm not what you think I am—I just try to be like that." Michael snaps, "Go on trying. But leave me out of it." Yet he knows he is caught like a male spider in the black widow's web (an image Welles planned to reinforce in the original crazy house sequence, where he "sees himself—insanely multiplied—as a scurrying homunculi [sic], a spider, all legs and eyes").

Such a brazen depiction of womanhood was anathema to the mogul, and Welles was obliged to work for six weeks more on the shooting script, ever modifying the thrust of the film. Joseph McBride's erroneous suggestion that Welles wrote the original screenplay in a seventy-two-hour session, after checking incognito into a hotel on Catalina Island, is wholeheartedly embraced by David Thomson as a means of *proving* that *Shanghai* "suffers from boredom, laziness, or impatience in its maker" (a charge one might level at Thomson, so lacking in research is his ostentatiously ignorant tome on Welles).

In fact, Welles seems to have devoted a great deal of time to the script, beginning work on it shortly after cabling Cohn at the end of April 1946; (co) writing (with William Castle) going on through June and into early July. The so-called *Black Irish* script was not completed until August 13; another script, called *Take This Woman*, is dated just six days later; and the "First Estimating Script," the raw version of the shooting script, carries the date September 20, 1946. Filming was due to start in Hollywood twelve days later, six months after Welles first read Castle's ten-page treatment. Yet the rewrites continued, covering a third of the script (which might have required a weekend in Catalina). Welles, though, did not consider this the end of the process and there are half-a-dozen scenes written between October 7 and 14, after filming had commenced. Crucially, almost all of the denouement in the "final" shooting script comprises revised pages, dated October 1 and in one instance October 3.

The compromise ending introduced in the revised script, presumably forced on Welles by Cohn, made Bannister the murderer of Grisby, and Grisby the murderer of Broome. The result was a lot of loose ends dangling in the wind. Having made Elsa retroactively innocent of both crimes, Welles was obliged to make Bannister instigate the shoot-out in the hall of mirrors, emptying his gun at Elsa but "fir[ing] mistakenly at her image instead of her." Elsa's own fate, given that she must die, is resolved by her being hit during the shoot-out, after she has fired back at Bannister and killed him.

Even in this version, though, Elsa still has the capacity to make Michael too "helpless to act or even to think clearly." Only after she thinks there is one bullet left in the gun and aims it at Michael, does he realize that she never loved him. He gently chastises her, "Oh my darlin' . . . you should never have done that. I might have believed you, if you'd let it be." He again appeals to her "better self" to let go of the gun, "Rosaleen! Don't pull that trigger! It's you I'm talking to, Rosaleen, the little girl there inside of you. The one I love, and always will—it's her I'm askin' not to pull the trigger. . . . Don't pull the trigger, Rosaleen. You've made enough hurt in the world." Elsa duly expires from the wound she has sustained from her husband, though not before asking Michael for one last screen kiss, "Kiss me, I think I'm going to die. Call me Rosaleen." It may well be Welles's closest approximation to a Hollywood ending, but it is hardly *Gilda*.

Already we have moved away from the dispassionate but gripping finale in *Black Irish* and toward the largely unsatisfactory version in the released film, which necessitated an unconvincing voice-over from Michael looking back at the way things turned out. Welles was understandably unhappy with the changes he was obliged to make. Indeed, Bret Wood suggests, in an article on the film entitled "Kiss Hollywood Goodbye," that "it is possible that Welles scripted this ending with little intent of filming it. Had he written the finale in which Michael coldly walks away from Elsa . . . Cohn would have probably never approved the film for production."

Not surprisingly, Welles's depiction of his personal love goddess in the film generated a great deal of scuttlebutt about his motives for humiliating his ex-wife so, followed by even more psychobabble about Welles's attitude to women, exemplified by this single film in splendid isolation. An attempt to bring the gritty realism of a contemporary novel to the screen was considered fair game for psychological analysis of the director, with the most disturbing hidden motives liberally applied. Even Barbara Leaming, the generally forgiving biographer of both Welles and Hayworth, viewed *The Lady from Shanghai* as something that "evolved slowly into Orson's guilt-ridden artistic meditation on the failure of his and Rita's relationship."

In fact, his Elsa was much the same character William Castle treated and Sherwood King devised. And Hayworth was perfect for the part. Indeed, part of her appeal to Welles, first as an actress and then as a woman, was that her persona stood "for everything a man strives after but cannot possess, [as well as being] the source of his destruction, [for she is] beyond reason, beyond morality, beyond responsibility." [JM] Aside from her riveting screen presence and siren status, she was willing to go through hoops for her hubby, even coloring her flowing locks at his request (inducing one of many fits from Cohn). As Earl Bellamy once said, "When Rita worked with Orson she was enthralled by him. Almost like she was hypnotized. She . . . would do anything he said."

It seems ironic that accusations of misogyny should be directed at Welles at precisely the point when he began to fall under the spell of "the White Goddess," Robert Graves's worshipful conception of the willful woman, who "scorns any claim on her person, or curb on her desires," of whom Elsa was an absolute archetype. A few critics seem perplexed to find Graves's influence evident in a film two years before *The White Goddess* was published, as if that work was Graves's first exposition of his grand conceit. In fact he had already depicted the white goddess in precise terms in two "historic" novels, *The Golden Fleece* (a.k.a. *Hercules, My Shipmate*) in October 1944 and, in September 1946, *King Jesus*. The latter work generated a great deal of controversy, prompting an eloquent defense from Graves in a New York paper. Given its premise, which depicted Jesus as a religious zealot who has come to defeat the power of woman (but fails), this was surely a must read for Welles in the fall of '46.

The influence of Graves would flower more fully in independent productions like *Othello* and *The Trial*. The two White Goddess novels, if they influenced Welles this early, simply reinforced a viewpoint there in the *Black Irish* draft of the script and in Welles's treatment for *Carmen*—woman as the destroyer. In *Black Irish*, Bannister even acknowledged his fate to Michael, in the crazy house finale, informing him, "Some day, of course, she'll kill me . . . I know she will—and yet I can't protect myself. There are women who do that to men. Look what she did to Grisby—he didn't have a chance."

The other themes Welles sought to address— transferred largely intact from the abandoned *Carmen*—reflect concerns that lay equally deep within the man. In one instance in the script he even seemed to be mocking his own "principled" stance versus the studios, as Sanford a.k.a. Bannister informs Michael in a Mexican bar, "You'll want something and you'll pay for it. You'll go to the market like any other fat little pig or hungry farmer and you'll make your deal." If Welles had himself made his deal with the devil, Cohn didn't like the inference and the scene was cut.

Welles's character in the movie, Michael O'Hara, can be seen in part as an idealized version of the roving blade who wandered around Ireland as a teenager, painting portraits until he came upon the Gate Theatre in Dublin, where he auditioned for the stage, got the part of a lifetime, and, as he says in *F for Fake*, "had been working his way down ever since." From the opening scene in Central Park, Michael is portrayed as a blundering romantic, an unwitting outlaw who fails to heed any warnings he may be given. In Welles's version, Elsa compares them at their first meeting with that other man out of time, Don Quixote, calling him her "knight errant," originally intended to also be the last words ever to play upon those lovely lips:

> THE GIRL: Rosinante was the old nag Don Quixote rode when he went out after those windmills. I think you're a lot like Don Quixote yourself, Michael. You haven't heard about the age of chivalry. It's out of business. . . . You'd better be careful. Things have changed, Sir Knight. Nowadays it's usually the dragon that lives happily ever after.
>
> MICHAEL: Don't the princess and the knight ever make it?
>
> THE GIRL (stopping and turning to him): Sometimes she gives him a kiss.
>
> Michael just looks at her, terribly embarrassed. A funny little spark comes into her eyes.
>
> THE GIRL (cont.): . . . You know what's wrong with being a knight errant?
>
> MICHAEL: No.
>
> THE GIRL: He's brave and bold because his heart is pure. But he's an awful fool—he doesn't know anything about women.

Welles delighted in the idea of the hero-as-fool-as-hero—in the released film Michael expresses the belief that "everybody is somebody's fool"—and while he still remained young and virile enough to pull it off, decided to make the part his own. His second romantic lead, after Rochester in *Jane Eyre*, it contained the usual parodic elements some critics mistook for bad acting. Just like Isabel Amberson, Michael O'Hara can't help but give himself away in song. As he is first seen walking in Central Park late at night, he is singing a song under his breath. It is an old Irish ballad about another outlaw who came a cropper when he took on the established order:

> Bold Robert Emmett, the darlin' of Erin
> Bold Robert Emmett, he died with a smile.

Michael is promptly reminded that little has changed since the days of Emmett, as "a blade of light stabs through the darkness and picks up his face, interrupting the song." It is a policeman's torch, which travels up and down Michael, assessing him on our behalf. Later, when the cop car again pulls alongside, one of the cops asks him why he might be singing. Michael's retort establishes him as a man used to living outside the law, "Is there a law now says a man can't be after whisperin' a little song to himself in the nighttime for companionship? And to keep himself from remembrin' that the world is full of cops?"

Throughout the remainder of the film *as shot*—now preserved solely within a January 1947 cutting continuity—there were continual reminders of the foolhardiness of Michael, his simplistic notion of the heroic. When he knocks a man down in a cantina, he is admonished by Elsa, who tells him, "You can't solve anything by knocking people down!" Michael's justification is that "he's a wicked man entirely." Though this retort goes unchallenged in the film, Elsa originally dispelled such a black-and-white view in a single sentence, "And I'm the princess in the fairy book . . . So you hit him and make a pretty speech to me and we ride off together into the sunset."

Yet despite herself, Elsa is fatally attracted to Michael's air of romantic fatalism, even if she knows that it spells death. At one point she pleads for Michael to "keep your dream—ride off into your sunset by yourself and look for windmills [another overt reference to Quixote]. I don't want to hurt you, Michael. I'm afraid for you. . . . You don't belong with us. You're alive. We're dead. . . . All of us are dead already!" Michael, though, is too wrapped up in his role as the knight errant to pay any heed, even as the sharks continue to harpoon their intended victim.

Certainly Elsa's husband, Bannister, is in no doubt as to Michael's likely fate. Like Elsa, he is perfectly willing to tell it to our hero, during one particular tavern conversation later removed, "A crust of bread and the open road and the song of the thrush at twilight, that's all you think you need, isn't it? You'll wake up out of your dream, Romantic Mike . . . but your kind always gets the worst of it." For Welles, the role represented a new challenge. As he commented later in life, his personality and demeanor usually resulted in him playing "authoritative roles," albeit ones in which he showed "the fragility of the great authority." Michael O'Hara held no such authority. Even when displaying a proclivity for fisticuffs, it only served, as Elsa observed, to "make everything worse."

If Welles's depiction of the Hayworth character has been seen by many folk as a grand revenge—on Cohn, on Rita herself, on Hollywood—it is Michael who represents the most obvious deconstruction of a Hollywood stereotype. In the same year that Howard Hawks successfully transformed Raymond Chandler's methodical detective Marlow into a man who never made a foolish move (in *The Big Sleep*), Welles's Irish Don Quixote made for an altogether less worldly innocent, adrift in a sea of sharks. That such a fool walks away at the end is little more than good luck.

The unsavory characters who populate the world into which Michael O'Hara blindly stumbles are all out for themselves. Without scruples, let alone morals, they fully understand each other's motivations. Michael, though, remains a mystery to these people who use verbal bayonets to spike their victims. Bannister at one point in the original script goads Grisby by reminding him of this power he has over him, "Blackmailer, now there's a real nice nasty name for you, but as it is, you'll have to be satisfied with partner." Welles had already described Grisby, in the shooting script, in terms that displayed a similar contempt:

> He is a hearty, silly ass, a racquet-club glamour boy in his late forties, an expensively togged out phoney with the look about him of always coming fresh from the barber's and the steam bath. A real pillar of café society, this—out of Groton and Harvard—and darn lucky to be out of jail.

Perhaps the most unsavory male character in the movie, though, is the detective Bannister hires to follow his wife. Broome is no Marlow, Chandler's or Hawks's. Broome's only interest is the one thing that Marlow seems to despise, money. Nor does he mind grubbing about in the muck and mire to get his hands on it. Like Grisby, he is introduced in the script with one of Welles's little verbal sketches:

> His blank face shows nothing but greed. A loose mouth sports a set of teeth the color of Camembert cheese. About two of these unlovely grinders are missing and this man Broome has a way of nursing a fat reptilian tongue through the gaping space with exactly the grimace of a sick lizard.

Broome expects the worst of people. With his current employers, he is rarely disappointed. Recognizing only the color of money, he is the only figure in the film not blinded by Elsa's beauty. As such, when Elsa (in the shooting script) acquired Michael's written confession from Grisby, Broome breaks into her bedroom at night, takes the confession out of the jewel box, and proceeds to read it. Elsa, seductively wrapped in a large Turkish towel, emerges out of the bathroom and asks him what he is doing in her room. Broome, though, is neither fazed nor embarrassed. He knows exactly how serious a threat she represents, and is the one man prepared to manhandle her:

> BROOME: I beg your pardon, Mrs. Bannister, I didn't mean to disturb you.

> She starts toward him.

ELSA: Give me that. . . . It's mine.

BROOME: Your name isn't signed to it.

She moves quickly to the other side of the dressing table. He jumps in front of her, seizes her, and throws her very roughly to the ground.

BROOME: Oh no you don't! I know about that gun. You ain't gonna use it. If anybody gets croaked around here it ain't gonna be me.

Atypically, Broome is proven wrong. He *is* going to get "croaked," almost immediately—for the "five grand" that Grisby is supposed to pay Michael to say that he killed him. But before he dies, it becomes his turn to warn Michael that he is in way over his head, while demanding the five grand that Grisby has now given to Michael. Michael wants to know what for and Broome replies, "A little piece of paper, that's what for. A confession." Upon seeing the confession, Michael gives the bleeding, dying man the money he craves, but will never get to enjoy:

Broome seizes it in greedy fingers sticky with blood.

BROOME (crooning in a kind of dying ecstasy): "Five G's . . . I worked hard for this . . . "

He slumps to the concrete floor—falls dead in a bloody morass of paper money.

After a minute, Michael forces himself into a search for the confession. Finds it in Broome's pocket. Puts it away in his own. Then he sees the money on the ground.

As one in a trance, Michael stoops and gathers up the precious garbage. Shovels the moist and dripping stuff into the car.

Bannister's prediction that even Michael will "go to the market . . . and make your deal" has come true. Even he has become tainted

by the blood money these human sharks are tearing each other apart
to get. A few minutes earlier, we were supposed to have seen a particularly dazzling visual representation of that earlier parable. When
Michael meets with Grisby to receive his money and arrange the
"fake" murder, the camera was to rise from the floor and focus on the
dashboard and right glove compartment, in which Grisby's gun has
been placed. Meanwhile Grisby's blood (the result of a car crash)
begins to drop onto the camera lens. The left-hand side of the screen
gradually starts to become blurred. As Grisby convinces Michael to
go through with his plan, "more drops of blood fall on the camera
lens, [as] the left half of the screen becomes progressively more
blurred." By the time Grisby is telling Michael to get out the gun,
"the left half of the frame is . . . completely blurred, [with] a fuzzy line
of demarcation between the left and right halves of the screen.
Michael's arm shoots out from this blurred dividing line into the
right half of the screen and raises the lid of the glove compartment.
He takes out a gun." The point, something about evil roots and
money, is driven home with typically Wellesian force, but it did not
make it to the finished film.

At least mirrors, and mirrored surfaces—so important in *Black
Irish*—continue to reinforce the idea that illusion and duplicity are
all that Elsa and her kind represent. The world these scavengers
have built for themselves is one great big ivory tower of illusion. As
Richard T. Jameson points out, the scene where Elsa dives off of the
rock "afford[s us] a glimpse of her poised against the sky; [but] what
we are really seeing is a reflection in the lens of a monocular—properly so, for Elsa's stock-in-trade is deception." Michael, though, fails
to see this world for what it is. Even after his first shattering
moment, during the fight with the court bailiff in the judge's chambers, when he throws a statuette at the camera itself, thus challenging *us* to see this world for what it is, one built on artifice, he
remains an innocent abroad. It takes the frenzied firing of Mr. and
Mrs. Bannister in that hall of mirrors to shatter that final layer of
unreality and reveal all.

That stunning shoot-out took all the resources of a studio like Columbia to capture. Charles Higham states, in his *Films of Orson Welles*, that the mirror maze contained 2,912 square feet of glass, that 80 plate glass mirrors were used along with 24 distorting mirrors, some of which had a "two-way" construction so that the cameraman could shoot through them. Such bald statistics barely hint at the real practical difficulties Welles faced, particularly as he planned to superimpose shots of Elsa over Bannister's multiplying image, and vice versa (two "gratuitous" close-ups of Elsa, inserted into the shoot-out, were the hack work of editor Viola Lawrence).

Welles had long wanted to shoot such a scene. As far back as August 1941, in the script he commissioned for the *Love Story* version of *It's All True*, we find Della and Hilda hiding out in a hall of mirrors, hoping to escape the unwelcome attention of rough-and-ready Rocco Stefani. When "a hundred reflections of Rocco Stefani appear in the mirror[s], Della turns . . . and whirls away from the images . . . straight into the arms of the real Rocco." Three years later, Welles attempted to sell a screenplay, *Don't Catch Me*, that was a comic adventure story in which a pair of newlyweds stumble on a Nazi conclave in the U.S. and are forced to flee to a deserted amusement park, into a maze of mirrors. There they are involved in a shoot-out with Nazi agents, before escaping through the tunnel of love.

When it comes to *The Lady from Shanghai*, the hall of mirrors shoot-out was a feature from its earliest extant draft (though it does not appear in King's novel). What was added to the scene, when Welles was obliged to make it a battle and not an assassination, was another layer of symbolism to an already unusually dark film, "compactly expressing the ruthless ambition and the self-destructive mania that has been evoked verbally in O'Hara's story about the sharks" [JN].

❖   ❖   ❖   ❖

If Welles was once again brimming with ideas, he surely knew that only some of them would survive the whims of a baffled boss. As late as December 1946, though, he was informing the *New York Times* "that Columbia had treated him with the utmost generosity . . . in matters of fiscal and artistic autonomy." It would last as long as Welles's services were still required. Cohn had come to realize something Welles had always known and expressed in print as long back as February 1941, "If an actor can do without a director, a camera can't. . . . It's the biggest job in Hollywood. ([Well,] it would be, except for something called a producer.)" Five years before working for Cohn, Welles had described a producer as "the man who interferes with a movie." He now needed to devise ways to militate against inevitable interference from King Cohn.

One tactic was to constantly change the script itself. William Castle's own diary of the shoot contains an entry for the twelfth of November that reads, "Orson started rehearsing. Actors, memorizing their lines, arrive on set to find Welles . . . doing a complete rewrite." According to Charles Higham, who interviewed a number of participants, this was a common state of affairs, with Welles "sometimes . . . deliberately upset[ting] them to make them give nervous, uneasy performances. He would even force them to forget their lines so that they would improvise new ones. Erskine Sanford, as a judge [sic] in a brawl in his chambers, cries out, 'This isn't a football game!' The line was made up on the spot because Sanford couldn't recall what he was supposed to say."

No one who ever worked with Welles would suggest that his reputation as a demanding director was undeserved, but *The Lady from Shanghai* seems to have been a particularly fraught shoot, in part because of tension in the air between a seemingly reconciled director and his anxious-to-please spouse, desperate to convince him to come back and try again. Welles's bullying of certain actors was clearly intended to extract appropriate performances from them. Thus Glenn Anders, as the loathsome lawyer Grisby, was made to feel so anxious by Welles that the crew dubbed him Glenn Anguish; while Erskine Sanford, as Elsa's jealous husband, was obliged to play a cripple so that he might become psychologically unbalanced enough to play this demanding role.

Welles had decided that, in order to ensure that he remained the "dominant personality" in such a necessarily collaborative process, he needed to keep everybody else unsure of their place. Associate producer William Castle found out, after a night spent viewing rushes that "again proved [Welles]'s brilliance" in a downtown theater in Acapulco, he was going to be left behind in Mexico to shoot additional footage. If Welles had always liked to introduce surprises into the filming process (notably his changed ending to *The Magnificent Ambersons*), from this point forward it became policy. As the assistant director on *Touch of Evil*, Terry Nelson, told one biographer, "He assumed absolute creative control by rewriting constantly so that nobody really had a firm fix on all the requirements except Welles."

A decade before *Touch of Evil*, Welles was already devising ways of second-guessing those who might undermine his grand design. Hence, part of Brecht's appeal. It was Brecht who had argued in "Theatre for Pleasure or Theatre for Instruction" that "an epic work, as opposed to a dramatic, [is where] one can as it were take a pair of scissors and cut it into individual pieces, [yet each] remain fully capable of life." Welles, who had already seen enough of his work cut to pieces, carefully constructed *The Lady from Shanghai* so that "each scene [worked] for itself."

This time, at least, Welles was not confined by budgetary restraints, even if the $2.3 million budget reflected Hayworth's standing more than his own. The memorable scene at the aquarium, where Michael and Elsa, having arranged a secret rendezvous, discuss their future against a backdrop of marine life in all shapes and sizes, was shot without any such tank. Instead, Welles relied on a simulation, shooting the tank separately and enlarging the creatures he wanted, before painstakingly matting the images into the frames, an expensive procedure but one that enabled him to synchronize the sights and sounds exactly. So Elsa's mention of her husband coincides with the shark swimming by, while the mention of his partner prompts a Congo eel to writhe into view. And so on.

Welles had not been able to use such resources since RKO. He had even set up what was apparently the longest dolly shot to date for the opening Central Park sequence, designed to establish that important frisson between Elsa and Michael. In this sequence Welles was supposed to carry on an intermittent conversation with Hayworth, in an open Victoria coach, while the horse trotted some three-quarters of a mile. This opening may well have been as worthy as that of *Touch of Evil*, ten years later, with Welles attempting to capture the series of brief encounters between Michael and the cops, Michael and Elsa, and Michael and the cops again, with one, omniscient camera on a crane, before his vision was cut to ribbons.

Once again, in the field of sound Welles proceeded to show the studios how much they usually underused their vast resources. One sequence Welles shot—which was still intact in the January 1947 cutting continuity—prefaced Grisby's unexpected request for Michael to murder him. During a climb up to the cliffs overlooking Acapulco, Welles planned "a series of elaborately choreographed traveling shots that express[ed] O'Hara's state of mind while at the same time showing the effects of Yankee capital" [JN].

In what would have been a tour de force of overlapping dialogue, Grisby's out-of-kilter conversation was designed to vie with the background conversations of American tourists, wholly obsessed with money. Thus, we would have seen a little girl attempting to get her mother to buy her a fancy drink, which "ain't even one dollar!" followed by a honeymoon couple walking across the screen. "Sure it's our honeymoon," the young man says, "but that's a two-million-dollar account." An older lady and her husband are seen arguing about taxi fare, with the lady claiming she "practically had to pay him by the mile." As they ascend the hill, a gigolo is speaking to a girl on a rock. "Fulco made it for her," he announces. "Diamonds and emeralds—must've cost a couple of oil wells. And she only wears it on her bathing suit." Another young couple walk up the steps from the beach, the man muttering, "But listen, Edna, you've got to realize pesos *is* real money." Meanwhile, Grisby continues burbling about the end of the world.

A hangover from Welles's various visits to Central and South America, this sequence's closest kin can be found in the "Mrs. Mallory" sequence in *The Way to Santiago*. Finally, O'Hara and Grisby reach the top of the hill, culminating in a fish-eyed view of the pair seemingly hanging in midair, like the long-suffering coyote in *Roadrunner* cartoons, as we finally get to hear Grisby's strange proposition. As it happens, all of Welles's careful scene setting counted for naught. Editor Viola Lawrence cut almost the whole of their climb up the hill from the beach and then dubbed on a painful discord to indicate, presumably, shock at Grisby's proposal. Welles may have told Cohn that he was looking for what he called "sound atmosphere," but his discordances were intended to make natural sounds startling, not merely odd.

According to Richard Wilson, Welles continued to experiment with recording certain scenes on audiotape, so that the dialogue could have the necessary intensity and volume. One of these was Grisby's first appearance in the launch, highlighted by Phyllis Goldfarb as one instance where the director "deliberately undermines space perception by mismatching the sound and its source. . . . [So,] in the middle of an intimate scene between Mike and Elsa . . . Grisby's voice intrudes in close-up while the sound of the launch he's in is distanced correctly. Grisby is nowhere near the couple . . . [but] the sound takes on a presence of its own." What better way to make Grisby's voice sound as creepy as the man himself?

The death of Broome was also subjected to its own series of discordances, prefaced by the horn on the car Michael is driving jamming—after crashing into a truck—so that the "irritating long steady drone of the horn cuts the night to ribbons." This cross fades into "the maddening whine of the phone" that is simultaneously ringing in Bannister's office. Broome is trying to get a hold of Bannister, but before there is an answer a high-angle camera shot takes us down into the street, where we hear "a faint but sharp textured gunshot! The noise ricochets off the granite faces of the empty buildings echoing remotely. . . . Precisely on the instant of the gunshot, the moving camera [has] . . . locked its focus in a fixed stare at the street below. . . . The minuscule shape of the man is seen to fall. . . . The phone bell clatters. . . . The man lies motionless." There follows a slow dissolve back to the horn on Michael's car, the ring of the phone merging "into the cry of the jammed auto horn and melting away under it . . . [as] Michael gets out of the car and lifts the hood." Plenty of sound atmosphere herein, but nowhere near enough Hollywood conventions being observed, so out it went.

It is doubtful whether Cohn ever understood what the movie Welles made was actually about. In one instance Cohn ordered a scene cut that showed Elsa driving to Grisby's house shortly before he was murdered, on the grounds that it was "misleading—she couldn't have done the shooting." He really can't have been paying attention. The implication is unmistakable—that she *did* kill Grisby (as she had in *Black Irish*). Only after Bannister's unconvincing confession at film's end are we supposed to believe her innocence of that particular crime.

Indeed, the famous anecdote in which Cohn at the end of a preview screening offered a thousand dollars to anyone who could explain the story to him, appears to have come *after* he ordered the film reedited. As such, Welles's admission that it made no sense to him either should surely be viewed as knowingly ironic. The cuts Cohn ordered to Welles's version of the film after he completed principal photography on January 22, 1947, simply served to *make* elements of the story nonsensical. Given that he almost cut the film in half (from 155 to 86 minutes), this was surely inevitable.

Part of what Cohn cut previously provided some necessary exposition. (Welles was ultimately required to do a voice-over to gloss over some of the more glaring dissociations in the narrative.) The director had been perfectly aware of the danger of losing his audience, and left little reminders as the plot unfolded. Broome, on the point of expiring, explains to both the gullible Michael and the curious viewer Grisby's motive for his own "faked" murder: "Bannister's dead, or he's gonna be when Grisby gets to him in Frisco. . . . That's why Grisby wants it to look like you're the one that croaked him. That way Grisby gets to kill Bannister, see, but clean, without nobody goin' after him. It's a swell alibi." It's also a swell (and necessary) explanation. However much he may have been mistaken about the actual outcome, Broome has provided a neat précis of this strand of the plotline.

Our suspension of disbelief was meant to continue even after Welles staged a performance in the self-consciously artificial Chinese theater that Brecht valued so highly, in which the two lovers (and the rest of the audience) are obliged to decide what is real and what is not. Elsa and Michael, under the pretense that they are discussing the plot of the play they are watching, set up the grand finale in their own little melodrama (again this vitally important scene was snipped during an interminable and costly period of post-production):

ELSA: I'll tell you the plot—the lady loves a man.

MICHAEL (still watching the play): Does she now?

ELSA: A poor sailor.

Michael darts a quick look at her.

ELSA: The poor sailor is accused of murder. But the lady's jealous husband . . .

MICHAEL (interrupting): I'll tell it.

She turns to him.

MICHAEL: The husband has a partner. The partner loves the lady, too . . . Everybody loves the lady. The partner plans to kill her husband and to put the blame on the poor sailor for the crime. . . . But the husband isn't murdered. There was money—partnership insurance. . . . That's the plot—but how does it turn out? With the partner dead, who is it gets the benefit of the insurance? Who stands to gain by killing him?

Having screened Welles's own cut of the film, the extent of the cuts Cohn ordered was draconian. The Central Park opening, the beach scenes in Acapulco, the campfire barbecue, the San Francisco Aquarium, the Chinese theater sequence, and the "hallucinogenic" "crazy house" finale all felt the swish of scissors. Retakes were also required, mostly a series of gaudy close-ups of Hayworth. The result was a picture that went $400,000 over budget, thanks almost entirely to eighteen months of postproduction, and ended up with a plot that made *The Big Sleep* seem like a fairy story.

None of these changes made the film abide by enough Hollywood conventions to make the ending "play"; but, hey, that's what happens when the whole story gets twisted off its axis to satisfy some pie-in-the-sky moral framework, where the bad get what's coming and the good walk away. In the end, as Andre Bazin observed, "the average American moviegoer couldn't forgive Welles for killing off Rita. Even worse, he let her die like a bitch on the floor of a hellish chamber while he walked out indifferently, eager to have things over and done with, without even obeying the elementary rule that the heroine should be paid the courtesy of dying in the arms of the rugged sailor."

For Welles personally, the greatest losses again came at the start and finish of this, his fourth Hollywood movie. To *Cahiers du Cinema*, he bemoaned the impoverished state of the opening ten minutes of the movie, which gave "the impression it wasn't me that made them. They resemble any Hollywood film." He was entitled to feel that way. The whole atmosphere that Welles went to great pains to cultivate, through an opening montage of New York on a hot summer night and the detective Broome's initial pursuit of Elsa to the Central Park encounter with our Irish romantic outlaw, was replaced with a flavorless cut-up that, as he once bitterly observed, "you could clip . . . into any old B [movie]."

The curtailed ending hurt the film even more. The crazy house sequence, in which "the protagonist's torments [are] monstrously reflected and his confused mental state . . . given cinematic expression" [BW], was, Welles believed, "*the* big tour de force scene." If, as

Naremore suggests, such "bizarre visual dissonances . . . serve[d] to mock Hollywood," they certainly prompted Cohn to distractedly ask, "What's all that about?" before dictating an instruction to go "from slide to mirrors, cutting out close-ups of girl with mask, also following shots." The "girl with mask" bore a particularly gruesome (wholly deliberate) resemblance to Elsa (stills are all that now exist of this sequence—see page 199). What is lost may well have been Welles's most nightmarish cinematic representation to date:

CRAZY HOUSE—NIGHT
A corridor like the corridors in dreams; a sloped tunnel diabolically gimmicked to bump and trip the visitor without mercy. Down this terrifying alley Michael makes his painful, bewildered way . . .
    A spring under his foot snaps a panel open with a sudden squeak as shocking as a scream in the night—a staring corpse falls out at him.
    The head of the corpse falls off the shoulders and bobbles hideously on a grotesque coil of wire . . . A second look shows Michael the dust on the wax figure, and, as he approaches it, his weight sets off a further mechanism: the dummy bolts back into the wall with an echoing bang of timber, there is a rattle of counterweights and the deafening complaint of tortured, rusty metal as the floor itself tilts slowly down and down and down.

Cohn complained, and out it went. Even this did not satiate Cohn, and after another miserable preview the film was further cut by Viola Lawrence and a largely new musical score inserted in which the hall of mirrors scene, in particular, was desecrated by the asinine soundtrack Lawrence superimposed. The director fired off one of his famous memos to Cohn, this one running to nine pages, in which he insisted that the shoot-out "*must not be backed with music.*" He also informed Cohn that the finale "is obvious to the point of vulgarity, and does incalculable injury to the finish of the picture." He later squarely placed the blame on "this terrible woman that [Cohn] brought in . . . [who was determined] to show that she'd made it different." After the Supercutter, cometh the Supersplicer.

A quarter of a century on, it still hurt. Introduced onto the *Dick Cavett Show* with the famous hall of mirrors shoot-out, Welles turned his face to the wall rather than watch what the studio had done. When Cavett questioned Welles about this, thinking it was some kind of projection fault, he was quickly set straight:

> I can't possibly fix it and I always see things wrong with it and I'd rather look back on these films as being much better than they were. . . . I know what I'd change from listening to it, which is the awful soundtrack. . . . After my version of it, which got its one preview, Harry decided to fix the music and he got a theme song. [This was] when people sang them on screen. We put that in—"Please Don't Kiss Me" or love me or something, not a bad song, and Peggy Lee, [who] was Rita's voice for that, was quite good—but Harry Cohn decided that the theme song would be nice in a sort of symphonic version under the shoot-out in the mirror scene, so instead of just hearing the crash of glass echoing and nothing else except ricocheting bullets and glass you have [that tune] all through it, which kind of louses up the proceedings.

Cohn's chosen song loused up a lot of proceedings. Welles, in his memo, felt obliged to point out that the film was "not a musical comedy," and that "this sort of music destroys that quality of strangeness which is exactly what might have saved *Lady from Shanghai* from being just another whodunit." Welles had planned to use a score which had "an atmosphere of darkness and menace, combined with something lush and romantic."

Presumably these two strains would have vied with each other throughout the picture, much as in *Citizen Kane*. Where relevant, these strains would have been intercut with regional tunes. The Acapulco scenes were to contain what Welles called "a very curious, sexy Latin American strain." But just one such sequence in the film can be seen to follow Welles's instructions. It comes as Rita is approaching Mike on the streets of Acapulco. Welles's penchant for "whorehouse pianos" and Brazilian dance music was evident in his instructions, the rapid cross fades reflecting his experience of radio:

> Nothing is heard but the solitary guitar. This plays through until we see through an arch on Rita's walk with Mike and see that there is a cabaret inside. As they approach that and would logically hear it, they hear—instead of the guitar—Cross fading into it, the Whorehouse piano. The Whorehouse piano plays through until Mike has punched Broome in the nose and Rita starts to run away. On the first cut of her crossing the street, there is a strong backlight on this. There is a Cross Fade in which (we) hear Fading out the sound of the Whorehouse piano and Fading IN over this Shot a very fast rhumba which is probably going to be the one from the Astaire picture [he means *Yolanda and the Thief*, confirming that he had indeed seen Astraire's sixteen-minute dream ballet]. It isn't important—a lot of drums and action. If that doesn't have one, pick Rita's from "Tonight & Every Night." This goes through the Quick Traveling Shot of Rita running and just as we come to the Shot of the band as she runs: a quick QUICK Cross Fade which takes us into "Palabras du Mohair" which plays through.

For self-styled iconoclast David Thomson, the Welles who made this film "is too superior, or too bored, to make a genre mood consistent and constructive. Working at the height of film noir, Welles is interested only in deconstructing the atmosphere. He lurches from one set piece to the next. His style is showy and jittery, never trusting the script or the actors, and the film is full of close-ups that do not quite fit the situation. The mood is always being broken." There is not an ounce of doubt in our David's mind that the above criticisms—most of them perfectly valid in and of themselves—should be placed at Welles's door. Despite knowing that Welles had no right of final cut, and that the film was cut from 155 to 86 minutes against his wishes, Thomson is convinced that the discontinuities are evidence of *his* contempt for Hollywood, and not the other way round.

To suggest that Welles, at barely thirty years of age, was bored with making films is, frankly, bizarre. As Welles put it to Tom Snyder when he had doubled his years on this earth, "The real renegade has to be a little short on that final 10 percent of ambition—he has to be more interested in what he is doing than what he is. In your early twenties there's a kind of arrogance and ego that drains away [later], but the love of what you are doing does not diminish." Nor did it.

Only with his experience on *The Lady from Shanghai*, though, did Welles realize that he was a "real renegade"; that there was no way he could ever reach any accommodation with the "studio method of moviemaking." In fact, the one cheap shot of Thomson's that hits an actual target is his observation that "the film is full of close-ups that do not quite fit the situation." Again, it had been Cohn who insisted on these close-ups of his sultry siren. However, this time Welles *does* adopt a superior, and satiric, attitude to the task. What Bret Wood calls "the two-dimensionality of movie glamour" is juxtaposed with the director's wide-angled view of the world, as "every sequence in which Hayworth appears is broken into crisp, deep, carefully composed wide shots [followed by] low-contrast, soft-focus, eye-level close-ups against a projected close-up." If this was the only satire Welles felt he could inject into the film—the courtroom scene excepted—it would have to do.

The experience, though, was a draining one. Once again, Welles found himself making a film where the "editing style is still discernible, but the final version of the film is not at all mine." Because he had learned (from Brecht) about the importance of shooting "each scene for itself," he still managed to make a movie that has "a considerable degree of formal narrative unity" [JN]. Unfortunately, it is another Welles film where, to (un)quote Bazin, "the kernel of meaning is [not] perceived . . . in its natural relationship to all the contiguous realities." Cohn, in the end, became the film's producer, not merely its financier. Welles, having expounded, back in 1942, on how "most producers manage, through the exercise . . . of the devious abilities which made them producers in the first place, to negate all other potential dominant personalities," can't have been *entirely* surprised.

The plot for *The Lady from Shanghai* in the end raises more questions than it answers. Unlike the altogether more coherent *Black Irish*, it fails to convey the sheer bloodlust of this particular school of sharks. But then neither did Howard Hawks's *The Big Sleep*, which opened at the end of August 1946 and proved to be a huge critical and commercial success. Of course, Hawks had been very careful to emphasize the romantic elements in the Bogart-Bacall relationship, the movie having been shot during their actual courtship; whereas Welles portrayed his own screen goddess, from whom he would be divorced before the film's release, as a lying bitch who deserved to die.

Perhaps this was not the time or the place for Welles to make what Naremore calls "his most misanthropic treatment of American life . . . [or] an allegory about [his] adventures in Hollywood." That adventure was all but over, at least for a decade or so. By the time *The Lady from Shanghai* was released, to poor notices and poorer receipts, he was already living in Europe and showing very little desire to return to his own shores, or put himself through the Hollywood mill again.

A PERFECT CROSS BETWEEN *WUTHERING HEIGHTS* AND *BRIDE OF FRANKENSTEIN*

[Macbeth; The Third Man]

Remember that every single way of playing Shakespeare—as
long as the way is effective—is right.

Orson Welles, *Everybody's Shakespeare*, 1934

Though the story behind the making, and (re)editing, of
Welles's penultimate Hollywood movie reflects many of the
problems he'd already encountered in Tinseltown, the movie
itself, a version of Shakespeare's *Macbeth*, is perhaps his least interesting foray into filmed adaptation. Dripping with atmosphere and
expressive cinematography, and with one of Welles's finest screen performances, it nevertheless fails to fully hold any but the already committed. Welles may have come to realize this. He showed an
uncharacteristic disinterest in the fate of the film after he had shot it,
and when he made his next Shakespearean film, with his own money
and in his own time, it had very little in common with *Macbeth*.

As Welles noted on many occasions, he viewed the 1947 *Macbeth* as an experiment. Ever since coming to Hollywood he had shied
away from Bill Shagspere, save for the odd radio cameo, despite
developing much of his reputation across most every other available
media from his adaptations of the Bard. By 1939, when not yet
twenty-five, he had already played Claudius, Fortinbras, and the
ghost of Hamlet's father in *Hamlet*; Brutus, Cassius, and Marc
Antony in *Julius Caesar*; Mercutio, Tybalt, and Chorus in *Romeo and
Juliet*; Malvolio and Orsino in *Twelfth Night*; and Shylock and the
Prince of Morocco in *Merchant of Venice*, often in the same productions (Peter Conrad suggests some deep-rooted egomania here,
rather than simple expediency, as if this kind of "multitasking" had
not been common on the Elizabethan stage).

Welles had even imagined an original dialogue with the Bard
himself, as a prologue to the *Twelfth Night* album, in which he
became the famous actor-producer Burbage. Only in one play, *Mac-*

beth, did he confine himself to a single part, and only on the fourth Mercury Text Record. On the stage, his fabled 1936 all-black "voodoo" production, under the auspices of the Works Project Administration, was the one theatrical Shakespearean production where Welles confined himself to directing.

By this point Welles was already the coauthor of a series of performance texts of Shakespeare plays (with his schoolmaster Roger Todd), produced initially in a private printing as *Everybody's Shakespeare*, then reprinted in the late 1930s as *The Mercury Shakespeare*. The plays presented in this format were *Julius Caesar*, *Twelfth Night*, and *The Merchant of Venice*. Welles, a precocious nineteen-year-old at the time, wrote a general introduction to staging Shakespeare, sketched the various illustrations, and presumably played his part in presenting a stageable version after Roger Hill had "blazoned away with a discreet and scholarly blue pencil."

From Hill, Welles seems to have acquired the belief that only by judicious trimming could one make "a popular presentation of Shakespeare." However, neither party was looking to bowdlerize the plays. Welles clearly states, in his essay "On Staging Shakespeare," "Dung isn't really dirty until you talk about it inside a house and it's fairly hard to be obscene out in the sunshine. But when the theater went hopelessly indoors . . . it became almost as immoral as the Puritans thought it was."

Macbeth, the theatrical version of which Welles liked to characterize as his greatest success, continued to occupy him even after he took off for Hollywood. It was the briefest of Bill's tragedies, and therefore requiring of the least blue pencil. It was also apparently the only Shakespeare play Welles thought could work as a Hollywood movie. He had told *Modern Screen* in April 1940, when Mankiewicz was still hard at work in Victorville, "I'm doubtful about Shakespeare for the movies. For while the movies do most everything better than the stage, they don't do verse better. But *Macbeth* and its gloomy moors might be grand. A perfect cross between *Wuthering Heights* and *The Bride of Frankenstein*." Even if we take this as an off-the-cuff comparison, elements of both genres, stormy romance and high camp melodrama, can be found in Welles's version of the tragedy.

And yet the audio version he recorded that month, for the fourth and last Mercury Text Record, hardly lent itself to such a cinematic synthesis, though it does retain many of the supernatural aspects of the 1936 production. Perhaps the aspect of that album whose absence Welles most keenly felt in the 1947 film was the immensely effective musical score by Bernard Herrmann. The 1940 album also allowed Welles-the-actor to concentrate solely on the words and, as Michael Anderegg observes, "he gives to the major soliloquies greater intensity and emotional variety than he [does] in the film."

For the next seven years, though, Shakspeer, Welles's first and foremost dramatic love, was sidelined, as was Welles's theatrical career, save for the triumphant *Native Son* in 1941 and the catastrophic *Around the World in Eighty Days* in 1946. His thoughts did not turn to the Bard's plays again until the winter of 1947, while finishing his own exasperating part in the postproduction of *The Lady from Shanghai*. At this time Welles and the Mercury received a request to present one of his famous Shakespearean productions at the Edinburgh Drama Festival. His thoughts didn't turn at first to *Macbeth*—nor any of the other Mercury Shakespeare texts—but rather to *The Tragedy of Othello: The Moor*. What Welles had in mind was to rehearse a production in the United States, put it on at the drama festival, and then film it on stage in color, releasing the result as a movie presentation. It was a radical, but not unprecedented idea. The Marx Brothers' first movie, *The Cocoanuts*, was a film of their stage show; and newsreel footage exists of the WPA production of *Macbeth* (which conveys some of the power the production must have held).

Welles hoped to convince British producer Sir Alexander Korda that the idea was sound enough for him to raise the necessary funding. Korda and Welles had been discussing ways of working together since the summer of 1946. They had actually entered into a three-film agreement in September 1946, worth $75,000 plus 10 percent of the producer's gross per picture to Welles. All they had to do now was agree on a movie. Korda continued to flatter Welles's ego with suggestions of suitable classics, having been obliged, in clause nine of their agreement, to legally recognize that the services Welles was offering were "of a special, unique, unusual, extraordinary, and intellectual character." A live shoot of *Othello*, though, represented too great a risk for Korda, and any formal collaboration between the gregarious pair was again held at bay by the ever-equivocating producer.

Meanwhile, Welles had received another offer to present Shakespeare on stage, and this one was not o'er the hills and far away. By the time it was announced that he would be directing and performing a Shakespearean tragedy at the Utah Centennial Festival at the end of May, it was *Macbeth* that was on offer, not the more demanding *Othello*. He undoubtedly realized that he already had the raw material to draw upon for a production of *Macbeth*, whereas *Othello* meant starting from scratch. He may also have believed that *Macbeth* presented the more viable commercial venture, at least when film and funds came from the States. Yet he had not entirely abandoned the idea of filming what was effectively a stage production of Shakespeare. He just planned to do it more along the lines of the second Marx Brothers movie, *Animal Crackers*, i.e. a cinematic representation of a stage play, but not actually shot "on stage."

Welles managed to convince a Hollywood studio to go along with his idea in surprisingly quick order, thanks to his good friend agent-producer Charles K. Feldman, who convinced Republic Pictures to come up with a B-movie budget for this off-the-wall project. Since Republic Pictures almost exclusively produced B movies, usually from the adventure or western genres, it seemed at first glance a bizarre alliance. But studio head Herbert J. Yates was prepared to do what no other more resourceful studio would—take a gamble on Welles. The "gamble," like Sam Spiegel's on *The Stranger*, was offset by many contractual restrictions—in this case largely budgetary—but Yates was hoping that a Welles version of a Shakespeare play might bring some much-needed credibility to the studio. And the sums involved hardly represented a mortgage on the entire studio's future.

For Welles, the $700,000 budget was quite a comedown. He was not as yet used to such restraints. His four movies to date had all received what one might typify as A-movie budgets (along with A-movie interference). What tipped the balance in Republic's favor was that for all their parsimony they *were* prepared to give Welles the right to the final cut—though not the final, final cut, as it happens. Welles personally stood to make $100,000 if the film came in on budget, but he was obliged to agree that any amount over $700,000 he would pay himself, presumably from his cut. The challenge was immense, but once again Welles hoped that he might "have a great success with it and . . . be allowed to do all kinds of difficult things as long as they were cheap." In his self-referential 1979 documentary *Filming Othello*, he claimed that he was "*gambling* [my italics] on [it] being a great success," suggesting that *Macbeth* was from the very first intended as a last roll of the Hollywood dice.

No longer sure what might work commercially, Welles was relying on the fact that *Macbeth* had been a great success for him once before. His idea was for the film to have "the same basic plan" as the voodoo production—"because it had worked." This was also undoubtedly how the scheme had been pitched to Republic studio head Yates. As it happens, though the WPA production *had* been a great success, it was despite the critics, not because of them. The "voodoo" *Macbeth* had drawn its fair share of barbs from harping (often overtly racist) theater critics. In keeping with most, the *New York Times'* Brooks Atkinson damned with faint praise aspects of the WPA production of this "voodoo show inspired by . . . *Macbeth*," while accusing the director of "miss[ing] the sweep and scope of a poetic tragedy." It was an accusation that would haunt the film far more than the play.

Welles, though, never subscribed to the notion of a perfect template to a Shakespeare play. As far back as *Everybody's Shakespeare*, he "doubt[ed] if there ever was a production of a play by Shakespeare, however expensively authentic . . . that was entirely worthy of its play." He believed, always, in the radicalization of these sacred texts, feeling that any great failure should be as wittingly embraced as the "great success." He said as much, and more, in a 1945 review of Margaret Webster's production of what was apparently his favorite Shakespeare play, *The Tempest* (a subtext to his comments about Webster can certainly be found by anyone who considers the unfavorable comparisons made by critics of his 1939 *Five Kings* production to Ms. Webster's acclaimed, but now forgotten, 1937 staging of *Henry IV*):

> Every season for quite some time now Margaret Webster has presented our theater with at least one Shakespearean revival. None of these productions has been very original or remarkable in any way, but all of them have met with unqualified success. Indeed, I think Miss Webster has avoided bad notices too long for her own good. . . . It's hard to resist Miss Webster's work, because she is a skilled and careful craftsman and has never presented anything to the public which is perfectly terrible. As a producer who has offered something perfectly terrible even more frequently than he's been panned in the press, I regard that infallibility with envy. . . . I really think Miss Webster ought to prove her merit as an artist by perpetrating an occasional flop. For this exception I . . . have nominated [her version of] *The Tempest* . . . [because] I [just] don't think charm is an adequate substitute for enchantment. I believe that *The Tempest* on the stage should be something between a magic show and a ballet.

Welles remained a man ever looking for that "enchantment." He also believed that he had the right to produce "something perfectly terrible" in the medium of his choice. As he once told Huw Wheldon, "If you take a serious view of filmmaking, you have to consider that films are not an illustration or an interpretation of a work, but quite as worthwhile as the original. . . . Film should not be a fully illustrated, all talking, all moving version of a printed work, but should be *itself*, a thing [in and] of itself."

With the Republic *Macbeth*, Welles was at his most radical, some would say un-Shakespearean. As Michael Anderegg suggests, "[He] retains just enough of Shakespeare's words to allow communication among the major characters, but not enough to maintain the verse structure, the texture of [Shakespeare's] poetic language." In this approach he was being wholly consistent, given that all three the-atrical productions to date—*Macbeth*, *(Julius) Caesar*, and *Five Kings*—had taken enormous liberties with the structure of the plays. In the case of *Caesar* he reduced the five-act play to a single act, which ran without an intermission.

Addressing the issue of authenticity many years later, while hard at work on his last Shakespearean film, *Chimes at Midnight*, Welles admitted to Kenneth Tynan that he was, "naturally . . . going to offend the kind of Shakespeare lover whose main concern is the sacredness of the text," even though no one dare criticize Verdi for "radically changing Shakespeare" (to the extent that he inserts a self-justifying soliloquy from Iago into his opera *Otello*). At this point Welles turns on Olivier, who he suggests "has made fine Shake-spearean movies that are essentially [just] filmed Shakespearean plays." He, on the other hand, does something entirely different and, by implication, far more daring, *"I use Shakespeare's words and char-acters to make motion pictures."*

With his 1947 *Macbeth*, the focus was on Macbeth himself, as Welles allowed himself no latitude for diversions, either textually or thematically. Critic Michael Mullin feels that, "by allowing Mac-beth's nightmare vision to control his setting and his cinematic tech-nique, Welles kept much of the play's eerie atmosphere, but almost wholly lost the sense of good and evil warring within a man's soul." It was a sacrifice Welles felt obliged to make in order to retain the primitivism and power in his necessarily condensed film "inspired by the Macbeth legend." As he snapped to one interviewer imperti-nent enough to question his judgment on *Macbeth*, "If I find a way of creating a primitivism which moves the public, which communi-cates with them, . . . why not do it?" Why not indeed?

Where Welles was more faithful to Shakespeare was in the set that he devised for his motion picture of *Macbeth*. Andre Bazin accused Welles of choosing "to recreate a universe that was artificial in every particular, a world closed in on its own incompleteness, like a grotto." Some (such as Michael Anderegg) have suggested a deliberate cheapness to "the film's *mise en scene* [which thus] calls into question the worth of Macbeth's ambition." In fact, Welles preferred to depict his *Macbeth* as "the first drama to be shot against abstract backgrounds. These sets could be nearly anywhere—or nowhere." He is here reiterating a view first expressed in print when he was just a teenager, "Poetry [in plays] has since [the Restoration and its opulent theaters] been neither necessary nor possible. . . . The Restoration chose to be literal, and because poetry is its own scenery, and because we've stuck to physical scenery . . . and thus isolated emotional excitement in the theater from the element of beauty, we've stuck to prose."

Welles's belief that the more the camera conveyed a glamorized reality the less it was able to concentrate on "*le sens* poetry" evidently sprung from a wide historical base. Where the challenge lay, after just four days of performances in Utah, and a further three weeks of rehearsals, was in complementing Shakespeare's gilded turns of phrase visually. The stark set, in its unvarying blackness and jagged ziggurats, was just part of Welles's design, though an important one. It enabled John L. Russell to photograph the characters surrounded by an unremitting darkness, without shade or relief.

For Welles, the play itself was black and white. Michael Mullin may consider "his depiction of Macbeth as the victim of the witches' powerful malevolence . . . reduc[ing] the play's complex moral issues to the neat black-and-white ethics of melodrama," but that appears to have been the director's precise intent. He believed that he could combine Gothic fiction and Elizabethan tragedy, as his comment to *Modern Screen* in 1940 suggests, using familiar motifs "to foreground what I thought was represented in the play."

In the 1936 production and especially the 1947 film, the key motif was "the struggle between the old and new religions." Welles had always painted the witches in particular as "represent[ing the] ancient religion, paganism," which had been "suppressed by Christianity." As Naremore notes this struggle is represented in the movie by two emblems, the Celtic cross representing Christianity and "the satanic forked staffs [the creed] of the witches." In the final battle we actually see the attacking army as a sea of crosses on long poles (also a cunning way of dispensing with a large number of expensive extras). Where Welles departs from his original theatrical template in the film is in the composite character he created—from other minor figures in Shakespeare—to represent this Christian value system. The Holy Father is no mere observer, but is made part of the endemic savagery and at the end is singled out for death by a Macbeth who senses his own time approaching.

As the bloody battle resolves itself, Macbeth attempts to place the responsibility for events at the door of the witches, crying, "Be these juggling fiends no more believed." But the fact that Macbeth believes he has been "juggled" by these witchy fiends in no way exculpates his deeds, at least in Welles's mind. The director does not perceive Macbeth to be a helpless vessel of fate, held in thrall by the witches' prophecies. Rather, he chooses to portray him as essentially "always a weakling," forever bound by wills greater than his own, whether his wife's or the weird sisters'.

Such was Welles's radical conceit. With a few subtle refinements of the 1936 production, and a few cinematic tricks, he carefully planned out how he could shoot the entire play in twenty-three days. Work began on the Republic lot on June 23, 1947. Richard Wilson, who would receive an associate producer credit on the film, informed *Theatre Arts* that the film was "a project in which preparation, mainly in the form of the stage presentation at Utah, and ten solid months of love, work, and tremendous ingenuity . . . was used instead of money which we didn't have." Much of that "tremendous ingenuity" was expended after the shoot, but Welles had learned from *It's All True* that it was important to leave as many options as possible open at the editing stage.

Welles devised a way of working within the restrictions effectively and economically. One rather ingenious innovation was the use of light, hand-held Eyemo cameras by members of the crew who were asked to join the throng and shoot any close-ups during the battle scenes, while Welles simultaneously supervised those trademarked long shots. In order to disguise these interlopers, he obliged them to wear reversed doublets and masks on their heads so that as long as they kept their backs to the main camera, they would blend into the shot. Welles also often ran three main cameras simultaneously. Jeanette Nolan, who held the challenging role of Lady Macbeth, told Charles Higham of how "there were sixty camera moves in one day, and everyone on the crew had said they could not be done. But he won everyone over with his camera brilliance; he held the crew spellbound."

Where Welles really radically reinvented his working methodology, though, was in his use of the long take. What had previously been an expensive exercise that brought him into conflict with even the more financially sound studios became, in *Macbeth*, a means of economizing. Abandoning the kind of intricate racking and reframing that had made *Heart of Darkness* impractical, Welles simply repositioned the actors "in the frame in relation to each other, chang[ing] from foreground action to background action, smoothly panning tracking and craning, though within a limited area" [BW]. In the case of one memorable sequence, the murder of Duncan, Welles's long take lasts a whole ten-minute reel, with the camera "guiding" the spectator as if at an especially large stage production of the play.

Richard France, in his *Orson Welles on Shakespeare*, also finds the continuing influence of Eisenstein, especially in the film's editing, and "nowhere is this more evident than in the scene depicting the execution of the erstwhile Thane of Cawdor—a scene that is not to be found either in Shakespeare or in Welles's script for the 'voodoo' *Macbeth*. Vertical, spaced staves carried by horsemen wearing circular horned headdresses are intercut with crowded round drums . . . A final thundering beat of the drums signals that the axe has fallen."

Macbeth was dead on schedule, July 17, 1947. After completing the filming, Welles almost immediately took off for Europe, and the prospect of a couple of lucrative acting paydays. In his own eyes he had achieved what he had set out to do, even if his "violently sketched charcoal drawing" (as he described the 1947 *Macbeth* to

246 ACT TWO: HOPE

an audience in Edinburgh in 1952) was never going to be "entirely worthy" of this "great play." The studio, though, was used to having their movies promptly edited, in the ubiquitous Hollywood style, and then dispatched into the movie houses to recoup their up-front costs. They were less than amused when Welles displayed a certain lack of urgency about the editing.

The Republic *Macbeth,* in Welles's mind, had never been anything more than a stopgap measure. In fairness to Welles, he probably did not want *Macbeth* appearing in movie theaters before the altogether more ambitious *Lady from Shanghai,* still undergoing its final Columbia cut—short, back, and sides. He had also once again been led to believe that Korda was ready to begin honoring their signed agreement.

In the end, on November 25, 1947, Republic took the hint and sent the unedited footage and a cutter to Rome so that Welles could supervise the "final cut," as specified in his contract. It would be the following March before the cutter returned, carrying what Welles still considered a "rough cut," having provided the cutter with a list of further changes he required made before the film's long awaited debut. This occurred on October 7, 1948, in Boston, where his disastrous production of *Around the World in Eighty Days* had opened eighteen months earlier.

Citizen Kane excepted, Welles could never be depicted as one of American critics' more favored sons, and the *Macbeth* reviews were predictably mixed. Unfortunately, among those who knew not what to praise and what to slam was a particularly vicious review in *Life* magazine, under the caption, "Orson Welles doth foully slaughter Shakespeare in a dialect version of his Tragedy of *Macbeth*." Never explaining what s/he means by "a dialect version," the anonymous reviewer depicts the film as little more than "a jumble of gallopings and sweaty close-ups and fog and bubbling cauldrons."

Another periodical that consistently welcomed any opportunity to give Welles a kicking, the *Hollywood Reporter,* joined in the fun, describing *Macbeth* as "one of the most disastrous of motion picture enterprises." Some in Hollywood thought Welles had done irreparable damage to his reputation. David Selznick attempted to dissuade Alexander Korda from casting Welles as Harry Lime in Carol Reed's *The Third Man* on the grounds that "one of the greatest disasters of all time in show business . . . [has now made Welles] far more of a damaging name than he has been in our worst fears to date."

Comparisons with Olivier's contemporaneous *Hamlet*—against which it was supposed to have competed at the Venice Film Festival in September 1948—undoubtedly hurt the film. Welles had in fact withdrawn his own entry on learning that the grand international prize was already earmarked for Olivier. He always resented any comparison made between what he saw as little more than a "filmed Shakespearean play" and his own, self-consciously radicalized interpretation. Nor did he appreciate the fact that "nobody seem[ed] to judge the picture on its own grounds: as an experiment achieved in twenty-three days and on an extremely low budget."

The select savagery of *Life* prompted an emboldened Herbert J. Yates to insist that the film was reedited before it went on general release. This decision appears to have found a welcome ally in the film's producer, and supposed friend of Welles, Charles Feldman. It was Feldman who sent a long memo suggesting that Lady Macbeth's first scene be cut because "she looks horrible and frightening, and everyone who has seen the picture, on the many occasions I have run it, was appalled at the looks of the girl. In her next scene she looks infinitely better—as a matter of fact she looks damned attractive, and I think this next scene is an infinitely better opening for Lady Macbeth. The soliloquy we lose may be of some importance, but I think it is of greater benefit to have the right opening for the girl." Feldman, who spoke the language of Hollywood, had little time for the one preferred by Shakespeare.

Thankfully, Welles's contract still gave him some say in the film's fate, and he insisted—successfully—that this "unimportant" soliloquy stay in. According to Richard Wilson, Feldman seemed to have memorized the *Life* review by heart, and spouted it whenever a view opposed to his own reared its head. As a result Welles was obliged to recut the film, losing a further twenty-six minutes from an already compact tragedy. The most brutal single cut was probably the one in which Macbeth instructed two of his thugs to murder Banquo, already singled out by *Life* in its laserlike critique.

More maddeningly still, the studio demanded that much of the dialogue be re-recorded, as the Scotch burr utilized for the, er, Scottish play sounded to one particular cretin at *Life* magazine like "the accents of Sir Harry Lauder on the vaudeville stage." As Anderegg properly concludes, "The criticism [by *Life*], taken so much to heart by Republic executives, . . . now seems incredibly petty and obtuse, underlining the irrational dislike Welles seemed to draw upon himself."

This time Welles's relocation to Europe worked to his disadvantage as he found that, save for his own role, he was unable to impose any real authority on the nature and scope of these overdubs. One memo fired off to the studio executives (presumably including Feldman)—and cited by Anderegg in his study of the film—shows Welles letting his feelings be known in no uncertain terms:

> When [Jeanette] Nolan moves from the Scottish speech (*in which she had been rehearsed*) to what she considers normal speech for Shakespeare, her vocal tone moves at least an octave upwards, and the entire personality of Lady Macbeth vanishes. . . . Her success in the role of Lady Macbeth was entirely based on her intelligence and on the vocal authority which informed and underlined the playing of all her big scenes. The unfortunate Montana whine, wheeze and scrape completely nullify this authority.

Welles had doubtless already surmised that such complaints would be disregarded, and this time one really does begin to sense this is someone who wished to wash his hands (sic) of the whole affair. He never shook the idea that the film was a failure—"the biggest critical failure I ever had"—even though among Europe's finest directors Welles's *Macbeth* was championed precisely because it offered far more challenges than Olivier's predictable effort. Marcel Carné, director of the equally challenging *Les Enfants du Paradis*, was in no doubt "that *Macbeth* has [the] greater cinematographic qualities"; but it was Jean Cocteau who provided perhaps the most incisive critique of all:

> Welles' *Macbeth* leaves the spectator [feeling] deaf and blind, and I can well believe that the people who like it . . . are few and far between. . . . [But] he wanted to retain a certain theatrical style, as proof that cinematography can put any work of art under its magnifying glass and dispense with the rhythm commonly supposed to be that of cinema.

Ironically, the film ended up making a profit, despite the unnecessary expense incurred due to the studio's reediting and redubbing. And, in the last decade and a half—since Republic turned up an authentically murky print of the original 112-minute version and issued it on video, laser disc, and DVD—the 1950 version has all but passed into oblivion, leaving Welles's original edit to become the standard-bearer for his first cinematic vision of Shakespeare.

◆　◆　◆　◆

On his second Shakespearean sortie Welles would not have to make any such concession to the studio system. It was time to do his own thing, even if he still required the studios to fund his first independent directorial venture, through the artificially inflated fees he demanded to play cameo roles that most actors of his caliber were unwilling to. Those roles, in the period between *Macbeth* and his sixth and final Hollywood movie, actually produced some of Welles's most entertaining, even defining performance as an actor. They also continued to make his name "bankable" when his directorial skills were not.

None of these cameos ever had quite the same effect as his Harry Lime in Carol Reed's *The Third Man*. It was Andre Bazin who made the point that though Welles "is on screen for only ten minutes [in the film], [he] . . . polarizes the whole moral meaning of *The Third Man* like iron filings around a magnet." Welles, though, never considered this small, but choice, part in Reed's film as more than another way of reminding producer Alexander Korda of his ongoing obligation to come through on their three-picture agreement, on which he pinned so many hopes in the mid-to-late 1940s.

It was this agreement that ultimately explains why Welles got the part of Lime over coproducer David Selznick's oft-voiced objections; and why Welles viewed it as just a building block in a relationship he was hoping to cultivate for some time to come. Korda had already advanced Welles moneys from their September 1946 agreement that he knew he would never see again if—as he was beginning to suspect—they never got a joint project off the ground. Indeed, Korda appears to have been partially funding Welles's extravagant lifestyle in Italy, presumably with the expectation that such sums would prove recoupable. Charles Drazin suggests, in his highly subjective history of the making of The Third Man, that Korda sanctioned payment through his production company's Italian office in April 1948—several months before The Third Man entered production—of three million lire to cover Welles's living expenses in Italy. According to Drazin, "Welles grossly abused this arrangement, diverting all his various bills, whether for hotels, film stock, or cigars, to London Films, with no obvious intention to pay them. Korda was happy to indulge Welles so long as there was a use for him, but began to tighten the purse strings once Welles had safely completed his role in The Third Man." So who exactly was using whom?

Welles played hard to get, proving almost as elusive as Lime himself, ducking out of hotels and onto trains, boats, and planes to avoid Korda's emissary. This was partially to make Korda aware that two could play this game; but also because he hardly saw Harry Lime as a central role in his career, and just wanted to see how much he might be permitted to get away with before he agreed to play the part. He was presumably unaware that Selznick wanted him replaced by Rex Harrison, and that Korda's implication that Welles had already signed to the role and that the role was open to him was one of Korda's little white lies. When he finally arrived on set and shook hands with his old friend Joe Cotten, there to play Reed's version of the blundering innocent abroad, he immediately began to make suggestions about his own dialogue.

The debate about the extent of Welles's input into *The Third
Man* has become largely detached from the merits of each director
on set at the time. Welles himself, contrary to Drazin's slant, never
suggested he directed his own scenes in *The Third Man* and repeatedly praised Reed as a "real director with a fine visual sense." His one
"criticism" of Reed, that he had "less sense of the architecture of a
plot," was Welles's way of relating Reed to his own sense of craft, a
compliment in itself given his usual view of contemporaries. Pointing out the one area where he felt his own strengths outweighed
Reed's hardly amounts to a denigration of the British director. Only
Drazin, who seriously suggests in *In Search of The Third Man* that
"Reed was Welles' equal as a director," might summon up the nerve
to disagree.

Unfortunately for Drazin, it is precisely this exquisite sense of a
film's architecture that certain cineasts find in *The Third Man*, but
nowhere else in Reed's work. Harlan Kennedy argues, in "Shadow of
a Debt," while exploring similarities between *The Third Man* and
Touch of Evil, that "for reasons we may never know, Carol Reed, who
was a craftsman-director, became infected with Welles's greatness/
madness in *The Third Man*. There is some baroque in *The Fallen Idol*,
some noir in *Odd Man Out*, some skewy angles and visual angst in
The Man Between . . . But the 'somes' in Reed don't add up to a
vision. The exception is *The Third Man*. Did Reed unprompted . . .
conceive the camera pushing through the flowers in Valli's window
toward the soon-to-be-Lime-visited night street? There is no
moment like it in any other Reed work. But there are many moments
like it in Welles."

I would argue that Lime's memorable debut finds a clear parallel in the scene in *The Stranger* shooting script where Meinike has a
vision of sorts on the streets of South America (see pp. 176–7).
Deleted from the film itself, it cannot have directly affected Reed.
Yet Welles describes that "Lime entrance scene" as "pure Carol." If
so, Michael Anderegg's belief that there are instances where Welles's

overbearing "presentation of self . . . in fact become[s] a form of direction, a way of imposing himself on the film," finds its purest vindication in this very scene.

For Welles, though, *The Third Man* was merely a lucrative diversion from his own project, a film version of *Othello*, the very project Korda had passed on eighteen months earlier. In fact, it could have been a lot more lucrative, almost single-handedly financing his second Shakespeare film. Though Korda was distancing himself from any actual collaboration with Welles, he still had that original September 1946 contract hanging over him. The only way to resolve it was to use Welles's services as an actor, and as early as June 1947 there is a reference in a list of provisional London Film productions to "a photoplay, as yet untitled, to be directed by Carol Reed, starring Orson Welles." *The Third Man*, this was not. The problem for Korda was that the terms of that contract with Welles, if applied to a mere acting part (and a cameo at that), were extremely generous. Welles stood to make not only a $75,000 fee for playing Harry Lime, but 10 percent of the producer's [i.e. Korda's] *gross* receipts. Though this wouldn't have included a share of the U.S. gross, which belonged to Selznick, it could still have solved many of Welles's financial problems, at the least in the short term.

To Korda's immense relief, when Welles turned up for filming he asked for a flat fee of $100,000 instead. Over the years the impression has been given that the actor was short of funds to start work on *Othello*, and so took an extra $25,000 instead of 10 percent of the gross on one of the most successful films of the era (Drazin makes this very faux pas). In fact, at the time that he was shooting *The Third Man*, Welles still believed he did not need to raise money to make his *Othello* because an Italian studio was interested. He just didn't think Reed's film would be a big hit. As he later ruefully observed to Barbara Leaming, "Picture grossed, you know, something unbelievable." This single decision meant that he would be living a feast-to-famine existence for much of the four years it would take him to complete his first independent film. Needless to say, he and Korda never did get to make that movie together.

ACT THREE:
CHARITY

THE JIGSAW PICTURES

[*Othello* and *Mr. Arkadin*]

I have lost years and years of my life fighting for the right to
do things my own way, and mostly fighting in vain. . . . Among
the pictures I have made I can only accept full responsibility
for one: *Citizen Kane*. In all the others I have been more or
less muzzled, and the narrative line of my stories . . . ruined
by commercially minded people. I came to Europe because in
Hollywood there was not the slightest chance for me (or for
anybody, at that) to obtain freedom of action.

Orson Welles, 1950

Such was Welles's "freedom of action" when he arrived in Italy in the summer of 1947 that he ended up directing parts of the movie in which he had come to play one of his cameos. *Black Magic* was the story of Cagliostro, an eighteenth-century French hypnotist. Aside from the $100,000 fee Welles demanded for playing the part, he apparently requested that he be allowed to direct his own scenes. Producer Edward Small agreed, and director Gregory Ratoff appears to have been too in awe of Welles to voice any opposition. One anecdote, related by Jackson Leighter to Leaming, suggests that Welles continued to "help out" even on scenes in which he had no personal involvement. Leighter arrived during the filming of a mob scene to find Welles barking orders from on top of a coach. Enquiring after Ratoff, Leighter was directed by Welles to the middle of the mob, where a fully costumed Ratoff was playing his part.

Despite all his previous trials and tribulations, Welles remained a commanding presence on set. His costar Nancy Guild, who played both Lorenza and Marie Antoinette in *Black Magic*, remembers that "he was extremely volatile. . . . Everything he said had an air of authority that made it sound true, even if it wasn't." She also found that Welles's moods seemed bound by whom she was playing that day, and whether his character was supposed to care for or deceive her. He seems to have been already preparing himself to browbeat some poor Desdemona into submission.

Much as Welles seems to have enjoyed hamming his way through this period piece, his mind was already working overtime on devising a film of *Othello*. And initially it looked like he would have the full backing of the most prestigious Italian studio, Scalera, based in Rome. The Italian producer Montatori Scalera had become dazzled by the Welles aura when he found him filming some scenes for *Black Magic* at the Italian producer's studio. He apparently informed Welles one day on the set, "We *have* to make *Othello*." Welles must have felt like he was reading his mind and began to plan out the production before he had even seen the color of Scalera's money. Welles later downplayed the seriousness of Scalera's intent, suggesting that the producer thought they were going to make a celluloid version of Verdi's *Otello*. This sounds highly unlikely. However, it may well be that Scalera's knowledge of the play was based almost entirely on Verdi's opera, and not Bill's original. As such, he would have found Welles's Iago a quite different creation from Verdi's.

Welles wanted none of Verdi's self-justification for the play's unregenerate villain. He greatly preferred what Samuel Coleridge called "the motiveless malignancy of Iago," a conceptual debt he acknowledged in his 1979 documentary, *Filming Othello*. In fact, Welles poured scorn on those who looked for Iago's motives in the text to the play. In a mid-1970s French television documentary, he insisted that he "agree[d] with Shakespeare: one doesn't need to provide [Iago] with motivations. . . . These days people simply don't believe in villains anymore. Since Freud, they think that *everyone* is sick!"

Again, Welles intended to "foreground" what he thought was there in the play in the first place. As he put it in *Filming Othello*, "The dizzying camera movements, the grotesque shadows and insane shadows, they are of Iago, for he is the agent of chaos." Welles had only recently played Shakespeare's prototype-by-proxy for Iago during his first year in Italy. Iago was originally conceived as the archetypal Machiavellian, a person for whom the end always justified the means.

The model for Machiavelli's *"il principe,"* in his famous political tract (which Shakespeare presumably read in translation), was Cesare Borgia, the most ruthless of those tin-pot princes who "divvied" up the many principalities that made up sixteenth-century Italy. And Welles had just delivered one of his most magnetic performances in *Prince of Foxes*, as the unregenerate Borgia, who tutors Tyrone Power's character, Orsini, in the politics of power play only for the latter to turn on him for love of a woman. Again Welles reveled in his role as villain of the piece, a cruel despot who was also an important patron to the true genius of the age, Da Vinci. He had, of course, just come up with his aphoristic summation of the Renaissance for the role of Harry Lime.

Interestingly, Welles's Borgia threatens Orsini with being suspended in an iron cage until he rots, the very fate which befalls Iago in his film (though not the play, which ends with his fate unresolved). Where the luxuriant Hollywood production also came in handy was in its gorgeous costumes, some of which were spirited off the set to reappear in *Othello*. The reason such "judicious borrowing" became necessary was that Welles almost immediately found himself with a script, a series of sketches, a crew, and a cast, but no studio to fund his second Shakespearean "experiment." Scalera had just gone bust:

> Orson Welles: Half a year of careful planning had to be thrown away. . . . Working together . . . over all those months, we designed a physical production in such a way that the entire picture [as conceived] had to be thrown away. . . . [It] would have been photographed in a relatively small number of camera set-ups. A whole scene, sometimes several scenes, would have been played without a single cut. But that method absolutely requires the full resources of a film studio. [1979]

The following day, back in the States, Mercury Productions lost all of its props and scenery to liquidators, after failing to pay the storage for more than a year. Richard Wilson jotted down a note on the relevant paperwork that said it all, "No dough among other things, so we lost it. End of an era."

Welles had a number of options, none of which held any immediate appeal. He could go back to Hollywood and play the part of the willing employee, go on playing unworthy roles abroad for inflated acting fees, or devise an entirely independent methodology that might yet establish a second career for him as a director. He chose the last two options, with the former funding the latter. If Hollywood was no longer the new frontier, he hoped that Europe— initially meaning Italy—might still prove to be so.

He expressed such a belief to an audience at the Edinburgh Festival in 1952, when he spoke of how "the new artist go[ing] out to Hollywood or Rome, or wherever it may be, may create something out of himself, something original . . . [but only] until the industrialists grow wise to him." He suspected that the studios had grown wise to his subversive ways. Unfortunately, as he admitted to the same audience, "being a filmmaker in the commercial world, and not in the documentary or avant-garde field, I need a million dollars to make a film. You have to be a businessman to handle a million dollars."

If there was one thing this extraordinarily multifaceted man was not, it was a businessman. For one thing, he held no great regard for making money (I'd like to think it was Welles who was responsible for that self-referential line in *Citizen Kane*, "It's very easy to make a lot of money, if all you want to do is make a lot of money"). Secondly, Welles never had the patience required to make the money men sweat. Witness the deal he made on *The Third Man*, which a night of restless thought would surely have convinced him made no sense.

Often Welles proved too anxious to get started, failing to work out in advance any kind of contingency plan *before* problems arose. With *Othello*, this had many hilarious consequences, but it also meant the process of filming was more tortuous than it needed to be. Only his sheer tenacity made him complete a film that seemed like another commercial blind alley for the man who once put the Hollywood train set to its greatest-ever use. But he was determined to prove a point, and this time he did.

His decision to continue with *Othello* even after Scalera's collapse was a typically Wellesian response to the vicissitudes of fate. He decided he had everything he needed to shoot the film—save money—and hoped against hope (and bitter experience) that he could get by until he found another backer. At this juncture, he certainly never conceived of making such a film himself. However, after a month of shooting, spanning the second half of June and part of July 1949, his own financial reserves were all gone and no backer had ridden over the horizon. Shooting was suspended, resulting in a "complete scattering of our forces," to quote Welles's Iago, Michael MacLiammoir, who now went from being Welles's first employer (as a teenage actor at Dublin's Gate Theatre) to his trusty employee.

Welles would have to suspend shooting on *Othello* a total of three times, on each occasion for between four and eight weeks, before completing filming, save for a handful of pickup shots, at the beginning of March 1950. The filming of *Othello* thus spanned almost nine months and involved the services of at least three Desdemonas: Lea Padovani, whom Welles claimed made him pay "for everything that I had ever done to women" in the nine months they were together, playing *him* for a cuckold much of the time; Cecile Aubry, direct from *The Black Rose*, who soon made her excuses; and Suzanne Cloutier. It also required at least two friends of sorts to become reluctant investors in the project.

The first investor Welles cajoled into contributing toward the fast-depleted coffers was one of those ubiquitous Russian millionaires whose fortune seemed to have a shady past (providing a possible inspiration for Welles's next antihero, Gregory Arkadin). Michel Olian, now relocated to Italy, initially played host to the ever-grateful Welles, who eventually summoned up the nerve to ask for a "loan" of $35,000, in return for a 50 percent general ownership of the film. Olian may have thought he had been made an offer he could not refuse, but in Welles's world, it was in for a penny, in for a pound. Olian would end up investing closer to $200,000 in the project before he actually had a claim on a commercial property.[*]

---

[*] It would appear that these percentage rights only applied until the loans had been repaid. Rights did subsequently revert back to Welles, and ultimately his executors, hence the 1992 restoration.

Using the proceeds of *Prince of Foxes* and a second Hollywood blockbuster with Tyrone Power, *The Black Rose* (which was filmed in North Africa between bouts of directing), Welles just about kept his Shakespearean ship from sinking for good off the coast of Morocco. But he was still obliged to take money from his purse, until it inevitably ran out again, and he was obliged to track down Hollywood producer Daryl Zanuck, then on holiday in Italy, and beg him for a "loan" of $75,000. A bemused Zanuck arranged for the money to be delivered (in sacks), and Welles returned to Venice, having apparently offered Zanuck a 60 percent interest in a film from which he no longer had three-fifths to give (to quote Gene Wilder's character in *The Producers*, after Zero Mostel has sold 2,000 percent of *Springtime for Hitler*, "You can only have 100 percent of anything!"). Zanuck's surprisingly generous gesture was enough to ensure that filming was completed, but not completion of the film.

In the fullness of time the tortuous nine-month filming process, which must have tried Welles's willpower in spades, became embellished by ever-more apocryphal delays and production difficulties, culminating in the legend of a four-year stint filming *Othello*. In fact, it was the *editing* of the film that would occupy Welles for two and a half of those years and would also try the patience of a number of Italy's finest film editors. Like a self-taught musician who finally feels the need to read the stuff s/he recites, Welles had decided to relearn his craft. The main result—aside from *Othello* itself—was an ever-more demanding perfectionist at the Moviola. In *Filming Othello*, he explained the aesthetic that he began to develop into an articulate theory while editing his first independent film:

> Movies aren't just made on the set. A lot of the actual making happens [with] a Moviola—[something that is] almost as important as a camera. . . . There's a rhythmic structure, there's counterpoint, harmony and dissonance [to] a film. [It] is never right until it's right musically. The Moviola is a musical instrument.

This new hands-on approach to editing may have been prompted in part by the damage that editors like Bob Wise, Ernest

Nims, and Viola Lawrence had inflicted on his films' "rhythmic structure," but it was also a necessary response to the economics of independent filmmaking. As he later expressed to *Cahiers du Cinema*, "It's more economical to make one image, then this image and then that image, and try to control them later in the editing studio. Obviously I would prefer to control the elements in front of the camera while I'm filming, but that requires money and the confidence of your sponsors."

Beginning with *Othello*, Welles self-consciously constructed a cinematic language that derived its terms from the musical and poetic forms he held dear. He also began to adopt a consistent vocabulary in interviews for what it was that he was trying to achieve. He had this to say to one interviewer, "With me the visual is a solution to what the poetic and musical form dictates. I don't begin with the visual and then try to find a poetry or music, and try to stick it in the picture. The picture has to follow it." To another, "I believe that the cinema should be essentially poetic." And to a third, "I'm looking for a precise rhythm between one frame and the next . . . for me, that's essential—the beat."

In his contemporary diagram of the major branches of cinema, Welles made "poets" one of his four categories (into which he put Chaplin, Murnau, Renoir, Flaherty, and De Sica, yet perversely placed himself elsewhere, as a nonclassifiable heir to D. W. Griffith and Eisenstein). Two aspects music and poetry share are rhythm and phrasing. Both are much in evidence in Welles's *Othello*, as William Johnson makes clear in his important essay, "Orson Welles: Of Time and Loss":

> The beginning of the [film's] action has a staccato rhythm as Iago and Roderigo follow Othello and Desdemona to their wedding and then rouse Brabantio. Calm is restored when Othello comes to justify his marrying Desdemona. But from this point on the staccato rhythm associated with Iago gradually imposes itself on Othello's stately rhythm, and the increasing complexity of the film's movements suggests the increasing turmoil of doubt in Othello's mind.

For Welles "*le sens* poetry" (and the poetry of film was never confined to mere dialogue) was more crucial than either narrative or dramatic development. He defined it in these terms, "Poetry should make your hair stand up on your skin, should suggest things, [should] evoke more than you see." Here he sought to graft the Brechtian notion of "what is *natural* . . . hav[ing] the force of what is startling" to Robert Graves's definition of "true" poetry—"the hairs stand on end . . . a shiver runs down the spine when one writes or reads a true poem." Jack Jorgens, in his 1976 essay, "Welles's *Othello*: A Baroque Translation," suggests that it is precisely Welles's attempt to apply "*le sens* poetry" to the film's visuals—establishing a new relationship between the image and the word—that prompted such diametrically opposed reactions on its release:

> It has been said that Welles's most notable achievement as a film-maker is his attempt to invest each shot with an impact and surprise which are greater than any relationship the shot bears to the dramatic content of the film. People who dislike Welles's *Othello* do so for this very reason. . . . On the other hand, those who find Welles's *Othello* a great film respond to it as poetry of the screen, a film whose style is much closer to the essence of Shakespeare than . . . [more] respectful adaptations.*

Jean Cocteau has recalled Welles telling him on one occasion "that the beauty of a film escaped ears and eyes, and did not depend on dialogue—or machines; that even with poor projection and poor sound it should not be possible to harm its rhythm." If ever a film tested this theory it was *Othello*, a film in which, by the director's own admission, "there was no way for the jigsaw picture to be put together *except in my mind* [my italics]." It was also dogged by sound problems that were never entirely resolved, in part because Welles

---

*Jack Jorgens's essay evidently struck a chord with Welles, as he adopted much of its point of view when making his 1979 documentary *Filming Othello*.

had to overdub a number of actor's voices himself and, without studio resources, the glitches sometimes remain rather audible.

For those brought up on the more prosaic Hollywood model,
Welles's *Othello* represented quite a shock. Charles Higham, his
first serious biographer, never got over it, suggesting that "In America the interior of Welles's films is as intricate as that of a prizewin-
ning watch; in Europe the springs hang out," a comment that can
be partially applied to *Othello* (and entirely applied to *Mr. Arkadin*),
but not really to the three movies Welles went on to make in the
1960s. As Michael Anderegg brings out in his own discussion on
Othello,

> Many of these supposed problems [with the film] can be attributed to
> intentionality. . . . In some sequences . . . the sound is not simply mis-
> matched; rather, the visual track and the sound track are deliberately
> conceived as *separate* entities. When, for example, Othello requires of
> Iago "oracular proof" of his wife's betrayal, Welles appears not to be
> speaking at all. Othello's lines are delivered when his back is to the
> camera, [which in fact] contributes to the [idea] that . . . his language
> is divorced from his essential self.

In this sense the 1992 "restoration" of the film—which "corrected" some of the supposed soundtrack problems, and rescored
other parts—is a revisionist view of Welles's "true" intentions,
adopting an aesthetic some way removed from the director's.
Indeed, it more closely resembles the Hollywood model, i.e. "that
acting should be psychologically credible, naturalistic, and invisible;
that a soundtrack exists primarily to support and clarify the images
and the narrative; [and] that the conventions of classical cinema,
transparency, coherence, clarity, motivated action, must be adhered
to" [MA].

With *Othello*, Welles became concerned not so much by what
could be put into his films as what he should end up leaving out,
arguing that "what you have to do is . . . evoke, to incant, to raise
up things which are not really there. . . . The interior conception of

the auteur, above all, must have a single shape."* In the case of *Othello*, that "single shape" sought to align visual poetics with Shakespeare's high-flown turns of phrase, creating a work that was baroque across every media.

To achieve such a departure Welles was obliged to draw shamelessly on the rich architecture of the Mediterranean cities themselves, relieving him of any need to build sets he could ill afford and ensuring that *his* film had none of the redolent artifice of big-budget Hollywood productions like *Black Magic* and *Prince of Foxes*. Yet this self-styled auteur preferred to downplay the creative largesse available to *any* director on set. In later years he claimed that "a great deal of what is applauded as creation is simply there, and it was there when he put the camera [there] . . . and you're [hopefully] intelligent enough to shoot it."

Othello was actually very carefully conceived. Welles just refused to tie himself to any initial image that may reside in his head. As he once wrote to Peter Cowie, "I plan every shot, then throw all the plans out. The images have to be discovered in the course of the work or else they . . . lack life." Michael MacLiammoir, in his published diary of the filming process, gives a sense of how Welles responded to circumstance when describing how they ended up shooting the famous "jealousy" scene:

> Spent all day on ferocious rendering of that portion of the jealousy scene in which Othello says "Villain, be sure thou prove my love a whore." Orson, beautifully dressed up and painted a dark chocolate brown . . . paced to and fro for hours thinking it all out on the edge of the farthest watchtower, among a thicket of cannons and anxious shivering technicians, black rocks and leaping waves below, and a tempest howling overhead. Finally, with warnings frantically hissed and shrieked at us by everyone, we assume stouty leather belts to which ropes are attached and, held fast by . . . members of the French crew (the Arabs

---

*As this was a French interviewer, and given the language adopted by Gallic cineasts, I believe that Welles would have used the word *auteur*, not author, as most translators have.

being considered too emotional for the job), hang at right angles from the battlements in order to play the scene, camera at dizzy levels conveying sense of terror and (not wholly unfounded) feeling of physical danger.

Freed of the need to produce a shooting script or conform to a shooting schedule, Welles was determined to discover images afresh every day. The constraints that remained, real as they were, came from a self-imposed overarching design. Regarding the above scene Welles specifically says, in *Filming Othello*, that he wanted "to create that sense of vertigo, a feeling of the tottering instability, culminating in Othello's epileptic seizure, the murder of Roderigo, and Othello's dizzying final fall." And he did.

The psychology of the tragic hero is constantly reinforced by the film's arresting imagery; as is the "motiveless maligancy" of Iago. It is no coincidence that we see a twisted gargoyle behind the Moor's head as Iago starts to feed Othello's jealousy. Or, "as jealousy begins to undermine him, [that] the shadows multiply until when [Othello] creeps towards Desdemona's bed chamber . . . he is no more than a grotesque silhouette on the wall."[PC] None of this can have been merely fortuitous, as MacLiammoir makes clear early in his diary, when he enthuses about "Orson's design for the growing dependence of Othello on Iago's presence, the merging of the two men into one murderous image like a pattern of loving shadows welded."

From the start of filming Welles laid down precise instructions as to what could, and could not, feature in any given shot. The director of photography on *Othello*, Oberdan Troiani, describes in the *Rosabella* documentary (see filmography) how the funeral scene that opens the movie, overwhelming the viewer with a sense of tragedy, required "gangways of varying height [to be] installed at a height of sixty foot. Then there were undulating wooden walkways along which the funeral procession passed, so [that] you never see the ground." Troiani also confirms how every aspect of the film's architecture was thought out in advance:

THE JIGSAW PICTURES 267

> [Welles] wanted black and white. He didn't like half measures. Gray
> didn't exist. We couldn't have any trees in frame the entire film
> because he didn't want trees; and he didn't want what he called rotun-
> dities. He wanted sharp angles. Therefore the photography had to be
> black and white, with very clear-cut images and no halftones.

Again, it is tempting to see Welles's decision to strip another of Shakespeare's plays of any halftones as being "under the influence" of Robert Graves's *The White Goddess*, published in 1948, one of two Graves titles (the other being *Greek Myths* [1955], a work that reinforced his mythopoeic view of ancient history) Welles felt Bogdanovich should read if he was going to understand his work. Certainly Graves was on his mind in 1949. After one day of filming he assured his Iago, MacLiammoir, that "a great dark Being like a bird . . . hung brooding over the Mediterranean; she [is] Death, the Goddess, the malevolent womb."

One related theme also carried over from *Macbeth*. During his 1979 documentary, Welles describes how the Venetian Christianity in the film is "overpowered by paganism. Christian imagery appears, but [the images] are put to perverse use." By implication, the virginal Desdemona is also "overpowered by paganism," in the person of the Moor, by first becoming his wife and then his victim. The scene of her actual murder gives Welles the opportunity to bring together a number of key motifs in the film, maintaining the black/white dichotomy that separates husband and wife from the altar to the grave. In fact, as the Moor enters her bedchamber we see "his shadowed form consuming the frame (three times throughout the scene). . . . He enters and douses the flames of the candles with his hand, one at an altar, one at their bed, and a third beneath a portrait of the Virgin Mary. . . . Othello goes to Desdemona and smothers her with an immaculate white veil, kissing her innocent, dying lips through the cloth" [BW]. The symbolic white veil refers us back to our first sight of the beautiful lady, as a corpse carried aloft in the film's prologue, with a transparent black veil draped across her features. That procession atypically establishes a number of these central motifs. The monks who accompany Othello's body are dressed in black, while Desdemona's cortege are draped in white. Meanwhile, Iago hangs suspended above proceedings in a cage, carrion for the birds, his "net that shall enmesh them all" having become bars of iron, an image reinforced as the film unfolds by the number of instances where "sharp angles" frame the very shots in which Iago is working his poison.

None of which is supposed to suggest that Welles was the first film director in history to understand the potency of visual symbols. Where Welles departed from the vast majority of his predecessors was in making certain motifs—like the pit, the maze, and the mirror—exist in their "natural relationship to all the contiguous realities" [AB]. Overseeing every aspect of the editing on one of his films for the first time, Welles could ensure that "events that are obviously charged with meaning [are] seize[d] . . . in their entirety." William Johnson is not alone in finding that "the binding force in Othello and in most of Welles's other films is his use of symbolism, [but] even the most explicit of Welles's symbols do not exist in isolation: they are rooted deep in the action of the film and share the same degree of reality."

This is what took Welles two years to resolve, and why it was not until May 1952 that Othello got to make its debut screening at the Cannes Film Festival, where it was awarded the grand prize. Having previously relied on a purely instinctual approach to editing, Welles "only learned about cutting when I got to Europe . . . [and] had to [learn to] fake things." The results spoke for themselves, even if he was given the usual faint-praise treatment in America, where Bosley Crowther again qualified his review of "this extraordinary picture" by calling it "an unliterate, inarticulate and hotly impressionistic film, full of pictorial pyrotechnics and sinister shadowy moods."

Though Welles was again condemned by those who believed he treated Shakespeare with a disrespect born of egotism—that, in Stanley Kauffman's phrase, "he is not capable of dedicating himself to an author, [but] just wants chances for virtuosity"—his Othello has come to be regarded "by some" as "a flawed masterpiece" (when

Leslie Megahey points this out to Welles, during his all-encompassing *Arena* documentary, he induces much mirth from the self-deprecating "would-be genius," who then concludes a discussion of *Mr. Arkadin* by inquiring whether that is also a "flawed masterpiece").

◆   ◆   ◆   ◆

After having had several films dismembered in the editing suite, Welles now believed that he could *make* a movie there. With all the fervor of the recent convert he began to use a variety of forums to expound his views on "the greatest medium since the invention of movable type for exchanging ideas and information," and its still largely latent potential. As he informed one audience in Edinburgh, what was needed now was "a way of making films . . . by which, if two or three million people see them, we have a return for our money."

Meanwhile, during the winter of 1955, he recorded half a dozen fifteen-minute monologues for BBC TV, hoping to provide "a way to satisfy my predilection for telling stories." *The Orson Welles Sketchbook* offered anecdotes about his introduction to the theater, critics, bureaucracy, Houdini, John Barrymore, the *War of the Worlds* broadcast and, in the final episode, a retelling of one story he had already filmed but hadn't been able to show the world, "My Friend Bonito."

Welles had already informed *Sight & Sound*, back in 1950, that he was now "only interested in putting my own stories on the screen." His "predilection for telling stories" was finally expressed in an original screenplay called *Masquerade*, which he had spent much of 1954 filming, before shooting *The Orson Welles Sketchbook*. In the film, Welles's own character, Gregory Arkadin, regaled partygoers with two little fables, the famous one of the scorpion and the frog and an even odder one about a graveyard and the nature of friendship (edited out of the U.S. version of *Mr. Arkadin*, it can be found in its less well-known European variant, *Confidential Report*).

While in Europe he had certainly been exercising his own imagination as never before. After completing the filming of *Othello* he had performed his earlier Hollywood fable, *The Unthinking Lobster*,

on stage in France with Suzanne Cloutier as the secretary elevated
to first lead actress and then sainthood (he eventually published the
text in French in 1952, along with another two-act play, *Fair Warning*). The following year Welles agreed to trade on, if not share in,
the extraordinary success of *The Third Man*, making thirty-nine half-
hour radio shows for the BBC, devoted to *The [Further] Adventures
of Harry Lime*. These popular weekly shows provided Welles with a
further injection of funds to help complete the editing of *Othello*,
courtesy of Lime. They also gave Welles a forum for original ideas,
nine of the thirty-nine stories being penned by him, two of them
triggering film scripts. *Buzzo Gospel* became a film treatment called
V.I.P. (which became in turn a French novel, *Une Grosse Legume*);
while *Greek Meets Greek* had by March 1953 become the film script
for *Masquerade*.

Welles had grown convinced that with the latter he finally had
an idea for a movie that "really should [be] a roaring success." He had
not abandoned the thought of commercial success, despite bewail-
ing the influence of "commercially minded people" on his films to
date. Even after *Mr. Arkadin* had become "the real disaster of my
life," he continued to insist that he "thought it could have made a
very popular film, a commercial film that everyone would have
liked." Where the film did untold damage was to Welles's continuing aspiration to put his "own stories on the screen." Though he had
the rather notable contrary example of Shakespeare—a man whose
plays, save for a single exception, only ever reworked existing story
lines—Welles always felt that he had a great "popular" story in him.

After he was again obliged to turn someone else's pulp thriller,
Badge of Evil, into his next movie, he pointedly claimed, "In my
trunks, [which are] stuffed with unproduced film scripts, there are no
thrillers." But then Welles never saw *Arkadin* that way. While still
in editing mode, he told the BBC that this film was "a tragedy with
melodramatic and comedic declarations. It pretends to be a thriller
but it isn't"—just as *Ambersons* pretended to be a psychological
drama. And yet Naremore views *Mr. Arkadin* as "a Hollywood
thriller seen from the vantage point of a European intellectual." At

the same time it is another film about someone seemingly (in this case only seemingly) in search of his past. To uncover that past, Arkadin hires an American smuggler to produce a confidential report. Why an American? Well, as Arkadin claimed in an early draft (though *not* in any of the versions of the film—at least five—released over the years):

> They dig up everything, absolutely everything. Not just facts, but inten-
> tions and motives. They take the circumstances into account. . . . It
> doesn't matter how long ago something happened. It doesn't matter
> what you may have done since. There's no canceling out, no forgive-
> ness. An event in a man's past remains for them as decisively impor-
> tant if it happened twenty years ago as if it happened yesterday. . . .

Welles self-consciously incorporated into his populist screenplay a number of elements from previous attempts at this kind of script. *The Way to Santiago* provided amnesia as a theme, with Arkadin actually using the opening line of that screenplay—"I don't know who I am"—though in his case the amnesia is feigned. He wants American smuggler Van Stratten to find out about his past so that he can erase it. In this sense he is a second cousin to Franz Kindler. On the other hand, Naremore sees *Arkadin* as "in many ways . . . a deliberately confusing, low-budget version of *Citizen Kane* and *The Third Man*" (it had, after all, begun life as a Harry Lime adventure). Bret Wood suggests its greatest debt is to *The Lady from Shanghai*, from which it appears to derive some of its architecture, i.e. "a root-less seafaring man . . . [takes] a job [that] turns into something more complex and soon the sailor is trying to avoid being killed by those who lured him into the web of deceit."

The barely adequate funding for the film was rustled up by another old friend, Louis Dolivet, who back in the 1940s had per-suaded Welles to write for the *Free World* magazine and to campaign for Roosevelt's reelection. After playing a small role in the formation of the United Nations, Dolivet returned home to France when it was safe to do so. With no experience as a film producer, Dolivet came up with an unusual, and potentially problematic, coproduction agreement between the French and the Spanish.

An unperturbed Welles began shooting in the winter of 1954 in Spain, France, and Germany. Unfortunately, two central roles in the film were assigned to unprepossessing actors. Welles's current girlfriend and future wife, Paolo Mori, became Arkadin's daughter. Untutored in movie acting, she exuded no great range or dramatic power, but was cheap and presumably willing. Robert Arden as Van Stratten was an unsympathetic male lead whose performance subsequently drew any flak that was not directed at Welles personally. Jonathan Rosenbaum suggests, in Arden's defense, that "it's the unsavoriness and obnoxiousness of the character rather than the performance itself that is responsible for most of this [abuse]. . . . Because [his] character occup[ies] the space normally reserved for charismatic heroes, we feel we're supposed to like and/or sympathize with [him], and when . . . [the] film make[s] this impossible, we wind up blaming either the actor or Welles's casting, rather than accept the premise that we're meant to have a difficult time with [Van Stratten]."

Rosenbaum, though, offers little in the way of defense for Welles's own performance, which is stiff and uncharacteristically lifeless. Again, it may well have been conceived that way, but it is hard to see how such an unendearing performance might help sell this "popular" story. Mr. Arkadin—especially in its more Wellesian variants—suggests that the director felt he could insert Brecht's "alienation effect" into a "popular story" and still have "a great success." He was wrong. Where the film transcended its limitations was in the set-piece scenes, not all of which survive in some of the variants. Thanks to the cameo performances of Michael Redgrave, Katina Paxinou, and Welles's old friend Akim Tamiroff we can discern, in their scenes, a real sense of what Welles thought he could achieve. Each of these vignettes is expertly framed and beautifully acted.

Welles predictably blamed a lot of Mr. Arkadin's deficiencies on the editing of the film, insisting that it was "blown, blown, blown by the cutting" and that what Dolivet "did to me was worse than anything Harry Cohn did to *The Lady from Shanghai.*" Familiar as this may all be starting to sound, there are enough variant versions extant to make a sensible judgment about the scale of damage incurred in the (re)editing. The essential problem seems to have been that the film's producer had no idea how long it took to edit a movie, especially when the director in question had only recently embarked on a whole new approach to editing that applied no set time limit to the exercise.

The two old friends rapidly came into conflict. Welles's version of events, as related to Leaming, suggested that he had been up front with Dolivet, telling him "all along that we didn't have a budget, that we were flying blind, and that we'd have to go on selling territories until we saw what we could bring it in for . . . And he turned on me because I take three days cutting to one day shooting. That's my ratio. And he wanted the picture about three weeks after it was finished."

Time must have flown by for Welles, locked away in the editing suite, for he had actually spent close to four months editing the film before being removed from the process by Dolivet just before Christmas 1954. Welles, it would appear, had barely completed the first third of the movie. According to the editor on *Arkadin*, Renzi Lucidi, he was working his way through approximately two minutes of finished film per week, so it would have taken at least a year for him to finish the job.

When Dolivet intervened, matters only became more complicated. Though Welles was not allowed anywhere near the Moviola, he continued to send instructions to Lucidi, who did his best to follow them. As Welles informed his biographer, originally *Arkadin* "was told in a very complicated and strange way—which is what made it, I think, more palatable and interesting." Just as with *Othello*, though, "there was no way for the jigsaw picture to be put together *except in [Welles's] mind.*"

His intention all along was to tell the story not merely "in flashback," but as a series of increasingly frantic flashbacks by Van Stratten, born of a desperate need to convince Zouk (Akim Tamiroff) that his life is in danger. Zouk, though, is fatalistic. After all, as he says when Van Stratten barges into his garret and informs him that someone wants to kill him, "I'm a dying man with no money. Somebody wants to kill me, he's wasting his time." In fact, the expression on his face in the instant before Van Stratten finds him, a deathly glaze, is perfectly replicated when Van Stratten later returns with his goose liver to find him dead.

According to one lucky individual, who caught a "preview" version of the film in England, in the summer of 1955, there was originally a brief prologue, in which "a cell door opened in a bright rectangle near midscreen, and an old man, Jacob Zouk, came blinking into the light. Because he was near death, Zouk was being released from a German prison, where he had been confined for fourteen years. As he stumbled reluctantly down the hall, Zouk complained that he didn't want to go outside, that he had forebodings. The jailer said, too bad, he was pardoned and had to go."

The character of Zouk was evidently intended to lie at the center of the story. Indeed, Welles told Bogdanovich that "in the full version . . . it was almost the leading part." It is the nature of this role that distinguishes the differences in the versions of the film available, the flashbacks (plural) not simply being intended as a bookending device. Rather, they intersect the story at crucial points, providing important expositional information to the audience.

Aside from the Spanish-language version that was part of the coproduction agreement, and actually features Spanish actresses in place of Katina Paxinou and Suzanne Flon, there are three versions of *Arkadin* in circulation, and at least one that once existed, but has seemingly disappeared. They are as follows:

1. *Confidential Report* Mark 1. The preview version screened in London in June 1955, this version opened not with the buzzing plane, but "a fade in of the nude body [of a] young woman lying on a beach, and then a close-up of her face, and open eyes." This is Milly, Arden's ex-girlfriend. As Arden speaks about her, his voice begins to trail off, interrupted by the buzzing plane,

which is followed by Zouk being released from jail. The credits came at the end of the film. Welles told Bogdanovich that *his* version began with a dead girl on a beach; and that it included two scenes where we see Arkadin "as a sentimental, rather maudlin Russian drunk."

2. *Confidential Report* Mark 2. The version that premiered in London on August 11, 1955, this was subsequently issued on Voyager laserdisc. At ninety-nine minutes, it retains the initial flashback as a device but none of Zouk's other interventions. Confusingly, we briefly see a shot of the dead girl on the beach immediately after Milly's drunken spat with Arkadin, though an explanation is only provided in the final moments of the film. The opening credits feature what appear to be papier-mâché bats. Though they make a further appearance at the masked ball, their significance is never explained in any of the released versions.

3. *Mr. Arkadin* Mark 1. Distributed in the United States through Corinth Films after its belated premiere in American cinemas in 1961. The delay resulted from a vexatious civil lawsuit issued against Welles by the production company Filmorsa, which was eventually dropped, though only after it fell foul of the then U.S. copyright registration requirements (hence its subsequent "public domain" status). This version was apparently even issued on video, though not on laser disc or DVD. Of the available versions, this one comes closest to Welles's conception, featuring several Van Stratten/Zouk flashbacks, including a unique insert immediately after Arkadin has made his proposal to Van Stratten. Other versions cut immediately to the chase. It would appear that the first third of this version of the film closely accords with Welles's own edit—though it is missing the "prologue" (see *Confidential Report* No. 1). It also runs for ninety-nine minutes.

4. *Mr. Arkadin* Mark 2. The ninety-three-minute version that seems ubiquitous as a "public domain" video and DVD. Reedited into chronological order and unframed by any flashbacks,

it begins down at the Naples docks, where Bracco has been stabbed, making it look like the work of our friend, the RKO janitor. The various scenes with Zouk are all bundled together in this bungled travesty of Welles's intentions.

If the maze makes its usual appearance as a Wellesian motif in *Confidential Report*, with Van Stratten having to negotiate one to reach Zouk, we still await the unraveling of the many Arkadins. Suffice to say, there are enough flashes of Welles's wit—a personal favorite coming when Milly is told that the robed procession are penitents "repenting their sins," and quips, "They must have sinned awfully badly"—to suggest that its logistical difficulties need not have made any more impression on the viewer than the man's *Othello*. The Christmas sequence certainly has a great deal going for it. The touch is sure-handed as Zouk reminisces upon hearing the street band play "Silent Night," unaware that this is precisely what Arkadin has in mind. Such genuine feelings of nostalgia were presumably intended to contrast with Arkadin's own maudlin sentimentality, the facade of a man who hates and fears the past. When we see Arkadin give Van Stratten the goose liver that Zouk craves for Christmas (thus answering Zouk's challenge to Van Stratten at the start of the film, "Who are you, Santa Claus?"), we know full well that Zouk is now forever silent. All the murders in *Mr. Arkadin* are silent. None of the murders are even committed on screen. The victims merely cease to speak, culminating in Arkadin's own static-filled suicide.

But for all of Welles's efforts, and his scarcely credible belief that he had a potential hit on his hands, *Mr. Arkadin* was one of cinema's greatest belly flops. If, as Welles claimed, he had "made quite a lot of pictures by then, and . . . knew exactly how long it takes to edit a picture," he perhaps should have made his timetable crystal clear at the outset. The coproduction agreement teetered too precariously to withstand such delays, and the producer decided he would rather have a travesty of Welles's intentions than, as an overweening legend already suggested, no film at all.

The film finally received its French premiere in June 1956—in God knows what version—where the French intellectuals embraced it to their bosoms, its impenetrability a challenge they welcomed. In America, though, the film was an unknown quantity for many years. When it was finally screened in the early 1960s, it was seen as a curio from Welles's European adventure, a memento from the other side of the pond made before his Hollywood homecoming.

That homecoming would be a long time coming. By November 1955 Welles had made it as far as New York, where he was in rehearsals for a return to the Broadway stage, as *King Lear* (a role he had played in a 1954 U.S. television production to great acclaim). When he was interviewed from his hotel room, for CBS, he admitted to having various projects in mind, "rather ambitious ones I'm afraid." Unfortunately, two bad breaks in rehearsals resulted in him playing Lear from a wheelchair, and the production closed after twenty-one performances. It would be his last appearance on the American stage, and he was soon back in London.

After fulfilling a commitment to make a second series of seven (this time thirty-minute) programs for ITV, entitled *Around the World with Orson Welles*, he finally returned to Hollywood in April 1956 and announced his intention to settle there for a while, with his new wife, recently retired actress Paolo Mori, and their newborn daughter, Beatrice. A stirring cameo as Father Mapple in John Huston's disappointing *Moby Dick* was a reminder of this natural orator's more obvious gift, and a hilarious appearance on *I Love Lucy* in October showed the man's hidden knack for comedy, but when an offer for a real movie part finally came from Albert Zugsmith at Universal, it was as a bullish bigot who attempts to frame a liberal sheriff for a murder.

At least the role of Virgil Renchler in *Man in the Shadow* was a lead role, not another of the cameos that were becoming Welles's stock-in-trade. And it convinced Zugsmith that he might be suitable for another part, as the crooked cop in a potboiler Zugsmith was planning to produce, for which Charlton Heston had agreed to play the law-abiding lead. If Welles had again temporarily reinvented himself as an actor for hire, he remained a legend to many actors, and Heston was one. He strongly suggested to the studio that they ask Welles to direct the film. Their response? "As though I'd asked to have my mother direct the picture." Not the creator of *Citizen Kane*.

A CANDID PARTISAN OF
THE OLD ELOQUENCE

[Touch of Evil]

Thanks to Europe, or at least thanks to European culture,
Welles became a conscious American, he discovered the pit
of savagery dissembled by the American facade.

Maurice Bessy

On January 3, 1957, Orson Welles received a phone call from the production head at Universal Pictures, Ed Muhl, asking him if he would be prepared to direct the movie *Badge of Evil*, for which he had already been cast as a corrupt cop. The job offer came with no (further) remuneration, not even a cut of the film's profits (though Heston was to receive 7½ percent for the unchallenging role of honest cop). Yet Welles leaped at the chance because, as he wrote the following year, he still had "a greedy need to exercise, in some way, the function of my choice: the function of a director."

Welles was presumably in the dark as to why Universal had made this offer, though he had launched a sustained charm offensive on producer Albert Zugsmith during the filming of *Man in the Shadow*, hoping that he might be given just such a chance (Zugsmith even took credit for the decision in an interview with Welles biographer Frank Brady, concocting a scene straight out of *The Producers*, with Welles drunkenly offering to direct the worst script the studio has, and Zugsmith handing him *Badge of Evil*).

The impetus had in fact come from Heston, in a New Year's Day phone call to Universal, followed up on January 3 by a further reminder. As Heston wrote in his journal, *Badge of Evil* was "only a police-suspense story, like the ones they've been doing for thirty-some years, but I think with [Welles] it might have a chance to be *something* [my italics]." Ed Muhl consulted Jim Pratt (and presumably Zugsmith). Pratt, who had worked on *The Stranger*, was now second in charge of production at Universal. Unaware of the unrepresentative nature of that particular film project, he had nothing but praise for Welles, and Muhl offered Welles the gig. The director had just one proviso attached to his acceptance: that he be allowed to rewrite the script.

Less than three months later, on April 2, 1957, Welles directed the final scene of the movie, now named *Touch of Evil*, in which his character is left floating in dirty water, dead as a dodo. At dawn, he retired to Charlton Heston's trailer for a champagne breakfast, and to sit and watch a television rerun of the director's previous Hollywood thriller, *The Lady from Shanghai* (doubtless with a running commentary for Heston's benefit as to what was cut). Afterward Heston wrote in his journal, "A hell of a picture to work on . . . I can't believe it won't be fine." In under three months, Welles had transformed a stereotypically ordinary Hollywood script from another slice of pulp fiction into "a hell of a picture."

It was the kind of resurrection devoutly to be wished for, and it began on January 8, when Universal notified Heston's agent that Welles had indeed agreed to direct the picture. The studio had been anxious to cast Janet Leigh as Heston's new bride. Welles immediately ensured that this would happen, fully aware of the likely effect on Ms. Leigh of a telegram from the former Boy Wonder:

> Janet Leigh: I came in one night, and there was a long telegram . . . I don't remember the exact words, but only he could have sent it, saying "I can't tell you how much I'm looking forward to working with you. . . . Could we possibly meet so that we could start our discussions immediately? Signed: Orson Welles." What's he talking about? I thought. But it did exactly what he wanted it to do, because I called my agent and said, "What's this?" and he said, "Oh Christ. They shouldn't have talked to you yet, because we're still negotiating." And I said, "I don't care what you're negotiating, I want to do the picture with Orson Welles."

The remainder of the casting for the movie could wait. It was time to go to work on the screenplay. Welles later claimed that he never read the novel, only the Universal "scenario," which he typified as "ridiculous." In fact, as John Stubbs establishes in his detailed comparison of Welles's screenplay with both the original novel by Robert Wade and William Miller (under the joint pseudonym Bret Masterson) and the previous screenplay by Paul Monash, the recently assigned director must have at least perused the original novel. Much of the dialogue Welles gave Manolo Sanchez, the Mexican shoe clerk accused of the murder of Rudy Linneker, is taken directly from the book, yet is absent from the Monash screenplay.

Six days after Welles was confirmed as director of *Badge of Evil* he had his first meeting with Heston, who was perhaps the first to see a draft of the new screenplay. If *The Lady from Shanghai*, contrary to legend, was no weekend's work, *Touch of Evil* seems to have been produced in the white light/white heat of inspiration. That first draft took just five days; the shooting script less than three weeks; yet what Welles ultimately constructed out of Monash, Miller, and Wade bore about as much resemblance to—and warranted about as much comparison with—its sources as, say, Shakespeare's *Romeo and Juliet* did to Arthur Brooke's 1562 poem, *its* ostensible source.

The original Monash screenplay had been commissioned by Universal back in the summer of 1956 (the finished script is dated July 24), and according to Albert Zugsmith, "had [been] written from [the] novel in four weeks, on a flat[-fee] deal." It was a perfectly competent script, tailor-made for the kind of B movie that Monash (and Universal) expected *Badge of Evil* to be, and some of its premises were intriguing enough. Indeed, certain features in the released film stem directly from Monash, the most crucial of which was the transformation of the corrupt cop into a large, heavyset figure by the name of Thomas (not Hank) Quinlan. (Perhaps Universal already had Welles in mind for the part?)

Monash also changed the name of the gang that threatens the novel's hero, and his wife, from the Buccios, responsible for a lucrative bar license scam, to the Grandi family, making for a sinister, mafioso undertone that Welles, to a large extent, sends up. At the same time Monash made the shoe clerk framed by Quinlan for Linneker's murder guilty, thus ensuring that Quinlan warranted his epitaph—"He was a good detective . . . but he was a bad cop"—originally delivered in its entirety by police chief Gould (Tanya, the tart-with-a-heart, has yet to emerge from Welles's imagination). However, the Monash screenplay also contained a statutory allocation of clichés from the Hollywood hacks' handbook, starting with an opening shot that, as Stubbs describes it, sounds like one of those silent movies where every other cut is a reaction shot in close-up:

> Monash's first shot reveals the killer's car speeding along a cliff road. The car stops above the cabana; the killer takes dynamite from the trunk; and he descends toward the beach house. Cha-cha music can be heard coming from the cabana. Inside, Linneker watches Gail dance, joins her in the dance, and then leads her to a couch. When the dynamite is thrown into the cabana, Linneker has to struggle almost comically to free himself from the uncomprehending woman's grasp to lunge for the dynamite. The woman's scream as she sees the dynamite coincides with the explosion.

The novel, likewise, begins with the death of Rudy Linneker in a violent explosion. However, there is no nightclub dancer present. Everything happens unobserved, as "a hand reache[s] through the window and drop[s] a package of dynamite inside." An explosion follows.

When it came to Welles, aspects of both the novel and Monash's script provided necessary triggers, but the result was uniquely his. He had always appreciated the cinematic necessity of a grand entrance. As he later said in *Filming Othello*, "A movie has to have a great opening—it must command attention. . . . You don't ever want to open a play at the top of your best, but a movie should open at the top of its best. It must—because this damn thing is dead. . . . You cannot bring the thing alive unless you seize the people at the beginning. The riderless horse has to come in."

In Welles's February 5 script the silent assassin has been carried over from the novel, though this time he is planting a time bomb in Linneker's car. In the background, we are supposed to hear "the brassy thump and blare which accompanies the bumps and grinds of a typical blow off in a striptease." The nightclub dancer added by Monash emerges out of the Grandi-owned Rancho Grande, with a "beefy bald-head in an expensive-looking gabardine suit." (Originally there would have been a brief scene inside the club, but Welles realized it would dilute the impact of his opening.) The stripper nuzzles up to Linneker, while the music blares out from every point of the compass, all but blotting out the steady ticktock—though not for the attentive viewer, from the godlike vantage point on the camera crane, imperiously looking down on the passage of the car, a.k.a. ticking time bomb, on its way through Los Robles, across the border and—boom!

Heston's comment in his journal for January 14 conveys astonishment at what Welles had already achieved: "In five days on the picture he's rewritten the script. Almost all of it's different, and almost all of it's better." Heston had already been informed of a change in his own character's point of view, providing him with a more challenging role, thanks to a phone call from Welles "three days into a rewrite of the entire script. . . . It was a vast improvement. . . . He'd turned my character into a Mexican attorney. . . . His name was Vargas . . . the very bright first son of a wealthy Mexican family . . . on the fast track for high office in his country. None of this was in either the script or the picture, but, inventing his background, we could begin to invent the man."

This was Welles's usual method—to make actors feel involved in the process of creating their own characters (but to keep them in the dark as to his grand design). He had already, in this first draft, begun to immeasurably deepen the most important dynamic in *Touch of Evil*—the one between Vargas and Hank Quinlan. At the same time, he developed an idea Monash had incorporated into *his* script's character list—that "between [Vargas] and Quinlan there is a certain parallel." Welles's own character list, which prefaces *his* script (a useful practice, now largely abandoned), portrays Ramon Miguel Vargas as "an idealist, but not at all of the impractical starry-eyed variety. . . . His dislike of the abuses of police power is every bit as intense as his opposition to crime itself."

Heston soon realized that Welles had turned the film from a detective story about Vargas's relentless pursuit of a corrupt cop into the tragedy of Hank Quinlan. However much Welles's transformation of Vargas into a high-ranking Mexican official added an all-important third dimension, the story now became Quinlan's, and Vargas was merely the catalyst for the man's fall; leading on from Wilson in *The Stranger*, O'Hara in *The Lady from Shanghai*, and Van Stratten in *Mr. Arkadin*.

Welles always insisted that his own instincts lay with Vargas, that his "position in the political or moral sense is completely anti-Quinlan," and yet he invests Quinlan with such resonance that an audience cannot help but identify with him. As Maurice Bessy wrote, in his *Orson Welles: An Investigation into His Films and Philosophy*, "Welles occasionally has spokesmen in his films who express his personal point of view: [notably] Vargas . . . but these spokesmen have a very feeble voice indeed when compared with the roar of the Princes of Darkness whom Welles has so often incarnated. . . . His moralistic declarations carry little weight against the reality of his characters."

In his character list, Welles certainly made it clear what an amoral monster Quinlan was, describing him as someone who "regards himself, not as a servant of the public, but as an almost divinely inspired instrument of justice." He proceeds to put the kernel of the film in its nutshell: "Before his story [it is now *his* story] is over [Quinlan] has become not only a criminal, but a murderer, but this is not because of any compromise or defection from his own perverted principles—it *develops logically from the extension of those principles*." It is this tragic flaw, in the Shakespearean sense, that brings Welles's antihero down, not mere chance or fate. For all its mazelike manner, *Touch of Evil* "develops logically" toward its conclusion. The introduction of the principled Vargas is all it takes to show black from white, a lie from the truth.

In one very rare instance, an interview with Andre Bazin and his compadres from *Cahiers du Cinema* in 1958, Welles met interviewers who simply would not accept his professed view. They harried him to concede that there was more to Quinlan than he was initially prepared to admit. Though he calls Quinlan "hateful—there is no ambiguity about that," Welles is pushed to consider the possibility that his latest, greatest monster, might also be his most sympathetic:

> Quinlan is sympathetic because of his humanity, not his ideas: there is not the least spark of genius in him. . . . Quinlan doesn't so much want to bring the guilty to justice, as to murder them in the name of the law. . . . Of course there's one thing I gave Quinlan, which I must love him for: that is, that he did love Marlene Dietrich, and that he did get that bullet in the place of his friend, the fact that he has a heart. But his beliefs are detestable. . . . [But] I always have to be bigger than life. It's a fault in my nature. So you mustn't believe that there is anything ambiguous about the way I approach these parts. It's my personality which produces these effects, not my intentions.

Welles continued to distance himself from Quinlan, even after Francois Truffaut, a director he admired, heralded his achievement in "making the monster more and more monstrous, and the young protagonist more and more likable, until we are brought somehow to shed real tears over the corpse of the magnificent monster." To another French interviewer, he confessed that "most of my friends and most critics who comment on *Touch of Evil* believe Quinlan has an essential goodness, while I think he's a scoundrel."

And yet it was Welles (and Welles alone) who "humanized" Quinlan, who made him take that bullet for Menzies (in the novel, it is his partner who is crippled); turned him into a reformed alcoholic; introduced two women whom he had loved; and, by inventing the "half-breed" who killed his wife and got away, provided him with his thirst for "justice," no matter how misguided. Welles insisted, to Megahey, that he did all of this because "the further you explain his villainy—not psychiatrically, not because mama didn't love him, but . . . [the more] you humanize him—the more human you make the monster, the more interesting the story must be."

It was also unquestionably Welles who made Quinlan into the monstrous beached whale *he* had yet to become, crippling him physically as well as morally, like Bannister in *The Lady from Shanghai* or Shakespeare's Richard III. He it was who invested the character with a deep-rooted sense of self-loathing (he even trades on popular perception in the film by letting Tanya/Dietrich tell him to "lay off those candy bars").

In many a mind's eye, Welles now looked like Quinlan. He even told Megahey one of those amusing anecdotes about a party he threw during the filming of *Touch of Evil*, to which he turned up late, still in makeup and padding, to be greeted by old Hollywood friends, all telling him how well he looked. It is a typical Welles anecdote, wryly revealing and self-deprecating at the same time. Welles, at barely forty, was actually still a strikingly good-looking, if heavyset, man. The possibility that he might become as physically monstrous as this character clearly troubled him. And yet, as with his depiction of George Amberson, he chose to address it head-on in film.

If in that original discussion with Bazin, shortly after the film's release, he did finally come clean—admitting to being "more interested in character than virtue"—the character of Quinlan remains one of his most rounded. Despite all that he has perverted, and become perverted by, he is "the most sympathetic Welles hero until Falstaff. . . . [Indeed] the enormity of the gulf between Quinlan's intentions and his actions helps Welles make one of his most lucid philosophical presentations. . . . Quinlan dies in a world so foul that his malignity almost seems, because of its unsparing candor, to be a virtue" [JM].

For all his protestations regarding a separation of effect and intention, Welles was too self-conscious an artist for such a stance to be a credible one. As he admitted in later life, "There is no such thing as becoming another character by putting on a lot of makeup. . . . What you're really doing is undressing yourself, even tearing yourself apart, and presenting to the public *that part of you* that corresponds to what you're playing. And there is a murderer in each of us, a villain in each of us, a fascist in each of us, a saint in each of us."

Welles never got to play a saint (unless Cardinal Wolsey counts). But Quinlan was assuredly a murderer and a villain, as Kindler was a murderer and a fascist. In both cases they got to commit murder/s "in the name of the law." In both cases, they failed to recognize themselves as criminals. Yet Quinlan shared one characteristic with Welles that even he would not have denied—a contempt for lawyers. One scene in the Grandi-owned Rancho bar, in which Menzies unwittingly affirms Vargas's deepening suspicions, was later trimmed of the most revealing part of dialogue:

> QUINLAN: The key to this whole thing is the dynamite. . . . The killer didn't just want Linneker dead—he wanted him destroyed—annihilated.
>
> MENZIES: Like that axe slaying in '39?
> (to the others)
> I'll never forget how Hank discovered the ax—after we'd all given up searching. I swear, he's got him a nose for evidence like a regular old bloodhound . . .
>
> QUINLAN (breaking in—with great sincerity): What I've got is a nose for guilt. . . . Guilt! (with contempt) Evidence is for the lawyers.

Welles intended Quinlan's repeated use of "guilt" and "guilty" to come back and haunt him. The studio thought different and he was obliged to explicate his design, in one of his famous memos: "As I planned it, after Quinlan was shot and Schwartz had turned on the recording device, there were to be two or three very significant lines coming through the little speaker: the accusing echo of the dead Menzies, and finally Quinlan's hoarsely repeated cry, 'Guilty, guilty, guilty. . . .' The tinny little voice of condemnation was meant to be a general comment on the story itself." After it was explained to them, the studio finally took this suggestion on board.

If Quinlan and Vargas took on new characteristics in Welles's rewritten script, the other characters were also deployed differently. The hero's wife in the novel (and original script) had been Mexican-born, though little had been made of any racial angle. At the same time as her husband became Mexican, she was transformed into an American tourist, who met Vargas at a diplomatic party six weeks earlier. Her name was duly changed from Connie to the all-American Susan.

Susan is characterized in the script as "extremely attractive and quick and bright. Her alert and almost world-wise air in no way reduces an essential freshness and innocence in her personality; a peculiarly American combination, this mingling of cleverness and simplicity—it still sometimes bewilders her Latin husband." In such a volatile situation this agglomeration of "cleverness and simplicity" means that she is also a loose cannon. The shooting script refers at one point to the fact that "caution . . . is not a virtue of Susan's, and curiosity is her guiding vice." This is immediately made plain, as she agrees to follow a strange young man who takes her to meet "Uncle Joe Grandi," whom she mocks when he tries to act tough, telling him, "You've been seeing too many gangster movies." The script suggests he may have seen just one movie—*Little Caesar*—a few too many times.

The head of the Grandi family, Uncle Joe, bears little comparison to the one in Monash's construct. Welles seems to have (re)written the part specifically for his old friend Akim Tamiroff, hoping he'd carry on where he left off with Zouk. Shots of Tamiroff accompanying Welles and Russell Metty as they scouted out locations (see page 279) suggest that his presence fulfilled an important psychological need in Welles (one that doubtless also prompted cameos from Joseph Cotten, Mercedes McCambridge, and Marlene Dietrich). The "Uncle Joe" character, according to the description in the character list, has assumed control of the Grandi "family affairs with great uneasiness—even with something like hysteria. He is not built to be a commanding general (even in this provincial gangland). . . . He is vain, a cowardly little man with a dirty and ingenious mind." It may be a promotion for Zouk, but he meets much the same silent fate.

The other key character in *Touch of Evil*, Pete Menzies, is Quinlan's loyal partner. He is described at the outset as "the third idealist in our story, his idealism having been channeled into the worship of his chief." Though he begins the film as "a reflection of Quinlan, consciously striving to imitate his thoughts and equal his deeds," he has, by the film's end, become a true Brechtian, "brought to the point of recognition . . . made to face something . . . [and] his capacity for action . . . arouse[d]." (In giving him a name with a Mexican flavor, Welles may have been implying that Menzies must bear some of the contempt Quinlan feels in general for Mexicans and "half-breeds.")

There is a fourth idealist in the film, also a Mexican. But the shoe clerk's love for the daughter of Rudy Linneker, described by Welles as "intensely real and deeply passionate," has no chance. Marcia, who barely figures in the finished film, was originally portrayed as "spoiled, stupid, vicious, and pretty." For all her looks, she would have had a lot more in common with Elsa than Susan. If Susan does have an alter ego in the film, it would have to be Tanya, the character Welles introduced after he decided that the brothel owner as originally sketched did not conform to a necessary archetype. The world-weariness of Mother Lupe, as she was known, was carried over more memorably to Tanya, even if it was Mother Lupe who initially witnessed Quinlan falling off his self-imposed wagon:

> A tatty little "parlor" with dusty painted velvet hangings on the walls, rickety wicker-work furniture and a profusion of tattered silk-covered lampshades. These lamps are still lit, but the dawn sky shows in the windows, the color of dirty dishwater.
>
> Mother Lupe herself, a venerable figure, snoozes near the player piano. Quinlan is slumped at a table facing the door. His whisky bottle is almost empty. Suddenly the music stops. Mother Lupe stirs.
>
> QUINLAN: Fix it.
>
> MOTHER LUPE (rising with a weary grunt): It's getting tired. It's old. Like us.

With a dry chortle of laughter she starts adjusting the mechanism.

QUINLAN: I need another bottle.

MOTHER LUPE: Liquor's all put away, dearie. It's daylight. You oughta go to bed.

QUINLAN: Another bottle.

The music starts again, and the old woman, shrugging, leaves the room. Camera tightens on Quinlan, whose bleary eyes focus on something off scene.

In the February 5 script Welles had moved a long way in the right direction, but he still required the characters of Tanya and the night clerk to complete his troupe and realize an ambition he had held since starting work on *Arkadin*. About that film, he later said he had "wanted to make a work in the spirit of Dickens, with characters so dense that they appear as archetypes." Those archetypes, mishandled in *Mr. Arkadin*, had largely materialized when shooting began on *Touch of Evil* on February 18, 1957.

A series of rewrites (and cuts) had occupied much of the interim. On January 26, Orson had met with producer Albert Zugsmith to cut some twenty-five pages from the already lean script. On or about February 5, the studio execs got their first real sight of the new script, prompting the first mutterings of concern. Heston's February 8 journal entry reads, in part, "There is a stirring of unrest out at Universal about the way Orson's going about the film. They seem to fear what I hope: that he'll make an offbeat film out of what they'd planned as a predictable little programmer. . . . [Thankfully,] Orson is holding firm."

What perhaps concerned the studio most was the whole bordertown element Welles had introduced (both the previous versions had been set in San Diego). American attitudes to Mexico, and Mexicans, were a subject still largely taboo in Hollywood, seventy miles from the border but two whole worlds away. For Welles, though, Mexico was a second home, cinematically speaking—the location for *The Way to Santiago*, "My Friend Bonito," and the opening part of *The Lady from Shanghai*, and already earmarked as the place where he would begin shooting his version of *Don Quixote*.

Welles was fully aware that the new script represented a challenging departure, and that it might lead the studio to voice disquiet. What they failed to conceive was just how radical he intended to be. As Terry Comito's introduction to the published screenplay states:

> In transferring the story's action to the Mexican border, Welles suggests a more subversive vision. Los Robles is the sinister foreign place we discover on the margins of our own world, just over the border from the comfortingly familiar. . . . To our discomfort, Welles engineers our complicity in violent fantasies, sexual and racial, of the most devious sort, at the same time he appeases the liberal in us with safe homilies on the evils of prejudice. . . . The most precarious boundary is one overseen by no friendly customs man. It is the boundary between the apparent solidity of our rational daylight world and the dark labyrinth in which, if we yield to its solicitations, we will lose our way. Welles's "Mexico" is a place of the soul.

Given the sheer sleaziness of Welles's border town, and his depiction of the Grandis and the shoe clerk, he cannot have been unduly surprised when the Mexican government refused to grant location approval for the film. The fact that he was clearly condemning the racism, much of it unconscious, of the American characters, was lost on the Mexican authorities, and the director was obliged to find an alternate location where he could recreate his border town "of the soul."

The ideal location already existed within the confines of the city of Los Angeles, but it took his old friend Aldous Huxley to suggest it—Venice, California. It had that ideal fin de siècle feel. The whole place reeked of decay and when Welles saw the bridge crossing over what Heston called "that damn antique travesty of a Venetian canal," with the oil derricks in the distance, he apparently told cameraman Russell Metty that he was going to rewrite the entire ending of the film. The whole rotten place seemed to already exist in 35 mm monochrome, a twilight zone amid the smog.

◆   ◆   ◆   ◆

Welles knew that the budget was not about to stretch to Technicolor or Cinemascope, and even if it had, he probably would have fought tooth and nail to keep the familiar ratio, in monochrome. As he wrote at the time for a film annual, "We never wake from a nightmare shrieking because it has been in Vistavision." Welles's view, which never really altered, was that "black and white separates the men from the boys . . . because we have removed one element of reality. We were luckier before, when we didn't [even] have sound." With Russell Metty he had a cinematographer of the old school, a master at helping visualize every aspect of Welles's baroque imagination, and entirely in his element in this black-and-white world. When *New York Times* film critic Howard Thompson accused Welles of using "camera tricks" to achieve the nightmare vision that was *Touch of Evil*, he was quickly set right:

> There is no attempt to approximate reality [in *Touch of Evil*]; the film's entire "world" being the director's invention. . . . While the style . . . may be somewhat overly baroque, there are positively no "camera tricks." Nowadays the eye is tamed, I think, by the new [Technicolor] wide screens. These "systems" with their rigid technical limitations are in such monopoly that any vigorous use of the old black-and-white, normal aperture camera runs the risk of seeming "tricky" by comparison. The old camera permits of a range of visual conventions as removed from "realism" as grand opera. This is a language, not a bag of tricks. If it is now a dead language, as a candid partisan of the old eloquence, I must face the likelihood that I shall not again be able to put it to the service of any theme of my own choosing.

Welles left little doubt that this was the same man who reinvented the parameters of cinematography with Gregg Toland in '41, praised Eisenstein in '45, and collaborated with Brecht in '46. His insistence that this was "a language, not a bag of tricks" was one more assertion of independence from Hollywood, still shackled to its glossy sheen of naturalism. This independence he reiterated in an article for *Esquire* the year after *Touch of Evil*, in which he described himself as "one of those who got away. I chose freedom—and . . . quite a while ago." *Touch of Evil* was a stopover, and shooting the bulk of the film in Venice, California, was one way of maintaining that independence. Not that he breathed a word of his strategy to any, save perhaps some old, old friends.

Janet Leigh was one of those who thought that "when we started the picture we were only supposed to have ten days of night shooting. But once he got down to Venice in California . . . he kept saying, 'Oh we'll do that scene here,' and finally switched the whole thing so we did the whole picture right down there in Venice—all night long." Heston also seems to have been slow on the uptake, writing in his journal on March 18 of how "we moved inside the hotel down in Venice, covering a scene scheduled for a set at the studio, in the DA's office. Orson never liked that set and when the rain washed out our night exteriors, he grabbed the chance to shoot this moving through the hotel lobby, into the elevators, up two floors, and along the hall."

In his autobiography, Heston recalled another occasion when "we were shooting in this crummy hotel in Venice, and at three o'clock in the morning . . . we were down in the basement of this old hotel, peeing in a drain . . . and [Welles] said, 'Gee, these pipes and this boiler . . . we should do the scene with Joe Calleia here—where he shows you the cane.' He zipped up his fly and said to the first assistant, 'Get Joe Calleia down here.' They said, 'Jesus, Orson, we were gonna do that scene on Friday; they've got it set up at the studio.' He said, ' . . . We're going to do it down here. We'll do it right now.' . . . And he did." Welles eventually came clean to Leaming, admitting that he had always secretly intended to remain in Venice until he had near-as-dammit finished the picture. He knew all along what he was doing, but was now wise enough to be wary, keeping his overarching design to himself.

He preferred to depict himself as a man responding to happenstance (his definition of a movie director in *Filming Othello* would be "the man who presides over accidents"). Those around him who did not know his working ways invariably bought into this persona. Heston has referred to the way he would "get an incredible idea about how to solve a scene, or a piece of casting, or a bit of writing, or an editing problem, but rather than polish it to perfection, [was at least as] likely to substitute still another idea." Janet Leigh believed that "the only problem with that picture was that Welles, having complete authority, would go off at a kind of tangent and lose what the film was trying to say."

Welles, though, only introduced new ideas when the architecture was already in place, and in instances malleable enough to withstand the change. Thus, the introduction of characters like Tanya and the night watchman took the film where it needed to go, never anywhere that he knew not. The last important decision before filming began—to shoot on location in Venice—gave Welles all the architecture he needed, and without a set to build. Venice's resemblance to the world of Raymond Chandler novels only served to inspire the man to produce the last great noir thriller, a valediction to "a dead language." As Naremore says, the film "deals with racism, police corruption, and sexual confusion in an atmosphere so gorgeously sleazy that the very air is filled with blowing garbage."

And yet Welles still manages to make the border town seem like a lost world, an Eden Quinlan lost somewhere on the road to purgatory. Hence, a blinking neon sign in the Los Robles arcade announcing Paradise, actually a tatty tits 'n' ass dance hall, serves to spark all kinds of memories for him. As Quinlan attempts to regain the Eden in his past, he comes upon Tanya's brothel, from which he can hear a familiar refrain calling him home. As Terry Comito notes, "The pianola theme . . . is a summons from the past, its simple and repetitive theme cutting with a quiet insistence through the jagged brass and bongos of the rest of the film's score." Its closest points of reference in Welles's work are Herrmann's original score for *The Magnificent Ambersons* and that equally evocative zither theme in *The Third Man*.

Venice also provided that "quality of strangeness" that Welles hoped might stop *Touch of Evil* "from being just another whodunit." Quinlan dunit. This had been his world and, until now, he had been its potentate, "an almost divinely inspired instrument of justice," who is not used to being questioned about his judgments (in either sense). Hence the shock and bewilderment when Vargas threatens to take his suspicions to a higher authority, and the explosion of bile, "Thirty years of dirt and crummy pay . . . Thirty years I gave my life to the department—and you let this lousy publicity hound accuse me, right in your office . . ." He would rather abdicate from his kingdom than face down his accuser.

As Quinlan's world tilts off its axis, he loses his balance. The cane that provides a physical crutch is mislaid, and in being mislaid proves to be his undoing. His attempts to cover his tracks are now as doomed as Kindler's. In the last third of the film we sense how, in Comito's telling phrase, "the film's center of gravity shifts from the trials of Susan Vargas to the figure of Quinlan himself, [and] we begin gradually to see not only the terror and perplexity of the labyrinth, but also its moral and psychological dimensions." The borderline where two worlds collide, which has succored and nurtured Quinlan for so long, has now begun to close in around him.

Welles has locked Quinlan in a world in which the kind of "quality of strangeness" make anybody "weirdly out of key" appear normal. Whereas in *The Lady from Shanghai* and *Mr. Arkadin*, his larger-than-life characters stick out from the crowd, in *Touch of Evil*, they are suffused by the fetid air around Los Robles. In such a world, all frames of reference have been removed. As Comito says, it is "a world, where violence is the norm rather than the exception: where the only context is disruption, where even "the 'safe' American motel turns out to be . . . perched on the edge of nothing."

In this world, a one-legged man may be king, but only the physically blind may truly see. Hence, the atmospheric scene in the blind woman's shop, where Vargas attempts to hold an intimate conversation with his wife, but can feel the gaze of this strangely arresting woman, who seems to be "the bearer of some knowledge we are unlikely ever to share"[TC]. She is a character lifted straight out of one of Robert Graves's *Greek Myths*.

As Welles was again obliged to explicate for the execs in *that* memo, "She was not there by accident. Her presence embarrasses Vargas and inhibits his phone conversation with Susan . . . [who is] in the strange motel speaking with drowsy sexiness to her husband . . . His discomfort at the quiet, oddly attentive figure of the blind woman [was one of those] elements in a rather carefully balanced little plan . . . *It was meant to be peculiar* [my italics]." As with the vignettes involving Billy House in *The Stranger*, the scene served an important function, but no purpose, at least in Universal eyes. Hence, their attempt to blow up the image of Vargas in the telephone booth "in such a way as to eliminate the blind woman in the foreground," thus provoking Welles's understandable ire.

Initially the studio seemed thoroughly delighted with Welles's progress and professionalism: "It was roses all the way—until that gate closed on me [again]." Welles even went out of his way to make it clear to the studio that he knew what he was doing. Heston likes to tell the story of how, on day one of shooting, Welles had arranged to film the interrogation scene in Sanchez the shoe clerk's apartment. It is a long scene, a good five minutes, with a great deal going on, and Welles intended to shoot the whole thing in one dolly shot, without a single cut. As Heston says, "We never turned a camera all morning or all afternoon, the studio brass gathering in the shadows in anxious little knots. By the time we began filming at a quarter to six, I know they'd written off the whole day. At seven forty, Orson said, 'OK, print. That's a wrap on this set. We're two days ahead of schedule.'"

It was a classic display of bravura, designed to get the execs off his back, and off the set. The scene was one Welles preferred to the more famous opening shot in the movie, because he felt it achieved at least as much in a less ostentatious way. He no longer felt he needed to show the entire contents of his box of tricks for a film to work. He did, however, need people around him who understood something of what he was trying to do, and on March 7, after three weeks' work, Heston noted in his journal that "Orson fired his cut-ter today." The firing of the cutter was the first sign that Welles and Universal had different agendas and that the director's technical demands did not recognize the same limits.

The studio, though, grew ever more delighted as they saw first-hand the kind of clout Welles could still command in the colony. On the same day he fired the cutter, the director introduced a new actress to the crew. In an inspired touch, he had asked Marlene Dietrich if she would be willing to play the brothel owner, formerly Mother Lupe. It seemed that Dietrich, like many of Hollywood's better actors and actresses, had far more sense of Welles's achievements than the studio heads, and when the call came, "no" was not an option.

In her autobiography Mercedes McCambridge wrote of how she also received just such a "command," to play a butch gang leader in the motel "gang rape" scene: "That's what it is like to work for Orson Welles. A phone call or a cryptic telegram giving no information whatsoever serves as the summons, and if you are like me, you drop everything and go wherever Orson is . . . —no [copy of the] script, no talk of money, billing, nothing . . . go!"

But it is Dietrich whose image lingers longer than any of the other fine actresses in *Touch of Evil*, even if the studio knew noth-ing of her presence until they saw the rushes. Tanya evokes every-thing that Quinlan had and lost. It was, as Welles suggested, her "last great performance." Nor is it a coincidence that their scenes feature only the two of them—as if Quinlan is indulging in a private reverie with the one woman who might have saved him from "the hooch," and the self-loathing he drank to drive away. Her brothel represents his one safe haven. When he leaves it for the last time, it is because he has been summoned by his partner, whom he now sus-pects has become another of those "starry-eyed idealists."

The other important character introduced to proceedings dur-ing the actual shoot was an altogether more eccentric creation—

the night watchman at the motel to which Susan flees to escape Los Robles. Though he can be found in the shooting script, it was a bit part for a bit-part actor. When Welles brought in Dennis Weaver, then still in *Gunsmoke*, he immediately began to conceive of a far more offbeat figure. As he later observed, it seemed to him "as though the horrific atmosphere by which [the night watchman] is surrounded could not of necessity bring forth anything but a fantastic creature of this kind, an Elizabethan figure . . . somewhat related to those sketched-in characters that turn up in old ghost stories."

If the motel itself was teetering on the edge of a precipice, so was Weaver's performance as this sexually repressed oddball. Indeed, when the studio arbitrarily decided to remove the first half of Vargas's confrontation with the night watchman, presumably on the grounds that Weaver's gibbering characterization was verging on the incomprehensible, Welles was required to explain the basis on which he (and Weaver) had created this "fantastic creature":

> The exchange is [meant to be] painful; in a spooky sort of way. . . . Slowly Vargas himself begins to realize that this man he's talking to is crazy. . . . As it is now, Vargas appears, asks for his wife, gets one fumbling reply and then, abruptly, without any feeling of chill, we're faced with that word "party." . . . Unless we follow [the night watchman's] startled, neurotic, scrabbling progress from the position where he's first cornered, to the door through which he wants to escape, his sudden, wild behavior must strike us . . . as being wholly arbitrary. This scene [with the motel clerk] is balanced on a perilously delicate point . . . [and] the question of rhythm is absolutely central. Each one of Weaver's scenes was . . . fully rehearsed . . . [and] painstakingly built up in terms of what I can only describe as a "sound-pattern."

Welles temporarily prevailed and the scene was restored, only to be chopped again when the film went on general release, lest the public thought they had seen a character out of one of those old ghost stories. Hitchcock would take Welles's sexually repressed night watchman and turn him into a far more sinister figure the following year, as the Master Bates of *Psycho*.

The "sound-pattern" that Welles was trying to achieve with Weaver's perilously positioned performance was one of an intricate array of sonic subtleties, as the director again had the means to create a truly challenging sound scape. This time, though, his use of sound had none of the flash-bang-wallop of *Citizen Kane*. Instead, as Phyllis Goldfarb has observed, "In [*Touch of*] *Evil* an element integral in one scene is present in, and brings us to, the next."

Reflecting the learning curve he had undergone in Europe, Welles was prepared on occasions to view the soundtrack and the picture as entities that could be divorced. In fact, a great deal of *Touch of Evil's* dialogue is conducted off camera; and, like *Othello*, the soundtrack was often at odds with the visuals in ways that reflected the disorienting nature of the film. One particularly effective instance comes during the interrogation scene, when Vargas retires to the bathroom just as it becomes evident how brutal Quinlan's methods are. As the script indicates, "The sounds of the brutal grilling can be heard faintly even [in the bathroom]. Mike tries to drown it out by running water loudly in the basin." Ironically, it is Vargas's attempt to shut out this sound that leads him to knock over the shoe box that is currently empty, but in a couple of minutes will be found to contain sticks of dynamite. Vargas is thus obliged to confront a truth that his act of running water had been designed to deny.

The way that Welles inserts the ticking bomb into the soundtrack at the outset of the film is one more example of the audience being let in on information denied the town of Los Robles. The script indicates that "we hear a very faint ticking sound. This muted, menacing little noise persists . . . scarcely audible . . . It continues—unnoticed by the other characters—whenever the convertible is close to the camera." This was evidently Welles's intent before he ever devised the crane shot, probably since another studio removed a similar idea from *The Stranger*.

Welles, as per, also had very specific ideas about the score, which he passed on in a memo to the then relatively unknown Henry

Mancini. Yet to enter the top ten with "Peter Gunn Theme" or win an Oscar for "Moon River," Mancini had scored a couple of biopics of jazz greats Benny Goodman and Glen Miller. He was someone the studios only thought of in terms of heavily jazz-oriented scores. Welles wanted nothing of the sort. Nor did he want any of the stock Latin American sounds that the mention of Mexico usually induced in American film composers. He instructed Mancini to avoid at all costs "the usual 'rancheros' and 'mariachi' numbers" and said he would indicate the few instances "where traditional Mexican music is wanted." What he essentially wanted was "a great deal of rock & roll," but not of the Elvis variety:

> Because these numbers invariably back dialogue scenes, there should never be any time for vocals. This rock & roll comes from radio loud-speakers, juke boxes and, in particular, the radio in the motel. . . . What we want is musical color, rather than movement—sustained washes of sound rather than tempestuous melodramatic or operatic scoring.

Mancini was allowed to give vent to a form of fusion in the motel scenes, where an ersatz jazz-rock (long before the term was coined) plays interminably through the hotel intercom. Only after the gang members enter Susan's room, confirming that she has entered her worst nightmare, is the music finally shut off. All that remains is a claustrophobic silence.

The so-called "gang rape" scene is perhaps the moment in *Touch of Evil* when the audience realizes that everything and everyone in the film is tainted by its amorality, as we are tainted by our voyeuristic interest in Susan's fate. Terry Comito described *Touch of Evil* as being "about a nice couple from Hollywood movies who stumble into a film by Orson Welles," and that about sums it up.

The casting of Janet Leigh as the Hollywood pinup girl about to be (or not to be) defiled by these "hoods" was an inspired touch. Like Rita Hayworth in *The Lady from Shanghai*, she provides a perfect fantasy image as she lounges around in her lingerie—only for Welles to deconstruct the fantasy. Leigh suggests that she found her motel experience disturbingly real, "The scene in the motel room was one of the most frightening, insidious scenes I've ever done: it scared me when I was doing it. We shot it in a real motel room out of town in some deserted place, and it looked exactly the way it was."

Welles still understood when to give imagination precedence over visualization. As he informed Dick Cavett, some years later, "You cannot make a film masterpiece which is pornographic because the material is antipathetic to the film. . . . Exciting [people] sexually is changing the subject so completely that you have no narrative form." It was a line that got thinner in his later films, but it still held. On this occasion, he plays with feelings (Susan's *and* ours) of lust and fear, desire and denial, which he proceeds to set "off against the vivid stereotypes of a racist and sadomasochistic imagination" [JN]. We, the audience, are required to experience all of this from Susan's point of view.

Before everything comes to a head, so to speak, Welles knows enough to cut away. Having through careful editing and staging prolonged "the moment of violation . . . Welles implicates us in her violation, . . . the dark side of our own voyeurism . . . throw[ing] us off balance" [TC]. Only later do we discover that there was no violation, that the hoods had merely intended to scare Susan witless. Thus Welles managed to retain all of the scene's impact on the viewer, while at the same time ensuring that it was not yanked out of the film by the censorious arm of American cinema. Where he was not quite so successful was in retaining the entire buildup to the "moment of violation." The script version of Susan's conversation through the wall with the girl gang members was compressed for the movie, presumably at some censorious individual's insistence (the cut part is italicized):

GIRL'S VOICE [whispering through the wall]: You Know what Mary Jane is?

(Susan starts to say something.)

Know what a "main-liner" is?

SUSAN (still whispering): *Somebody who takes heroin by needle, isn't it?* (breathlessly) But what's that got to do with me?

GIRL'S VOICE: Not the muscle honey, you take it in the vein.

SUSAN: You're trying to tell me these men are drugged? Is that why—?

GIRL'S VOICE: Shhh!

[Silence . . . Susan stands with her face pressed to wall . . . waiting . . .]

SECOND GIRL'S VOICE (not whispering like the other but in low, thick-sounding tones): They brought us here to have a party.

FIRST GIRL (in her whisper): A real, wild party—you know the kind, honey—where anything goes.

SECOND GIRL'S VOICE (words blurred): They want you to join us.

FIRST GIRL'S VOICE (still whispering, but sharply): They're comin' back!

Susan turns to the door. There is the sound of a key turning in the lock.

The next time Susan regains consciousness, she sees the staring eyes of a decidedly dead "Uncle Joe." Her waking nightmare has become infected by the same contagion as Quinlan and the Grandis. We never find out how, or if, her experiences in and around Los Robles irredeemably alter her, but presuming her to be a true Brechtian, then the answer would undoubtedly be "*si*." Not so Vargas, in his blunderingly black-and-white view of the world. He informs his wife, as the body of Quinlan floats in the filth, "It's all over. . . . I'm taking you home." Wherever that might be.

The story has come full circle, with the oil derricks that we saw first when Quinlan drove up to inspect the smoking wreckage of Linneker's car now providing the backdrop to Tanya's mournful eulogy. But there is one last Wellesian irony to be added, as Schwartz tells us that the shoe clerk has just confessed to killing Linneker. Quinlan's instincts have proved to be true. So maybe all we have to show for the bullheaded intervention of Vargas is the death of two detectives and one "half-breed."

Welles never resolves the question of whether the confession was true, or how it was extracted. When asked about this very point, he dismissed it as unimportant, "[Quinlan] was wrong in spite of everything." By then, the roar of this particular prince of darkness had been stilled. Never a fan of the moralistic coda, Welles preferred to leave it up to the viewer. As he told the audience of a television pilot he made the same year *Touch of Evil* was released, "This story hasn't any moral or any message of mine tied to it. It's about morals and messages though, and I was serious when I said I hoped you'd draw your own conclusions."

In a surprising display of conformity to continuity, Welles even shot the final scene of his film on the last night of the shoot. The film was one day over its thirty-day shooting schedule, and $31,000 over its $900,000 budget. It had cost only fractionally more than *Citizen Kane*. Everyone seemed elated by the experience. Heston, in his journal, described Welles as "the most exciting director I've ever worked with. . . . Maybe it will all really begin to happen now." He is talking about himself, but on that day, and at that time, the sentiment could have equally applied to the film's overseer.

A DARK TURGID AFFAIR

[Touch of Evil]

The film . . . was shot strictly within a most precise pattern
involving rather special arrangements of sound and silence.
The crescendo of suspense was to depend more on the
soundtrack than the images. The decision to shuffle those
images in a new, and much more obvious order could never
have been made except in ignorance of this basic scheme.

Orson Welles, memo to Universal, December 1957

W elles always claimed a certain bemusement at what transpired after he finished filming *Touch of Evil*. He felt that
he had done all that was required of him, and that the film
was taken away from him arbitrarily. According to his version of
events, the executives "saw a rough cut of it, and they were so hor-
rified that they wouldn't let me in the studio . . . [Maybe it was] a little too black. But that's a guess." It must remain a guess, because
that version is now done gone. There are others, some involved in
making the film, who see its sabotage by the studio as being primarily down to Welles. Charlton Heston came to feel that there was
within the man, "some kind of perverse, suicidal refusal to deal with
the people . . . who are going to give him the money to make the
movies. I think he disdains them . . . and [is] outraged that they nevertheless control what he does."

David Thomson, in the dumbest line in a rather dumb book, suggests, apropos of *Touch of Evil*, "It is never an excuse in Hollywood to
say you've been betrayed. You have to take that possibility for
granted, and plan accordingly." The previous chapter shows how well
planned the film was and how carefully Welles set about ensuring
the minimum amount of studio interference. Quite how "planning,"
though, might compel a studio to let one have the time and resources
to complete editing a movie made "within a most precise pattern,
involving rather special arrangements of sound and silence," Thomson can't quite bring himself to convey. The idea that Welles's mul-

tilayered way of making films might be anathema to the Hollywood system never patters across the man's crinkled cranium.

Touch of Evil was not taken away from Welles because he insulted the bosses, or proved incapable or unwilling to play second-guess the subterfuge. It was taken away from him because the studio had no idea what he was doing, and why he was taking so long to do it. Even though Universal discovered in the fullness of time, as had RKO and Columbia before them, that their own attempts to reconstruct the film only made matters worse, they, like RKO and Columbia, persevered without Welles and released a film that failed on both counts, being neither representative of its "dominant personality" nor a commercial success. On this basis, it should have been these decision makers who were fired as a result, not the director.

None of which lets Welles off the hook here. He screwed up. Or more accurately, he got screwed up. Seeing an instant replay of previous catastrophes pass before his eyes, he allowed a personal despair to get the better of him, at least temporarily. When he subsequently tried his damnedest to resurrect the film, and his reputation, it was too late. That gate had already closed on him.

When Welles wrote his famous fifty-eight-page memo in December 1957, in which he pleaded for the studio to at least take account of the "visual pattern to which I gave so many long hard days of work," the film had already passed from his hands. And he knew it. This memo—which ironically now forms the basis of what looks set to become, as of 1998, the "standard" version of the film—came at the end of a six-month process that resulted in as many as six different *Touch of Evils*, none of which attempted to replicate the instructions in the "memo," and only two of which have survived. Only by tackling these in turn can we discern how and why Universal decided to dismantle Welles's painstakingly conceived *Touch of Evil*.

The July 22 Edit

Welles began work on the editing of *Touch of Evil* shortly after the final day's shooting, in mid-April 1957. He was anxious to start stitching together his precise pattern and knew from experience that it might be a drawn-out process. As he told Andre Bazin a few months later, he already knew that "in the editing room I work very slowly. . . . I don't know why it takes me so long . . . [but it] always enrages the producers who tear the film from my hands."

It was Truffaut who memorably described the films of Welles as being "shot by an exhibitionist and cut by a censor." At the same time, he painted Welles as someone who "criticizes himself pitilessly on the editing table." In fact, the director's reputation across the editing suites of the world was of someone more likely to criticize the work of his fellow editor(s) "pitilessly." Bill Morton, who was principal editor on *Othello*, remembers Welles once snapping at him, "Your job as a film editor is not merely to get from one shot to another. There is a living part to this film and a dead part. Please eliminate the dead." Sound advice, tersely expressed.

Unfortunately, the first editor assigned to *Touch of Evil*, Virgil Vogel, struggled to follow Welles's line of reasoning, let alone his aesthetic. The director kept banging on about the rhythm of the cuts, while paying little attention to the narrative line, exposition, or continuity. Vogel may have been none the wiser had he read Welles's views on editing—with particular emphasis on this very film— expressed to *Cahiers du Cinema* the following year: "As far as I'm concerned, the ribbon of film is played like a musical score, and this performance is determined by the way it is edited. . . . The images alone are insufficient. They are very important, but they are only images. The essential thing is how long each image lasts, [and] what follows each image."

At one point Vogel was apparently perplexed by the absence of a discernible audio track from a particular actor and asked Welles what the lines were meant to be. Welles informed him that it was none of his business and to concentrate on the "pictorial value" and, of course, the rhythm. The sequence in question may have been the fabled crane shot, at the end of which the border guard asks to see Linneker's passport, a piece of dialogue that the bit-part player in question kept blowing. Welles finally told him not to say anything, but to just move his lips, as he'd rather not keep reshooting a three-and-a-half minute scene for a single actor's benefit.

According to Welles, Vogel eventually just "froze up" and the director was obliged to replace him. His replacement, Edward Curtis, was no better equipped to deal with the demanding director and, while Welles was in New York in early June to appear on *The Steve Allen Show*, the studio head Ed Muhl stepped in and appointed Aaron Stell to the task. Welles, who promptly returned to L.A., was less than happy with Muhl's choice. To start with, it had been imposed in a somewhat underhand fashion, and secondly, he had been asked to let Stell work alone, which went against his entire modus operandi.

And so Welles again found himself obliged to conform to standard Hollywood practice, rather than the other way around. As a result, he ended up projecting sections of film onto a screen, wherein he would make notes of any changes he wanted. He would then inform Stell in memo or conversation how and where to make them. According to Stell, "He constantly recast the editing sequence, providing different interpretations of whole scenes by transpositions, frequently disrupting the continuity." Although Stell claimed that he worked with Welles for several months, it can only have been for six weeks at best. He also says that "in all the months they worked together, Welles never once entered the cutting room," which shows that Muhl had got his way—without the editor's foreknowledge. Stell also observed, to Charles Higham, that Welles had already started to act "ill, depressed, and [generally] unhappy with the studio's impatience."

Stell later claimed (this time to Frank Brady) that Welles never even watched the "one partial cut that [he] ran for him." In fact, there was a rough cut of sorts *completed* by Stell, which was screened for the studio. According to Brady, though not Leaming (who probably relied unwisely on Ernest Nims's selective memory), Welles attended this screening—though only after fiercely complaining to Muhl that it was like yanking the last page out of a novelist's typewriter before he was given a chance to revise it. Welles clearly felt he was very close to finishing *his* film (a valedictory reference appears, in his December 1957 memo, to "the edited version I was

so near to finishing last July"). In attendance at the July 22 screening, aside from Welles and presumably Stell, were studio head Ed
Muhl, studio exec Mel Tucker, producer Albert Zugsmith, and apparently Ernest Nims, the Supercutter on *The Stranger*, who was now
head of postproduction at Universal. It was March 16, 1940, all over
again; except that Welles seems to have been present to hear what
the studio thought.

Once again Nims felt he had incisively isolated the problem:
"He had really messed up the first five reels . . . He was making those
quick cuts—in the middle of a scene you cut to another scene, and
then come back and finish the scene, and then cut to the last half
of the other scene." Given that Welles hadn't actually finished editing the picture any such criticism was premature, but Muhl made it
anyhow. He appointed Nims to work at resolving these "problems,"
i.e. he took the picture out of Welles's hands and again "requested"
that the editor be left to work on his own. Welles was powerless to
prevent Nims doing another number on one of his movies.

That first rough cut may well have contained elements lost altogether from subsequent Universal-appointed edits. Welles, on at
least two occasions, referred to "a whole section of the film which
was rather surrealistic, a mad, sort of dark, black comedy," that was
cut out (if so, it was presumably improvised on the spot as it does not
appear in the shooting script). Producer Albert Zugsmith later
claimed that "his first cut kept going on and going on. Orson kind
of takes off, you know, he lacks discipline," equating those Wellesian
digressions with taking one's eyes off the continuity prize.

The August 28 Edit

To his dying day Ernest Nims always talked up his relationship with
Welles in interviews. According to Walter Murch—who edited the
1998 "remake"—Nims even claimed to have "memos that Welles
had written to Ernie about their strategy for the film, how to outwit
the studio." If so, he did not show them to Barbara Leaming, who
interviewed him for her biography, but makes no mention of such

memos, though she does refer to a letter from Nims to Welles, "in response to Orson's telegrams about when he could come back to work." Welles evidently felt he had been ostracized for good.

The Nims edit of *Touch of Evil* was finally screened for Welles on August 28. In the five weeks between the July 22 screening of Welles's edit and the "Nims" screening, Welles disappeared from the Hollywood radar. It was during that time that Nims instigated the process of dismantling the director's sixth (and last) Hollywood excursion, while Welles questioned whether he had the strength to get up and take another shot. One Welles character trait highlighted by Alessandro Tasca di Cuto, executive producer of *Chimes at Midnight*, worked against him here: "Sometimes, when he could have asserted himself, he didn't; and other times, for no good reason, he behaved like a bull in a china shop, smashing everything." On this occasion, when the latter should probably have been his chosen course, he mutely headed for Mexico, a land that always reconnected him to his wellspring.

According to Zugsmith, with whom Welles endeavored to retain cordial relations, he "was staying in his favorite place, Caesar's. I don't know whether his liver started bothering him, or what," before suggesting that "Welles was so crushed by the adverse studio criticism and the fact that the control of the film had been virtually taken away from him that he went on what might be considered a month-long psychological bender." If Welles notified the producer that he was not a well man, he did not hold him personally responsible for what seems to have been a very deep trough of depression.

When such moments came upon him, Welles really did feel he was in the depths of the abyss, and "neither faith nor philosophy" could touch him as he lay "beneath the ruins." Audrey Stainton, who started working as his secretary shortly afterward, says that "the image of Welles" she retained was "of a man devastatingly alone. In his good moods, in company he enjoyed, no one could be wittier or more charming, but what I remember most are his long silences." Michael MacLiammoir, another confidant who knew Welles well, also wrote of how his "own shadow, which has nothing to do with leaves, branches, or birds, broods constantly within him, a dark turgid affair. It spreads when things go wrong."

Well, things had gone catastrophically wrong—yet again—and Welles couldn't help but question the choices he had made. As he told his biographer, disaster "repeated itself enough to look like a character failing of mine. And I keep thinking maybe it is. It's like somebody who every time he goes out gets struck by lightning." He even began to think the unthinkable—abandoning film—informing Bazin at Cannes the following year, "I've be[come] too disillusioned. I've put in too much work, too much effort for what was given to me in return."

His sense of despair was real, but not new. As far back as *Citizen Kane*, he had developed a habit of disappearing for a few days at a time, remaining incommunicado throughout. He would then reappear without explanation and work would resume. Two weeks after opening in Richard Wright's *Native Son*, in the spring of 1941, his last real triumph on the New York stage, he admitted himself to a private sanitorium, where he stayed for a couple of days to recuperate from the rigors of his helter-skelter schedule.

Evidently failure was not a requisite for the dark shadow to descend. In this instance, though, he felt that he had come close to restoring his reputation. To see it snatched away, in that old familiar way, was doubly heartbreaking. He knew the stakes. As he eloquently observed in a letter to Charlton Heston in November, when his worst fears seemed to be coming to pass, "If I were now directing another picture—or about to direct one—and if I hadn't been away so long, I might be tempted to write off my own investment as a bad loss. But as things are with me in this industry, I simply cannot afford to sustain [another] such . . . blow."

On August 28 Welles saw the Supercutter's work. He seemed surprisingly positive about what Nims had done, admitting in his memo that "the whole problem of the opening reels is one of clarity. There are different sets of characters and innumerable relationships which must be very clearly established and set off one from the other. I believe that the criticism of my own, unfinished version of these opening reels was entirely justified and, as I told him, Ernie Nims made dramatic progress in reducing this confusion." Such a concession was not enough for the pugnacious Muhl, and he decided that some additional scenes were needed for exposition purposes. Welles, not unreasonably, requested the opportunity to direct these scenes. He was turned down, and so concluded, again not unreasonably, that the studio intended to take the film still further away from his intentions.

The "November 4 Edit"?

From this point the sump only gets dirtier. No additional scenes were shot for over two months. Nor does there seem to have been any concerted attempt on Universal's part to get the film finished and released, even though this had been the ostensible reason for (prematurely) screening Welles's rough cut in July. With Welles excluded from the process—and his acting not required, it is hard to see how this delay can be put down to him (he was in Louisiana and Mexico, acting in one film and directing another).

The suggestion made in a number of books, that the studio had agreed to consider any suggestions Welles might choose to present in writing, and that his supposed tardiness in offering these led to a delay on the reshoots, is simply not a credible one. Those who accuse Welles of willfully refusing to provide suggestions after seeing the Nims edit do so on the slenderest of evidence, conveniently disregarding the fact that the studio had already screened an unfinished rough cut and enforced changes on that basis; imposed two editors, both unsuitable, on the director; and refused to allow him to supervise any reshoots on his own movie. So why would Welles have any reason to think that they might take the slightest notice of any further suggestions?

The language Welles chooses to use in the December memo makes it clear that he felt himself to be persona non grata: "Where there's simply a difference of taste between your editing and mine, I have resigned myself to the futility of discussion, and will spare you my comments." This hardly reads like the sentiment of a man for whom the door remained ajar. Later in the memo Welles tells us something of what has already gone down against his wishes: "In the light of the decision [already taken] to deny me permission to direct these scenes, to write the dialogue for them or to collaborate in that writing, or indeed even to be present during your discussions of the matter, I must . . . face the strong probability that I am the very last person whose opinion will be likely to carry any weight with you." His subsequent heartfelt plea to "open your mind for a moment to this opinion from the man who, after all, made the picture" sure sounds like the last recourse of a man who had already been repeatedly ignored.

There *was* a first memo from Welles: it ran to nine pages and, according to his longer December memo, it dated from "last summer." According to the studio it did not arrive until November 4, which was the same day that a version of the movie was screened for Heston and presumably other cast members' benefit. The film that Heston says he saw that day "has flaws. Unscored, undubbed, it seemed uneven in tempo and unclear in the opening sequences. Universal feels a day or so of additional shooting is necessary to clarify some ambiguities. Maybe so."

But did Heston see the Nims edit, or had Universal made further inroads into the film? One thing is certain. Even if Welles had failed to send—or Universal had mislaid—this original memo and Muhl did not see it until November 4, the studio head still had time to reevaluate his decision to keep Welles from directing the reshoots, or to at least write the dialogue, in the interests of some kinda consistency of tone. To reconsider, or not to reconsider, that was the question.

One thing was for certain. This was *not* panning out to be *Ambersons* revisited. Indeed, Muhl faced the possibility of an out-and-out rebellion from the two stars he needed for the reshoots. Initially, the studio had managed to convince Heston that the problem lay with Welles, who he was led to believe was sulking in his tent "like Achilles." However, when on November 7 he got to hear the director's version of events firsthand, Welles assured him that he was "eager to do any retakes they want, and do them free as well." Heston became adamant that he would not do any reshoots without

Welles. Leigh, too, had thrown her hat into the ring and was obdurately siding with Welles.

Welles took to furnishing Heston with a copy of the nine-page memo and a personal plea for support. In his letter to Heston, he referred to "rumors of Muhl joining [the unemployed] continu[ing] to spread." He also suggested the possibility that "a certain throbbing of war drums has reached their ears at last, and they intend to make a convincing show of cooperating with my suggestions [in the memo] in the hope of spiking my guns." (This is essentially what Muhl ended up doing.)

At this point, any levelheaded studio head would have made the best of a bad job and made the magnanimous gesture. The fact that Muhl didn't suggests that the whole thing had probably at some point become personal. Heston later asserted that he had seen Welles "deliberately insult studio heads," which strongly implies that Muhl and Welles did at some point lock horns (contacted by Rick Schmidlin in the mid-1990s, Muhl dismissed Welles "as a poseur who never made a film that earned any money," apparently unaware how much of an earner *Touch of Evil* had become over the years).

By November 11, it was being made absolutely clear to Heston (and presumably Leigh) that the studio heads "really don't *want* Orson to do the work." After Heston canceled one reshoot in a last-ditch attempt to resolve the situation in Welles's favor, he was reminded of his contractual obligations. In the face of "Universal's apparently implacable determination that Orson will *not* direct" the reshoots, he finally folded. On November 19, three or four new scenes were shot by television director Harry Keller. In these scenes Keller's patent unsuitability is lit large, as he replaces Welles's mise-en-scène with a mess on-screen. Despite instructions to "duplicate the style of Orson Welles"—and his own claim to have done so—Keller's scenes merely confirm continuing employment for the RKO janitor.

Not surprisingly, Welles struggled to keep a tight rein on his true opinion of Keller's technical gifts in his long memo. Despite the "scrupulous care" with which he sought to "avoid those wide and sweeping denunciations of your new material to which my own position . . . sorely tempts me," there is one moment when the anger he is undoubtedly feeling threatens to break through. It is a bracketed and single-spaced aside in which his feelings run close to the surface: "(You may be sure that I have strong opinions on the quality of all the new dialogue, the texture of the photography and the direction and playing of the new scenes . . .)." As the one and only time that he reverts to single-space typing, it suggests he probably had to Typex out another, altogether more scathing version.

The "Kellerized" Version

Sometime in late November, Welles was finally given an opportunity to see what Universal had done to his film. Not only had the new scenes by Keller been inserted, but there appears to have been further editing, as Welles expresses dissatisfaction with the way they had apparently recut Nims's own edit of those "messy" first five reels, as shown to him in August. At the same time, he expressed pleasure "that the brief scene between Susan and Vargas on the hotel stairway has been restored." Whether these changes predate the November 4 screening is not known.

Much has been made of the fact that Welles wrote his powerful memo after just a single screening. However, he still had his original nine-page memo to draw upon, which the later memo often simply embellished. According to his letter to Heston, the studio had already "expressed willingness to follow the main lines of the [original] memo." But, as Welles astutely observed, "the big question . . . is just what the [studio's] 'majority' [of changes] will really turn out to be." The second, longer memo was thus largely intended to reinforce points made in that first memo and to forcefully restate the case for changes. Walter Murch, the eminent editor primarily responsible for the 1998 "restoration," spoke for Welles in a recent interview, when he said:

> I can only imagine how he felt, sitting there, writing away furiously in the dark. By the morning he had typed up fifty-eight pages of comments—astute, insightful, restrained, boiling with passion under the surface. But he was aware he was addressing his thoughts to the heads of the

studio—notably Ed Muhl—who were his declared enemies. So you can see him trying not to express outright blame for what had happened, no matter what he thought privately. It's heartbreaking to read.

The first outlets for Welles's barely contained invective were two of Keller's scenes, a brief scene in the hotel lobby between Vargas and his wife and one in which Susan attempts to get her husband to concentrate on her needs in the car on the way to the motel. Even though Welles attempts to keep a lid on his true feelings, he accuses the "director" of making the leading lady appear "flighty to the point of feeblemindedness" in the former scene, while pointing out just how unlikely it is that "two cars . . . just happen to meet" in what "seems to be a pretty out of way corner of the wilderness" in the latter. Keller had roundly ignored Welles's warning against "the vestigial remnants of the old [story] line . . . remain[ing] in too obvious conflict with your added material," something alluded to in that original "summer" memo.

Welles's comments in the memo about the lobby scene—which lasts less than a minute—are most revealing. The addition of a nonsensical line from Vargas to his wife telling her to lock her door (which she self-evidently fails to do) suggests feeblemindedness, not so much on Susan's part as on Keller's. As Welles points out, even if the intent behind the scene is simply to provide "added footage for Miss Leigh and Mr. Heston," it does so at the expense of sense: "This particular new scene goes directly against the intentions of the . . . original line of the story . . . [as it] makes the later scene . . . in which Susan packs and stamps out of her hotel room, completely arbitrary."

Obliged to reiterate what the film he had made was actually about, Welles proceeds to explain the central husband-wife dynamic: "A honeymoon couple, desperately in love, is abruptly separated by a violent incident . . . which, although it had no personal bearing on either of them, the man considers as a matter of his urgent professional concern. This feeling of responsibility by Vargas [represents] . . . an expression of the basic theme of the whole picture." Applying conventional motivations and narrative form to persuade the stubborn Muhl, Welles seems on the verge of revealing to the studio head what a fundamentally subversive movie he had made:

> By sweetening their relationship . . . at precisely that point where the distance separating the man and woman should be at its greatest, there is a sharp loss in dimension, and both Vargas and Susan emerge as stock characters—the sort of "romantic leads" to be found in any program picture. . . . The separation of the newlyweds . . . doesn't come about through the arbitrary mechanics of the detective story, but develops as an organic progression of events implicit in the characters of the people.

His reference to "an organic progression of events" reveals a self-conscious artist, who knows exactly what he'd like to say but must for now hold back. Likewise, in the "sleepy seduction" scene on the way to the motel, Welles gives the studio the option of retaining their preferred implication, but expressing it his way: "If the purpose here is to warm up the sex interest, why not finish the scene on the kiss, with the police car interrupting the embrace (as in the original version)?" Welles's real motive was to provide a reason for the studio to adopt the original method by which Vargas's car meets Uncle Joe's. He fully admits to being baffled as to their motive "for cutting the footage in which Grandi's tailing operation was made clear to the audience." He personally felt that such a cut detracted from the film, especially in the soundtrack department:

> The [original] plan (as indicated in my original memo) was for a quite interesting pattern of newscasts to be heard on the radios of the two cars and in the two languages. When Vargas switched stations, there was to be a dreamy, old-fashioned Mexican waltz. . . .. This pattern was to be rudely broken by the aggressive siren of Quinlan's car, and then—after Vargas's departure in that car—the gently picturesque lullaby would soothe Susan toward sleep as Menzies drove off with her. . . . This music . . . would all be part of a most intricately worked out sequence in which sirens, dynamite explosions, and various radio voices . . . would play their different roles. . . . What was meant to be a tour de force in

the rather sadly neglected dimension of the soundtrack, now cannot be anything more interesting than a succession of straight plot scenes, all quite necessary to our story, but of no special value in themselves.

However, the point where Welles came closest to blowing his cover, as a concerned fellow worker in the great cooperative venture, was in his comments regarding the early scenes and the editing thereof. The opening of the film had evidently been a source of disagreement from the very first screening. Muhl seemed to feel that Welles had forsaken every precept of movie storytelling simply to achieve some perverse "quality of strangeness." For Welles, disorientation need never be at the expense of exposition; and he remained adamant that a return to the burning car, where Vargas awaits the entrance of Quinlan, should be delayed by the sequence where Susan is accosted on the street and taken to meet Uncle Joe. Again, he summoned up the Gods of Continuity and Clarity to come to his aid:

> Resigned as I am to the fact that a great majority of my previous notes and suggestions have been disregarded, the case of the scene between Grandi and Susan is one of the few issues I feel justified in reopening. This scene is just exactly a thousand percent more effective played, as it was first arranged, in two parts, with a cutaway to the scene of the explosion between those two parts . . . I think that moving the conflict between Quinlan and Vargas closer to the street scene in front of the hotel will aid clarity and much improve the narrative line. . . . This is in the best, classic tradition of movie continuity, the clinching virtue of which is the fact that in this arrangement we would never stay away from either story—Susan's or Vargas's—long enough to lose their separate but relating threads of interest. . . . What's vital is that both stories—the leading man's and the leading woman's—be kept equally and continuously alive; each scene, as we move back and forth across the border, should play at roughly equal lengths leading up to the moment at the hotel when the lovers meet again. This simple but drastic improvement—added to the body of Ernie Nims's clear and concise version of this opening section . . . will put the identification with the characters in a just proportion.

How much of Welles's original edit Ernest Nims had left intact is undocumented, but the director chose to keep his old nemesis—who was, after all, head of postproduction at Universal—convinced that he respected his input. Thus in the long memo, though he criticizes the way that the studio edited together the Susan/Uncle Joe scene(s) (presumably Nims's handiwork), he "recognizes" that this "was born of an overall desire for simplification and clarity." The version told in Leaming's "authorized" biography, though, states that Welles "was aghast at what he saw as Nims's having undone all his painstaking labor in the editing room."

Welles suggests the benefit of his own approach in one of the more minor requests made in his memo, suggesting that the second hall of records scene, in which Vargas confronts Menzies about his boss, should not be followed by Menzies calling Tanya (which it does not in the released versions, so evidently this one wish was respected). In Welles's eyes, if left as it was, the result would have been not so much "a really drastic befuddlement, just a mild series of short circuits in the logic of the visual progression. . . . There's no real dislocation but rather an insensible loosening of tension," the kind that comes about when a film becomes the disjointed projection of two (or more) dominant personalities.

Knowing that he was faced with "the antithetical approach to moviemaking" [BL] practiced by Keller, Muhl, and Nims, Welles was obliged to be disingenuous in a number of his given explanations. As Murch suggests, he was still "addressing his thoughts to . . . his declared enemies." Rick Schmidlin, in an interview with Lawrence French, cited a particularly subtle example of Welles's subterfuge, in the same scene as above, that it took the restoration itself to reveal:

> One of the smaller changes we made, but one with the largest repercussions, was the removal of a close-up of Menzies, Quinlan's sidekick. It is particularly interesting that Welles, in asking for this change, phrased his request in technical terms—he wanted the shot removed, he wrote, "because of a mistaken use of the wide angle lens which distorts Menzie's face grotesquely." . . . At first, this note appeared to me to be some-

what out of character for Welles, because there are many other "weird close-ups" in the film that use the same lens . . . But I did what he asked, and it was only when viewing the film as a whole that I saw the real reason for the note, which he carefully avoided telling the studio. The close-up occurs in a scene between Vargas and Menzies, at a crucial point in which Vargas has confronted Menzies with evidence of Quinlan's duplicity. Menzies, who has been standing, collapses and his agony is revealed in this close-up. Almost instantly, he jumps back to his feet and defends his boss, but the damage has been done: Vargas has seen him acknowledge the truth, and more to the point Menzies has seen Vargas see this. As a result, everything that Menzies does in the film's last half hour is done under duress. . . . Menzies has a metaphorical leash around his neck. By cutting this close-up, we also cut the leash. . . . As a result, everything that Menzies does from that moment on—and he plays a crucial role in the undoing of his boss—is done authentically: he chooses to do it, rather than being coerced.

Such subtleties had been the man's trademark for nearly twenty years, invariably conveying a "feeling of many actions, visual and aural, occurring simultaneously" [JN]. The sophistication of studio resources gave him the facilities to realize his ideas, albeit at the cost of independence in thought and deed. Thus, in the sequence between Vargas and Schwartz in the racing car, Welles always intended for the final shot to be Vargas's hand reaching for the radio: "The idea here was for the music to be suddenly raised in volume. Then, when the camera cranes up, and the car pulls violently ahead, there would be an interesting reverse pattern in the sound, with the 'chase music' abruptly fading as the car speeds off into the distance." By highlighting this example of "the rather sadly neglected dimension of the soundtrack" Welles at least succeeded in getting this aspect restored to the film, making for one of the most Wellesian moments therein.

The changes that *were* made on the basis of Welles's memo were selective, never substantive. In those instances where the studio took on board the vast cinematic experience Welles brought to bear in his memos, their criteria seems to have been wholly economic—if the change Welles requested was simple and cheap, it was made. If it involved a rethink about the film's direction, or cast doubt on their own postproduction, it was quietly ignored, just as Welles had previously predicted in his letter to Heston.

Given the spirit in which Welles wrote his fifty-eight-page memo—"in recognition and full acceptance of the fact that the final shape and emphasis of the film is to be wholly yours"—i.e. the studio's—it is supremely ironic that the 1998 *Touch of Evil* "restoration" has been presented as some kind of "director's cut," the movie as Welles intended it (indeed, emblazoned across the front of the DVD is the apocryphal legend, "Restored To Orson Welles's Vision"). This was not the case, and the wider dissemination of the memo might have helped reinforce this vital distinction.

In Welles's mind, the film he felt he had been so close to finishing in July was no more. As he says halfway through the great memo, when another change makes no(n) sense of the story, "I'm passing on to you a reaction based not on my conviction as to what *my picture ought to be,* but only what here strikes me as significantly mistaken in *your picture*" (the italics are Welles's own). Though Welles told the studio that he still "want[ed] the picture to be as effective as possible . . . now, of course, that means effective in *your terms.*" In this sense, he was already disowning the results—whichever changes they decided to take on board. It was their picture that Universal now set out to release.

The UCLA Version

At this point Welles had little choice but to wash his hands of the film. In a letter to the *New Statesman,* six months later, he sought to inform a wider audience for the first time of "the wholesale reediting of the film by the executive producer, a process of rehashing in which I was forbidden to participate . . . further confounded by several added scenes which I did not write and was not invited to direct." He was never even advised which of his suggestions the studio ultimately elected to adopt. When he was asked by the *Cahiers du Cinema* contingent, the same month as the above missive, what Quinlan meant when he told Menzies that this was the second bullet he took for him, Welles was genuinely bemused. He knew that "his" film explained that his limp was the result of a bullet he had received when saving Menzies's life. By the time it made it to France (in its sixth incarnation), no such explanation remained to clarify Menzies's hero worship.

If the scenes executed by Keller remained intact, the reediting of the film—in particular, its opening twenty minutes—was now linear enough to insensibly loosen much of the film's latent tension. Even if producer Zugsmith believed that all "Universal did to the film, beyond what Welles might have wanted, was to sharpen his grammar, dot his *i*'s and cross his *t*'s," they had i' truth brought in Beaumont and Fletcher to rewrite parts of *Hamlet*.

Though Universal finally had a 108-minute version of the film ready for release, they decided that another preview was in order. It was previewed at the Pacific Palisades at the end of January 1958 and again we are reliant on Charlton Heston, who "sneaked" in to take a peek, for a contemporary reaction to this version. He thought that what he saw was "simply not a good picture. It has the brilliance that made each day's rushes look so exciting, of course . . . but it doesn't hold together as a story." (In an editorial aside to his published journals, composed in 1978, Heston stated that he was "at a loss to explain this gloomy estimate.") He was clearly not alone in his initial assessment. The general reaction at the preview was sufficient for the studio to decide that another edit was in order.

The General Release

Though all the "preview" version really needed to succeed on its own terms was a little resequencing and some judicious exposition, the studio's solution—trimming a further fifteen minutes (including some of the reshoots that vexed Welles so) and hang the story's internal logic—beggars belief. An ongoing lack of attention to detail meant that the unexplained limp, from that "first bullet," was just one of a plethora of incongruities the film left swinging in the breeze. Not surprisingly, the press noticed. As *Variety's* reviewer vocalized, "There is insufficient orientation and far too little exposition, with the result that much of the action is confusing and difficult to relate to the plot."

Once again a studio had decided to reedit Welles in a way that dissipated but failed to dispel "that quality of strangeness." The result was something strangely strange but oddly normal. Ever since *The Stranger*, Welles had been constructing films that could not be easily recast by some other "dominant personality." For all of Universal's rejigging, the atmosphere was still all Welles. As Howard Thompson wrote in the *New York Times*, Welles had "generat[ed] enough sinister electricity for three such yarns . . . staging it like a wild, murky nightmare." The film even drew the fire of Soviet director Sergei Gerasimov for decadently displaying "the 'aesthetics' of filth and blood." The film's gorgeous atmospherics were also enough to win Welles the first prize at the Brussels Film Festival that spring, but Universal refused to mount any kind of campaign to promote what they had wrought. Indeed, according to Welles, they promptly fired the individual who put the film in for the Brussels competition.

Something about our Orson had got under their skin, but no one at the studio was man enough to admit that they never really understood what kind of film he had made. According to Rick Schmidlin, Universal compiled some nineteen different distribution plans, one of which "made it look like a prostitution-slavery movie that Orson Welles was making in Mexico and . . . that the movie couldn't be shown in California or Mexico because it was too close to what was going on in the border towns there!"

It took the discovery in 1976, by a UCLA professor, of the fuller "preview" version to provide a degree of validation for Welles's complaints about this general release version. Again his instincts were destined to receive a belated vindication, as the extent of the damage done by the studio's ham-fistedness stood partially revealed. By 1982, when the "preview" version had all but replaced the ninety-three-minute general release on television, on video, and at film festivals, *Touch of Evil* was one of three Welles films included in *Sight & Sound*'s top twenty films of all time (the only director to figure in this list more than once).

In 1998 the film was reedited according to Welles's long memo, allowing viewers to see a film without codirection by Keller. The first twenty minutes were finally edited in such a way that "both stories—the leading man's and the leading woman's—[are] kept equally and continuously alive . . . put[ting] the identification with the characters in a just proportion and in a form which . . . is irresistibly interesting." More shocking still was that remarkable opening minus its title credits (and Mancini's music!). Sadly, even this restoration was never going to be what Welles felt his "picture ought to be." The necessary elements had long been consigned to the Universal dumpster.

Touch of Evil represented a watershed in Welles's career, not only in his relations with Hollywood, but also in his expositions on the thriller genre. As he pointed out to an English periodical less than two months after the film went on general release, he had "only twice been given any voice at all as to the 'level' of my subject matter," and neither of these were thrillers. There would be no more thrillers to be found within those well-worn "trunks stuffed with unproduced film scripts." Time to leave it to Hitchcock, who eighteen months after the Palisades preview came up with a film in which Janet Leigh is holed up at a motel on the outskirts of town, where she meets an unhinged hotel clerk who freaks her out; all beautifully shot by John L. Russell, the camera operator on *Touch of Evil. Psycho* was gauged to be a most welcome return to form from the increasingly erratic king of suspense. Welles, though, continued to be the leper of the colony.

Some of this can be put down to what Naremore identifies as Welles's "fairly steady movement away from the conventions of cinematic reality toward the bizarre and surreal . . . [whereas] Hitchcock, whose films have several parallels with his own, [uses] imagery [that] is always lucid and orderly." It may be that Welles simply refused to learn the same lesson Howard Hawks claimed he did from the commercial failure of *Bringing Up Baby*, "There were no normal people in it. . . . They were all way off center. . . . I think it would have done better at the box office if there had been a few sane folks in it." Welles's explanation for his movement away from the center ground was simple—he felt obliged to "occupy positions that aren't occupied because, in this young medium of expression, it's a necessity."

After his Universal experience, Welles began to distance himself from the "dream factory," insisting that he no longer "venture[s] back behind the chromium curtain . . . without a return ticket to the outside world." As he made his last notable acting cameo in a Hollywood movie, for Daryl Zanuck's *Compulsion*, he seemed overwhelmed with nostalgia for the Tinseltown he first knew back in its ostensible golden age. The same month *Compulsion* was released, March 1959, he contributed an article for *Esquire* entitled "Twilight in the Smog," which was almost a valedictory for the old Hollywood he had left "quite a while ago":

> In its golden age . . . the mood and manner [of Hollywood] were indeed much like that of a gold rush . . . [with] the same cheerful violence and cutthroat anarchy. . . . In this unlikely outpost—unfettered . . . a motley crew of show folk, in spirit far closer to the circus, to burlesque and the commedia dell'arte than to the starchy stage world of that epoch, was gaily producing a new art form. . . . All of that Western turbulence has been silenced now; the wild and woolly charm is just a memory. . . . It's just recently that we began to employ that very middle-class word, "profession." This was when the mention of art began to embarrass us, and this was the beginning of our fall from grace.

Welles even began to talk about a career outside film, and in the winter and spring of 1960 he put on stage productions of Ionesco's *Rhinoceros* and his Falstaff play, *Chimes at Midnight*, in London and Dublin respectively. By this time, though, he had become the darling of European cineasts. For all his talk of no longer "wasting my life trying to express myself in film," he continued to explore ways of raising funds to film his prismatic vision of the world.

At the turn of the decade, while being interviewed for the BBC's *Monitor* program as a prelude to the U.K. television debut of *Citizen Kane*, Welles still clearly retained an enthusiasm for the medium, if not the mass-marketers who seemed to have taken over his home country's film industry. As he informed Huw Wheldon, "I'm very much an American and I deeply regret my inability to make films on American subjects, because they're the ones that interest me the most." This was a statement of intent, confirmed by everything to come, that he felt his days as an American filmmaker were assuredly over—even if his directorial career was not.

12

OUTSIDE THE SYSTEM

[The Trial; Don Quixote; Chimes at Midnight; The Other Side of the Wind]

What's valid on the . . . screen is never a mere professional
effort and certainly not an industrial product. Whatever is
valuable must, in the final analysis, be a work of art . . . [and]
originality is one of the essential definitions of any work of art.
. . . Just as obviously, the industrial system, by its nature,
cannot accommodate originality. A genuine individual is an
outright nuisance in a factory.

Orson Welles, "Twilight in the Smog," March 1959

By the time Welles next crossed the Hollywood radar it was
1975 and he was accepting a Lifetime Achievement Award
from the American Film Institute (AFI). Though he had ten
years' more breath in him, he would complete no more films after
this award ceremony. Welles himself attended the event in the hope
that he might, by this very public reminder of his achievements, be
able to raise enough interest (and, therefore, funds) to complete his
latest (and last) satire on "the college graduates from the conglomerates" that represented the New Hollywood. He had spent the past
few years shooting *The Other Side of the Wind* on and off in the arid
Arizona desert, with a cast of willing cronies, headed by John Huston as film director Jake Hannaford, and featuring every raggle-tag-
gle gypsy he could cajole.

At this AFI tribute Welles spoke eloquently of his maverick
nature, calling up Samuel Johnson on the subject of contrarieties:
"There are goods so opposed that we cannot seize both; and in trying, fail to seize either. Flatter not yourself with contrarieties. Of the
blessings set before you, make your choice." Regarding the choices
he had made, he spoke as an arch-maverick, who "may go his own
way, but he doesn't think that it's the only way or ever claim that it's
the best one—except maybe for himself. . . . It's just that some of the

necessities to which *I* am a slave are different from yours." However, no offers were forthcoming and *The Other Side of the Wind*—which according to Welles's latter-day collaborator, Oja Kodar, was filmed in its entirety—would never be finished, leaving a last question mark at the end of the man's career to be seized upon by those for whom his life was one big question mark.

Yet the seventeen years that separated *Touch of Evil* from Welles's AFI award had seen Welles continue to hone his craft in myriad ways. In the 1960s he had completed three films—*The Trial, Chimes at Midnight* (a.k.a. *Falstaff*), and *The Immortal Story*—that were at least the equal of his 1950s triumvirate, as well as working on two long-term projects, *Don Quixote*, which soon became the stuff of legends, and *Sacred Beasts*, which eventually became *The Other Side of the Wind* (and *then* the stuff of legends). In the 1970s, finally feeling the call of home again, he returned to the United States to settle there, but not before he had furthered the cause of the contrary in foreign lands.

Throughout the 1960s Welles remained a productive force in cinema, while self-consciously rejecting the Hollywood approach, on the grounds that there was "no madness in their method." He had seemingly come to terms with the fact that "in my films, I demand a very specific interest on the part of the public." Though he informed one set of budding auteurs at a 1982 French forum that they should remember "other branches of moviemaking are just as much fun and are just as important and, above all, much less of a headache," he placed himself with those "who believe that they have something to tell the public, besides a diversion." Nor were any of the movies he completed between 1962 and 1968 subjected to the editorial interference of others, even if purse strings remained permanently stretched to the breaking point.

In this decade Welles placed himself outside the system because he no longer saw the slightest benefit in conformity. As he said back in 1952, while putting the finishing touches to his first independent experiment, *Othello*, "To conform to a system is neither a duty nor a discipline." By 1963, he was no longer convinced that "the only problem" the moviemaker faced was "to interest" one's audience, nor that "once they are interested, they understand anything in the world." His vocation had become essentially a selfish one. As he told Dilys Powell of the *Sunday Times*, "You can make my [kind of] movies without having to think of the public at all—if only because that public is unthinkably big, inconceivably many-faced. A great blessing. [So,] yes, I make movies for myself."

In one fabled instance, this quite literally became the case. Over the years, Welles actually seemed to delight in the very inaccessibility of his film version of Cervantes's *Don Quixote*. He even gave it a sardonic alternate title, *When Are You Going to Finish Don Quixote?* Asked about the film at Rome airport in the mid-1960s, he came over all proprietorial. "That's my own movie. . . . Is there such a thing as a home movie [in this sense]? . . . It's an experimental movie, a [type of] work that I love. . . . When I'm finished with it, I'll release it." An interesting choice of phrase, methinks. Welles speaks here of being "finished *with* it," not merely having "finished it."

But then *Don Quixote* was, in the words of Audrey Stainton, Welles's secretary through much of its filming, "intensely private and personal—almost a secret psychoanalysis of Orson Welles. Besides, he was not a hundred percent sure that *Don Quixote* was the masterpiece the world expected of him." That concern stayed with him—had perhaps haunted him since *Citizen Kane*—and became in itself an excuse for never finishing with it. He suggested as much in 1966, while putting the finishing touches to a less flawed masterpiece, *Chimes at Midnight*. He claimed to be well aware that *Don Quixote* "will please no one. This will be an execrated film . . . If [my previous film] *The Trial* had been a complete critical success, then [perhaps] I would have had the courage to bring out my *Don Quixote*." Perhaps not.

His film of Cervantes's panoramic satire on chivalry began life as just another project, this one confined by a paltry television budget. CBS had come up with some money for Welles to film a thirty-minute drama-documentary about the figure of Don Quixote.

It originally comprised a continuation of a genre Welles had been experimenting with since the mid-1950s, and the six-part ITV series *Around the World with Orson Welles*; its never-finished seventh installment, "The Tragedy of Lurs" (which was later reworked, after Welles's death, by Christophe Cognet, as "The Dominci Affair"); and the one-off *Portrait of Gina* (1958). The word Welles gave to the form was a French one, *essayage*—a personal essay on film.

It was this project that Welles was apparently working on in the fall of 1957, when he had left Universal to their edit of *Touch of Evil* and headed down to Mexico for several weeks of filming. However, when a CBS executive was shown a partial rough cut of the film he was less than impressed and no further moneys were forthcoming to aid its completion. Welles was apparently unfazed by the rebuff, secretly relieved that he would be able to use the footage in an altogether grander reworking of Cervantes's monumental work.

Welles duly began to conceive of a full-length film that would be framed by scenes featuring him as narrator, opening with him sitting, reading Cervantes in the lobby of a hotel in Mexico. A brash young American girl, to be played by Patty McCormack, approaches him and asks, "Are you the famous Orson Welles?" She proceeds to ask what he is reading and, placing her on his lap, he begins to tell her the story. According to one source, "the plan was for Welles's voice to periodically reenter to provide continuity. As the film's structure continued to evolve, Welles [planned to add] a documentary subplot exploring Spanish history and culture. In one scene shot in front of a bullring, the subject of bullfighting is introduced [after] McCormack asks Welles, 'Was Don Quixote a bullfighter?'"

Any of this sound familiar? A similar premise had been used by Welles as the basis for his last bona-fide treatment of *It's All True* in September 1943. If *It's All True* was his unfinished pan-American odyssey, *Don Quixote* was to be its Hispanic equivalent. Even the bullfighting element carried over from *It's All True*, as Welles again sought to capture something Homeric in Latin culture. As with *It's All True*, though, Welles struggled to formulate a method that he was prepared to pursue consistently. In one instance, he talked about making a film "made of things we found in the moment, in the flash of a thought, but only after rehearsing Cervantes for four weeks . . . so that the actors would know their characters . . . [and it would be] an improvisation supported by these rehearsals, by the memory of the characters." This version, clearly based on the premise underlying the commedia dell'arte, was planned as "a silent film," in keeping with its cinematic origins. The idea was subsequently transposed to an altogether different film project, *Sacred Beasts.*

In a subsequent reconfiguration Welles planned to place Don Quixote in modern Spain and leave him to fend for himself. In this version, according to Stainton, the deluded knight "charges into a movie theater and plunges his sword into the screen, slashing it to shreds in his effort to defend a damsel in distress in the film being shown." This was presumably one of Welles's private little displays of piqué at the critics who metaphorically slashed his work to shreds, but the scene itself does not appear in the 1992 "composite" version. However, stills from the sequence, recently posted on the Internet along with the hotel lobby scene, confirm that it *was* filmed.

By the winter of 1964 Welles had allowed himself to be sidelined into making a series for Spanish television, providing them with little more than home movies of his trips to Spain. It was called *In the Land of Don Quixote.* He still didn't seem sure whether to make his *Don Quixote* one extended *essayage,* an *It's All True* take two, or something that might "represent what that author would desire done in a film if he were alive today." Meanwhile, the actors originally cast to play the main characters were aging, even dying. The process itself began to take him over. As Stainton says:

> It was his perpetual dissatisfaction that was his undoing, his perpetual craving for perfection. "There's always a better way," he used to tell another editor, Renzo Lucidi. . . . And it was in search of that "better way," in all his work, that Welles would go on chopping and changing, rewriting and recutting, till he had spent more than he or anyone else could afford. . . . [But] I [now] know what a privilege it was to type and retype all those pages [of script], to have the opportunity to watch and

learn from the way he corrected and corrected again, shooting out spikes in all directions pointing to new words and new ideas, until the original snippet of text began to look like a hedgehog and it took a certain gift of telepathy to decipher the mess. All his writing was done in this way, each page a kernel of inspiration. He never began at the beginning of a script and worked through to the end; he went straight to the heart of the drama and gradually developed it outwards from the core.

There may well have been as much method as madness in the man's approach. If *Don Quixote* was an indulgence, Welles knew that it was so; and, as his films to date had proven, any ideas not realized could be stored away for future projects. He certainly seems to have gone to extraordinary lengths to ensure that *Don Quixote* remained 100 percent his, even in its unfinished state. Just as he had suggested to the hotel guest in that September 1943 treatment, he sensed that he could make a thousand films around the notion, and he was not about to settle for just one. On one occasion editor Mauro Bonanni asked him why he divided up all the reels in *Don Quixote* and he replied, "If someone finds them, they mustn't understand the sequence, because only *I* know that." Resequenced reels were then given names like Sheep, Television, Dreamers, Fake. No one else was going to present *their* idea of *his* movie(s). His new approach, represented by this film in particular, appeared to stem from something he had said at Cannes, the year after *Touch of Evil*, "I'm not interested in . . . posterity, or fame, only in the pleasure of experimentation itself. It's the only domain in which I feel that I am truly honest and sincere."

Just as a number of other twentieth-century popular artists have re(de)fined their artistry until they are seemingly experimenting for experimentation's sake, often alienating their audiences in the process, so Welles no longer seemed to conceive of his film career in terms of the public, or even the art of it all. He suggested to Kenneth Tynan, in 1967, that he sometimes felt there was very little point in doing anything worthy "because of this ridiculous [personal] myth, [which means] that when I try to do something serious, something

I care about, a great many critics don't review that particular work, but me in general."

Determined to continue honing his rhythmic methodology, he even began to develop a method of postsynching that he called "prevoicing," in which he "recorded the dialogue, sequence by sequence, 'wild,' which means without screening the film and regardless of the actors' lip movements. In this way, he established the rhythm he wanted his editor to follow in cutting the film. The editor had to adapt the image to the voice, instead of vice versa. Only after this was done, and Welles was satisfied with the rhythm of the sequence, would he study the lip movements on the Moviola and adapt his own speech accordingly" [AS].

Not surprisingly, the footage of *Don Quixote* that Welles left behind—and there were apparently hundreds of cans left in storage—proved impossible for anyone else to process, even though someone (in this case Jesus Franco, second unit director on *Chimes at Midnight*) was willing to try. In 1992 a seventy-six-minute version of *Don Quixote* had selected screenings around the world. Like the "reconstruction" of *It's All True* released the following year, Franco's *Don Quixote* was essentially of academic interest. Little of the cinematic flair that Welles *might* have brought to these splintered fragments was in evidence.

Perhaps this was Welles having a little chortle at our expense, while providing a banquet for worms, and *Don Quixote* was merely this auteur's way of maintaining his cinematic chops between projects, realized *and* unrealized. Unfortunately for Welles, his little pet project soon became another rod with which to beat him. As the Welles Wars broke out at the end of the 1960s, *Don Quixote* became conclusive "proof" that this director suffered from a fear of completion. Despite the extraordinary lengths to which he went to finish *It's All True* and *Othello*, it took only one crackpot theorist, in this case Charles Higham, in his 1970 picture book *The Films of Orson Welles*, to decide "that all his blame of others for wrecking his work is an unconscious alibi for his own genuine fear of completion." Coworkers' words (not always in context) were marshaled to the cause of Higham's grand thesis. It wasn't the studios, it wasn't the producers, it wasn't his finances, it was Welles all along, for his "is the tragedy of a man who fears the conclusions tragedy reaches: that men are mortal, their works imperfect, their lives and arts doomed." The one man in Hollywood who had addressed such tragedies time and time again turned out to be the one figure whose fear of them drove him to destroy everything he touched. Sic.

The real tragedy was that Higham's thesis—such a neat little box in which to wrap any enigmas the work itself threw up—drew a great deal of attention and, according to Welles, cost him at least one potential investor for one of his projects. His record of finishing films against the odds was not about to be allowed to speak for itself. Welles himself always knew the difference between a real job and a private indulgence (like Don Quixote), and he never allowed his pet project(s) to interfere with an opportunity to direct a real film, which meant to the death. As Welles told Bogdanovich, when discussing Higham's "theory," "Not finishing a job is not really to do it at all—which isn't suicide, but murder."

Yet, at a time when his own record in film was being twisted back upon itself, few returned to Welles's own words. In 1963 he had articulately lamented his inability to change any of the finished articles of faith he'd already made: "In the cinema, once a film is finished, it's finished forever; there are no revised editions. [So] it's torture to sit in a movie house and watch the mechanical repetition of your own work—a work that can never be altered, never improved. And all the time the reaction of the live audience to that dead thing up there is teaching you what's wrong, and there's nothing you can do about it."

An inability to affect the outcome is what gave Welles shivers, not the process itself. Because of this understandable aesthetic concern, Welles did indeed hate to see the finishing line; and the condition, in keeping with many contemporary artists, grew worse as the years went by. On one level he came to feel—with some cause—that this might be the very last film he would ever get to make. Whither then?

Pet projects, like *Don Quixote*, like his abridged *Merchant of Venice*, which he fiddled with ad nauseam, were always viewed as diversions, to occupy his time when beefier fare was not on offer. In meatier instances, Welles shared King Vidor's definition of a good director as "a fellow who doesn't go on trying to get everything right, who knows when to walk away from something, and when to stay with something." When specifically asked about his so-called "fear of completion," as he was by Tom Snyder on the *Tomorrow Show*, shortly after the AFI award, Welles lucidly distinguished between feelings of regret and actual fear of a film's final resting state: "You always hope you can make it better [but] there comes a time when you have to leave it alone. . . . [But, yes] I hate every kind of goodbye and every time those lights go out it's a little death. I hate to see it 'cause that's the proof of how all your suspicions [about flaws] were right."

Welles's "solution" to the irrevocable nature of these finished articles was, in his own words, "to keep the screen as rich as possible, because I never forget that the film itself is a dead thing, and for me, at least, the illusion of life fades very quickly when the texture is thin." That "richness," that "seven-layer-cake profusion," was Welles's way of dealing with the finality of a film, rather than indulging some deep-seated desire to abort all that he done.

In fact, Welles's next project was completed, on budget and a week under schedule, in circumstances almost as grave as those that had afflicted *Othello*. If his version of *The Trial* provided a whole set of logistical and financial challenges for the man himself, it also demanded much of his seemingly diminishing audience. Proof positive that he meant it when asserting that he now made movies for himself, Welles in 1962 made his most avant-garde statement to date and enthusiastically put it out into the world, hoping it might be able to "compete commercially."

However "difficult" the movies he had made in the past twenty years appeared to some, not one of them had been made with such a challenging intent. *The Trial* was different. As he told Huw Wheldon, on a return visit to BBC's *Monitor*, "What's remarkable is that *The Trial* is being made by anybody! It's such an avant-garde sort of thing. . . . [But] what matters is that a difficult and on the face of it an experimental film got made, and is being shown [around the world]." This statement—and the "experimental" film Welles refers to—appear to be the antithesis of all that our would-be populist had previously professed. The change, more evolutionary than seismic, came of a recognition that *Touch of Evil* was not just another mutilated movie, but was a line in the sand; and that if he was going to keep making films, they must be made "for no public, [and] for every public."

The Trial was as avant-garde as Welles ever got. It still remains his most radical as well as his most unrelenting film, and it prompted at least one Welles expert, Bret Wood, to suggest it showed what happened when "Welles's talent [was] methodically applied, [but] allowed to run free of any conventions of filmmaking. . . . [It] can be called a masterpiece and there is much to learn about the director's art from viewing it, but it is the least enjoyable of his films." Others have expressed similar sentiments. Peter Bogdanovich nagged at Welles to explain the film to him in the hope that he might learn to enjoy it (he says that he finally did); and, in his nagging, perhaps elicited from Welles one of the most honest comments he ever made about (one of) his films, "You are supposed to have a very unpleasant time. That's the idea . . . to give you a rough time there in the theater. . . . Here I go and make [a] movie that I want people to see and not like. [But] that's the paradox at the heart of *all* my work."

Yet the funding to make such a blatantly uncommercial work came about, in part, because of Welles's growing reputation as one of the Hollywood greats. The 1962 *Sight & Sound* poll of international film critics, asked to vote on the greatest movie ever made, for the first time placed *Citizen Kane* at its pinnacle (where it has remained ever since). This was a great help to producers Alexander and Michael Salkind, then attempting to prize funds from affluent would-be investors. Thankfully, it was not Welles himself who set out to raise the $1.3 million needed to shoot *The Trial*, as he was of the opinion that "only people with nothing to lose could make such a film."

The choice of this particular twentieth-century novella by Welles was an interesting one. Kafka was not a figure who had previously featured in his burgeoning collection of lost projects. *The Trial* had also only been published after the author's death. According to Welles, it appeared on a list of literary works for which producers Michael and Alexander Salkind believed they could secure film rights, and from which list he was invited to select a subject. If Kafka represented a new challenge, not just for Welles but for Western cinema, "popular" artists previously namechecked by Welles, like Dickens and Tolstoy, were on the Salkinds' list; as was Dostoevsky's *Crime and Punishment*, about which Welles says he thought long and hard. In the end he felt that he "could do nothing [with it], and the idea of being content to illustrate it did not please me at all. . . . I like to make films in which I can express myself as auteur, rather than as [a mere] interpreter."

The Trial offered an opportunity to stretch himself again, and Welles no longer worried unduly about how others viewed his "violations" of the original work. For him, such criticisms were old hat and left him unapologetic: "It's a film inspired by the book, in which my collaborator and partner is Kafka . . . and although I've tried to be faithful to what I take to be the spirit of Kafka . . . I've tried to make it my film because I think it will have more validity if it's mine."

His version of *The Trial* certainly made several departures from its novelistic source, of which the most important to Welles was ensuring that "the character of Josef K in the film doesn't really deteriorate, certainly doesn't surrender in the end." The fears that overwhelm Welles's K, effectively played by Anthony Perkins, are quite different from those that had plagued Kafka's bemused innocent. Welles's film concerns itself with a guilt that is never verbalized by "the system," but is taken as read. As he once commented concerning Josef K, in contradistinction to Kafka's conception, "He's guilty as hell!!" And, as he confessed to his biographer, "I think if you're guilty of something you should live with it." There is a sense that K is carrying some huge secret burden, like the one in a recurring dream Welles once shared with his French secretary, Maurice Bessy:

> Every year, the night before Palm Sunday, he is obsessed by a particular dream. He is alone, in the streets of a tiny English village, alone and in flight. From behind, statues pursue him, huge statues, some of marble but mostly bronze, streaming with verdigris. The same cortege has accompanied him for thirty years, a heavy troop of giants, frozen in eternity. Such visions graphically illustrate what great riches remain choked in the soul.

The Trial was another nightmare within a labyrinth. As the narrator originally observed at the end of the film's opening parable, "The logic of this story is the logic of a dream. Do you feel lost in a labyrinth? Do not look for a way out." Welles edited this speech, probably *because* it gave the audience too much information before the movie has even begun to unfold. The sense of disorientation for the viewer should be as gradual as Josef K's.

Like the worst nightmares, this one begins when Josef K awakens one morning to find that he is still alone in the existential sense, but not alone in his bedroom. Throughout the film K tries to find out what he has done and how he might avoid being put on trial. Unlike Kafka, though, Welles went to great pains to explain, for those unsure as to the nature of Josef K's crime: "His crime is surrendering to the system that's destroying his individuality. Yet he tries to fight it . . . I couldn't put my name to a work that implies man's ultimate surrender. Being on the side of man, I had to show him, in his final hour, undefeated." Josef K discovers, in the events leading up to his death, a truth Welles already knew, that "a genuine individual is an outright nuisance in a factory."

For the first time, Welles gave that sensuality half-glimpsed in *The Lady from Shanghai*, *Othello*, and *Touch of Evil* full flight. Thomson is right, for once, when he posits the possibility that "the half-buried guilt in Joseph K is that he is unfit for women: his trial is being exposed to the lascivious invitation of Jeanne Moreau, Elsa Martinelli, and Romy Schneider—Welles's greatest witches, and the sexiest women in all his work."

In fact, the witchiest representative of the triple goddess was cut from *The Trial* on the eve of its premiere (it has recently been added to the French DVD edition). The Scientist, as she is called, is played by Katina Paxinou, whose task it is to tell K which crime he is "most likely to commit." When K asks what it might be, she names the mortal sin of suicide. Welles commented at the time, "The subject of that scene was free will." His description in the shooting script makes clear her relationship to the white goddess: "The woman in charge of the night shift is as old as the world. Immutable, vaguely disquieting, this venerable lady of science is the archetype of the priestess serving a powerful, millenary mystery."

Though Welles played only a cameo (the Advocate) in the film, he claimed it was "the most autobiographical movie that I've ever made." *The Trial* was also a film he was (rightly) proud of, describing it to Huw Wheldon as "the best film I have ever made."

And yet, like previous independent productions, it suffered from a form of financial hemorrhaging that threatened to render the whole production stillborn, only to prove a spur to Welles's inventive mind. When money earmarked for the sets failed to materialize two weeks into production, Welles once again used his febrile imagination to conceive of a way to use an empty Parisian railway station he glimpsed from the window of his hotel. As he described it, "At five in the morning I went downstairs, got in a cab, crossed the city, and entered this empty railway station, where I discovered the world of Kafka." The Gare d'Orsay gave Welles a set of challenges that couldn't fail to inspire a man who claimed that, though he designed a film in advance, it was with the intention of "throw[ing] all the plans out. The images have to be discovered in the course of the work."

Such difficulties were there to be overcome, even if there were a few losses. One involved the scene where Josef K is confronted by Inspector A outside the opera house, and forced to meet the Interrogation Commission. In Welles's original scheme, the opera house was to be seen as "part of a complex of interconnected buildings, all in some way concerned with officialdom: cultural affairs, town planning, or local government. They are monumental in aspect but dilapidated, sinister, and cold. They exude the melancholy atmosphere of all public institutions. In a low-angle shot of the columned vestibule we see [the] Inspector [appear]." The weight of these institutions was meant to bear down on K, but the oppressive, ceilinged station was obliged to provide a makeshift alternative.

Welles again used long takes as a means of economizing, but not at the expense of the film's architecture. Most of these long takes occur early in the film, when Josef K's world still retains its parameters. The fast cuts and "editing [that] is obvious and jarring, with handheld camera work and frequent cutaways to close-ups, [like those] of the eyes of the young girls who stare at K through the cracks in the walls" [BW], are reserved for the second half of the film, where the nightmare becomes fragmentary and labyrinthine, and K loses all control of his destiny. If the cutting of the film once again proved "a terrible chore," Welles's first film in four years was very much his own, being wholly "unspoiled in the cutting."

Sadly, spotty distribution and uncomprehending reviews again plagued an important Welles film, and he was left asking the same old question: how might he make such an independently minded film next time around? The Salkinds were chastened by the experience, having discovered the true cost of such experimentation. Welles himself was not about to raise the poisoned chalice of Hollywood to his lips. In fact, he had a yearning to tackle Shakespeare again, and he already knew how well that name went down in Tinseltown.

◆　　◆　　◆　　◆

Though it had been over a decade since he had tackled Shakspeere on film, Welles had not given up on the Bard in the interim. Rather, he had returned to the stage—from whence he came—performing *Othello* in England in 1951, *King Lear* on U.S. television and the New York stage in 1954 and 1955 respectively, and presenting a condensed version of his unwieldy 1939 production of Shakespeare's Henriad, *Five Kings*,* now called *Chimes at Midnight*, in Dublin in 1960. It was the last of these that Welles now began to talk up as a possible film project, until he convinced a Spanish producer, Emiliano Piedra, that he could make a film version "on the cheap" on location in Spain, while simultaneously completing a movie of the ever-popular classic *Treasure Island*.

Whether Welles ever intended to make the latter is open to doubt (it did get produced seven years later using Welles and his script, which suggests a start had been made in 1964–65). Yet Keith Baxter, who had played Prince Hal in the 1960 Dublin production, and was the only actor Welles now recalled for the film, believes the version of *Treasure Island* was merely a ruse. Welles had once told the audience on Steve Allen's television show, "I would like to do Shakespeare but Steve would like to do magic, and he owns the shop." Well, he no longer cared to kowtow to his sponsor.

And so, using sets that were meant to double as venues for *Treasure Island*, Welles began shooting his third radical interpretation of Shakespeare on celluloid in Spain during September 1964. Though the script had been honed over a quarter of a century, it was to all intents and purposes the same play viewed by Irish audiences four years earlier. Welles found other ways of making the filming process spontaneous. Baxter recalls how "Orson would [frequently] go marching off with the viewfinder to find a shot for the next scene, followed only by the lighting man and the camera operator, while we all waited around having a cup of coffee."

At the same time, slowly but surely, the story began to assume a form of its own, one with which Welles was experienced enough to go along. At the heart of the play(s) had always been the figure of Falstaff. And, in Baxter's words, "it was [Welles's] life's ambition to . . . play Falstaff. He wanted this to be his statement. You felt that there was a great deal of him in Falstaff—this sort of trimming one's

---

*The four Shakespeare plays that constitute the Henriad are *Henry IV* parts one and two, *Henry V*, and *Henry VI*.

sails, always short of money, having to lie, perhaps, and to cheat." The allusions were there to be indulged. When the chief justice accusingly berates Falstaff, "Your means are very slender and your waste [a pun on waist] is great," one can well imagine Piedra the producer nodding in the wings.

Falstaff had always been an idealized creation for Welles, a good-humored wit, the life and soul of the party—Merry England person-ified. Welles even thought that he had a handle on what kind of archetype Shakespeare's stout figure represented. Now, though, the darker side of the Falstaff-Prince Hal relationship began to move to the fore; as it had in Shakespeare's *2 Henry IV*, which was not so much a second part as a second take. Just as Shakespeare discovered, when writing his sequel to the popular *Henry IV Part One* circa 1599 (three years after its predecessor), Welles found that the character of Falstaff had far more dramatic potential than the sterile vessels of ambition that were Henry IV and V (Welles described young Henry to Baxter during shooting as "a most awful shit"). The problem for Welles, as he recognized at the time, was that "comedy can't really dominate a film made to tell this story, which is all in dark colors."

A rethink was needed, in which Falstaff was depicted as a reluc-tant jester, "obliged to sing for his supper, [who knew he] had to earn everything he ate by making people laugh." The imagery of the film became winter itself—so much so that Welles was obliged to film the scene in which Falstaff, Shallow, and Silence are running to Hal's coro-nation "in the snow" by placing white sheets on top of the Spanish soil, because it was the spring of 1965 by the time this scene was shot:

> Keith Baxter: Orson realized, halfway through the shooting, that this was a very sad film, much sadder than he intended it to be. But what he himself was, and what the film expressed about him, had taken over. . . . Orson [once] said to me, "You know, we don't have one scene of summer in this film, Keith." And we tried to shoot one, rid-ing to the Gadshill robbery . . . but it didn't work. . . . By then he had begun to realize that winter, and the movement of the film toward win-ter and cold and bleakness, was in fact what he wanted.

It seems likely that Welles caught Anthony Quayle's Stratford production of these plays in the autumn of 1951, when he was also playing Shakespeare on the English stage; and as the man whose own stage version of the Henriad stumbled at the first hurdle. At the very least, he would have read about Quayle's desentimentalized depiction of Falstaff. He was determined to go to the other extreme. For him, Falstaff was "that most unusual figure in fiction . . . an entirely good man."

Though the Falstaff Welles shows in *Chimes* retains much the same flaws Shakespeare gave him, his essential goodness is always made to shine apparent. When Hal uses an extempore play in the tavern to tell Falstaff a few home truths, he visibly wilts under the barrage, refusing to recognize the person the prince reveals (for some weird reason this scene reminds me of Laurel and Hardy's *Chump at Oxford*, where a concussed Stan becomes an upper-class toff who takes to calling Ollie "fattie"). In this sense Falstaff is a metaphor not only for the loss of innocence, but for a lost England that Welles admitted to Michael MacLiammoir—while filming *Othello*—never actually existed, "being but a memory dreamed by the Forest People. . . . Even in Chaucer's day it was imagined as a thing of the past." But Falstaff *was* in Chaucer's day. Indeed, his death is made to signal the end of the Middle Ages and the advent of the modern age (symbolized in the film by Poins eating an apple as Falstaff's coffin is prepared).

With the focus firmly on Falstaff, Welles was obliged to lose his original opening to the film, the murder of Richard II by Henry IV's lackeys. Though Welles claimed that it was cut because it "looked like the murder of Thomas a' Becket," its omission reflected the film's unabashed concentration on Hal's rejection of Falstaff, not his validation as the legitimate heir of a cold-blooded usurper. In 1960, when asked about the imminent Dublin stage production, Welles insisted that "the basic idea" was to "take the main theme [of the plays] and stay with it." But Shakespeare's main theme in part one is not carried over to take two, suggesting a conflict that Welles was obliged to resolve in favor of Falstaff, whose final rejection rather overshadows Hal's crowning glory.

That rejection is telegraphed on a number of occasions by the prince. According to Welles, "Having made a film which contains [Falstaff's] rejection and death, I felt I had to prepare for it. And I prepare for it from the very first moment of the film . . . you see the rejection enacted in parody form two or three times, and you see it foreshadowed." Of these, the most subtle is when Hal rides off to find out if his father still lives and calls out, "Falstaff, good (k)night." It is the last time that he will feel or know such camaraderie, as the prince is lost in one of the many swirls of mist that the film is bathed in (Baxter comments on how "incense was used all the time . . . so that the light would be diffused").

In Welles's version of history even the "kernel of inspiration" for the film's centerpiece—a reenactment of the Battle of Shrewsbury—is not the chivalric duel between Hal and Hotspur, and the powerful death speech of the vanquished latter, as Shakespeare appears to have intended, but Falstaff's "catechism" on "honor" that prefaces the battle. It is Falstaff's question, "Who hath [honor]? He that died a Wednesday" that truly informs Hotspur's vainglorious duel, not Hal's valediction. The director achieves his intent with what Naremore recognizes as "the finest example of rhythmic montage in Welles's career," a disquisition on the death of chivalry that needs no words.

Even though throughout this period Welles vainly hoped he might be allowed to make the film version of Joseph Heller's *Catch-22*, it is here that Welles delivers an equally effective antiwar "sermon," beginning with a little dig at Olivier's *Henry V*, a belated revenge for *Macbeth* that was born of genuine aesthetic disagreement. As he said in 1966, "No matter how convincing the set, whether it's a real place or made out of cardboard [surely a reference to *Macbeth*], as soon as people in costume ride out on their horses it's suddenly banal. . . . In *Henry V*, for example, you see the people riding out of the castle, and suddenly they are on a golf course somewhere, charging each other."

The golf course in *Chimes at Midnight* very soon becomes the Somme, an allusion that appears to have been entirely deliberate (according to Martin Gabel, a Mercury assistant on the original 1939 *Five Kings*, the stage set for this battle came about from "imagin[ing] the medieval battlefields as a sort of no man's land, like in World War I"). Welles snips more and more pieces of film, fragmenting the field of battle until it dissolves into a mass of disembodied limbs struggling in the mire and there is nothing honorable left. The victor, again, is the usurping, beady Bolingbroke, a man without honor.

The Battle of Shrewsbury proved Welles's assertion that one could make a film in the cutting, even if he had to abandon his original intention, which "was to intercut the shots in which the action was contrary, so that every cut seemed to be a blow, [then] a counterblow." In fact, for all its allusions to Ford (and Eisenstein)—which prompted Pauline Kael to suggest that it showed what Welles could still do when allowed to "edit, not to cover gaps and defects, but as an artist"—this was not *Stagecoach* in Shropshire. The beauty of the shot of Hotspur outlined against the sky before the battle holds no more sway in the film than Hotspur himself will in battle.

As the director said at the time, "I don't go around like a collector picking up beautiful images and pasting them together. . . . What I am trying to discover now in films is not technical surprises or shocks, but a more complete unity of forms, of shapes." This meant the usual two minutes of edited film per week, and though Welles concluded shooting on *Chimes at Midnight* in April 1965, he was thirteen months away from approving an edit of the film. According to Keith Baxter, even that gesture was extracted under duress. "He could never bear to leave a picture alone. He'd cut and cut and cut. Luckily, the man who was then running the Cannes Festival . . . saw a rough cut . . . [and] wanted the film for the festival . . . so Welles was pressured into finishing the editing."

One presumes that Welles "inadvertently" forgot to inform Piedra, and executive producer Alessandro Tasca, that one of the tasks he was obliged to fulfill in postproduction was postsynching almost an entire film's worth of dialogue. Baxter claims that "there isn't a word of the film that was shot in direct sound." I find this hard to believe. John Gielgud's speeches appear far too well-synched when compared with those of Welles himself and of Margaret Rutherford, which we know were largely overdubbed. And Gielgud was hardly likely to appreciate a request for overdubbing his already word-perfect delivery of the Bard's lines. However, Welles clearly felt he had refined the technique of "pre-voicing" (with which he had been experimenting since *The Magnificent Ambersons*) well enough to use it throughout *Chimes at Midnight*.

The results were only partially satisfying, and reviewers—even those full of praise for the film—were unanimous in their criticism of the film sound, which Pauline Kael quickly noticed "doesn't match the images." Some also suggested the film lacked a consistency of tone, a criticism that really should have been leveled at Shakespeare, who never reconciled the two parts of his story, rather than Welles, who ironed out a fair number of discordances between the plays. But *Chimes at Midnight* gradually began to accrue enough good press, and word of mouth, to suggest that the maverick's gifts were still intact.

His attempt to "foreground" Falstaff had produced a truly Wellesian film on "the central theme in Western culture: the lost paradise." As with his portrayal of Hank Quinlan, Welles's depiction of Falstaff suggested a man old before his time. Barely forty-nine years old, the actor's whitened hair and widened girth gave added poignancy to the role, while also suggesting a man already reconciled to a curtailed career as a lead actor thanks to his increasingly unwieldy frame. His next role, which was filmed in September 1966, just four months after the premiere of *Chimes at Midnight*, seemed to complete some kind of cycle.

The story of Charles Clay, from a novella entitled *The Immortal Story* by Welles's favorite author (next to Graves), Isak Dinesen, was an alternate ending to the biography of Charles Foster Kane. A rich, lonely old man who has made his fortune at the expense of other people arranges to experience vicariously the lust of a young man before he dies (which in the final reel—not unexpectedly for Welles—he does). If the made-up Clay resembles any previous Wellesian figure, it is the figure of Death itself, from the silent "home movie" *Hearts of Age* he had made in the summer of 1934 with his then-wife Virginia Nicholson. Welles looks utterly dissipated, a shell of a man, waiting on death.

The film itself was really a filmella, a short film of a short story made for French television. But it was put on limited cinema release in the summer of 1968. It is the least well known of Welles's movies— as well as his first venture into color as a director. As such, it is tempting, if slightly unfair, to view it as little more than a beautifully shot afterthought to more challenging statements like *The Trial* and *Chimes*. That Welles found himself, at fifty-two, reduced to making films for government-sponsored television stations suggests just how bereft of options his principled approach to filmmaking had left him.

Though Welles would make a couple of *essayages* (personal essays on film) in the next decade, funds for projects like those he had made in the first half of the 1960s were never forthcoming again. All the while he worked away at an idea for a movie that he had been thinking about for a number of years (since at least 1958, when he outlined the story to writer Peter Viertel in Biarritz). *Sacred Beasts* began life as a film ostensibly about bullfighting, though as Welles said, it "is not [really] the story of a bull or a bullfighter. It [just] has this world . . . as its background. . . . It has to do with a kind of voyeurism. I would call it emotional parasitism. It has to do with the whole mystique of . . . the he-man. . . . This whole picture is against he-men."

In the summer of 1966, fresh from the artistic triumphs of *The Trial* and *Chimes at Midnight*, Welles endeavored to raise funds to begin work on his most radical experiment in filmmaking, fusing many of the preoccupations found in his personal projects with "a more complete unity of form." He again imagined a low-budget, quick-fire shoot. "It can't take too long. I think the whole thing is eight weeks at the most, 'cause it's got to be that time, the time it really took." Eight years later he was still shooting. By then *Sacred Beasts* had been transplanted to the other side of the pond, having become *The Other Side of the Wind*.

Those to whom Welles had pitched his original idea had not been moved by his eloquent speech, captured on film by the Maysles brothers at Welles's behest, even though it represents some of the most heartrending footage of the great director ever shot. The footage in question comes from a meeting with potential investors in Madrid in June 1966, when the afterglow of positive press for *Chimes at Midnight* still lit the way. With the camera rolling, and presumably a degree of preparatory staging, Welles proceeds to describe the idea behind *Sacred Beasts*. It is a brilliant speech, the wine is flowing, and he seems in no way weary of his vocation or the ridiculous demands it has placed on him, but one senses from the faces of the flushed financiers that there will be no happy ending here either. Welles, though, still has faith in his powers of persuasion, as he launches into his sales pitch:

> Our story is about a pseudo-Hemingway, a movie director. So the central figure . . . you can barely see through the hair on his chest; who was frightened by Hemingway at birth. He's a tough movie director who has killed three or four extras in every picture . . . [but is] full of charm. Everybody thinks he's great. In our story he's riding around following a bullfighter, and living through him . . . but he's become obsessed by this young man who has become . . . his own dream of himself. He's been rejected by all his old friends. He's finally been shown up to be a kind of voyeur . . . a fellow who lives off other people's danger and death.

All well and good, but then Welles slips in one of his verbal counterpunches. "We're going to shoot it without a script. I've written the script. I know the whole story, I know everything that happens, but what I'm gonna do is get the actors in every situation, tell them what has happened up to this moment, who they are and I believe that they will find what is true and inevitable from what I've said. We'll photograph that, and go on to the next moment."

One can already sense that this is not an audience conversant with the commedia dell'arte. What we hear instead is a (possibly planted) voice asking the director concernedly, "Have you done that kind of thing before?" Welles states the obvious, "Nobody's ever done it." Though he had improvised scenes here and there in all of his films, he still yearned to "take a story and see if it'll work [out]." After informing his fellow imbibers that he has the screenplay written, he announces, "I'm gonna hide the script. I don't want [the actors] to know that [version]. . . . We get [image-conscious] actors together and say, 'There's the situation. Here's what you did yesterday, here's what you did twenty years ago, here's what you know about him, [let's] start shooting.'"

His frustration at the limitations of the medium now bubbles to the surface as he talks about how "we've been cranking along in movies too long the same way. You know, it's the most old-fashioned industry on earth." The love of improvisation, which had initially drawn Welles to the theater, he now hoped to impose on this less malleable medium. Again a voice of concern is raised, "Aren't you afraid that the end result won't have any control or any form?" He insists he is not. However, any would-be investors were.

The project lay dormant for the remainder of the decade, before work began again in America in 1970. The film was still about the same thing it had been since at least 1962, when Welles first voiced the idea to a French interviewer—"death, the portrait of a decadence, a ruin"—but he no longer intended to play the lead. *Sacred Beasts* had become *The Other Side of the Wind*, with the he-man now played by John Huston and the setting transplanted to Hollywood. But this was not the Hollywood he had known. The nature of the enemy had changed. In the New Hollywood both his lead, Jake Hannaford—a has-been director for whom success was everything—and the auteur himself were as strangers.

Inevitably, the film as shot contained its fair share of satire on the Hollywood of "the college students from the conglomerates" (to use Welles's phrase), including a hilarious conversation between one such fresh-faced assassin and a Hannaford stooge (played by Norman Foster) in a screening room, while rushes from Hannaford's latest movie play on the screen. But the setting remained as much of a backdrop as when Welles envisaged a Spanish bullring.

Welles had told those earlier investors, "If you see a man [truly] on his way to death . . . you may have many choices about how that may happen, but that end is as clear as anything in the world. . . . There is a terrible pull. This is a picture about the love of death." Coming from a man who told Tom Snyder in 1975, "I'm very interested in death, and always have been," it was perhaps fitting that his final film should be "half in love with easeful Death." Only half in love, though. In his 1962 discussion of the idea behind *Sacred Beasts*, Welles refused to accept "that genius disappears with old age. . . . Fitzgerald [like Hemingway] . . . was rotted with the same anguish. That attitude is death." It was the process of creation that kept Welles alive and kicking.

As with his other work from the autumn of his career, Welles envisaged the theme of *The Other Side of the Wind* developing out of a cast of people "experiencing life and death and sex in a secondhand way." As such, the story was bound to be as dark as the moods that those close to the man knew, and which he could no longer disguise in his work. As the darkness crept into the very crevices of his films, Welles began to prefer that "unity of form" to the self-consciously radical stylization of yesteryear, no matter how uncommercial the results might be deemed. Certainly he (and after his death, Oja Kodar) managed to scare off a number of potential investors from the West Coast colony, including a couple of actor-directors who owed him an incalculable personal debt, by the simple expedient of showing them scenes from the unfinished film. "Too dark—but that's only a guess!"

For Welles, "the pleasure of experimentation" was now all that was left to him. But it was the greatest of pleasures. After filming one shot for *The Other Side of the Wind*, witnessed by Joseph McBride, in which the spray of actors "rose in fancy curlicues, beautifully backlit by colored filters," Welles shouted, "Cut! We can't film that. . . . Too baroque—even for a Welles film." It was a little joke at his own expense, to relieve the sense that he and that audience he had aspired to reach in Hollywood's heyday had duly gone their separate ways. Maurice Bessy, one of those intimates who saw his dark reflection in the mirror, explained Welles's ultimate fate—and his commercial impasse—in just these terms:

In considering the baroque/decadent nature of Welles's art, we may have arrived at the source of Welles's resounding failure with the general public, while people of highly developed sensibilities were so enchanted by him. People in this latter group, whatever their other failings may be, can love a work of art that restores reality to them, whatever that reality might be; whereas the mass of people can only respond to a work that testifies to a faith and gives them hope. But Welles's work is the sumptuous, hallucinogenic, and baroque re-creation of a world in the process of disintegration.

If Welles preferred to describe himself as "a petit-maître of an art form which has not yet entirely proved itself to be an art form," he never clarified whether he meant simply filmmaking, or specifically "the sumptuous, hallucinogenic, and baroque re-creation of a world in the process of disintegration." In fact, the term "baroque" has been applied to Welles's work in both a pejorative and a praiseworthy sense, suggesting something intrinsically contradictory about the man's life and art. Peter Bogdanovich captured it best when he wrote about "the tension between the essential pessimism of his outlook and the exhilirating optimism inspired by the brilliance of his style."

Welles himself never attempted to reconcile those contradictions. As he once told Kenneth Tynan, "Everything about me is a contradiction, and so is everything about everybody I know. We are made out of opposites, we live between two poles . . . You don't reconcile the poles. You just recognize them." That is indeed what he did—highlighting the contradictions in the human condition by amplifying them in characters who were themselves larger than life. As Henri Angel concluded:

Just as he is visibly ravaged by genius, . . . in him the exaggeration, the tumultuous and frenetic atmosphere characteristic of baroque style reach a peak of extraordinary magnificence. . . . It would be . . . ridiculous to reproach Welles for his contradictions or for the incertitudes of his ethic, because the very essence of baroque has its source in the dynamism of this split.

Welles never accepted that *Citizen Kane* was the best he could do. Nor was it. But he recognized the uniqueness of its happenstance. As he pointed out to Huw Wheldon, "Nobody else will make that sort of picture under those ideal circumstances [either], until another man . . . give[s] a studio's facilities to an artist, to make the film he wants to make. It sounds terribly simple, but it *literally* never happens." When the one-off nature of the opportunity stood revealed, Welles had nowhere to go. He was obliged to become, as Peter Wollen says, "a filmmaker who rejected the whole idea of making a Faustian bargain with Hollywood," lest he *become* Faust.

Inevitably, that legend of the would-be genius dogged him throughout his directorial career. Every time he shrugged it off long enough to make another film, it was in less "ideal circumstances," so he merely reinforced it. Like many an artist, Welles was obliged to constantly rewrite his own history simply to avoid being interred by it. For instance, when raising the money to make *The Trial*, he wryly observed, "It's rough to be thought of as the fellow who had it— once. I could easily have gone on the sauce. Then I found a solution. For years I'd been telling people they were wrong about Welles. I tried a new tack. I'd give 'em a steely look and say, 'You were right. Only I've changed.'"

For a while he hoped that similar doses of self-deprecating humor might turn things around. At the end of his first appearance on *The Dick Cavett Show*, in July 1970, when he was back in the States trying to reinvent himself as the cinema's cuddliest maverick, the credits ran as follows: "Entire production conceived, produced, directed, written, staged, choreographed, built, designed, lit, managed, rehearsed, contracted for, and criticized by Orson Welles." In the midst of the Welles Wars, it was a wonderful riposte, but it did not help dispel the myth. To break out of the caricature, he would have had to abandon the only means he had of making a living, as an actor selling his and others' wares.

Perhaps he had always had a premonition that this was the way things would turn out. Back in February 1945, when he was still three months the right side of thirty, already a legend and well on his way to becoming unemployable, he wrote two columns in the *New York Post* that spoke of the dissolution of others, and the roads they could have taken. One was concerned with Hamlet, the one great tragic figure in Shakespeare that Welles never played on stage or in film. Welles's version of history, though, suggested that if the Danish prince had stayed in England "and avoided the ghost and graveyards . . . Hamlet would have lived to be old and fat. Indeed, I think that's just what happened. . . . [He ended up] exiled from tragedy and living sinfully in England. . . . I think Falstaff is Hamlet—an old and wicked Hamlet—having that drink."

If Welles was ever in a position to play Hamlet it was at the end of the war, before he went into exile and began "living sinfully" in Europe. That he never did, I suspect, was not because it conjured up too many personal ghosts, as Carringer posits, but because he remained in awe of the Hamlet that his great idol and friend John Barrymore once performed on stage (he had apparently been given Barrymore's own signed copy of the play when he joined Katherine Cornell's acting company as a callow teenager in 1933). Barrymore's is generally viewed as a wasted life, his profligate talent pissed away. Welles, though, had a different theory, that spoke for him:

> They used to tell [Ethel Barrymore] that [her son] Jack couldn't act, and he wanted to prove that they were wrong. He proved it [one night]. The rest of his life was anticlimax. There wasn't anything left to do except go on imitating, as accurately as possible, that one great evening. When Jack got tired of that he began to satirize. Finally he burlesqued. When it wasn't sad, it was hilarious. . . . I began to guess that what he hated was the responsibility of his own genius.

BIBLIOGRAPHY

The primary resource for Wellesiana remains the Richard Wilson collection, which was sold to the Lilly Library at the University of Indiana in 1979. The material spans the full period of the Mercury, i.e. up to the completion of *Macbeth*. Other unpublished material that I have drawn upon has been principally derived from private collections. However, the Museum of Modern Art was kind enough to allow me access to the shooting scripts for *The Magnificent Ambersons* and *The Stranger*.

As for published works, the most essential general volumes are those that present Welles "in his own words," though equally important is Frank Brady's thoughtful and meticulous biography of the man, belatedly published in 1989. Of the numerous critical studies, the earlier volumes have most to commend them. Those that gave me the greatest insights were those of Bazin, Bessy, and Naremore; though there is also much worth to be found in the two Focus volumes (edited by Ronald Gottesman).

Of the specialist volumes that concentrate on a single film or theme, Carringer's *Kane* volume set the standard. Comito's *Touch of Evil* comes close to it; as do the works of Richard France and Michael Anderegg. Sadly, there is no single volume that collects together the thoughts of perhaps the finest American contemporary commentator on Welles, Jonathan Rosenbaum. As for those mythmakers who have entered the field, I have already had my say in the main body of the text. Suffice to say, there is still much work to be done to dispel the miasma they have sought to wrap around the man and his work.

—CH.

Reference Works:

Berg, Chuck, and Tom Erskine. *The Encyclopaedia of Orson Welles.* Checkmark Books, 2003.

Milne, Tom, ed. *The "Time Out" Film Guide.* Longman, 1989.

Thomson, David. *The New Biographical Dictionary of Film.* Little, Brown, 2002.

Wood, Bret. *Orson Welles: A Bio-Bibliography.* Greenwood Press, 1990.

Critical Studies:

Anderegg, Michael. *Orson Welles, Shakespeare and Popular Culture.* Columbia University Press, 1999.

Bazin, Andre. *Orson Welles: A Critical View.* Harper and Row, 1978. [AB]

Bessy, Maurice. *Orson Welles: An Investigation into His Films and Philosophy.* Crown, 1971. [MB]

Bogdanovich, Peter. *The Cinema of Orson Welles.* MoMA, 1961.

Carringer, Robert L. *The Making of Citizen Kane.* University of California Press, 1985.

Comito, Terry, ed. *Touch of Evil.* Rutgers Film in Print, 1985. [ToE]

Conrad, Peter. *Orson Welles: The Stories of His Life.* Faber and Faber, 2003.

Cowie, Peter. *A Ribbon of Dreams: The Cinema of Orson Welles.* A. S. Barnes, 1973. [PC]

France, Richard. *Orson Welles on Shakespeare: The WPA and Mercury Theatre Playscripts.* Routledge, 2001.

Goldfarb, Phyllis. "Orson Welles' Use of Sound." In Gottesman, *Focus on Orson Welles.*

Gottesman, Ronald, ed. *Focus on "Citizen Kane."* Prentice-Hall, 1971. [FoCK]

———, ed. *Focus on Orson Welles.* Prentice-Hall, 1976. [FoOW]

Jameson, Richard T. "An Infinity of Mirrors." In Gottesman, *Focus on Orson Welles.*

Johnson, William. "Orson Welles: Of Time and Loss." In Gottesman, *Focus on "Citizen Kane."*

McBride, Joseph. *Orson Welles: Actor and Director*. Jove Publications, 1977.

———. *Orson Welles*. Da Capo, 1996.

Naremore, James. *The Magic World of Orson Welles*. OUP, 1978. (Revised ed. Southern Methodist University Press, 1989.)

Prokosch, Mike. "Orson Welles: An Introduction." *Film Comment*, Summer 1971.

Simon, William G., ed. *Persistence of Vision #7*, 1989. [PoV]

Thomson, David. *Rosebud: The Story of Orson Welles*. Little, Brown, 1996.

Biographies:

Brady, Frank. *Citizen Welles: A Biography of Orson Welles*. Anchor, 1990.

Callow, Simon. *Orson Welles: The Road to Xanadu*. Jonathan Cape, 1995.

Fowler, Roy. *Orson Welles: A First Biography*. Pendulum, 1946.

Higham, Charles. *The Films of Orson Welles*. University of California Press, 1970.

———. *Orson Welles: The Rise and Fall of an American Genius*. St Martin's Press, 1985.

Leaming, Barbara. *Orson Welles: A Biography*. Viking-Penguin, 1985.

Interviews:

Interviews below are in Estrin, Mark W. *Orson Welles: The Interviews*. University Press of Mississippi, 2002. [OWI]:

Richard O'Brien. *New York Times*, November 14, 1938.

Thomas F. Brady. *New York Times*, December 8, 1946.

Francis Koval. *Sight and Sound*, December 1950.

Andre Bazin and Charles Bitsch. *Cahiers du Cinema*, June 1958.

Andre Bazin, Charles Bitsch, and Jean Domarchi. *Cahiers du Cinema*,
    September 1958.
Huw Wheldon. *Monitor*, BBC-TV, March 13, 1960.
Juan Cobos, Miguel Rubio, and J. A. Pruneda. *Cahiers du Cinema in Eng-
    lish* 5, 1966.
Kenneth Tynan. *Playboy*, March 1967.
Richard Marienstras. French TV series, 1974.
Leslie Megahey. *Arena*, BBC-2, May 18, 21, 1982.*

The following books also contain copious interview material:
Leaming, Barbara. *Orson Welles: A Biography*. Viking-Penguin, 1985.
Welles, Orson, and Peter Bogdanovich. *This Is Orson Welles*. Harper-
    Collins, 1992; rev. ed. Da Capo, 1998. [TIOW]

Writings:

Welles, Orson. "Citizen Kane Is Not about Louella Parsons' Boss," *Friday*
    2, February 14, 1941.
————. Article in *Stage*, February 1941.
————. *Kane*, press statement. January 14, 1941. In Brady, *Citizen Welles*.
————. Lecture, New York University, October 20, 1942.
————. Article in *New York Post*, February 10, 1943.
————. "Orson Welles Almanac." *New York Post*, January 22,
    1945–November 6, 1945.
————. *Lundberg vs. Welles*. Transcript of deposition, Federal Records
    Center, NJ, 1947.
————. "The Third Audience." Lecture, Edinburgh Festival, 1952. In
    Cowie, *Ribbon of Dreams*.
————. "The Major Branches of the Cinema." In Bessy, *Orson Welles*.
————. "Ribbon of Dreams." *International Film Annual* 1, 1957.
————. Letter to *New Statesman*, May 24, 1958.
————. "Twilight in the Smog." *Esquire*, March 1959.
————. "The Creation of Citizen Kane." *The Times*, November 17, 1971.

---

*The *Arena* interview used in OWI is mistranscribed in several places; and in such instances
I have preferred to rely on my own ears.

————. Acceptance Speech, AFI Award Ceremony, 1975.

————. Obituary of Jean Renoir, *L.A. Times*, February 18, 1979.

————. "Proposal for *King Lear*." In Welles and Bogdanovich, *This Is Orson Welles*.

Welles, Orson, and John Houseman. "Repertory 38," *Billboard*, November 26, 1938.

Documentaries:

Chabat, Charles, and Rosemary Wilson (producers). *The RKO Story Part 4: It's All True*. BBC, 1987.

Franco, Jess. *Don Quixote*. El Silencio, 1992.

Giagni, Gianfranco, and Ciro Giorgini. *Rosabella: la storia italiana di Orson Welles*. Tape Connection, 1993.

Graver, Gary. *Working with Orson Welles*. Sidney Niekerk, 1993.

Lennon, Thomas, and Michael Epstein. *Battle Over "Citizen Kane."* American Experience, 1996

Megahey, Leslie. *Arena: The Orson Welles Story*. BBC, 1982.

Rodriguez, Carlos. *Orson Welles In the Land of* Don Quixote. Canal + Espana, 2000.

Schmidlin, Rick (producer). *Retouching Evil*. Universal, 1998.

Silovic, Vassili, and Oja Kodar. *One Man Band* a.k.a. *The Lost Films of Orson Welles*. Pit Riethmuller, 1995.

Welles, Orson. *Filming "Othello."* 1978.

————. *Filming "The Trial."* 1981.

Wilson, Richard, Myron Meisel, and Rosemary Wilson. *It's All True*. Paramount, 1993.

SOURCE NOTES

All sources are in alphabetical order except the interviews and the material from the Richard Wilson collection, which are in chronological order. Abbreviations refer to entries in the bibliography.

Preface

Welles interviews:

Peter Bogdanovich. *This Is Orson Welles*.
Leslie Megahey. *Arena*, BBC-2, May 18, 21, 1982. In OWI.
Barbara Leaming. *Orson Welles: A Biography*.

Other sources:

Bazin, Andre. "L'Apport d'Orson Welles," *Cine-Club* 7, May 1948. In MB.
Callow, Simon. *Orson Welles: The Road to Xanadu*. Jonathan Cape, 1995.
Welles, Orson. Letter to *New Statesman*, May 24, 1958.
———. Obituary of Jean Renoir, *L.A. Times*, February 18, 1979.

Chapter 1: Definitely Not Love in the Tropics

Welles interviews:

Richard O'Brien. *New York Times*, November 14, 1938. In OWI.
Andre Bazin, Charles Bitsch, and Jean Domarchi. *Cahiers du Cinema*, September 1958. In OWI.
Dilys Powell. *Sunday Times*, February 3, 1963.
Juan Cobos, Miguel Rubio, and J. A. Pruneda. *Cahiers du Cinema in English* 5 (1966). In OWI.

Kenneth Tynan. *Playboy*, March 1967. In OWI.

Peter Bogdanovich. *This Is Orson Welles*.

Charles Champlin. *L.A. Times*, May 12, 1973.

Michael Parkinson. *Parkinson*, BBC-TV, November 17, 1973.

Tom Snyder. *The Tomorrow Show*, September 1975.

Leslie Megahey. *Arena*, BBC-2, May 18, 21, 1982. In OWI.

Question-and-answer session. *L'Avant-Scene Cinema*. July 1982.

Barbara Leaming. *Orson Welles: A Biography*.

Primary source material:

(i) Material from the Richard Wilson Collection, University of Indiana Lilly Library:

Orson Welles to Diana Bourbon, telegram re *Campbell's Playhouse*.

Conrad, Joseph. *Heart of Darkness*, great modern short stories ed., annotated copy by Orson Welles, used in preparation for 1939 film.

Unsigned, undated to RKO, memorandum, "Camera," re *Heart of Darkness*.

"Mercury" to RKO, memorandum, "Heart of Darkness," September 15, 1939.

Orson Welles to Herb Drake, memorandum, October 18, 1939.

Cast list for *Heart of Darkness*, October? 1939.

Eddie Donahoe to Orson Welles, memorandum, December 7, 1939.

Shooting schedule and cast list for *Heart of Darkness*, November 28, 1939.

Welles, Orson. *Heart of Darkness* screenplay, November 30, 1939.

Welles, Orson. *The Smiler with a Knife*, January 9, 1940.

Welles, Orson. *The Way to Santiago/Orson Welles* 4, March 25, 1941.

(ii) Contemporary press:

Hollywood Reporter, January 8, 1940.

Hollywood Reporter, January 13, 1940.

Hollywood Reporter, September 26, 1939.

(iii) Other primary source material:

Conrad, Joseph. *Heart of Darkness*. Penguin, 1973.

Cotten, Joseph. *Vanity Will Get You Somewhere: An Autobiography.* Columbus Books, 1987.

Houseman, John. *Run-through: A Memoir.* Simon and Schuster, 1972.

Sturges, Preston. *On Preston Sturges.* Faber and Faber, 1991.

Welles, Orson. [Untitled]. *New York Post*, February 10, 1943.

———. "The Major Branches of the Cinema." In MB.

———. "Proposal for *King Lear.*" In TiOW.

———. "Twilight in the Smog." *Esquire*, March 1959.

———. "Welles Writing About Welles." *Stage*, February 1941.

Welles, Orson, and John Houseman. "Repertory 38." *Billboard*, November 26, 1938.

Secondary source material:

Callow, Simon. *Orson Welles: The Road to Xanadu.* Jonathan Cape, 1995.

Cantril, Hadley. *Invasion from Mars.* Princeton University Press, 1940.

Carringer, Robert L. *The Making of Citizen Kane.* University of California Press, 1985.

———. "The Scripts of Citizen Kane." *Critical Inquiry*, Winter 1978.

Debona, Guerric. "Into Africa: Orson Welles and Heart of Darkness," *Cinema Journal*, Spring 1994.

Dunaway, David King. *Huxley in Hollywood.* Bloomsbury, 1989.

Gomery, Douglas. "Orson Welles and the Hollywood Industry." In PoV.

Lasky, Betty. *RKO: The Biggest Little Major of Them All.* Prentice-Hall, 1984.

Chapter 2: The Wellesian Mosaic

Welles interviews:

New York Herald Tribune, September 11, 1951.

Andre Bazin, Charles Bitsch, and Jean Domarchi. *Cahiers du Cinema*, September 1958. In OWI.

Huw Wheldon. *Monitor*, BBC-TV, March 13, 1960. In OWI.

Dilys Powell. *Sunday Times*, February 3, 1963.

Dick Cavett. *The Dick Cavett Show*, September 14, 1970.

Peter Bogdanovich. *This Is Orson Welles.*
Leslie Megahey. *Arena,* BBC-2, May 18, 21, 1982. In OWI.
Barbara Leaming. *Orson Welles: A Biography.*

Primary source material:

(i) Material from the Richard Wilson Collection, University of Indiana Lilly Library:

Welles, Orson, and Roger Hill. *The Marching Song* script, 1932.

Mankiewicz, Herman, and Orson Welles. *John Citizen USA* draft, Spring 1940.

Mankiewicz, Herman, and Orson Welles. *Citizen Kane,* final script, June 18, 1940.

Affidavit from Richard Baer regarding authorship of *Citizen Kane,* May 1941.

(ii) Contemporary press:

[Untitled]. *Friday,* January 8, 1941.

[Untitled]. *Newsweek,* September 16, 1940.

[Untitled]. *Time,* March 17, 1941.

[Untitled]. *Variety,* March 8, 1941.

Belfrage, Cedric. "The Clipper #1." In FoCK.

Herrmann, Bernard. "Score for a Film." In FoCK.

Lean, Tangye. "Horizon #4." In FoCK.

O'Hara, John. Review of *Citizen Kane, Newsweek,* March 17, 1941.

Powell, Dily. Review of *Citizen Kane. Sunday Times,* 1946.

Toland, Gregg. "How I Broke the Rules in Citizen Kane." In FoCK.

"Wellesapoppin." *Friday,* September 9, 1940.

(iii) Other primary source material:

Bogdanovich, Peter. "The Kane Mutiny." In FoOW.

Cotten, Joseph. *Vanity Will Get You Somewhere: An Autobiography.* Columbus Books, 1987.

Herrmann, Bernard. Interview by Ted Gilling, *Sight and Sound,* Winter 1971.

Herrmann, Bernard, and George Coulouris. "The Citizen Kane Book."
    Interview by Ted Gilling, *Sight and Sound*, Spring 1972.
Hoge, Ralph, and James G. Stewart. Interview. *The RKO Story Part 4: It's
    All True*.
Houseman, John. *Run-through: A Memoir*. Simon and Schuster, 1972.
Huxley, Aldous. *After Many a Summer Dies the Swan*. Folio Society, 1980.
Mankiewicz, Herman, and Orson Welles. *The Citizen Kane Book*. Little,
    Brown, 1971.*
Meryman, Richard. *Mank: The Wit, World and Life of Herman
    Mankiewicz*. William Morrow, 1978.
Truffaut, Francois. "L'Express." In FoCK.
Warrick, Ruth. "Introduction." In Berg and Erskine, *Encyclopaedia of
    Orson Welles*.
Welles, Orson. "Citizen Kane is not about Louella Parsons' Boss." In FoCK.
———. "The Creation of Citizen Kane," *The Times*. November 17, 1971.
———. Lecture, New York University, October 20, 1942.
———. *Lundberg vs. Welles*, transcript of deposition, Federal Records
    Center, NJ.
———. "Orson Welles's Almanac." *New York Post*. February 27, 1945.
———. Press statement, January14, 1941.
———. "Proposal for *King Lear*." In TIOW.

Secondary source material:

Bordwell, David. "Citizen Kane." In FoOW.
Callow, Simon. *Orson Welles: The Road to Xanadu*. Jonathan Cape,
    1995.
Carringer, Robert L. *The Making of Citizen Kane*. University of California
    Press, 1985.
Carroll, Noel. "Interpreting Citizen Kane." In PoV.
Kael, Pauline. "Raising Kane." In *The Citizen Kane Book*, by Herman
    Mankiewicz and Orson Welles. Little, Brown, 1971.

---

*Includes third revised final script, July 16, 1940; as well as the cutting continuity, February 21, 1941.

Lasky, Betty. *RKO: The Biggest Little Major of Them All*. Prentice-Hall, 1984.
Lebo, Harlan. *Citizen Kane: The 50th Anniversary Album*. Doubleday, 1990.
Mulvey, Laura. *Citizen Kane*. BFI Film Classics, 1992.
O'Doherty, Brian. "Kane's Welles: The Phantom of the Opus," *Art Forum*, December 1987.
Pizzitola, Louis. *Hearst Over Hollywood*. Columbia University Press, 2002.

Chapter 3: Journey Into Darkness

Welles interviews:

Huw Wheldon. *Monitor*, BBC-TV, March 13, 1960. In OWI.
Kenneth Tynan. *Playboy*, March 1967. In OWI.
Peter Bogdanovich. *This Is Orson Welles*.
Leslie Megahey. *Arena*, BBC-2, May 18, 21, 1982. In OWI.
Barbara Leaming. *Orson Welles: A Biography*.

Primary source material:

(i) Material from the Richard Wilson Collection, University of Indiana Lilly Library:
Welles, Orson. *The Way to Santiago/Orson Welles #4*, third revised continuity, March 25, 1941.
George Schaefer to Orson Welles, cable, March 21, 1942.
(ii) Contemporary press:
[Oscar report], *Variety*. March 4, 1942.
Crowther, Bosley. Review of *Citizen Kane*. *New York Times*. May 2, 1941. In FoCK.

(iii) Other primary source material:
Carringer, Robert L., ed. *The Magnificent Ambersons: A Reconstruction* University of California Press, 1993.*
Cotton, Joseph. Joseph Cotten to Orson Welles, March 28, 1942. In TIOW.
Herrmann, Bernard, interview. *Miklos Rozsa Society Newsletter*, Summer 1974. Quoted in Naremore, *Magic World of Orson Welles*.

---

*Includes cutting continuity for Welles's *The Magnificent Ambersons*.

MacLiammor, Michael. "Orson Welles," *Sight and Sound*. July–September 1954.

Selznick, David O. *Memo From David O. Selznick*. Edited by Rudy Behlmer. Modern Library, 2000.

Stewart, James G. Interview. *The RKO Story, Part 4*.

Truffaut, Francois. *Hitchcock*. Secker and Warburg, 1968.

Welles, Orson. Lecture, New York University, October 20, 1942.

———. *The Magnificent Ambersons*, estimating script, August 15, 1941.

———. "Orson Welles's Almanac." *New York Post*, September 11, 1945.

———. "Welles Writing About Welles." *Stage*, February 1941.

Welles, Orson, and John Houseman. "Repertory 38." *Billboard*, November 26, 1938.

Wilson, Richard. "It's Not Quite All True." *Sight and Sound*, Autumn 1970.

Secondary source material:

Bordwell, David. "Citizen Kane." In FoOW.

Carringer, Robert L. *The Making of Citizen Kane*. University of California Press, 1985.

Farber, Stephen. "The Magnificent Ambersons." In FoOW.

Harvey, James. *Movie Love in the Fifties*. Da Capo, 2002.

Higham, Charles. *The Films of Orson Welles*. University of California Press, 1970.

Kamp, David. "Magnificent Obsession," *Vanity Fair*, January 2002.

Lasky, Betty. *RKO: The Biggest Little Major of Them All*. Prentice-Hall, 1984.

Perkins, V. F. *The Magnificent Ambersons*. BFI Film Classics, 1999.

Chapter 4: The Spoiled Brat Gets His Comeuppance

Welles interviews:

Andre Bazin, Charles Bitsch, and Jean Domarchi. *Cahiers du Cinema*, September 1958. In OWI.

Huw Wheldon. *Monitor*, BBC-TV, March 13, 1960. In OWI.

Dilys Powell. *Sunday Times*, February 3, 1963.

Peter Bogdanovich. *This Is Orson Welles*.

Leslie Megahey. *Arena*, BBC-2, May 18, 21, 1982. In OWI.
Barbara Leaming. *Orson Welles: A Biography.*

Primary source material:

(i) Material from the Richard Wilson Collection, University of Indiana Lilly Library pertaining to **The Magnificent Ambersons:**
Review comment cards for first preview, March 17, 1942.
Jack Moss to Orson Welles, cable, March 23, 1942.
Orson Welles to Jack Moss, cable, March 25, 1942.
Orson Welles, eight-page cable, preliminary list of *Amberson* cuts, March 27, 1942.
Bob Wise to Orson Welles, letter, March 31, 1942.
Orson Welles to Jack Moss, four-page cable, further suggested changes to *Ambersons,* April 18, 1942.

(ii) Material from the Richard Wilson Collection, University of Indiana Lilly Library pertaining to **It's All True:**
John Fante, *It's All True: A Love Story,* August 1941.
Orson Welles, *It's All True* treatment, March 11, 1942.
Tom Pettey to Herb Drake, letter, March 27, 1942.
Orson Welles to George Schaefer, cable, April 12, 1942.
George Schaefer to Orson Welles, cable, April 13, 1942.
Orson Welles to George Schaefer, cable, April 15, 1942.
George Schaefer to Orson Welles, cable, April 16, 1942.
[Richard Wilson] to John Hay Whitney, memo, report on Welles's activities in Brazil, April 27, 1942.
[Richard Wilson,] memo regarding Lynn Shores, April 27, 1942.
Richard Wilson to Herb Drake, letter, May 5, 1942.
Maurice Bernstein to Orson Welles, May 14, 1942.
Memo to Coordinator's Office on "Welles Activities" from May 5 through May 23, dated May 30, 1942.
Herb Drake to Orson Welles, cable, June 1, 1942.
Herb Drake to George Schaefer, June 3, 1942.
Jack Moss to Charles Koerner, letter, June 15, 1942.
Charles Koerner to Jack Moss, letter, June 16, 1942.

RKO, memo "On the Lynn Shores Matter," undated.
Richard Wilson to Phil Reisman, letter, August 11, 1942.
RKO Studio to Orson Welles, letter, October 19, 1942.
It's All True script, September 2, 1943.

(iii) Contemporary press:
Angora, Gatinha. *Cine-Radio Journal*, May 20, 1942.

(iv) Other primary source material:
Carringer, Robert L., ed. *The Magnificent Ambersons: A Reconstruction.* University of California Press, 1993.
Cotton, Joseph. Joseph Cotten to Orson Welles, March 28, 1942. In TIOW.
Endfield, Cy, interview by Jonathan Rosenbaum. *Film Comment,* 1992.
Fanto, George, and Elizabeth Wilson. Interview. In *It's All True* by Richard Wilson, Myron Meisel, and Rosemary Wilson. Paramount, 1993.
Otelo, Grand. Interview. In *The RKO Story, Part 4: It's All True.*
Selznick, David O. *Memo From David O. Selznick.* Edited by Rudy Behlmer. Modern Library, 2000.
Shores, Lynn. Lynn Shores to Walter Daniels April 14, 1942. In *The RKO Story Part 4: It's All True.*
Welles, Orson. "Orson Welles's Almanac." *New York Post*, February 13, 1945.
———. Radio broadcast, 1942. Quoted in PoV.
Wilson, Richard. "It's Not Quite All True." *Sight and Sound*, 1970.

Secondary source material:

Garcia, Maria. "Re-inventing Orson Welles," *Films In Review*, 1990.
Kael, Pauline. "Raising Kane." In *The Citizen Kane Book* by Herman Mankiewicz and Orson Welles. Little, Brown, 1971.
Kamp, David. "Magnificent Obsession." *Vanity Fair*, January 2002.
Lasky, Betty. *RKO: The Biggest Little Major of Them All.* Prentice-Hall, 1984.
Perkins, V. F. *The Magnificent Ambersons.* BFI Film Classics, 1999.

Rosenbaum, Jonathan. *Movie Wars: How Hollywood and the Media Conspire to Limit the Films We See.* A Cappella, 2000.
Stam, Robert. "Orson Welles, Brazil, and the Power of Blackness." In PoV.

Chapter 5: The Nature of the Enemy

Welles interviews:

Thomas F. Brady. *New York Times*, December 8, 1946.
Peter Bogdanovich. *This Is Orson Welles.*
Barbara Leaming. *Orson Welles: A Biography.*

Primary source material:

(i) Material from the Richard Wilson Collection, University of Indiana Lilly Library:

Welles, Orson. *The Way to Santiago/Orson Welles #4*, third revised continuity, March 25, 1941.
Orson Welles to Nelson Rockefeller, letter, October 20, 1942.
Nelson Rockefeller to Orson Welles, letter, November 10, 1942.
Orson Welles to Fernando Pinto, letter, December 1942.
Orson Welles to Fernando Pinto, letter, February 26, 1943.
Welles, Orson. *It's All True* script, September 2, 1943.
Welles, Orson. Rough draft treatment for *Carnival in Rio* a.k.a. *Samba*, Spring 1945.
Anthony Veiller to Orson Welles, letter, May 22, 1945.
Orson Welles to Bob Hall, letter, May 30, 1945.
Contract for *The Stranger*, signed by Welles, September 20, 1945.
Indemnification agreement for *The Stranger*, September 20, 1945.

(ii) Other primary source material:

Chandler, Raymond. "Writers in Hollywood," *Atlantic Monthly*, November 1945.
Rodriguez, Carlos. *Orson Welles In the Land of Don Quixote.* Canal + Espana, 2000.
Sturges, Preston. *On Preston Sturges.* Faber and Faber, 1991.

Welles, Orson. Acceptance Speech, AFI Award Ceremony, 1975.

———. Deposition in Lundberg case, 1947.

———. Lecture, New York University, October 20, 1942.

———. "Orson Welles's Almanac." New York Post, January 30, 1945.

———. "Orson Welles's Almanac." New York Post, February19, 1945.

———. "Orson Welles's Almanac." New York Post, March 16, 1945.

———. "Orson Welles's Almanac." New York Post, March 29, 1945.

———. "Orson Welles's Almanac." New York Post, April 12, 1945.

———. "Orson Welles's Almanac." New York Post, April 17, 1945.

———. "Orson Welles's Almanac." New York Post, April 24, 1945.

———. "Orson Welles's Almanac." New York Post, May 7, 1945.

———. "Orson Welles's Almanac." New York Post, May 16, 1945.

———. "Orson Welles's Almanac." New York Post, May 25, 1945.

———. The Other Side of the Wind, excerpt. AFI Award Ceremony, 1975.

———. The Stranger screenplay (final shooting script), September 24, 1945.

Welles, Orson, and John Huston. The Stranger screenplay (temporary draft), August 9, 1945.

Secondary source material:

Benamou, Catherine. "It's All True as Document/Event." In PoV.

Truffaut, Francois. Foreword. In AB.

Wood, Bret. "Recognizing The Stranger." Video Watchdog 23.

Chapter 6: A Date with the Supercutter

Welles interviews:

Andre Bazin, Charles Bitsch, and Jean Domarchi. Cahiers du Cinema, September 1958. In OWI.

Peter Bogdanovich. This Is Orson Welles.

Richard Marienstras. French TV series, 1974. In OWI.

Leslie Megahey. Arena, BBC-2, May 18, 21, 1982. In OWI.

Barbara Leaming. Orson Welles: A Biography.

Primary source material:

(i) Material from the Richard Wilson Collection, University of Indiana Lilly Library:
Shooting schedule and scene synopsis for *The Stranger*, September 27, 1945.
"Work To Be Finished on *The Stranger*," November 12, 1945.
RKO to International Pictures, accounting ledger for *The Stranger*, February 24, 1949.

(ii) Contemporary press:
Kerr, Walter. *Theatre Arts*, September 1951.

(iii) Other primary source material:
Brecht, Bertolt, and John Willett, ed. *On Theatre*. Hill and Wang, 1964.
Nims, Ernest. Interview. *American Cinemeditor*, Winter/Spring 1982–3.
Welles, Orson. Letter to Peter Cowie. In *A Ribbon of Dreams: The Cinema of Orson Welles*, by Peter Cowie. A.S. Barnes, 1973.
———. "Orson Welles's Almanac" *New York Post*. April 17, 1945.
———. *The Stranger* screenplay (final shooting script), September 24, 1945.
Welles, Orson, and John Huston. *The Stranger* screenplay (temporary draft), August 9, 1945.

Secondary source material:

Anderegg, Michael. *Orson Welles, Shakespeare and Popular Culture*. Columbia University Press, 1999.
Leaming, Barbara. *If This Was Happiness: A Biography of Rita Hayworth*. Viking-Penguin, 1989.
Wood, Bret. "Recognizing *The Stranger*." *Video Watchdog* 23.

Chapter 7: That Quality of Strangeness

Welles interviews:

Thomas F. Brady. *New York Times*, December 8, 1946. In OWI.

Andre Bazin, Charles Bitsch, and Jean Domarchi. *Cahiers du Cinema*,
  September 1958. In OWI.
Juan Cobos, Miguel Rubio, and J. A. Pruneda. *Cahiers du Cinema in Eng-
  lish* 5 (1966). In OWI.
Dick Cavett. The Dick Cavett Show, July 28, 1970.
Peter Bogdanovich. *This Is Orson Welles.*
Tom Snyder. *The Tomorrow Show*, September 1975.
Leslie Megahey. *Arena*, BBC-2, May 18, 21, 1982. In OWI.
Barbara Leaming. *Orson Welles: A Biography.*

Primary source material:

*(i) Material from the Richard Wilson Collection, University of Indiana
  Lilly Library:*
Fante, John. *It's All True: A Love Story*, August 1941.
Welles, Orson. *Black Irish*, draft script, August 13, 1946.
———. *Take This Woman* (*The Lady from Shanghai*), first estimating
  script, September 20, 1946.

(ii) Other primary source material:
Brecht, Bertolt. *On Theatre*. Edited by John Willett. Hill and Wang, 1964.
Castle, William. Personal diary (of filming of *Lady from Shanghai*). In
  Frank Brady, *Citizen Welles: A Biography of Orson Welles*. Anchor,
  1990. [CH—please confirm]
———. *Step Right Up!* Putnam, 1976.
Graves, Robert. "Intimations of the Black Goddess." In *On Poetry: Col-
  lected Talks and Essays*. Doubleday, 1969.
Meryman, Richard. *Mank: The Wit, World and Life of Herman
  Mankiewicz*. William Morrow, 1978.
Welles, Orson. Letter to *New Statesman*, May 24, 1958.
———. Orson Welles to Mr. Cohn, 1947. In TIOW.
———. "Orson Welles's Almanac" *New York Post*. April 23,1945.
———. "Welles Writing About Welles." *Stage*, February 1941.

Secondary source material:

Bazin, Andre. "L'Apport d'Orson Welles," *Cine-Club* 7. In MB and AB.

Leaming, Barbara. *If This Was Happiness: A Biography of Rita Hayworth.* Viking-Penguin, 1989.

Naremore, James. "Between Works and Texts: Notes from the Welles Archive." In PoV.

Rosenbaum, Jonathan. "Notes on *Lady from Shanghai.*" In TIOW.

Wood, Bret. "Kiss Hollywood Goodbye." *Video Watchdog* 23.

Chapter 8: A Perfect Cross Between *Wuthering Heights* and *Bride of Frankenstein*

Welles interviews:

Modern Screen, April 1940.

Francis Koval. *Sight and Sound,* December 1950.

Derek Grigs. "Conversation at Oxford," *Sight and Sound,* Spring 1960.

Huw Wheldon. *Monitor*, BBC-TV, 1962.

Kenneth Tynan. *Playboy*, March 1967.

Peter Bogdanovich. *This Is Orson Welles.*

Richard Marienstras. [name of French TV series], 1974.

Leslie Megahey. *Arena*, BBC-2, May 18, 21, 1982.

Contemporary press:

Atkinson, Brooks. Review of *Macbeth. New York Times*, April 15, 1936.

Hollywood Reporter, October 11, 1948.

Life, October 11, 1948.

Other primary source material:

Selznick, David O. *Memo From David O. Selznick.* Edited by Rudy Behlmer. Modern Library, 2000.

Welles, Orson. *Filming Othello*, transcript, 1979.

————. "On Staging Shakespeare." In *The Mercury Shakespeare*, Harper, 1939.

————. "Orson Welles's Almanac." *New York Post*, February 2, 1945.

————. "The Third Audience." Lecture, Edinburgh Festival, 1952.

Wilson, Richard. *Theatre Arts*, June 1949.

————. "Welles and Shakespeare." *New York Herald Tribune*, October 3, 1950.

Secondary source material:

Anderegg, Michael. *Orson Welles, Shakespeare and Popular Culture.* Columbia University Press, 1999.

Brady, Frank. *Citizen Welles: A Biography of Orson Welles.* Anchor, 1990.

Cocteau, Jean. "A Profile of Orson Welles." In AB.

Drazin, Charles. *In Search of the Third Man.* Methuen, 1999.

France, Richard. *Orson Welles on Shakespeare: The WPA and Mercury Theatre Playscripts.* Routledge, 2001.

Kennedy, Harlan. "Shadow of a Debt: *The Third Man* and *Touch of Evil.*" *Film Comment.*

Mullin, Michael. "Orson Welles' *Macbeth*: Script and Screen." In FoOW.

Chapter 9: The Jigsaw Pictures

Welles interviews:

Francis Koval. *Sight and Sound*, December 1950. In OWI.

Press conference, BBC-TV, January 14, 1955.

Person to Person, ABC-TV, November 25, 1955.

Andre Bazin and Charles Bitsch. *Cahiers du Cinema*, June 1958. In OWI.

Derek Grigs. "Conversation at Oxford," *Sight and Sound*, 1960.

Huw Wheldon. *Monitor*, BBC-TV, September 16, 1962.

Peter Bogdanovich. *This Is Orson Welles.*

Richard Marienstras. [name of French TV series], 1974. In OWI.

Question-and-answer session. *L'Avant-Scene Cinema.* July 1982.

Contemporary press:

Crowther, Bosley, review of *Othello. New York Times*, September 13, 1955.

Other primary source material:

Fraser, Alex. "Orson's Noirish Gooseliver," http://www.eopinions.com

Graves, Robert. *On Poetry: Collected Talks and Essays.* Doubleday, 1969.

MacLiammoir, Michael. *Put Money In Thy Purse: The Making of Othello.* Virgin, 1994.

Troiani, Oberdan. Interview. In *Rosabella, La Storia Italiana di Orson Welles,* directed by Gianfranco Giagni and Ciro Giorgini. Tape Connection, 1993.

Welles, Orson. *Filming Othello,* transcript, 1979.

———. Letter to *New Statesman,* May 24, 1958.

Welles, Orson. "The Major Branches of the Cinema." In *Orson Welles: An Investigation into His Films and Philosophy,* by Maurice Bessy. Crown, 1971.

"Welles, Orson." *Mr. Arkadin: The Novel.* W.H. Allen, 1956.*

———. "The Third Audience." Lecture, Edinburgh Festival, 1952.

Wilson, Richard, note scribbled on bill for liquidation of items in storage, July 25, 1949. Richard Wilson Collection, University of Indiana Lilly Library.

Secondary source material:

Anderegg, Michael. *Orson Welles, Shakespeare and Popular Culture.* Columbia University Press, 1999.

Cocteau, Jean. "A Profile of Orson Welles." In AB.

Jorgens, Jack. "Welles's *Othello*: A Baroque Translation." In FoOW.

Kaufman, Stanley. "The Trial." In *A World on Film,* Harper and Row, 1966. Also in MB.

Rodman, Howard A. "The Last Days of Orson Welles." *American Film,* June 1987.

Rosenbaum, Jonathan. "The Seven Arkadins." *Film Comment,* January–February 1992.

Chapter 10: A Candid Partisan of the Old Eloquence

Welles interviews:

Andre Bazin, Charles Bitsch, and Jean Domarchi. *Cahiers du Cinema,* September 1958.

---

*The authorship of this novelization of *Mr. Arkadin* continues to be a source of dispute. The most likely culprit is Maurice Bessy, working from Welles's own draft scripts.

Juan Cobos, Miguel Rubio, and J. A. Pruneda. *Cahiers du Cinema in English* 5 (1966).

Kenneth Tynan. *Playboy*, March 1967.

Dick Cavett. *The Dick Cavett Show*, July 28, 1970.

Peter Bogdanovich. *This Is Orson Welles*.

Richard Marienstras. French TV series, 1974.

Leslie Megahey. *Arena*, BBC-2, May 18, 21, 1982.

————. Question-and-answer session. *L'Avant-Scene Cinema*, July 1982.

Other primary source material:

Heston, Charlton. *The Actor's Life: Journals 1956–76*. Allen Lane, 1979.

————, interview by James Delson. In ToE.

————. "Touch of Genius." *National Review*, February 3, 1992.

Leigh, Janet. "Psycho, Rosie and A Touch of Orson," *Sight and Sound*, Spring 1970.

Masterson, Bret. *Badge of Evil*. Dodd-Mead, 1956.

McCambridge, Mercedes. *The Quality of Mercy*. Times Books, 1981.

Schidlin, Rick (producer). *Retouching Evil*. Universal, 1998.

Silovic, Vassili, and Oja Kodar. *One Man Band* a.k.a. *The Lost Films of Orson Welles*. Pit Riethmuller, 1995.

Welles, Orson. *Badge of Evil* screenplay, revised final script, February 5, 1957.

————. *Filming Othello*, transcript,1979.

————. *Fountain of Youth*. TV pilot, 1958.

————. Letter to *New Statesman*, May 24, 1958.

————. Orson Welles to Henry Mancini, 1957. In TIOW.

————. Orson Welles to Ed Muhl, December 1957. In TIOW, in edited form; in its entirety in *Touch of Evil* DVD, 2000.

————. "Ribbon of Dreams." *International Film Annual* 1, 1957.

————. "Twilight in the Smog." *Esquire*, March 1959.

Zugsmith, Albert. *King of the Bs*. E.P. Dutton, 1975.

Secondary source material:

Collet, Jean. "Etudes Cinematographiques #24–25." In ToE.

Comito, Terry, ed. *Touch of Evil*. Rutgers Film in Print, 1985.

Comito, Terry. "Welles's Labyrinths: An Introduction to Touch of Evil."
   In ToE.
Stubbs, John. "The Evolution of Touch of Evil from Novel to Film." In
   ToE.
Truffaut, Francois. "Arts." In ToE.
Wollen, Peter. "Foreign Relations, Welles and Touch of Evil." Sight and
   Sound, 1998.

Chapter 11: A Dark Turgid Affair

Welles interviews:

Andre Bazin and Charles Bitsch. Cahiers du Cinema, June 1958. In OWI.
Huw Wheldon. Monitor, BBC-TV, March 13, 1960. In OWI.
Dick Cavett. The Dick Cavett Show, September 14, 1970.
Peter Bogdanovich. This Is Orson Welles.
Leslie Megahey. Arena, BBC-2, May 18, 21, 1982. In OWI.
Barbara Leaming. Orson Welles: A Biography.

Contemporary Press:

Review of Touch of Evil, Variety, March 14, 1958. In ToE.
Gerasimov, Sergei. Film and Filming, 1959.
Thompson, Howard. Review, New York Times, May 22, 1958. In ToE.
Truffaut, Francois. Foreword. In AB.

Other primary source material:

Bogdanovich, Peter. Who the Devil Made It. Knopf, 1997.
Giagni, Gianfranco, and Ciro Giorgini. Rosabella, La Storia Italiani di
   Orson Welles. Tape Connection, 1993.
Heston, Charlton. The Actor's Life: Journals 1956–76 Allen Lane, 1979.
———, interview by James Delson. In ToE.
———. "Touch of Genius." National Review, February 3, 1992.
MacLiammoir, Michael. "Orson Welles." Sight and Sound, July–Septem-
   ber 1954.
Nims, Ernest. Interview. American Cinemeditor, Winter/Spring 1982–3.

Stainton, Audrey. "Don Quixote: Orson Welles' Secret." *Sight and Sound,* Autumn 1988.

Welles, Orson. Letter to *New Statesman,* May 24, 1958.

———. Orson Welles to Charlton Heston, November 17, 1957. In TIOW.

———. Orson Welles to Ed Muhl, December 1957. In TIOW.

———. "Twilight in the Smog." *Esquire,* March 1959.

Zugsmith, Albert. *King of the Bs.* E.P. Dutton, 1975.

Secondary source material:

Murch, Walter. *The Conversations.* Knopf, 2002.

Schmidlin, Rick. Internet interview by Lawrence French. Posted on Welles.net

Stubbs, John. "The Evolution of *Touch of Evil* from Novel to Film." In ToE.

Chapter 12: Outside the System

Welles interviews:

Andre Bazin and Charles Bitsch. *Cahiers du Cinema,* June 1958.

Andre Bazin, Charles Bitsch, and Jean Domarchi. *Cahiers du Cinema,* September 1958.

Huw Wheldon. *Monitor,* BBC-TV, March 13, 1960.

Huw Wheldon. *Monitor,* BBC-TV, Septmeber 16, 1962.

Dilys Powell. *Sunday Times,* February 3, 1963.

John Kobler. "Citizen Welles Rides Again." *Saturday Evening Post,* December 8, 1962.

Juan Cobos, Miguel Rubio, and J. A. Pruneda. *Cahiers du Cinema in English* 5 (1966).

Juan Cobos and Miguel Rubio. *Sight and Sound* 35.

Kenneth Tynan. *Playboy,* March 1967.

Kathleen Halton, *The Movies,* BBC-TV, April 10, 1967.

Dick Cavett. *The Dick Cavett Show,* July 28, 1970.

Peter Bogdanovich. *This Is Orson Welles.*

Richard Marienstras. French TV series, 1974.

Tom Snyder. *The Tomorrow Show*, September 1975.

Leslie Megahey. *Arena*, BBC-2, May 18, 21, 1982.

———. Question-and-answer session. *L'Avant-Scene Cinema*, July 1982.

Barbara Leaming. *Orson Welles: A Biography*.

Contemporary press:

Kael, Pauline. Review of *Chimes at Midnight*. *New Republic*. June 24, 1967.

Other primary source material:

Allen, Steve. *The Steve Allen Show*. May 5, 1957.

Giagni, Gianfranco, and Ciro Giorgini. *Rosabella, La Storia Italiani di Orson Welles*. Tape Connection, 1993.

Baxter, Keith. Interview by Bridget Gellert Lyons. In *Chimes at Midnight*, Rutgers Films in Print, 1988.

Bogdanovich, Peter. "Is It True What They Say About Orson?" *New York Times*, August 30, 1970.

———. "Introduction." In TIOW, rev. ed. Da Capo, 1998.

France, Richard. *Orson Welles On Shakespeare: The WPA and Mercury Theatre Playscripts*. Routledge, 2001.

Lyons, Bridget Gellert, ed. *Chimes at Midnight*. Rutgers Films in Print, 1988.

MacLiammoir, Michael. *Put Money In Thy Purse: The Making of Othello*. Virgin, 1994.

Rodriguez, Carlos. *Orson Welles In the Land of Don Quixote*. Canal + Espana, 2000. (Includes Welles short *The Sacred Beasts*, Madrid, June 1966.)

Stainton, Audrey. "Don Quixote: Orson Welles' Secret." *Sight and Sound*, Autumn 1988.

Welles, Orson. Acceptance Speech, AFI Award Ceremony, 1975.

———. *The Cradle Will Rock: An Original Screenplay*. Santa Teresa Press, 1994.

———. *Hearts of Age, Citizen Welles*. DVD. Focus Films, 2001.

———. "Orson Welles's Almanac." *New York Post*, June 2, 1945.

————. "Orson Welles's Almanac." *New York Post*, February 15, 1945.

————. "The Third Audience." Lecture, Edinburgh Festival, 1952. In PC.

————. *The Trial*. Lorrimer Publishing, 1970.

————. "Twilight in the Smog." *Esquire*, March 1959.

Welles, Orson, and Oja Kodar. *The Big Brass Ring*. Black Spring Press, 1991.

Secondary source material:

Angel, Henri. *Les Grandes Cineastes*. Editions Universitaires, 1959.

Gagné, Nicole. "Where Is the Other Side of the Wind?" *Cineaste*, Winter 2003.

Rodman, Howard A. "The Last Days of Orson Welles," *American Film*, June 1987.

THE FILMS OF ORSON WELLES

A Digital Versatile Discography

Citizen Kane. (RKO Pictures, 1941)

119 minutes.

Though initially issued on single DVD, this classic has warranted two different double-disc editions in the U.K. and U.S. Of the pair, the U.K. edition has more going for it, the U.S. edition devoting its entire second disc to the less-than-earth-shattering *Battle Over Citizen Kane* documentary (see below). The U.K. edition instead prefers to provide viewers with a brief documentary by respected film pundit Barry Norman, entitled *Anatomy of a Classic*, as well as the fabled *War of the Worlds* radio broadcast. Both versions are "full frame" (4:3), an inexact substitute for the correct film ratio but no worse than most such "fudges."

The Magnificent Ambersons. (RKO Pictures, 1941)

88 minutes.

An American DVD edition of this "lost" masterpiece, hopefully akin to its feature-packed laserdisc twin (issued by Criterion and produced by Robert Carringer), continues to be cited as "imminent." However, for the moment cineasts must rely on the perfectly splendid print issued in France, in the Cahiers du Cinema series, which comes with some fascinating audio extras; or a less-enhanced Japanese edition.

The Stranger. (International Pictures, 1946)

95 minutes.

Because of its public domain status, which means that it can be issued by anyone with a print and a pressing plant, *The Stranger* circulates on DVD in more editions than any other Welles film. There is apparently even a colorized copy. Of those currently available in the U.S., the best print appears to be the one issued by the Roan Group. However, versions issued by Matinee in the U.K. and by MGM in France and Germany are eminently respectable. All of these include the hilarious original U.S. trailer. Misleading or what?!

The Lady from Shanghai. (Columbia Pictures, 1948)

87 minutes.

Available in the Columbia Classics series, the DVD of Welles's fourth film is bereft of bonus material but is blessed with an exquisite looking print.

Macbeth. (Republic Pictures, 1948)

107 minutes.

In keeping with the version issued as a fiftieth-anniversary laserdisc and video, the DVD edition of this strange ol' film is the uncut 1948 original. The bastardized 1950 version has now seemingly been supplanted for good. What would have been nice, as a bonus audio on this full-price, bonus-free DVD, would have been an audio of the 1940 Mercury album.

Othello. (1952)

90 minutes.

Othello is the first of Welles's films to require any true aficionado to go beyond its DVD self, splendid a representation of the 1992 "restoration" as it may be. Unfortunately, this restoration does not fully reflect Welles's own intentions, for which viewers are advised to seek out the laserdisc edition issued by Criterion in the eighties, which accords with the 1952 original in most respects. Of course, it is only one of at least three edits Welles made at the time. Indeed, the French version of the film is different enough to warrant its own DVD edition.

Mr Arkadin a.k.a. Confidential Report. (1955).

99 minutes (93 minutes).

Another Welles film where definitive versions do not, and like as not cannot, exist. In this instance, its public domain status has probably dissuaded the more estimable DVD companies from attempting a thorough revamp, given its ubiquitous availability in bargain bins worldwide and its lowly place in the critical canon. In fact, a "restored" version would be one of the most rewarding ventures left to those so inclined, especially as (by far) the best version extant—the so-called Corinth version—has never made it to either laserdisc or DVD. Likewise unavailable is a digital version of the Spanish edit, itself a radical departure, though at least one website has recently suggested that a Spanish DVD may be about to appear.

What should certainly be avoided at all costs are any of the U.S. public domain DVDs to date, all of which adhere to the chronological, 93-minute Dolivet-inspired abortion—and not even a good print thereof. At least the Europeans have preferred the "bat credits" version for their public domain DVD, presumably taken from the laserdisc issued by Voyager (which includes the original episode from the BBC radio series among its bonus goodies).

Touch of Evil. (Universal Pictures, 1958)

111 minutes (108 minutes)

As with the 1992 Othello, the 1998 restored Touch of Evil certainly misrepresented itself in much of the publicity surrounding its limited cinema release and subsequent DVD edition. To re-edit the movie according to a memo Welles wrote some five months after he was removed from the editing process is not to "restore" Welles's vision for the film. There are also many fans who cannot get over the loss of Mancini's overture. Nevertheless, this version provides for an altogether more symmetrical film, along with the welcome death of Harry Keller, film director, and is likely to become the "standard" version, as has the 1948 Macbeth. Where it does fall down is on its trimming of the original image to fit standard TV screens, something that the 1976 UCLA "preview" issued on laserdisc is less guilty of.

The Trial. (1963)

118 minutes.

Another movie that has suffered a plethora of public domain editions that do scant justice to Welles's carefully choreographed cinematography; this has been rectified in part by recent single-disc editions in the U.S. and U.K. from Studio-Canal, both of which give prints of the film a spring clean. However, the premium DVD edition to date has to be the French two-disc set, also by Studio-Canal, which includes two versions of the film (both with English audio-tracks), one the 1963 original, the other a revised edit from 1984 (presumably approved by Welles), as well as two scenes deleted from the film (sadly, minus any audio, but including the oft-rumoured "Scientist" scene). Both versions of the film are in their original widescreen, and look spectacular.

Chimes at Midnight. (1966)

119 minutes.

Currently only available on DVD in Spain, and likely to remain that way unless contractual "difficulties" are resolved between Welles's estate and the original producers. Thankfully, those sensible Spaniards have produced an edition that contains both the Spanish dialogue (with optional English subtitles) and its English equivalent.

The Immortal Story. (ORTF, 1968)

57 minutes.

Amazingly, this film was issued on DVD in 2003, by RHV, in Italy only; and in a print that is as good as one has any right to expect. The bad news is that, though it contains an English audio version, this also comes with (unremovable) Italian subtitles plastered across the screen. Nor does an Italian version, also included on the single disc, allow one to bask in the full movie, being pruned of ten minutes in its curious, re-edited state. Still, for now, it'll have to do.

F For Fake. (1973)

85 minutes

Issued on laserdisc in the U.S.—along with its nine-minute trailer—*F For Fake* has yet to appear on DVD Stateside. However, the French and the Japanese have again obliged with reformatted DVD editions.

◆　◆　◆　◆

Documentaries About Welles

Some of the most useful work on Welles since his death has been done by documentary makers around the world, often providing an important corrective to published revisionists. Welles himself left behind two discursive documentaries about films of his, one of them unfinished. Sadly, neither of these has made it to any kind of commercial release. Nor has the Megahey documentary, or its Spanish and Italian equivalents, all of which provide vital perspectives on Welles's film career.

Filming *Othello*. (1978)

Director: Orson Welles.
85 minutes.

Only rarely seen on the big screen, this documentary is Welles's most conscious exposition on his own craft extant. A vital insight into the film *and* the man.

Filming *The Trial*. (1981)

Director: Orson Welles.
83 minutes.

As it stands, this "documentary" is simply a filmed record of a discussion Welles conducted with an audience of American film students, after a screening of his 1963 film, but it is fascinating nonetheless. Save for screenings at film festivals, almost never screened.

Arena: The Orson Welles Story. (BBC, 1982)

Director: Leslie Megahey.
165 minutes.

The definitive documentary on Welles, this two-part Arena special, directed and produced by Leslie Megahey, incorporates a wide-ranging interview with the man himself. An edited version was screened by ABC in America, though a commercial release would seem in order.

The RKO Story Part 4: It's All True. (BBC, 1987)

Produced by Charles Chabat & Rosemary Wilson.
65 minutes.

This episode from a five-part series on RKO Studios is devoted entirely to Welles's association with the studio. It represents the best account on film of the *It's All True* saga, even though it predates the following . . .

It's All True. (Paramount, 1993)

Directors: Richard Wilson, Myron Meisel, and Bill Krohn.
88 minutes.

A disappointing documentary that is part history, part reconstruction, but falls between its two chosen stools. Issued on laserdisc at the time.

Don Quixote. (El Silencio, 1992)

Post-Production Director and Editor: Jess Franco.
76 minutes.

Franco's film gives very little sense of the scope of Welles's vision, being little more than a random collection of sequences from the never-completed film. It has, nonetheless, been issued on DVD in Spain and France, with both English and Spanish audio tracks.

One Man Band a.k.a. The Lost Films of Orson Welles. (Pit Riethmuller, 1995)

Directors: Vassili Silovic and Oja Kodar.
90 minutes.

A very personal testimony by Oja Kodar to her late partner and collaborator, this is a fascinatingly eclectic series of glimpses into the unrealized projects that occupied Orson in his last two decades.

Working with Orson Welles. (Sidney Niekerk, 1993)

Director: Gary Graver.
94 minutes.

A disappointingly lightweight documentary from the cinematographer on whom Welles relied for the last fifteen years of his life. Issued on DVD.

Rosabella, La Storia Italiana di Orson Welles. (Tape Connection, 1993)

Directors: Gianfranco Giagni and Ciro Giorgini.
56 minutes.

An excellent account of Welles and the work he did in Italy, largely in Italian(!), but blessed with English subtitles.

Orson Welles in the Land of Don Quixote. (Canal + Espana, 2000)

Director: Carlos Rodriguez
89 minutes.

A companion piece to *Rosabella*, and an equally valuable account of Welles and his work in Spain. Includes the Maysles brothers' *Sacred Beasts* "promo."

Battle Over *Citizen Kane*. (American Experience, 1996)

Directors: Thomas Lennon and Michael Epstein
113 minutes.

Available on DVD in the U.S., as part of the double-disc *Citizen Kane*, this has everything you'd expect from a contemporary American TV documentary—a gratingly annoying narrator, blindingly obvious historical "insights," overstatements and understatements in almost equal proportions, and the kind of cutting better reserved for the pop videos its directors doubtless once directed. Even when it digs up a valuable piece of footage—as in the clip from the WPA's *Macbeth* production—it is needlessly edited (the entire three-minute segment has been issued on DVD, though only as part of an eleven-DVD boxed-set!). High production values wasted on such twaddle.

Retouching Evil (Universal, 1998)

Produced by Rick Schmidlin.
58 minutes.

Originally scheduled to be part of the DVD edition of the 1998 restoration, but omitted for legal reasons, this doubles as both a good "making of" documentary and an invaluable breakdown of the changes wrought on the film by its new editors. Broadcast alongside TV screenings of the new *Touch of Evil* on both sides of the pond, this documentary puts a good case for the changes they made.

ACKNOWLEDGMENTS

Firstly, I must thank Jaime Marzol, a true authority on Welles's work, who generously shared both archive and insights. Gratias, too, to Mike Conner, who meticulously transcribed the 92-page draft of *John Citizen USA* on my behalf, hopefully laying Kael's thesis to rest for good; and to Alex Fraser, for his memories of *Arkadin*.

Next in this roster of thanks must come James Naremore, whose own book on Welles was a constant inspiration, but who also went out of his way to find me a reliable, industrious, and enthusiastic researcher to help access some necessary gems from the Lilly Library's Welles Collection. This researcher, Jonathan Haynes, also deserves undying thanks for the efficient and thorough way he applied himself to the task.

I'd also like to thank Robert Carringer and Jonathan Rosenbaum, whose suggestions were not always followed, but were always appreciated. In New York, I imposed upon the ever-generous Ron Simon at the Museum of TV and Radio and on Ron Magliozzi at the Film Study Center for the Museum of Modern Arts, who gave of their time and knowledge unstintingly. High fives also to the staff of the Lincoln Center Library of Performing Arts; while in London, Andy O'Dwyer was a man on a mission through the archival aisles of the BBC.

Messy buckets are also extended to the British Film Institute, the Lilly Library, and MoMA for access to their impressive collections of publicity stills and production photos.

Friends and fellow fans gave up time to hunt down audio-visual material on my behalf, as well as trying to look convinced by my occasionally dodgy ideas. A nod of gratitude and a gratis cappucino for Simon Gee, Glen Korman, Bob and Tanya Strano, and Steve and Sara Shepherd.

Finally, and in no way begrudgingly, handshakes all round to my long-suffering editors, Yuval Taylor at Chicago Review Press and Andy Miller at Canongate. I hope the end result fully reflects their faith.

—CH.

INDEX